P9-DJL-171

RESEARCHING
Audiences

# RESEARCHING
## Audiences

**Kim Schrøder**
**Kirsten Drotner**
**Stephen Kline**
**Catherine Murray**

A member of the Hodder Headline Group
London
Distributed in the United States of America by
Oxford University Press Inc., New York

P
96
A83 R47
2003

# 52056715

8-15-05

c. 1

First published in Great Britain in 2003 by
Arnold, a member of the Hodder Headline Group,
338 Euston Road, London NW1 3BH

http://www.arnoldpublishers.com

Distributed in the United States of America by
Oxford University Press Inc.,
198 Madison Avenue, New York, NY10016

*British Library Cataloguing in Publication Data*
A catalogue record for this book is available from the British Library

*Library of Congress Cataloguing-in-Publication Data*
A catalog record for this book is available from the Library of Congress

ISBN 0 340 76275 6 (HB)
      0 340 76274 8 (PB)

1 2 3 4 5 6 7 8 9 10

Typeset in 9.5/12.5 Baskerville Book by Servis Filmsetting Ltd, Manchester
Printed and bound by MPG Books, Cornwall

What do you think about this book? Or any other Arnold title?

Please send your comments to:
feedback.arnold@hodder.co.uk

# Contents

## Section Six    Experimental Audience Research

## Section Seven    The Dual Challenge of 'Convergence' in Audience Research

# Preface

This is a book that preaches and practises methodological pluralism in the area of audience research. The spirit of interdisciplinarity and cross-fertilization – buzz-words in media studies for a number of years – calls for a decisive rejection of the methodological segregation that is still not entirely a thing of the past.

*Researching Audiences* defines audience research within a theoretical framework of 'discursive realism'. Methodologically we present and discuss four main approaches to audience research: media ethnography, reception research, audience surveys and experimental audience studies. We regard these approaches as complementary and compatible instruments available to researchers interested in exploring social and cultural meaning processes and social practices in our increasingly mediatized societies.

A mediatized society is one in which the communication media play an increasing, even overwhelming, role in the way we think about everything and thus in what we do in all contexts of life. Think of the young mother going to see the family doctor about her daughter's obesity problem: on her mind will be a collage of the coverage in print and broadcast media of this issue, going back years; before going she may have consulted the NetDoctor website; and most likely she has talked to family and friends about the topic too. The way she perceives and responds to the doctor's advice will be moulded by how she has seen doctors and the health system portrayed on TV news and in TV serials. In other words, the way she and the doctor talk about and try to resolve the problem is endlessly entangled in – and interacting with – media meanings that have affected and will continue to affect how she thinks about and acts on this issue. We wish to equip the students reading this book to better understand this mother and audiences in general, through methodological awareness and fieldwork skills, so that they may offer their services to public and private actors wishing to intervene in social and cultural processes, for human betterment or private gain.

More conceptually speaking, the mediatized society is affecting us in whatever social roles we have to fill in everyday life. As citizens, we are concerned about the organization of society, our priorities for the present and the future. As consumers we have to take care of our material, intellectual and wider cultural needs. As human beings we have to organize our private lives as individuals, couples or families on a daily, weekly and yearly basis; we have to move between home and work, preserve our physical and mental health and well-being, educate ourselves, bring up our children, seek diversion from routines and constraints, etc.

The decisions we have to make in all these respects must be made under conditions of increasing detraditionalization: we are being liberated from the constraints of traditional social structures, becoming more mobile in terms of geographical and sociostructural space. But with liberation comes choice and dilemmas: with apparently many options in matters big and small, how do we make up our minds – what do we want to do with our lives? And to what extent are we perhaps not as free as the ruling ideological climate would have it?

The dilemmas often appear as risks. At the macro-level we may wonder what exactly our civilization has done to the climate and ecological balance of our planet, spilling over into daily dilemmas of consumer choice at the micro-level. At the same time, more and more experts offer more and more conflicting 'research-based' analyses and advice in all areas of life. In all this, the media and other kinds of institutional communication play an ambivalent role for their audiences and users: they educate us and confuse us; they empower us and control us.

Audience and user research is necessary in order to explore and understand what we do with all the communicative inputs offered to us. How do we make sense of the world around us? How do we become capable citizens, discriminating consumers and whole human beings? This book is founded on the need to study the way we, as audiences and users, appropriate, make sense of and act on the media we receive, and how, in doing so, we ourselves become actors who influence communicative micro- and macro-social processes.

The book is based on our experiences in teaching practice-oriented media audience courses at the universities where we have worked over the years. We hope we have succeeded in writing a book that will address the learning needs of mature undergraduate students taking a course that aims to equip them with the theoretical frameworks and methodological tools necessary in order to carry out their own empirical projects, small or big, in the area of media audiences.

We have written the book at a time when the phenomenon of 'audience' is changing, as the age of the *recipient* of print and broadcast media is being superseded by the age of the *user* of converged media, requiring an increasing measure of user interactivity. We have incorporated this notion of the changing audience in our discussions throughout the book, but we have also devoted one chapter to a fuller discussion of the implications of convergence and interactivity for the study of contemporary audiences (Chapter 18).

We have also written the book at a time when it is being realized in academic circles that quantitative and qualitative methods are indeed complementary. Until recently the qualitative/quantitative divide has been a victim of the laws of academic inertia, and thus has been permitted to live on for much longer than the epistemological disagreements might warrant. This is in large part due to the knee-jerk mutual distrust that new generations of students and scholars have been socialized into, to some extent based on a widespread ignorance in each camp of the methodological Other – often aggravated in the qualitative camp by a lack of fundamental statistical prerequisites or a lack of discursive training in the quantitive camp.

We hope to be able to remedy this situation, not least by providing a foundation chapter written as a primer to initiate novices into the fundamentals of quantitative measurement (Chapter 10). Even if this chapter may not be able to equip cultural studies students to undertake ambitious large-scale surveys on their own, we hope that it will at least enable them to understand and value the contributions offered by audience research in the survey and experimental traditions, and thus to draw on their findings in the way they design their own studies.

The spirit of methodological complementarity is fundamental to the book as a whole, but in addition we devote one chapter to delineating the contours of the traditional divide (Chapter 2), one chapter to the theoretical anchorage of methodological complementarity, under the label of *discursive realism* (Chapter 3), and one chapter to the presentation of the way different methods can be brought together for greater explanatory power in concrete research projects (Chapter 17).

The book is structured in four main sections, each of which offers a thorough introduction and discussion of a major, well-founded approach to audience research: media ethnography, reception research, audience survey research and experimental audience studies. The order in which we present them is determined by the differing degrees of openness and control with which they approach the encounter between researcher and human subject: from the most naturalistic to the most controlled research situation (see further in Chapter 3).

Each main section (Sections 2, 3, 5 and 6) portrays its approach in three chapters. The first presents a hopefully eye-opening full case study of *the research approach in practice*, an exemplar that epitomizes how the approach does research at its best. The second *defines the field* by providing an overview of the approach, including its historical emergence and consolidation, and a discussion of the main theoretical and methodological debates among its practitioners that have had a formative influence on the development of the tradition up to the present day. The third, the 'toolbox chapter', is a practice-oriented guide for prospective researchers wanting to use the approach in a study of their own. It is our hope that, separately and together, these four sections will enable students to think about, plan and carry out research projects that analyse and interpret audience behaviour in different social and cultural contexts and illuminate the inevitable methodological trade offs to be made in choosing between and within approaches.

We wish to thank the many generations of students who have served us in two important ways. Some have unwittingly been the guinea pigs for a lot of the material in the book, served in classes at varying stages of completion. Others have inspired us through their own empirical work on audiences, in class projects and dissertations, as will be evident from the way we have used quite a few of their findings and insights as examples in the book.

Our thanks are also due to the many colleagues whose ideas and advice have had a formative influence on the way we think about audiences in the book. We hope that this book will be able to inspire them and others in their audience research in years to come, in fulfilment of our common ambition to better illuminate the practices of media audiences and users.

*Kim Schrøder, Kirsten Drotner, Stephen Kline, Catherine Murray*
*November 2002*

# Section 1

# Contours of Audiences

# Chapter One

# Approaching media audiences ☐

The audience of a modern television entertainment programme format like *Big Brother* may engage in a wide range of audience activities, only one of which can be said to be obligatory in order to belong to the '*Big Brother* audience': the watching of the TV programme 'itself' when it is broadcast as a daily part of the channel's flow of programmes.

However, even this notion of the programme 'itself' may turn out to be a hazy one, since *Big Brother* is broadcast both as a daily or weekly taped summary of the residents' life in the house, as a live broadcast of crucial moments such as the voting out of a resident, and as a talk show in which the residents and their antics are subjected to critical comment by viewers and experts. As audience researchers we shall therefore have to ask ourselves whether a viewer who watches only the daily or weekly summary can really be said to belong to the *Big Brother* audience in the full cultural sense of the word. In other words, even within the boundaries of the TV schedule, the audience of a contemporary 'reality show' like *Big Brother* must regularly follow a range of different TV discourses in order to be properly constituted as the audience of this programme.

While these discourses all require audience members to take on the role of 'viewer', there are a great many potential additional activities that take them far beyond this role: if they are watching 'the programme' in the company of others, the interactional roles required by the situation will influence their negotiation of programme meaning. Outside of the viewing context they may feel that the *Big Brother* experience is a rather depleted one if they don't also regularly read the coverage of the show in newspapers and magazines, ranging from hype and gossip to critical commentary, depending on the taste profile of the publication in question. In a British context, tabloid newspapers like the *Sun* ('Official paper of *Big Brother*') may report on the previous sexual conquests of a resident Casanova, while a broadsheet paper like *The Times* may analyse the programme as a scathing verdict on a depraved culture of voyeurs and exhibitionists.

Viewer-readers may expand their daily dose of gossip by joining the *Sun*'s mobile phone message service that provides hourly updates with fresh gossip, or become sources of juicy gossip themselves, if they know any of the contestants, responding to the paper's invitation to call or email the *Sun*. They may also place bets with the country's leading bookmakers (in shops or on the net) on the winner of the contest, or on the likelihood that a same-sex affair will develop in the house before a male/female one.

Through sms messages or email they may also take part in the voting about which resident should be the next one to be evicted from the house, or they may vote an additional participant into the house. They may visit the programme's official website, where a palette of communicative options present themselves: they may seek further printed information about the show and the contestants; they may use the web-TV option and become the fly on the wall by choosing one of the many camera positions surveying the participants anywhere in the house 24 hours a day; they may email the contestants directly, giving sympathy, advice or abuse; and they may join virtual chat groups in order to discuss with other fans who is the most likeable of the remaining residents – if they do not prefer to reserve such conversational interaction for their interpersonal encounters with friends and family in real everyday life.

Finally (or maybe you can think of additional distinguishable activities that viewers may engage in), they may produce their own personal presentation video and submit it with an application to become a contestant in the next season of *Big Brother*. Such applications may be archived by TV production companies and used to recruit participants for other, future programme initiatives.

The modern audience experience, in other words, is becoming increasingly multidimensional and multiply interactive. The classic media audience, particularly in the case of broadcasting, would fulfil its role as audience by receiving, actively but with more or less concentration and involvement, a message beamed at them from an institutional sender, and processed from a reclining position in the context of their living room. The usual metaphorical stereotype accompanying this kind of audience practice is that of the couch potato.

The contemporary and future media audience, on the other hand, as described above in the (still somewhat extreme) case of *Big Brother*, is more aptly characterized as a semiotic juggler, keeping many communicative balls in the air, and frequently throwing them to and receiving them from other real and virtual jugglers. The notion frequently used to encapsulate this state of affairs is *interactivity*.

In the network society of the future characterized increasingly by communicatively hyper-complex phenomena like *Big Brother*, only an approach based on methodological pluralism, with a toolbox including a variety of methods, will be able to grasp the multifaceted nature of media audiences. But already the mediatized society of today is complex enough to warrant a pluralist approach to the study of how media audiences use and negotiate the conventional media ensemble. We therefore devote the four main sections of this book to a presentation, demonstration and discussion of what we see as the four main approaches to audience research: media ethnography, reception research, survey research and experimental research. In addition, we devote a chapter to explaining how these seemingly incompatible approaches may be brought on to a common epistemological platform that we call 'discursive realism'.

One important purpose of the book is to demonstrate how a solid knowledge of the main approaches to audience research may enable prospective researchers to understand the roles of the media and their audiences in a larger sociocultural picture. Within such a framework, media audiences are studied in order to increase public knowledge about how the old and new media may contribute to vital social processes like the social construction of identities, the building of social relationships, the citizen's ability to participate in democratic decision-making, the potential for cultural enlightenment through television, and so on. In the case of *Big Brother* we would be interested in illuminating the way people negotiate identities and roles, as well as norms of social interaction, as they engage with the programme's invitation to join a mediatized emotional democracy characterized by first-person forms of address (Dovey 2000).

But it is an equally important objective of the book to demonstrate how the different approaches may help professional communicators reach their audiences more effectively. We return to this objective later in this chapter.

## MEDIA AUDIENCES AND EVERYDAY LIFE

It is axiomatic for the argument of this book that people's media use is anchored in the contexts of everyday life in which people live their lives as members of partially overlapping large and small groups, at the global, national, regional and local levels. The way individuals use and make sense of media material is determined by the identities and communicative repertoires they are socialized into as a result of their membership of these groups in the course of their life history.

People develop their cultural identities and communicative repertoires throughout life in a variety of intersecting socializing institutions such as the family, the school, clubs and associations, and, last but not least, peer groups. Some of these groups are natural sites of media consumption. Over the last couple of decades, the peer group has assumed an increasing importance as a prominent context of media use for adolescents, but it is still the case that the family by far overshadows any other social institution as the most important context of media use.

### FAMILY TELEVISION

In the audience research classic *Family Television*, the British researcher David Morley claimed that 'the changing patterns of television viewing could only be understood in the overall context of family leisure activity' (Morley 1986: 13). He even went on to suggest that one should take 'the dynamic unit of consumption to be more properly the family/household rather than the individual viewer' (Morley 1986: 15).

Readers who respond to this suggestion with scepticism should take a look at Michael Arlen's small slice-of-life portrait of the morning rituals of an average American family in the mid-1970s (Box 1.1; Arlen 1982). Clearly a fictional and humorous account of this family's interpersonal communication around the TV set, the portrait nevertheless comes across as a mock field-note fragment of an ethnographer's reporting from an observation study of family behaviour.

## Box 1.1 Slice-of-life portrait of the morning rituals of an American family (Arlen 1982)

[. . .]

'I can't find my shirt anywhere,' said Father.

'Here's your orange juice,' said Mother.

'Good morning, I'm Bill Beutel,' said Bill Beutel, his jacket flickering in alternating shades of green and yellow. 'The Westminster Kennel Club Show is opening in New York, and in a few moments we're going to be talking to you about that.'

'Don't you want your orange juice?' Mother said.

Father took the glass of orange juice and held it in his hand [. . .].

'I saw it in the closet only last night,' he said. 'Joey, you leave the set alone.'

[. . .]

'Clarice, you do the toast,' said Mother.

'Mother, I have all this *homework*. I have a quiz in social studies.'

Bill Beutel said, 'Johnny Miller's 69 keeps him out front in the Bob Hope Desert Classic. As of this moment it looks as if the women are going to boycott Wimbledon.'

Father switched channels. Frank Blair said, 'Yesterday, in Cambodia, a direct hit was scored upon this school in Phnom Penh.'

Father said, 'I guess I'll go look for it myself.'

[. . .]

'Clarice, remember the left side of the toaster doesn't work,' said Mother.

'Mother, I *know*,' said Clarice.

[. . .]

On the television set, Fred Flintstone was rolling a stone wheel down a long hill. [. . .] Father watched as the wheel rolled down the hill and then along the back of the dinosaur until it hit him on the head. 'Who turned this on?' Father asked.

'Mom asked me to,' said Joey.

'I did no such thing, Joey,' said Mother. 'Eat your eggs before they're cold. Clarice, come eat your eggs!'

Father switched channels. Stephanie Edwards said, 'Nearly the entire central part of the country is in the grip of a cold-air mass. In Oklahoma City, the high today will be thirty-seven, the low around twenty.'

'Did you know that thirty-two degrees is freezing, Mom?' said Joey.

[. . .]

'You run along now, boys,' said Mother.

> There was the sound of the storm door slamming, then reopening, then slamming. Mother changed the channel on the television set and started collecting the dishes. [. . .] The refrigerator clicked on. The dishwasher churned. The telephone began to ring. 'Hi, Beth,' Mother said. 'Wait a minute while I turn the TV down. We were just listening to the morning news.'

Like the mother, the other members of this American family would probably report having 'watched the news' on this as on every other morning. As media researchers concerned with the use of news as a democratic resource, however, we would normally understand the activity of watching the news as a more concentrated activity in which the viewer engages with the news programme in a more concentrated manner. The way in which the TV news serves as a kind of background wallpaper for this family might not qualify therefore.

Yet when TV meters measure the TV audience, the distracted viewing of this family would be registered and disappear into average ratings figures along with the concentrated viewing of other viewers. And when we carry out interviews about a news programme for a reception study, we may show informants a news programme and solicit their experience of news items that they would have paid little or no attention to in a natural viewing situation. An ethnographic observation study of authentic news viewing thus may provide a necessary supplement, or even corrective, to the results produced by less naturalistic research methods.

The mock observation data of Arlen's family portrait do not enable us to determine what proportion of the news broadcast is actually processed by the family members. We can only see that of all the news broadcast during their breakfast there are only two items that provoke any kind of response from the family members, one being the remarks about the temperature in Oklahoma City. No one reacts to the information that a school in Cambodia received 'a direct hit', even though this family itself has two schoolchildren.

The reason is, quite simply, as with a large part of TV viewing in the modern family, that media use is often completely overwhelmed by the routines of everyday life. Each family member pursues his or her own urgent morning projects, as the father worries about his lost shirt, the mother makes an effort to get everyone breakfast, and Joey manoeuvres to secretly switch the dial to his own favourite channel.

The 'observation data' enable us to observe how family members commute between distracted and concentrated viewing; how differences of taste according to gender and age cause family members to struggle about channel choice; how TV material may sometimes surface as a topic of conversation, and thereby how the morning news may have a kind of agenda-setting effect for the family. But many aspects of the way in which the family members make sense, individually and interpersonally, of the morning ritual around the TV set are not observable. In order to put together a complete picture of the situational use of a mediated communication process like 'watching the news', therefore, we need to employ the optics of different empirical methods, not least methods in which viewers are asked to verbalize their experiences and practices.

## AUDIENCE ROUTINES

We have just seen how the use of a particular media product, in this case morning television, is embedded within social rituals of the family dating from long before the arrival of television, which constitute a kind of matrix that television must fit itself into rather than vice versa. This is true of the media generally and means that we should think of audiences as individuals who don't always make a conscious choice to 'expose' themselves to a specific media product. There are obvious exceptions to this rule, one of them being the movie theatre experience, which does have the status of a special occasion for many people. But most media uses have the distinctive character of the ordinary – that is, people enact a number of chronologically organized routines that follow the temporal units of the year, the week and, most importantly, the day, into which the different media are fitted.

In many countries, people's overall consumption of television, for instance, follows the natural cycle of summer and winter, so that they watch considerably less television during the summer when increased daylight invites more outdoor activities in private gardens and public sports grounds. Television stations in the US and other countries respond to this by offering few new productions during the summer months, leaving faithful viewers with a diet of re-runs of the past year's programmes. In Denmark the most popular daily evening news programme for most of the year is broadcast by TV2 at 7 p.m. During the three summer months, however, the main competitor, DR1, whose evening news is broadcast at 9 p.m., soars to the top of the ratings. Finally, many people look forward to the special programming in connection with annual national and international sports tournaments, and in connection with annual holidays like Christmas.

Apart from the well-known scheduling practice by TV companies operating fixed day and time slots for most of their serialized fare, the weekly patterning of TV use consists mainly of the division of the week into weekday viewing and weekend viewing. On weekdays the ratings curve starts to decline from its primetime plateau somewhat earlier than during weekends, when viewers can watch what they like as late as they like because they don't have to get up the next morning. For the same reasons many families have a more relaxed attitude to children's viewing on Fridays and Saturdays, 'letting them watch until they drop'. Similarly, heavy Sunday newspapers with half a dozen supplements try to meet the readers' need for domestic relaxation on the last day of the week.

For many people, daily life on working days displays a remarkable degree of routinization, right down to the single movements of the toothbrush or the items on the breakfast menu. The activities of the working day have become conventionalized into a routine pattern with little room for deviation. Even though people may value some of their recurring media experiences highly, they are generally accorded a secondary importance compared to the daily activities that take care of material necessity such as work, shopping and cooking. In practice this means, for instance, that if time pressure emerges in one's material obligations, the reading of the newspaper may be cut down, postponed or cancelled for that day. And a TV serial episode may be recorded for later watching, while a late news programme may be substituted for an early one.

It may be instructive and consciousness-raising with respect to the routinized distribution of the different media in one's own daily practice to register them in tabular form, as exemplified in Table 1.1. The table shows the correspondences of everyday activities and media uses during the working day of a 35-year-old middle-class male, married with two children, who drives his car to work at an office 25 minutes away.

Table 1.1   A day in the life: media use on a typical weekday of a 35-year-old middle-class male, married with two children, who drives his car to work at an office 25 minutes away

| Everyday activity | | Media exposure/use |
| --- | --- | --- |
| Out of bed | 7.00 | Morning paper headlines |
| Breakfast | | |
| Pack lunch | 8.00 | Radio news |
| Taking kids to school | | |
| Car ride to work | 9.00 | Talk/music radio |
| WORK | 10.00 | Intranet/email/www |
| Car ride home | 16.00 | Talk/music radio |
| Picking up kids, homework | | |
| Coffee | 17.00 | CD music |
| | | Morning paper articles |
| Shopping | | Food product posters, muzak |
| Cooking | 18.00 | Children's TV, TV news (cursory) |
| Family meal | 18.30 | |
| | 19.00 | |
| Kids' night rituals | 20.00 | |
| | 20.30 | Morning newspaper articles |
| Relaxation | 21.00 | TV news hour |
| | | OR |
| Relaxation | 22.00 | TV news, sports |
| | | Recorded TV programme |
| Relaxation | 23.00 | Professional journal, magazines |
| Bedtime | 24.00 | Local newspaper |
| | | Book on the bedside |

Before we leave the subject of the media and everyday life it is necessary to mention a change that is developing in the consumption of television. This is the gradual emergence of multi-set families or households in which each family member has access to their own TV set. This means that TV use, especially among adolescent family members, has become individualized to a point where a considerable part of their TV diet does not have to be negotiated with other household members. This is a significant change, which means that the use of television has become a lot like the individualized use of newspapers, books and print media generally. However, there are still important collective uses of television in some spaces of the family household. And the general point about media use being embedded in the social and situational contexts of everyday life is equally valid with respect to individualized and collectively used media.

## GETTING ACROSS

We now turn to a different kind of audience research, which is designed to assist the communicators of specific messages to specifically delimited audiences. While the example above of the *Big Brother* audience emphasizes the need to understand audiences as situated in the social and discursive terrains of contemporary modern culture, the following case emphasizes the need for institutional communicators to understand the audience discursively, but in more strategic terms, as the 'targets' or beneficiaries of what, for short, we may call campaigns.

A few years ago a poster campaign was launched in all commuter train stations in Copenhagen, Denmark, with the purpose of informing people that it was possible to take a bicycle on the trains. The dominant element of the poster was a big photograph of a young man with a shaved head wearing a leather jacket, and with a pleased smile on his face. He is sitting on a train next to a bicycle with a basket on his lap. 'Ole is faster than Bjarne,' says the headline, and the copy says that you can take your bike with you on the commuter train free of charge on Saturdays and Sundays.

According to the manager of the railway operator, 'the poster shows a picture of a nice and clean-looking young man sitting in the commuter train next to his bike with a basket on his lap. In the basket we can see part of a book about wild mushrooms, in other words he is going out to gather mushrooms in the forest, taking his bike with him on the train' (quoted in the railway's monthly passenger magazine).

The headline plays on the cultural knowledge of the Danish audience that 'Bjarne' is the bicycle hero, Bjarne Riis, who won the Tour de France in 1996. In other words, the attempted joke is that 'Ole', the young man in the picture, is faster than even Bjarne Riis when he takes his bike with him on the train.

But not everybody interpreted the poster in this way. One passenger thought that 'the poster depicts a skinhead with a basket full of stolen goods, ready to testify that Bjarne is a lot smarter than Brian. The poster urges passengers to look after carefully their bags when travelling on commuter trains because they may meet half-criminal hooligans' (letter published by the passenger magazine).

This example plunges us directly into a number of issues that should be of interest to communicators whose job it is to address people in their capacity as citizens or consumers, and to communication researchers whose job it is to analyse and understand communication processes.

The first and very practical point is that the receivers of mediated verbal and visual messages often get something completely different out of a message than what the sender intended to communicate. We normally assume that meaning is a fairly straightforward thing, but the example shows that we have to consider carefully what we actually mean when we say that a text has a message. We simply cannot take for granted that the meaning intended by the sender is identical to the meaning actualized by the audience.

Second, and following directly from the first point, we will not get far in our attempt to understand media audiences if we conceptualize meaning as a fixed entity. In semiotic terms, the meaning of media messages is a multiple and diverse product of the interplay between signs and their users. With media messages, the main stages of this interplay are the 'encoding' process, taking place among the agents in media institutions, and the complementary 'decoding' process, taking place among the agents of everyday life – what we normally call the 'audience'. Media producers and consumers alike bring with them many-faceted communicative repertoires, rooted in their personal life histories and in the collective histories of the social and cultural groups they belong to; and they bring these repertoires to bear on specific communicative tasks. There is therefore no necessary fit between the encoded and the decoded meaning.

In the case of the passenger's understanding of the poster, we can observe how a middle-aged man responds with anxiety to the image of a young man whose attributes of clothing and hairstyle may be associated with the often-encountered media representations of deviance and mugging on metropolitan trains. His reading is probably anchored in an age-specific communicative repertoire, which may be quite 'wrong' in relation to the communicative intention, but which is nevertheless a fact of life that cannot be argued with.

The passenger's active communicative repertoire manifests itself in two supplementary ways: first of all it produces a meaning on the basis of the visual and verbal signs of the image that are actually there in the text; but it does more than that, as it imaginatively writes something *into* the text that is not 'there' – it transforms one of the names of the poster's narrative from Ole to Brian, and changes the poster's order of names and the descriptive adjective. The passenger's signifying process thus creates a scenario in which it is no longer Ole who is faster than Bjarne, but *Bjarne* who is *smarter* than Brian!

These transformations may be explained by the anchorage of the passenger's communicative repertoire in a Danish sociocultural context. For people who grew up in Denmark in the 1950s, the name Brian, which was then an innovative working-class adoption from English, connotes 'troublemaker', and in popular jargon, for instance, among schoolteachers, any obnoxious young male can be referred to as 'a Brian'.

The second point arising from the example is therefore a theoretical one: any investigation of media audiences must base itself on an adequate theory of the social production of meaning. In this book our theoretical platform builds on theories that have variously been described as 'social semiotic', 'post-structuralist' and 'constructionist'.

Third, and most importantly for a practical guide to media audience research like this one, the poster example may give rise to a number of methodological questions. What are the empirical methods we can use in order to produce knowledge about the way audiences make sense of and use the mediated messages they encounter in the different spheres of life? In this particular case, our knowledge about one individual's reading of the poster does not come out of a major empirical study. It was found by accident when one of the authors read the railway company's passenger magazine, in which a middle-aged male passenger wrote a letter to the editor complaining about the misleading poster.

The passenger had asked the staff at a station whether he could take his bike on the commuter train, and had been directed to the poster, which was exhibited on a nearby wall. He had noticed the poster before, he was motivated to receive a message about the possibilities of taking bikes on the train, and yet he had not read it because the way the picture was composed prevented him from realizing its relevance.

The poster, in other words, failed in its communicative purpose as far as this passenger was concerned. The question that might plague those who planned the campaign is obviously how many people shared this passenger's reading? The railway manager believes that 'the message is easy to interpret correctly – and that it has been interpreted correctly by the majority of our passengers' (quoted in the passenger magazine).

He may well be right, but one of the questions that concerns us in this book is how it might be possible to know with a greater degree of certitude whether the poster functioned communicatively according to the sender's intention. The discipline of audience research has a number of different tools to offer that can provide different kinds of insight into the poster campaign's communicative success, or lack of it.

For instance, within the framework of a *reception* study, the poster (and other posters from the same campaign) could be shown to members of the target group. People would thus be invited to talk in individual or focus-group interviews about the experience of and response to the actual campaign, and on the basis of these interviews the campaign planners would be able to assess the campaign's relative degree of success.

Such a reception study could combine the interview approach with a more *ethnographic*, observational approach in which researchers explored passengers' attention to the posters in station halls and on platforms, and engaged passengers who brought their bikes with them on the trains.

Another possibility would be to pre-test the campaign material before launching it, allowing campaign planners to make adjustments to the poster's verbal and visual elements if necessary. A pre-test procedure could be *experimentally* designed to present a number of different creative ideas to selected members of the target group, for instance, trying out their communicative responses to protagonists of different ages and genders, wearing different kinds of garments and other accompanying attributes, and different graphic realizations of headlines.

The three types of audience research exemplified so far have all been 'qualitative' (although experimental research usually uses quantitative methods). As such they are characterized by the production of quite detailed, in-depth information, leading to a rich understanding of the informants' experience. Qualitative research normally collects its data from a relatively small number of informants, typically one or two dozen individuals, and is therefore not statistically 'representative' of the target audience.

Some communicators of mediated messages therefore prefer to rely on a different, 'quantitative' kind of approach, which can handle large, representative numbers of respondents, even if it means having to sacrifice some of the depth of understanding offered by qualitative approaches. In the case of the poster campaign, the planners might want to evaluate the campaign's effectiveness by carrying out a large-scale questionnaire-based audience *survey*. In such a survey, hundreds of passengers could be invited to fill in their answers to a set of closed questions about their ability to recall the campaign posters, their understanding of the posters and their possible change of behaviour as a result of the campaign.

In the chapters that follow we aim to present, exemplify and discuss the four methodological approaches to the audience just mentioned: ethnographic research, reception research, survey research and experimental research into media audiences. For practical reasons we shall focus on these approaches separately in the major part of the book, but as we go through their respective strengths and weaknesses it will become clear that we do not consider them to be isolated tools.

In the history of media and communication research, the four approaches have often been used in a 'pure' form, in isolation from one another. And in the past the adherents of each approach have often seen the practitioners of the other approaches as belonging to antagonistic camps. However, in this book we will adopt a non-dogmatic, theoretical perspective in which the specific research methodology recommended depends in each case on the nature of the task at hand (Chapter 3). We thus have no difficulty with blending the different approaches into hybrid research designs that seem appropriate for specific purposes, just as we shall follow the by now common practice of using different approaches side by side in a so-called triangulation strategy (Chapter 17).

## TRANSMISSION OR DIALOGUE? TWO CONCEPTUALIZATIONS OF THE AUDIENCE

The lesson to be learnt from the campaign example in the previous section can be summarized neatly by quoting a passage from Brenda Dervin's plea for a reorientation of perspective within communication research. Her distinction between 'transmission' and 'dialogue' is related to Carey's distinction between the transmission and ritual aspects of mass communication (Carey 1989), and to Fiske's distinction between the 'process' and 'semiotic' schools of communication research (Fiske 1990):

> *Communication research cannot be conceptualized as transmission. Rather, it must be conceptualized in terms of both parties involved in creating meanings, by means of dialogue. The sense people make of the media messages is never limited to what sources intend and is always enriched by the realities people bring to bear.*
>
> (Dervin 1989: 72)

The poster example above demonstrated precisely how people may indeed 'enrich' the media message, although most campaign planners would probably have said that the message is 'distorted' by the audience, because they are concerned with getting through to the audience with *their* intended message.

We shall continue here for a few more pages to illustrate the general points we wish to make about media audiences, with lines of reasoning taken from the agenda of campaign planners. This is not because campaign research is the sole focus of this book – it is not – but because this agenda, with its need to reach the targeted audience, creates an acute dependency on audiences, which may highlight the fieldwork challenges facing any audience analyst.

Campaign planners are people who have the task of solving a social or communicative problem through a communication effort, usually through the mass media. It is their purpose to disseminate information so that the targeted groups may change their attitudes or their behaviour in a given area, such as joining blood donor schemes, quitting smoking or becoming users of community libraries. Due to historical and academic tradition, campaign planners have usually conceptualized their task in terms of a *transmission model* of communication.

When audience groups are addressed within such a model, communication tends to become one-way, so that campaigners see themselves as talking *to* people, informing them about unquestionable truths that it would be in people's best interests to accept and follow. Using a couple of conventional metaphors for describing this situation, we may say that audience groups are regarded as 'empty vessels' to be filled with information provided by experts, or that audience groups are seen as 'targets' that campaign communicators try to 'hit' with their supposedly beneficial information.

In either case, audiences are thereby depersonalized and objectified as amorphous groups, usually defined in demographic terms such as age, ethnicity, income, gender, etc., and with system categories forced on them. This is the case both when the campaign itself tries to get people, for instance smokers, to change fundamental aspects of their everyday life, and when people have to relate to and fill in the more or less straitjacket-like questionnaires that are sometimes used as an input to the creation of campaign strategy.

Campaigns that are conceptualized within such a framework often fail, because people don't notice them, misunderstand them, don't care about them or meet them with outright resistance because they see them as having little or no relevance to their daily lives. This is, in many cases, a pity, observes Dervin, because campaigners are often well-intentioned social engineers whose noble purposes could actually improve people's lives, and the well-being of society as a whole. She therefore suggests that communication campaigns should be approached in an entirely different manner, which 'requires a fundamental reconceptualization of both the *nature of audiences* and the *nature of campaigns*' (Dervin 1989: 69).

The alternative *dialogic model* of communication is one that recognizes from the outset that the 'truth' about social phenomena is always relative, because it depends on the contextual circumstances affecting people's lives. In this view, people from different social groups are seen as active in the construction of everyday truths that work for them in their daily lives. Campaign planners should therefore take an interest in how people themselves define their problems and goals, and be prepared to find ambivalences and contradictions of both motives and solutions. And the larger picture of the social landscape should be perceived in terms of a range of equally valid norms and values, leading campaign planners to recognize that the existence of competing perspectives may require a negotiation of solutions, rather than the imposition of official ones.

Negotiation implies dialogue and a mutual openness to change, and therefore calls for a qualitative research approach to campaigns, although Dervin also recommends the supplementary use of relevant quantitative methods. The essential feature of the dialogic approach is really the mutuality of the relationship between campaign planners and researchers on the one hand and the 'audiences' on the other.

In one of Dervin's case studies the objective was to get more people with a Hispanic background to use the facilities of a New York community library. Dervin argues that a conventional one-way information campaign targeted towards the Hispanic community would have fallen on barren ground and not led to the desired outcome. The dialogic approach gave the library staff a better understanding of the needs and interests of the Hispanic groups, and made them realize how a change of some library rules and procedures could overcome the barriers of access previously perceived by these groups.

Dervin takes up the radical position that we should perhaps stop talking about 'audiences' and 'campaigns': 'Adopting a communication-as-dialogue approach to audience research yields a fundamental change in the conception of the audience and the campaign. In one sense neither term is any longer applicable' (Dervin 1989:76).

This book is based on the belief that people who are going to work as professional communicators and communication researchers would not benefit from drawing this conclusion. We take the view that the communication process should be conceptualized through the optics of different models, and that within such an eclectic perspective there is a role to be played by both the transmission and the dialogic model.

In the chapters that follow we shall try to demonstrate that the purpose of understanding the ways in which people use and experience mediated communication may be served both by measuring the 'amorphous mass' of audiences in terms of demographic and lifestyle patterns, and by analysing in depth the social reality behind the numbers, i.e. the complex meanings and practices of people's everyday lives. In doing either, or both, it is vital to remember that the results produced by any form of communication research do not represent the truth. All we can claim is that our findings are a particular construction of social reality, which is offered as one contribution to ongoing public and professional discussions about the role of the mediated communication in contemporary society.

## THE RESEARCH CONSTRUCTION OF AUDIENCES

All audience research is obtrusive. We cannot study audiences empirically without at the same time interfering with the very phenomenon we wish to study – the everyday practices through which people use and make sense of the media – or interrupting people's lives for the duration of the research encounter. This is a characteristic that differentiates audience research from the types of media research that study media content, because the analysis of content can measure and interpret its object of analysis without affecting this object in the process.

One might therefore feel tempted to study the media exclusively through their content, were it not for the fact that even the most insightful of textual studies cannot tell us anything about how people appropriate the textual products offered by the media into their everyday lives, nor can they tell us how they make sense of the cultural meanings offered by these messages. It was precisely as an antidote to the often far-reaching claims made by content analysts – for instance, about the ideological effects of media representations on public understandings of controversial issues – that reception research was developed from the early 1980s.

As audience researchers, therefore, we have to come to terms with the fact that however we choose to engage audiences empirically, we shall be several steps removed from that which we wish to study: on the one hand, how people *use* the media as an integrated part of their daily lives, as a *social practice* alongside other social practices, and on the other hand, how the cultural meanings offered by the media are *made sense of* and may *gratify* people's needs for information and entertainment.

The moment we start to *observe* people's media-related behaviour we will be intruders in their lives and we will be affecting this behaviour in ways that are neither predictable nor controllable. This has been an ongoing concern about the method of participant observation among ethnographers, aptly expressed in the so-called 'Observer's Paradox', according to which the aim of ethnographic research is to find out how people behave when they are not being systematically observed; yet this can only be done by systematic observation (Labov 1972a: 209).

While the paradox cannot be solved, the ethnographic experience shows that there is no need to exaggerate its practical effects. As James Lull, one of the pioneers of modern media ethnographic studies, puts it in the context of his study of TV use in American families: although participant observation does constitute an 'intrusion into such a small and private social unit, . . . the presence of the investigator in the habitat of his subjects, the usual objection to participant observation research, need not severely disrupt the natural behaviour of the family unit' (Lull 1980). Moreover, the ethnographer's role as a stranger in the lifeworld he is studying may in some ways be seen as an enabling factor for the obtaining of insights about media-related behaviour. These issues are discussed in greater depth in Chapters 4–6.

The moment we start *talking* to people about their media experiences we complicate things even more, because we cannot take complete mutual understanding for granted, even when researcher and informant belong to the same language community and 'speak the same language'. The researcher's communicative repertoires, i.e. the verbal and cultural 'codes' at his or her disposal, may not match completely those of the informants, and in some cases may deviate considerably, due to differences of class, ethnicity, age, gender, etc. This is so because our communicative repertoires are intimately related to the various cultural identities we inhabit and the spheres of experience we are familiar with.

Therefore, even though there exists a considerable common core within a national language community, there are still plenty of possibilities of misunderstanding both as regards the meaning of individual lexical items and the 'traffic rules' of interpersonal inter-action. Language is constantly being innovated, and most so among young people. A middle-aged researcher might therefore completely misunderstand a young man of 20 speaking of a TV programme about a 'really sweaty hotel', not realizing that for young Danes the Danish equivalent of 'sweaty' has completely changed its meaning from 'seedy' and 'squalid' to the almost opposite 'glamorous' and 'high class'. The same point would apply to questionnaires, whose effectiveness as a research tool depends on the researcher's ability to produce questions that are decoded by respondents as meanings that correspond closely to those encoded by the researcher.

For these reasons, audience research can never claim to find the truth about audience practices and meanings, only partial insights about how audiences use the media in a specific context. In other words, *audience research always produces a social construction of audience practices and meanings*. The key moments of this construction and their interrelation may be visualized in the diagrammatic form of Figure 1.1, which shows the 'archetypal' audience research process as a multi-layered communicative signifying process.

For presentational purposes the model will be explained here using reception research of television programmes as the case. But the model may represent the generalized audience research process and readers may play with – and perhaps elaborate on – the model, sub-stituting other research approaches (survey research, experimental research, ethnographic research) and other media (newspapers, radio, cinema, the World Wide Web, etc.).

**Figure 1.1** Audience research as a multi-layered communicative signifying process

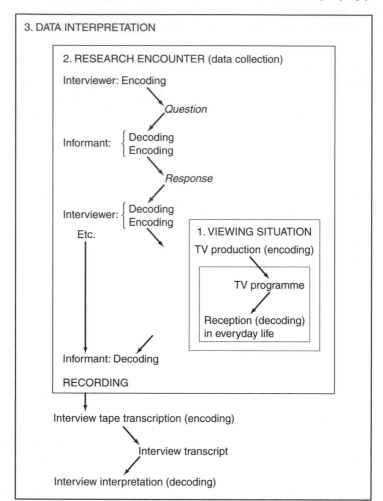

The model depicts the audience research process as a system of 'Chinese boxes', consisting of at least three communicative situations that are embedded into each other: the viewing situation in everyday life, the research encounter and the interpretation of the collected data. Each of these situations is conceptualized as a site of social meaning production, a series of interrelated communicative exchanges, each consisting of the three stages of encoding, text and decoding. Audience research is thus represented as a communicative process of situational embedding.

In the *encoding* process of each situation, the participants' communicative repertoires are actualized as a text, formed by cultural, social, political, situational and individual circumstances. The *text* is therefore a complex material manifestation of these communicative repertoires, organized semiotically along paradigmatic and syntagmatic lines. The *decoding* is the triggering by the text of the recipients' communicative repertoires as formed by cultural, social, political, situational and individual circumstances.

At the core, in the innermost box, we have the viewing situation and its cultural meanings, which is what we want to explore. The TV programme is produced ('encoded') by a multitude of cultural producers within the complex organizational framework of a media organization, and is transmitted (as a 'text') into the domestic context of the family, where it is accessed and experienced ('decoded') by family members in the context of everyday life. This is where audience meanings are constructed spontaneously and authentically through the programme experience.

Moving into the second box, we get to the domain of the research encounter where the data collection (and recording) takes place through some sort of personal encounter between researcher and informants, be that in an individual or a focus-group interview, in the informant's home or in an institutional setting. This personal encounter takes the form of an interpersonal communicative exchange, a 'turn-taking' process in which the participants collaborate, through the verbal performance of the pre-allocated roles of interviewer and informant, to illuminate the social practices and the meaning processes of the viewing situation.

The research encounter can, therefore, not be seen as a window on the viewing experience; rather it should be seen as a partial reconstruction of it, which is dependent on the informant's memory, selection of experiences and meanings according to their perceived relevance, and willingness to co-operate, and on the mutual communicative skills of researcher and informant.

The third box depicts the situation of data interpretation, although of course everything that goes on in the research encounter from planning to execution is obviously steeped in interpretative activity. The data analysis begins with the 'encoding', or fossilization, as a 'text', of the written transcript based on the audio or videotape recording of the research encounter. It continues with the 'decoding' – that is, the interpretation of the transcript – which is best considered as yet another partial reconstruction, now twice removed from the authentic situation of media use that we are studying.

Basically, this interpretative process seeks, on the basis of already existing scientific knowledge, to produce new scientific knowledge based on the interpersonal meanings that informants offered in the interview situation, when they talked about the everyday meanings evoked by the programme.

In an exhaustive model there could be several more boxes, in order to take account of the scientific and non-scientific construction processes that follow the analysis, such as the researcher's encoding of journal articles and books about his findings, offered for the critical decoding of colleagues and students within the scientific community. Such reports may sometimes find their way into the hands of journalists, whose articles or broadcast reports interpret and disseminate the researcher's findings to a wider community.

It has been the purpose of this model-construction exercise to demonstrate that the knowledge produced by audience research – as indeed by any other kind of social research – should be presented in a spirit of modesty and humility, but also with confidence in the insights that audience research is capable of providing.

There exists no empirical method that can provide rock-solid knowledge about human society and its social and cultural practices. But each method may claim its ability to deliver at least a partial picture of the complex mediatized reality we live in, and thereby to contribute to the platforms of knowledge that institutions, communities and individuals need as points of departure for interventions in the social construction of reality.

The methods we have, and are ever likely to get, for studying media audiences may not be perfect, but there is no alternative – except ignorance. If we want to understand audiences, we have got to study them empirically, with the methods that have been accumulated and refined in the discipline over the years.

It is the purpose of this book to heighten the critical awareness among students of media and communications about the precise manner in which the different tools available to audience analysts can be said to provide different kinds of 'partial pictures' of the worlds of audiences. Each approach has inherent strengths and weaknesses, enabling it to illuminate some aspects of audience practices while having little explanatory power for others. Being clear about those strengths and weaknesses is a first prerequisite for producing audience research that is credible and useful.

## CRITICAL EYE ON AUDIENCE RESEARCH

The critical awareness of the strengths and weaknesses of different methods advocated above should be applied both when we design our own research projects and when we use the research results produced by others. The conventional wisdom in communication studies, and in the social sciences generally, usually distinguishes between the strong and weak points of quantitative and qualitative methods: 'Quantitative observations provide a high level of measurement precision and statistical power, while qualitative observations provide greater depth of information about how people perceive events in the context of the actual situations in which they occur' (Frey et al. 1991: 99). This distinction is made on the basis of the traditional criteria of scientificness used in the social sciences, so that 'measurement precision', 'statistical power' and 'depth of information' are synonyms for, respectively, reliability, representativeness and validity.

These criteria may serve as a heuristic set of terms for evaluating the results produced by the range of communication research from the social sciences to the humanities. It should be borne in mind, however, that sometimes audience research projects, especially those conceptualized as ethnographic research, are deliberately designed to not live up to all of the criteria when they are pursuing objectives and knowledge interests that do not require them to do so.

Here we shall briefly demonstrate the usefulness of applying these criteria as a systematic way to evaluate specific examples of audience research, by discussing a questionnaire-based study of music videos (Brown and Schulze 1990). We will also take up the discussion of the criteria of scientific credibility later in the book, in connection with the presentation of each of the four research approaches, as well as in the chapter that discusses ways of combining and cross-fertilizing the different approaches (Chapter 17).

Brown and Schulze wanted to explore the effects of race, gender and fandom on audience interpretations of Madonna's music videos. Here we shall focus on those aspects of their study that deal with male and female, black and white, experiences of the music video 'Papa Don't Preach' (1986).

Briefly, the music video tells the story of a white adolescent girl (played by Madonna), who has apparently been brought up by a single father. After she falls in love with a young man, a romantic relationship develops, and a conflict arises between her and her father. The video is not explicit about the reasons for this conflict. We hear Madonna singing that she insists on 'keeping my baby' and that she feels that she is 'in trouble deep'. In one scene from her house we see her sitting on a bed clutching a pillow against her stomach; in another there is literally a wall between her and her father. Finally the father appears to give in, and father and daughter are reconciled.

Brown and Schulze did their study in 1988, two years after the release of the video, with 68 black and 118 college white students. The method used was questionnaires, with a few closed demographic questions in order to identify respondents' identities, and a number of open-ended content questions, all of them to be answered in writing. The content questions asked, for instance, 'How did this video make you feel?' 'What do you think this video is about?' and 'Complete the story – what happens?' The questionnaires were handed out and completed by the students in class.

In the analysis two coders read through all the responses and established a number of themes that appeared to be common to the respondents. Contrary to the norm in many survey studies, in which the researchers require respondents to relate to a set of pre-determined themes, the analytical themes in this study were audience driven. The main themes constructed were 'Mention of pregnancy' and 'Primary theme', the latter subdivided into 'Teenage pregnancy', 'Boy/girl relationship', Father/daughter relationship' and 'Independent girl/decision-making'. Once constructed, these themes guided the quantitative coding of the students' responses. The two coders' categorizations of the data into the themes were compared, and their agreement was established to be between 75 and 85 per cent. The findings are reported in Table 1.2.

The results show that whites were more likely than blacks to see this video as being about teenage pregnancy, and more likely to see this as the video's primary theme. In the words of the researchers, 'Even when Blacks "saw" a pregnancy, they were less likely than whites to focus on it as the central theme of the video' (Brown and Schulze 1990: 94). In line with this interpretation, blacks thought that the 'baby' of which Madonna sings is her boyfriend, not an unborn infant.

Table 1.2    Reactions to 'Papa Don't Preach' by race and sex; rounded percentages

|  | Black male (n=28) % | Black female (n=40) % | White male (n=54) % | White female (n=64) % |
|---|---|---|---|---|
| Mentioned pregnancy | 43 | 73 | 85 | 97 |
| Primary theme |  |  |  |  |
| Teenage pregnancy | 21 | 40 | 56 | 63 |
| Boy/girl relationship | 21 | 5 | 15 | 5 |
| Father/daughter relationship | 43 | 50 | 22 | 25 |
| Independent girl/decision-making | 14 | 5 | 7 | 8 |

Source: Brown and Schulze 1990: 95

The most important theme for blacks, on the other hand, was the father/daughter relation-ship, which they were twice as likely as whites to mention as the video's primary theme. Among the less important themes, males of both races were more likely to focus on the boy/girl relationship, and black males tended more to see the theme 'Independent girl'. The figures show a clear pattern of interpretation, but they show equally clearly that we are not dealing here with an either/or of audience interpretation.

The first point we wish to make about this study continues the discussion of audience research in the preceding section about the need for empirical audience research: no amount of sophistication in a textual analysis, qualitative or quantitative, could have predicted this pattern of audience interpretation of the Madonna video. Conceivably a textual analysis might have been able to spot the ambiguity of the word 'baby', but it could not have guessed that the young audience of this video is partly divided along racial lines of interpretation. Consequently, it could not have raised a discussion about the intersec-tion of media experiences and the wider social practices of American society.

Using terminology developed within audience research over the last decades we can say that a textual analysis might have been able to demonstrate the video's *polysemy*, i.e. the multiple possibilities of meaning offered by this cultural artefact. But it could not have predicted that the black and white students belong to different, but partially overlapping, *interpretative communities*, whose culturally anchored communicative repertoires appear to give different priority to the potential meanings offered by this video.

Brown and Schulze (1990) argue that the pattern of readings they found is clearly related to deep-rooted social concerns in the everyday life of the white and the black community in America, respectively. Blacks, especially males, do not see teenage pregnancy in the video because they don't see teenage pregnancy as the trouble most whites think it is, because it is not uncommon in the black community. For instance, unmarried mothers are four times more common among black teenagers than among whites, and 50 per cent of black mothers as opposed to 14 per cent of white single mothers have never been married. In other words, because teenage pregnancy is so much more of a disgrace in the white community, white students are much more alert to signs in the video that might have to do with this taboo subject. The blacks' focus on the father/daughter relationship is explained by Brown and Schulze by 'the currently more problematic nature of establishing lasting cross-sex relationships in black society' (Brown and Schulze 1990: 95), not least the absence of the father from many black families.

The second point has to do with the critical awareness that should always accompany social research: can we trust these findings, and what sort of questions should we ask of empirical research in order to pinpoint the issues of credibility? As indicated at the beginning of this section, it is often useful to look at the way a study was carried out, and to evaluate its methodology in terms of the traditional scientific criteria of reliability, validity and representativeness. The Madonna video study can be used to illustrate what such critical awareness may look like in practice – although we wish to stress once more that because different types of research operate within different epistemological frameworks, credibility standards also show variation from one methodological approach to another.

Without wishing to go into detail at this moment, *reliability* basically has to do with whether the procedure used in gathering and analysing one's data is systematic and consistent, so that arbitrariness is avoided. Brown and Schulze describe their data gathering and analysis very meticulously, leaving the reader with the impression that their results are indeed reliable. For instance, they describe how all the written qualitative data was interpreted by two pairs of eyes, whose level of agreement about the categorization of data into themes was high.

The concern with *representativeness* is relevant if we are interested in knowing whether the findings from studying a relatively small number of individuals apply to other individuals within the total population of a country, an organization or a community. Representativeness thus hinges on the size and composition of *the sample*, and usually the randomness of its recruitment. In the Madonna video study, the sample studied were college students, but the reader sometimes gets the impression that the findings are used to say something about 'blacks' and 'whites' in general, far beyond the college student community. The history of communication research is only too rich in examples of studies that have used college students, because they were convenient for the researcher, without showing sufficient restraint when reporting the findings as if they were generalizable to, for instance, a national population.

In the Madonna study, even if the researchers' conclusions are made only about the college student population in the US, we may object that the sample is really not big enough, especially with respect to the black respondents, to make a strong claim about the racial and gendered patterning of readings.

When we ask about *validity* we are questioning whether a study has accurately captured that which it intended to investigate, how 'true' the findings are. We may phrase this generally in terms of the model of the audience research process discussed above (Figure 1.1). What is at issue is whether our fieldwork design (i.e. the data gathering of the middle box) is likely to provide us with real insights about, say, the use and experience of TV news in everyday life settings (the innermost box). Was our questionnaire good enough? Did we succeed in setting up a productive focus group setting? Did our ethnographic design establish 'rapport' with important informants, so that people really let us into what they think and do when they watch the news?

In the case of the Madonna video study, we may ask if the choice of the classroom setting is perhaps less than ideal for exploring pop videos, which as a pleasure of leisure time belong to an entirely different realm of students' daily life. The choice of the rather formal written medium of data collection may pull the students' reported experiences in the same direction, by turning the articulation of a largely emotional experience in the direction of an intellectualizing school achievement.

These are just some of the critical methodological issues that can always be raised about any empirical study. Whether the objections are insignificant or invalidating is first up to the individual reader, second to fora of discussion available to the interpretative community of researchers, and finally to the decision- and policy-makers of the wider society, who rely on social research for their political initiatives.

The perfect, flawless fieldwork design does not exist. The researcher is inevitably faced with multitudinous methodological choices, from the overall design to the minutest detail, and with every choice something is gained and something is lost. But the more the researcher bases these choices on intelligent reflection, the more likely it is that the balance of methodological trade-offs will lead to illuminating and credible insights about the audience practices examined. It is the aim of the chapters that follow to provide would-be audience researchers with a platform for such intelligent methodological reflection.

## WHAT IS AN AUDIENCE?

In his theoretical overview of the conceptual history of audience research, Denis McQuail observes that:

> *there is an established discourse in which 'audience' simply refers to the readers of, viewers of, listeners to one or other media channel or of this or that type of content or performance. . . . Nevertheless, beyond commonsense usage, there is much room for differences of meaning, misunderstandings, and theoretical conflicts. The problems surrounding the concept stem mainly from the fact that a single and simple word is being applied to an increasingly diverse and complex reality, open to alternative and competing theoretical formulations.*

(McQuail 1997: 1)

The diverse and complex reality of the notion of audience is due on the one hand to the fact that *the technological and social conditions* under which different types of communication and media are used are very different. We need only think of the differences between the spectators of a theatre or sports performance, the audience in a movie theatre, the living-room viewers in front of the TV screen, the newspaper reader at the breakfast table or in the commuter train, or the visitor to a museum's website. These audience scenarios are characterized by different technological requirements, by different social and interpersonal relations, and by the different communicative competencies required by the different media.

On the other hand there are also several different *ways of conceptualizing audiences*. In the history of communication and media research, audiences have been conceptualized as a 'public' of informed citizens concerned about their democratic rights and obligations. They have also been seen by cultural critics as a manipulable 'mass' of alienated individuals who lead empty treadmill lives not worthy of humans. And they have been viewed by media industries as a landscape of intersecting sociodemographic 'markets', as dependent consumers rather than as communicative equals. More recently, with the advent of the more interactive technologies of the Internet, audiences have come to be conceptualized as interactive partners, who are in communicative control of their lives.

We shall deal in greater depth with different conceptualizations of the audience in the chapters that follow. For now, however, in talking about 'audiences' we shall rely on the reader's intuitive notions about the common core of the different meanings of the word. This is a book about audience research methodology, and the methods we present, demonstrate and discuss are ones that are especially useful for producing insights about the users of different forms of mediated public communication taking place under conditions of 'non co-presence'. In other words, we deal mainly with methods for studying communication processes where there is a separation in time and space between institutional communication producers and large groups of unrelated individual recipients – between the distinct but related moments of encoding and decoding.

There is an urgent need for research that explores these kinds of situation, because in such communicative relationships, unlike face-to-face interaction, senders cannot observe the receivers' uptake of their communicative activity, and nor can those concerned with the political, social and cultural consequences of such communication. The analytical approaches of the following chapters should therefore be of interest both to institutional communicators wishing to reach audiences with their messages, and to social analysts seeking a better understanding of the communicative processes that affect the future of our societies.

# Chapter Two

## ☐ The history and divisions of audience research: the received view

### A TALE OF TWO CAMPS

In the early 1990s, one of the authors of this book participated in the annual conference of an American academic association in the field of communication studies. In one of the working groups he presented a research paper about a qualitative study of British informants' experiences of and attitudes to corporate image advertisements in the printed press. The paper was positively received and discussed by the members of the working group, not least the discussant, who ended his evaluation of the paper by saying, 'I really liked your paper. I'm sure you could easily do a quantitative thing on it if you wanted to publish it.'

We have chosen to start this chapter about the history of audience research with this anecdote from the real world of academic communication research because it reveals a fundamental rift that has characterized western communication studies for half a century, and to some extent still does, making and breaking the careers of individual scholars (Holbrook 1987). Although the anecdote puts the quantitative research environment in the dock as the ungenerous culprit of scientific apartheid, we hurry to add that over the years the qualitative research community in audience studies has harboured an equally persistent methodological fundamentalism that easily matches that of the anecdote (see for instance Ang 1991). Audience research, in other words, has witnessed a division between two competing scholarly paradigms – a paradigm being defined as 'a tendency of thought' that identifies as important certain areas of social and cultural exploration, and prescribes a certain methodology, which leads to results acknowledged by the paradigm's members to hold legitimate explanatory power (Gitlin 1978). The division has often assumed the character of open and mutual hostility, although we rush to emphasize that the contemporary spirit in both paradigms, as in this book, is turning towards dialogue and cross-fertilization.

Clearly, in the scholarly universe of the anecdote, a methodological bias exists that simply does not recognize qualitative work as truly scientific in its own right. Here a qualitative study of a communicative phenomenon like corporate advertising is seen, at best, as a pilot study necessary in order to create a legitimate, quantitative research instrument, such as a survey questionnaire.

The shorthand characterization of the paradigms has traditionally used the methodological labels of 'quantitative' versus 'qualitative'. But much deeper questions are at issue underneath the garb of methodological disagreement. It is quite obvious that in talking about methodologies, the adherents of each paradigm have also always been speaking from the alternative epistemological and political foundations of, on the one hand, a positivist, administrative and functionalist conceptualization of knowledge and science, and a phenomenological, hermeneutic and critical conceptualization on the other (Gitlin 1978).

Over the years it has been almost fashionable among media and communication scholars to create their own labels for the binary landscape of not just audience research but media and communication research in general. Fiske (1990), following Carey (1989), describes the division as being between two 'schools' of communication research: on the one hand, a social scientific 'process school' seeing communication as the efficient transmission of intentional 'messages' from senders to receivers; on the other hand, a 'semiotic school' seeing communication as the socially ritualized production and exchange of meanings resulting in the creation of ideologies and cultural identities.

Fiske's account, which has points in common with Dervin's distinction between a 'transmission' and a 'dialogic' approach (see Chapter 1), can be seen as an attempt to explain the difference between a kind of communication research that functions under an obligation to make communication work in practice, and another kind that emphasizes the collective processes of meaning-making that constitute a society and a culture through relations of dominance and acquiescence.

The emerging developments within and the dialogue between the two paradigms, therefore, are ultimately between epistemological entities, not just methodologies. However, as Jensen and Rosengren (1990) observe in their discussion of the main research traditions within the field of audiences:

> *In simplified terms, the sets of theories available in the area may be divided into the humanistic type and the social science type, which are the legacy of 'arts' and 'sciences', respectively. . . . These two mainstreams of general methodology are often referred to in terms of the distinction between quantitative and qualitative approaches. While much of the discussion that is premised on this distinction has obscured rather than clarified the similarities, dissimilarities and interconnections between the approaches, for want of a better terminology we use it occasionally.*

(Jensen and Rosengren 1990: 214, 219)

While being in general agreement with these authors, we believe that in a book specifically designed to present and discuss research methodologies it is appropriate to use the methodologically labelled distinction more generally. After all, it is through their operationalization into methodological practices and procedures that the epistemological positions must ultimately be evaluated by the various research communities and, not least, the wider society: can the findings produced with this or that methodology be considered interesting, relevant and useful to social and cultural concerns, or not?

Also for many new scholars, and college students, methodology precedes epistemology in the sense that the new generations in both paradigms are imperceptibly socialized into the methodological canon of their department or programme, 'the way we do things around here'. In this way the methodological lenses given to new members of research communities simply have built into them epistemological biases so as to render many issues a priori 'unresearchable', and many findings a priori 'unscientific'.

Gitlin (1978) illuminates, through an imaginary anecdote, the way in which the methodological lenses may become an epistemological straitjacket for what may count as knowledge about human culture. He imagines the following dialogue between two of the grand old men of American sociology, C. Wright Mills and Paul Lazarsfeld, representing the interpretative and the positivist paradigms respectively:

> *One of my favorite fantasies is about a dialogue between Mills and Lazarsfeld in which the former reads to the latter the first sentence of* The Sociological Imagination*: 'Nowadays men often feel that their private lives are a series of traps.' Lazarsfeld immediately replies: 'How many men, which men, how long have they felt this way, which aspect of their lives bother them, do their public lives bother them, when do they feel free rather than trapped, what kinds of traps do they experience, etc., etc.'*

(Gitlin 1978: 91)

While it is certainly possible to be humorous, from the safe distance of many decades and a secure career, about the historical conflicts between the paradigms and their practitioners, it should be remembered that this history has also been characterized by fierce and bitter struggles for scientific hegemony within the field of communication and media research (Holbrook 1987). In North American communication research, until fairly recently the social science paradigm and quantitative methodology constituted the almost uncontested 'dominant paradigm' (Gitlin 1978), even when the field of American sociology in general could boast considerable methodological pluralism from quantitative to qualitative approaches. Through the 1990s, however, there have been signs of a 'qualitative turn' as the interdisciplinary effort associated with cultural studies has made inroads into the authoritative platform of quantitative research (Grossberg et al. 1992).

In European media and communication research, the dominance of quantitative approaches within a social science framework has characterized the situation in most countries (southern Europe, Norway, Sweden), where the development of interpretative research has been an uphill struggle, though with some recent success. In some countries, notably Britain and the Netherlands, the relationship between the two paradigms is more aptly characterized as two forces of more equal strength, while media and communication research in Denmark has been the only example of the reverse situation of an all-dominant humanistic and cultural studies tradition, and an almost non-existent quantitative paradigm.

The authors of this book come out of both of these paradigms. We take a pragmatic perspective on their sometimes bitter conflicts, acknowledging that the agendas of both have followed specific and, to some extent, inevitable logics in the larger landscapes of societal and academic politics.

Looking on the bright side of life, we could even say that the absolute separation of the paradigms has enabled them to refine their respective scientific perspectives to a point of no return from which it only makes sense to explore the complementarities in a spirit of cross-fertilization. As previously indicated, such a mutual openness has now existed for some years, and cross-fertilization has become not just a buzz-word but an observable fact within the international communication research community.

In the following chapters we structure our presentation of the four approaches in accordance with their historical separation, as we move from the more interpretative and subjectivist end of the spectrum to the more positivist and objectivist approaches. Each approach will be presented in a fairly hardcore fashion, although the emergent signs of inter-paradigm dialogue and the authors' shared discursivist vision of audience research will inevitably have left their traces on the presentations. In Chapter 3 we shall discuss discursive realism as the shared epistemological foundation of the book. Towards the end of the book (Chapter 17) we will systematically address the question of methodological complementarity, as we consider side-by-side research designs (often referred to as 'triangulation') and begin to explore the possibility of a more ambitious methodological integration of research designs.

## QUALITATIVE OR QUANTITATIVE?

We have already quoted a succinct assessment that expresses the conventional wisdom in wide scholarly circles about the respective strengths and weaknesses of quantitative and qualitative approaches: 'Quantitative observations provide a high level of measurement precision and statistical power, while qualitative observations provide greater depth of information about how people perceive events in the context of the actual situations in which they occur' (Frey et al. 1991: 99). Before we go on to comment on the elements of this assessment, we want to briefly characterize the two paradigms in terms of, first, their data collection and analysis, and, second, their epistemological premises.

*Quantitative observation* employs numerical indicators to count the relative size or frequency of something, as when communicative phenomena are categorized, measured and calculated statistically and the results presented in absolute numbers, percentages or indices in tabular form. In audience research this is the chief methodology employed in the traditions labelled effects studies and uses and gratifications studies (see below), where a variety of (in particular) survey questionnaires are used (telephone-administered, mailed self-administered or location-administered in lecture halls, shopping malls, etc.).

In quantitative audience research, originating in an empiricist conception of science, it is common to speak about empirical work as 'data collection', because the reality of communicative processes is often not problematized: the phenomenon to be analysed (a media-related behaviour such as a voting intention in a general election, or a perceived media gratification such as watching television in order to avoid boredom) is, so to speak, regarded as being readily available in the world of the audience for objective collection through the analyst's questionnaire. This view originates in the natural science-inspired approach to social research that forms the epistemological heritage of the quantitative methodology. In its scientific roots – from which many of its present-day practitioners in communication research may have distanced themselves considerably – it is deductive, hypothesis-testing, seeking the causal relations between hard-and-fast independent and dependent variables, and insisting on the necessary separation of analysis and interpretation (see Chapter 10).

Research involving *qualitative observation* constructs records by employing words and images in order to register and interpret the salient verbal and visual features, manifest and latent, of communication processes, and in order to categorize them into different types. In audience research this is the chief methodology used in the cultural studies tradition (see below), where a variety of qualitative tools are used for different purposes, e.g. semiotic analysis and discourse analysis of media as text, participant observation of media consumption and various kinds of verbalized accounts of the audience experience elicited in face-to-face interviews with individuals or groups.

Qualitative analysts usually speak about 'data construction' rather than 'data collection', because they regard all social phenomena as discursively produced in specific situational contexts and hence as, in principle, ephemeral. This also means that the fieldwork situation can never be detached from the influence of the researcher, who is thus a priori deprived of the possibility of observing the communicative phenomena (such as the negotiation of the meaning of a news broadcast or peer-group enjoyment of a rock concert) objectively.

This view of the fieldwork springs from the epistemological roots of the qualitative methodology in a hermeneutic and phenomenological conceptualization of the social production of meaning in a discursively constructed social reality: audience research is thus fundamentally the analyst's interpretation of people's interpretations of their own social practices involving the media. It follows, moreover, that far from demanding the separation of analysis and interpretation, analysis can only be carried out through interpretation.

In spite of these differences of epistemological origin, most qualitative and quantitative researchers share the verdict of Frey et al. quoted above about the strengths and weaknesses of the 'other' approach as well as their own. Rephrased in terms of the traditional criteria of scientific credibility, what they say is that quantitative approaches are strong on reliability ('measurement precision') and generalizability ('statistical power'), whereas qualitative approaches are relatively stronger on validity ('depth of information'). These criteria of scientific soundness will be dealt with in greater detail below in connection with each of the four approaches, where we may better do justice to the specific interpretations and inflections given to them as a consequence of the different knowledge interests pursued by ethnography, reception research, survey research and experimental research.

Most researchers also agree that, as a consequence of these differences, quantitative and qualitative approaches should be used for different kinds of inquiry. If we are permitted to propose a general recommendation based on what may be called 'predominant methodological suitability', we suggest that questionnaire-based quantitative methods be used especially for the investigation of the more factual aspects of communicative behaviour, such as questions about the frequency and duration of media exposure, genre preferences, cultural tastes, etc. Interview-based qualitative methods, on the other hand, should be used to explore issues that involve more complex cultural meanings, such as the ambivalent negotiation of the meanings of various forms of media output. They are also necessary for any research that recognizes the potential discrepancy between the researcher's and the informants' categories for making sense of a social domain and wishes to understand the latter.

These recommendations have to do both with the properties of the phenomenon under study and the inherent properties of the methods. The lived complexity of media experiences expressed by even a handful of informants in a qualitative depth interview may be so multi-faceted as to almost defy accurate interpretation and meaningful generalization. Nevertheless we do need small-scale qualitative research that reminds us of the micro-reality of confusingly kaleidoscopic everyday experiences.

At the same time we also need large-scale quantitative research that is capable of reducing the dizzying complexity, thereby enabling us to discern the larger contours of the social and cultural landscape. On the other hand, however, survey questions that evoke too frequent responses of 'That depends on . . .' are maybe not really suitable for quantitative measurement.

Then again, irrespective of the distinction between factual aspects and complex meanings, the choice of method depends on the level of precision needed. If it is the job of audience research to provide us with 'maps' of the landscapes of audiences, it is the desired scale of the map of findings that should decide the methodological issue. Roe has argued that this topographical metaphor enables us 'to bypass the sterile controversy which surrounds the issue of "quantitative" versus "qualitative" method', because maps:

> can be made on different scales covering larger or smaller regions, with lesser or greater detail . . . the real question becomes whether the level of generality which a researcher employs is appropriate to the problem at hand, and whether the details are sufficiently accurate to solve it.

(K. Roe 1996: 89)

Sometimes, as argued above, researchers have not had a real choice of methodology, because this issue had been decided once and for all by their academic peer group. At other times, the choice of methodology has been made in the shadow of dominance cast by quantitative research, which – in spite of occasional challenges, especially in recent years – traditionally carries more authority and respectability in both the scientific community and wider society, with implications for the success of applications for research funding.

Silverman presents two lists of terms drawn from the speakers at a conference on research methods, showing 'how imprecise, evaluative considerations come into play when researchers describe qualitative and quantitative methods' (Silverman 1998: 78–9):

| *Qualitative* | *Quantitative* |
|---|---|
| *Soft* | *Hard* |
| *Flexible* | *Fixed* |
| *Subjective* | *Objective* |
| *Political* | *Value-free* |
| *Speculative* | *Hypothesis-testing* |

The lists show how there is a clear tendency to associate quantitative research with real science ('objective', 'hypothesis-testing'), whereas qualitative research appears to be less than systematic ('flexible'), subjective and typically influenced by the researcher's political orientation.

While this is still the common way in which public opinion judges the two paradigms, it should be mentioned as a partial corrective that there has been a marked change of climate in certain sections of the private sector's research community: especially in market and public relations research, there has been a growing recognition of the usefulness of qualitative methods, especially focus-group interviews, to provide access to the complexity beyond the numbers (Morgan 1988; Bloor et al. 2001). Also large media corporations have started to use focus groups both in connection with the pre-testing and fine-tuning of TV programmes, and in order to obtain a more detailed general understanding of how audiences actually use the media in contexts of everyday life.

We shall conclude this section with a table, based on Danermark et al. (2002: 162), which sums up the methodological points made so far, through a comparison of the characteristics of quantitative and qualitative research.

Table 2.1   Characteristics of qualitative and quantitative research

| Point of comparison | Qualitative research | Quantitative research |
| --- | --- | --- |
| Focus of research | Quality (nature, essence) | Quantity (how much, how many) |
| Philosophical roots | Phenomenology, symbol interaction | Positivism, logical empiricism |
| Associated phrases | Fieldwork, ethnographic, naturalistic | Experimental, empirical, statistical |
| Goal of research | Understanding, description, hypothesis generation | Prediction, control, description, hypothesis testing |
| Design characteristics | Flexible, evolving, emergent | Predetermined, structured |
| Setting | Familiar, natural | Unfamiliar, artificial |
| Sample | Small, non-random | Large, random, representative |
| Data collection | Interviews, observations | Questionnaires |
| Mode of analysis | Inductive | Deductive |
| Findings | Comprehensive, holistic, expansive | Precise, narrow, reductionist |

Source: based on Damermark et al. (2002: 162)

All the concepts used in the table will reappear in the general discussion of methodology in the following chapter, and will be elaborated on in the context of each of the four approaches in the rest of the book.

As we have stated before, with such complementary strengths (and weaknesses) it only makes sense to use the two paradigms (and their richly equipped toolboxes) in conjunction. The viability of such a multi-methodological research design is guaranteed by the increasing acceptance within contemporary communication research of the shared epistemological premise that all scientific methodologies are steeped in interpretation, all 'leading to cumulative generalizations which can always later be refuted' (Silverman 1998: 95).

Quantitative or qualitative, all that any research tool can hope to produce is a temporary snapshot 'version' of a corner of social reality.

## A BRIEF HISTORY OF AUDIENCE RESEARCH

People have always been interested in the media and their influence on social and cultural life, and for many different reasons. Sometimes this interest, as expressed by political and cultural guardians, has been rooted in concern over, or even fear of, the potential disruption of social traditions and norms ostensibly caused by the media (Postman 1985;

Drotner 1992), while reformers and radicals have been critical of what they saw as the media's reinforcement of ideologies benefiting the wealthy and the privileged, and stifling any tendency towards fundamental social and political reorientation (Adorno and Horkheimer 1947/1972; Schiller 1969; Smythe 1977; Hall et al. 1978).

In the realm of business communication, the interest in audiences has especially focused on the ability of corporate communicators to influence consumer behaviour through effective marketing communication, not least advertising, with the objective of increasing corporate profitability in the interests of owners and shareholders. Finally, there has always been a more curiosity-driven disinterested academic and intellectual focus on simply increasing the level of human knowledge about how media influence social and cultural processes.

These diverse but related interests have been taken care of within a number of academic disciplines and from a variety of perspectives, which have explored audiences directly or indirectly, and which may be seen as the predecessors of and sources of inspiration for contemporary audience research.

Researchers who see themselves as audience researchers are thus indebted to a range of historical research traditions in the interdisciplinary field of media and communication research, although few of them, if any, would regard the labels used to designate these traditions as an adequate expression of their individual scholarly identity.

In the following we provide a (very) brief outline of three such traditions (effects research, uses and gratifications research, cultural studies), which we believe to have been seminal to the *mélange* of contemporary audience studies as such, even though their respective scientific perspectives and procedures have affected individual audience researchers in quite idiosyncratic combinations.

It can be discussed what the exact formal status of these three 'traditions' is today, and has been in communication research history, and we invite our readers to do so. Two of them (uses and gratifications research, cultural studies) have been self-declared 'schools' that have struggled at particular historical moments to establish their once innovative perspectives in the academic pantheon of respectable approaches. One (effects research) has only come to be seen as something like a 'school' at a safe retrospective distance, from which its many internally distinguishable groups blend into a blurred common entity (Chapter 15). All three are constructed here as the predecessors of, and formative influences on, contemporary audience research, not as solid, universally valid monuments in the scientific landscape.

The overview presented on the following few pages is necessarily sketchy – some would say rudimentary – but for students with limited previous knowledge of the field it will hopefully serve as a heuristic introduction to the history of audience research. We hope that with this light historical baggage, readers will find it easier to understand the heavier treatment of the four approaches in the rest of the book, which elaborate on many theoretical and methodological aspects introduced here. Students with a deeper interest in the history of audience research are advised to consult other sources on the traditions of communication research in general and audience research in particular (see McQuail 2000 and the references therein). The following account of the major landscapes of audience research largely follows the framework set out in Schrøder (1987), Jensen and Rosengren (1990) and Lewis (1991).

## EFFECTS RESEARCH

The easy way to define the effects tradition is to quote an often-quoted phrase according to which effects research has the purpose of answering the question 'What do the media do to people?' Effects research thus capitalizes on the last element of Harold Lasswell's famous if banal definition of the concerns of communication research: '*Who* says *what* in *which channel* to *whom* with *what effect?*' (Lasswell 1948). The dual roots of the tradition lie in the 1920s and 1930s, in the growing social concern with the role of the media in the democratic process and the need of business corporations to effectively influence consumer decisions.

With the advent of the then new medium of radio, politicians were suddenly able to simultaneously reach every eye and every ear of the voting population, an opportunity that was eagerly taken up by democratic and anti-democratic political leaders alike: in the US, Franklin D. Roosevelt began a regular practice of radio 'fireside chats', broadcast nationwide with weekly addresses to the American people; while in Germany, Adolf Hitler used radio as one element of his efficient propaganda machine. The more general interest in the political effects of the media has been pursued in numerous studies that have tended to equate politics with elections and focus on short-term media-induced changes in voting behaviour (Negrine 1996). This research has virtually ignored the day-to-day political coverage and the possible long-term effects of the reiteration of deep-rooted ideological positions, which has instead become one of the hallmarks of cultural studies-oriented analyses of the political coverage of the media (see below).

Since the 1950s, in addition to the continuing interest in the political and commercial effectiveness of the media, the overriding concern, if not obsession, has been with the effects of media violence, especially on young minds, and millions of dollars and other currencies have been devoted to illuminating the complex causal question about the relationship between mediated and real-world violence (Klapper 1960; Halloran 1970; Comstock et al. 1972).

In the 1990s, such research has been used in the US as a political lever for introducing legislation requiring television manufacturers to supply TV sets with a so-called V-chip device, which enables parents to block children's access to TV programmes that show excessive violence, sexual material and abusive language. In the late 1990s, a global Unesco clearing-house for monitoring and coordinating media violence research was set up at the University of Gothenburg, Sweden (Carlsson and Feilitzen 1998).

One of the more sophisticated studies of the social and cultural effects of television, including violence, is that carried out by George Gerbner and his associates in the 1970s, under the name of 'cultivation research'. The research consists of two interrelated parts: 'message system analysis', monitoring the world of television drama; and 'cultivation analysis', 'determining the conceptions of social reality that television tends to cultivate in different groups of child and adult viewers' (Gerbner et al. 1978: 177). The correlations between the message system of television, audience perceptions of social reality and audience social behaviour is based on a sophisticated hypothesis that traces the effects of television by studying the differences between heavy and light viewers in the following manner: 'Heavier viewers of television, those more exposed than light viewers to its messages, are more likely to understand social reality in terms of the "facts of life" they see on television' (Gerbner et al. 1978: 194).

One part of the research findings contributes to the understanding of the effects of violence in the traditional sense of the term, as heavy viewers more often than light viewers respond that they find it acceptable, if provoked, to engage in violence against others (to hit someone) (Gerbner et al. 1978: 196), but the more wide-reaching findings have implications for the way television cultivates general social attitudes and political allegiances. It is found, for instance, that television viewing affects people's general perception of danger: rather than making them violent, heavy viewers become more fearful of walking in the city and their own neighbourhood at night, and therefore more likely to support law-and-order policies.

Theoretically effects research has undergone a series of significant changes since the early days of the metaphorically labelled 'hypodermic needle' and 'bullet' theories. These were actually never seriously suggested by effects researchers as descriptions of their theoretical outlook, but have become shorthand expressions for a framework of understanding that tends to believe in strong media effects, i.e. media effects that are immediate and direct.

Research being carried out around 1950 started to question this view of effects and, in a number of seminal studies, demonstrated the greater explanatory power of the since renowned theory of the two-step flow of media influence (Katz and Lazarsfeld 1955). According to this work, media effects are weak, delayed and indirect, because the way media messages may contribute to an individual's change of opinion on some political issue is mediated by so-called 'opinion leaders' – that is, significant others whose opinion carries decisive weight in the individual's social network. From here it is only a small step to less mechanistic contemporary theories that see the process of influence as characterized by multi-step and multi-directional flows, as media discourses intermingle in complex ways with interpersonal discourses in everyday life (Windahl et al. 1992: 51ff.; Gamson 1992).

The history of effects research since the 1970s has seen the relaunch of a strong effects perspective, as researchers have demonstrated the strong agenda-setting powers of the media (McCombs and Shaw 1972). According to this research, the media cannot tell us what to think, only what to think *about*, as they set the social agenda for public debate, for instance, effectively silencing issues that they define as irrelevant or that are awkward for economic and political elites (Herman and Chomsky 1988).

Methodological effects research, which relies both on survey and experimental research, belongs firmly in the social science mainstream, whose staunch positivism requires data collection and analysis to deal only with objective, observable phenomena that can be broken into countable units. This means, for instance, that the question of the effectiveness of advertisements must be translated into the measurable question of recall. The effect of an advertising campaign is thus considered to be very strong if the respondent can recall having seen it without any prompting (unaided recall), weak if prompting is necessary (aided recall).

This example may also be used to throw critical light on the tradition's weaknesses. In accordance with the general critique of the validity of much quantitative work, we may ask whether recall can really be seen as a valid measure of effectiveness, as there may be no connection between present recall of a particular campaign and future purchase of a particular product, presumably the ultimate test of effects. The widespread phenomenon of people being able to recall ads for well-known products that were not advertised in the media at the time of the study may also caution us that the relationship between media messages and audience meanings is indeed a complex one. For a more developed theoretical and methodological critique of cultivation research, see Newcomb (1978). Chapters 14–16 deal with effects research in greater detail.

## USES AND GRATIFICATIONS RESEARCH

The preferred way to characterize uses and gratifications (U+G) research in the scholarly literature is to apply the rhetorical figure of 'chiasmus' to the conventional description of effects research, standing it on its head, so to speak, by asking: 'What do people do with the media?' In other words, the U+G perspective introduces the notion of the 'active audience', who seek to satisfy various individual and social needs through the mass media. On the one hand, this complete reversal of the agenda of effects research heralds the emergence through U+G research of a revolutionary innovative perspective on audience research. Our understanding of anything the media might 'do' to their users is thus grounded in the intentional practices of people motivated by their individual dispositions, and at least in principle also by the situational environments and the wider social contexts in which people encounter the products of the media.

On the other hand, however, the reversal implied by the chiasmus has often resulted in the painting of a misleading picture of U+G research, because the phrase implies a clean break with effects research, whereas it is closer to the truth to say that the U+G perspective, pioneered by researchers brought up in the effects tradition (Katz 1957), grew organically out of the then dominant tradition – as indeed new paradigms always do. The very distinction in the two-step flow conceptualization of media effects, between gatekeeping opinion leaders and other people interacting in social networks, implies that people use the media in different ways and that these uses are deeply embedded in interpersonal relationships that precede any possible role played by the media.

For historical scholarly reasons, U+G researchers chose to focus on individually motivated media uses, leaving it to later traditions to explore the situational and social–contextual determinants of media use. It is common to associate U+G research with studies being carried out in the late 1960s and early 1970s, coming to full maturity in the authoritative paradigm-building volume, *The Uses of Mass Communication* (Blumler and Katz 1974). In a sense, however, U+G research dates back to the 1940s, when important studies of the text/listener relationships of radio daytime serials and quiz programmes were carried out. Herzog's study of daytime serial listeners, for instance, was based on the conviction that in order to address the question of the probable effects of 'escapist' media material, social scientists must both study the content of the serials and the listeners themselves in order to determine 'what satisfactions . . . they say they derive' (Herzog 1944, quoted in Klapper 1960; see also Warner and Henry 1948).

Strangely, however – or perhaps not so strangely given the often ruthless character of academic power struggles – these early examples of qualitative audience research went into oblivion as the quantitative paradigm became dominant in social science communication research, imposing the straitjacket of questionnaire-based surveys on those who wanted to be admitted to the respectable research community. Radio gratification studies became the victim of a scholarly spiral of silence, because they began the empirical exploration of what the mainstream considered to be unresearchable, i.e. cultural meanings and interpretations.

The authoritative programmatic platform laid out for U+G research by the retrospective founding fathers (Blumler and Katz 1974) is comprehensive and spacious, and there is nothing in the wording that appears to impose a methodological orthodoxy. According to the platform, it is the intention of U+G research to explore (1) the social and psychological origins of (2) needs, which generate (3) expectations of (4) the mass media or other sources, which lead to (5) differential patterns of media exposure (or engagement in other activities), resulting in (6) need gratification and (7) other consequences (Katz et al. 1974: 20). Readers interested in finding out how U+G researchers have pursued and developed this agenda may consult the two collections of articles that demonstrate, in the mid-1970s and the mid-1980s respectively, the range of work that has been produced within the tradition (Blumler and Katz 1974; Rosengren et al. 1985). For an insider's assessment of its merits, see Gantz (1996).

Theoretically, U+G research rests on the same positivist foundation as effects research, according to which the only way to carry out an objective analysis of media-related behaviour, uncontaminated by the researcher's subjectivity, is to carve social reality into measurable units. Consequently, 'what has come to be known as uses and gratifications research is . . . virtually synonymous with questionnaire surveys' (Zillman 1985: 225).

In practice, most U+G research has focused on patterns of media exposure and on the gratifications people say they get from using various media and genres, because these aspects lend themselves most easily to quantitative measurement. As an example, the uses of television have been explored in a number of studies by many different researchers (Katz et al. 1973; Greenberg 1974; Rubin 1981). Usually such studies present respondents with a questionnaire list of 20 or so possible gratifications derived from qualitative pilot studies, accompanied by the following instruction:

*Here are some reasons that other people gave us for watching TV. We want to know how much each reason is LIKE YOU. Please tell us if each reason is a lot like you, a little like you, not much like you or not at all like you.*

(Greenberg and Hnilo 1996)

One study (Greenberg 1974) found that the watching of TV is gratifying mainly because it is a 'habit', because it is a good way to 'pass the time' and because it provides 'companionship' when there is no one else to talk to, that is, mainly for non-programme-specific reasons. Another study (Rubin 1981) found that people's main reasons were to do with programme content – they watch TV primarily for specific programmes, while 'entertainment', 'relaxation' and 'habit' range considerably lower. In other words, Rubin's study shows that TV viewing is related to the active choice of favourite programmes.

It is of course possible to reconcile such apparently contradictory findings by seeing them as complementary insights about people's motives for watching TV. Another, more critical view, might end up questioning the validity of studies that expect people to be able to respond meaningfully to over-generalizing, de-contextualized questions about why they 'watch TV'.

Most of the critique against the U+G tradition has focused on its individualistic bias, which leads it to see people as rationally motivated and problem-solving individuals, and on its overriding concern with psychological needs rather than the contextually and socially differentiated needs created by the social formations that frame people's lives (Elliott 1974; Morley 1980). Other critics, from a position within the tradition itself, have pointed to the inherent shortcomings of a questionnaire-based approach to research questions dealing with cultural meanings and ritualized behaviours. In connection with a study of young people's 'gratifications' from a rock concert, Lull thus objects that there is 'simply no way to represent numerically the essence of what thousands of young people had experienced during the concert or what the cultural meaning of music is to them generally' (Lull 1985: 219).

With such motivations, some researchers have pushed the frontiers of the tradition towards more qualitative and ethnographic territories.

## CULTURAL STUDIES

Nowadays the meaning of the academic label of 'cultural studies' has been all but usurped by one particular variant within the many academic disciplines that focus on the study of culture, namely the innovative research agenda that rose to prominence at the Centre for Contemporary Cultural Studies (CCCS) at the University of Birmingham, England, in the 1970s, often associated with the names of its founding directors Richard Hoggart and Stuart Hall (Hoggart 1957; Hall 1980). Today, due both to its continuing academic excellence and the general logics of publishability in the Anglo-American academic world, this school, once critical of academic canons, has established its own canon and out-manoeuvred most of its competitors on the global scene of 'cultural studies' (Ferguson and Golding 1997).

## THE FRANKFURT SCHOOL

Before we succumb to the Birmingham School's hegemony, however, we are obliged to mention one other, and earlier, influential school of cultural studies, the Frankfurt School, which rose to prominence as a brilliant environment of critical social and cultural studies in Germany in the 1930s (Adorno and Horkheimer 1947/1972), and continued to do so after returning from its American exile during the Second World War, from the 1950s onwards (Habermas 1962; Marcuse 1964). Outside Germany the Frankfurt School, not least the work of Herbert Marcuse, served as a major source of analytical inspiration in the 1960s and 1970s for oppositional academics and youth movements in northern Europe and North America.

Often including a psychoanalytic perspective on mass society and mass culture, the Frankfurt School is most often associated with what would now be called a rigid political economy perspective on culture. According to this view, the cultural industries, including the mass media, function under a capitalist production logic which ensures that the masses, who already live under impoverished economic and cultural conditions, are ideologically enslaved by the clichéd and standardized media fare. The end result of cultural production – as seemingly confirmed by the rise of populism and fascism in a number of European countries in the 1920s and 1930s – is thus mass seduction, achieved by deluding the working classes about the democratic nature of a fundamentally unequal and unjust society, and by narcotizing them with escapist daydreams and ideologies, away from the necessary struggle for a classless society with true freedom and equality for all (Strinati 1995).

As the vocabulary used here shows, the work of the Frankfurt School is clearly an example of a radical politics, equally characteristic of Europe in the 1930s and 1970s, but it has always shared its fundamental cultural pessimism with cultural critics of less radical, even with conservative, observations (Postman 1985). The audiences and users of the media are seen as the powerless victims of mass seduction, arising as a consequence of both the intentional attempt by the privileged and powerful to deceive in order to stay in power, and – more importantly – the economic logics of cultural production that result in cultural products that pander to the lowest common denominator of taste.

It is not least as an antidote to this view that reception research, to some extent building on the insights of uses and gratifications research, began to explore the possibility of 'active audiences'. This antidote has immediate methodological implications, since Frankfurt School analysis of the media uses a broad linguistic/semiotic/literary approach that simply deduces audience impact from the analyst's introspective reading of the media texts.

As an example, the meaning of a magazine advertisement for Calvin Klein Obsession from the 1980s, picturing half a dozen naked human figures positioned in stylized fashion on an ensemble of giant white blocks, was analysed by Larsen (1988). He sees them as 'a swelling human pyramid on a soaring edifice *reminiscent of* Mussolini architecture and nazi sports palaces', which makes the advertising image an expression of 'the worship of Kraft-und-Schönheit'. And 'in an instant a series of historical images *flash across the spectator's mental screen*' (Larsen 1988; our translation, emphases added).

While this is certainly one valid interpretation for one reader of the ad's images, the question nevertheless remains as to the validity of the analysis for the signifying processes of the thousands of actual readers who encounter it in the magazine. Frankfurt School textual analysis, as the quotation shows, does not hesitate to make the leap from the analyst's reading to a general claim about each and every reader's reading, implying that readers who find pleasure in this ad harbour a hidden inclination towards a fascist aesthetic. Therefore, scholars who see those white marble blocks differently – as perhaps a museum of modern art, a sophisticated sculpture, or just a theatrical set-piece – start to wonder just what the diversity of readings might be out there among actual readers, and to develop an approach that can explore this diversity empirically.

## THE BIRMINGHAM SCHOOL

The greatest difference between the Frankfurt and the Birmingham Schools of cultural studies lies in the latter's conceptualization of culture as a struggle. This cultural struggle may be an unequal one between dominant and repressed social classes and groups and their cultural practices, but fundamentally its outcomes cannot be predicted.

The origins of the Birmingham School are to be found in a concern with the direction of the cultural processes of modernity in post-war Britain, especially the way in which the popular culture of the working classes was being overrun by the popular culture of an entertainment-oriented and increasingly Americanized consumer society. In a sense, the early core concern of the Birmingham School may be said to be with the duality of the term 'popular', the tensions and struggles between the authentic culture of working *people* developed through generations on the one hand, and the artificial, partly imported, super-ficial consumer and media culture that quickly achieved widespread 'popularity' among these very working classes on the other (Hoggart 1957). A main pioneering achievement in this context was the rehabilitation of popular mass culture as a legitimate object of sci-entific study – an achievement that itself had to be produced through fierce academic and non-academic struggle.

Theoretically, cultural studies have been balanced between a 'structuralist' perspective, according to which people's lives are determined by the socio-economic structures they live in, and a 'culturalist' perspective, according to which people possess social and cultural resources that enable them to create meaningful lives for themselves and to challenge the sociostructural determinants (Hall 1980). The main sources of theoretical inspiration have been drawn from central figures in structuralist and post-structuralist con-tinental political and cultural thinking such as Marx, Saussure, Althusser, Gramsci, Lévi-Strauss, Barthes and Foucault. The particular theoretical 'bricolage' performed on these

41

theories enabled the Birmingham scholars to produce groundbreaking work on many aspects of culture and society, although many have felt that sometimes the theoretical work was being discursively articulated by the devotees for its own sake and in prohibitively mystifying jargon (Williamson 1978; Hall et al. 1980).

The historically rooted knowledge interests and the continental theoretical anchorage led to two different methods of inquiry. First, *textual analysis* of a range of cultural phenomena, from works of acknowledged value taken from the English literary tradition, through the products of the cultural and media industries, to the cultural expressions of various youth subcultures read as 'texts' (Hall et al. 1976; Hebdige 1979). The focus was on the discovery of how texts 'position' readers in specific ways so as to reinforce ideologies that serve the status quo among the readers/viewers (much along the lines of Frankfurt School textual analysis; see, for instance, Gitlin 1979). Work with a gender-political commitment, always and still a strong voice in the tradition (*Women Take Issue*, 1978), has focused especially on the social and ideological repression of women, as it is articulated, for instance, in the inherent 'male gaze' of Hollywood cinema (Mulvey 1975).

Second, and of more lasting value to audience research, has been the School's ethnographic exploration of youth and ethnic subcultures since the mid-1970s (Hall and Jefferson 1976). In these seminal studies, the everyday practices of conspicuous youth cultural groups were interpreted as a symbolic resistance to the macro-social forces that threatened to take the meaning out of their lives by having nothing to offer but unrewarding jobs or, at times of recurring economic crisis, unemployment. For instance, the work of Willis (1977) was based on extensive fieldwork among teenage boys about to face the transition from school to work, with few prospects of 'the good life' that the gospel of welfare society seemed to promise everybody. The direct motivation for the study, as for other studies of youth cultures done at Birmingham, lay in a desire to face the objectifying label of 'deviance' that social researchers, politicians and the media attached to these groups, and to explore what it feels like subjectively to be a young working-class lad facing the prospect of spending the rest of one's life under the bleak conditions offered by class-dependent social arrangements. Parallel work on adolescent female cultures was carried out by McRobbie (1978).

The same desire to give voice to the perspective of ordinary people underlies the emergence of qualitative reception research of the media within cultural studies. Here the objective was to explore what people do with the media, but – contrary to uses and gratifications research – in a manner that emphasized the signifying processes surrounding the nexus of media and everyday life, and that related these meanings closely to the historical, political and social context in which media consumption takes place.

Early cultural studies-oriented reception research was indebted to the textual analysis tradition for its interest in exploring the signifying *power* of the media, as audiences engage the ideology-laden meanings offered by the media – for instance, in news and current affairs programming (Hall et al. 1976; Morley 1980) and in fiction and entertainment (Hobson 1982; Radway 1984). The reception perspective was soon extended into an ethnography-inspired series of studies based on qualitative interviews, looking not just at the audiences' negotiation of media meanings, but also at the way media technologies and meanings are embedded in gendered family interaction (Morley 1986; Gray 1987; Silverstone and Hirsch 1992).

As this brief historical outline has demonstrated, the historical roots of audience research are diverse, theoretically and methodologically. Therefore let us conclude with a quotation that summarizes the empirical credo that has been the driving force behind all audience research:

> *[If you ask me] I may well, of course, lie to you or otherwise misrepresent my thoughts or feelings . . ., but at least, through my verbal responses, you will begin to get some access to the kind of language, the criteria of distinction and the types of categorizations, through which I construct my (conscious) world. Without these clues, my TV viewing (or other behaviour) will necessarily remain opaque.*

(Morley 1989: 25)

## Chapter Three
☐ Methodological pluralism: the meta-theoretical foundations of discursive realism

This book is based on the conviction that we shall be able to better understand media audiences if we equip ourselves with a comprehensive toolbox based on interdisciplinarity and methodological pluralism. We therefore offer two major qualitative approaches to audience research and two major quantitative ones. In order to do that, in the first place, nothing more is required than a willingness to provide for a peaceful coexistence of traditionally rival approaches.

But we wish to move further than a research policy based merely on a tolerance of the epistemological 'Other'. We wish to argue, and to demonstrate through the way we describe and explain the four approaches, that they are both complementary and compatible. Such an argument, however, can only be put convincingly if we can base it on a meta-theoretical foundation capable of uniting the approaches, and the quantitative and qualitative paradigms, under a common knowledge claim, which does not privilege one approach as inherently superior and more 'scientific' than others, as has often been the case with the traditional inside perspective of both the quantitative empiricist paradigm and the qualitative interpretativist paradigm.

## TOWARDS DISCURSIVE REALISM

Such a meta-theoretical platform has been emerging in the social sciences under the label of 'critical realism' over the last decade or two, in a fruitful dialectic between theorists in the philosophy of science and empirical researchers involved in concrete social research, including media and communication research (Bhaskar 1978; Deacon, Pickering et al. 1999; Danermark et al. 2002). As a parallel development in the humanities and psychology, a constructionist and discourse analytical approach has emerged with similar epistemological foundations (Potter and Wetherell 1987; Fairclough 1992, 1995; Potter 1996), and independently of these, a discursive turn has also made an impact in political science (Laclau and Mouffe 1985; Laclau 1990). What is common to all these developments is the decisive role played by language and discourse in human knowledge acquisition (Jørgensen and Phillips 2002). For this reason, and because of the dual origins of the authorial team in the social sciences and the humanities, we have decided to label our meta-theoretical platform *discursive realism.*

The discursive realist platform brings quantitative and qualitative methodologies into epistemological alignment as research methods with the same claims to knowledge and explanatory power, although with different, complementary roles to play in social and cultural analysis; the different methods are suitable for different analytical tasks, and as we argued in Chapter 1 it is 'the nature of the object under study which determines what research methods one may use' (Danermark et al. 2002: 11).

The essence of discursive realism consists in the belief that there is a social reality that exists independently of language, but our only access to knowledge about this reality goes through language and other sign systems. This position is in contrast to both the empiricist belief in our ability to acquire true knowledge about a reality unaffected by the human understanding of it, and to the interpretativist belief that reality *is* our discursive understanding of this reality. While this point about the nature of knowledge and reality could at a first glance be seen as an esoteric philosophical concern of no importance for practical research, it becomes important the moment we address the issue of the explanatory power of our analytical findings: here, empiricist researchers would seek to generalize their findings and to make an absolute truth claim for them, while the pure interpretativist researcher would adopt a relativist position emphasizing the case-specific and situationally bound nature of their findings.

A discursive realist will take 'the third way' between these two (Pavitt 1999), agreeing with the interpretativist that the findings – quantitative or qualitative or both – represent no more than interpreted 'versions' of reality, but agreeing also with the empiricist that some form of generalization may be desirable and necessary, and that some versions of reality are better – *more* 'truthful' – than others: 'Though we can only know it through our concepts, there is nevertheless a *real* subject for our inquiry, which is not entirely spirited away by our admission of its relativized position' (Willis 1980: 91). Or as critical realists put it, 'It is possible to gain knowledge of actually existing structures and generative mechanisms, albeit not in terms of a mirror image . . . but certainly in terms of theories, which are more or less truthlike' (Danermark et al. 2002: 10).

This issue of truthlikeness must, then, be resolved through scientific negotiation by the community of scholars, through an evaluation of the theoretical and methodological soundness of the empirical work. The best accounts of the reality of media audiences, for instance, are those that are based on solid and insightful theories about audiences, in general and in the particular area studied, and on systematic and inventive (quantitative or qualitative, or both) methods of study.

Critical realists often emphasize that third-way social research operates through a different analytical mode than both empiricist and interpretativist research (Danermark et al. 2002: 808f.). Typically, empiricist research starts out with 'universal' laws, then forms hypotheses about how social behaviour takes place in accordance with these laws, and proceeds to test the hypotheses through strict hypothetico-*deductive* analytical procedures. Equally important in the empiricist tradition, however, though often ignored in methodological critiques, is the inductive research process that works in the opposite direction, from numerous specific observations to universally valid conclusions about a whole population. Interpretativist research also works mainly according to an *inductive* mode of analysis, although without the generalizing ambitions, remaining at the level of the 'thick description' of a handful of cases. What characterizes both of these analytical modes is that they are, at least in principle, if not in practice, not capable of delivering truly new knowledge, as they merely test existing knowledge (deduction), or accumulate empirical facts (induction).

The essential analytical mode of critical realist social research, which supplements the deductive and inductive modes, is often labelled 'abduction', a concept originally invented by the American semiotician Charles Peirce. What this concept, which is notoriously difficult to understand, essentially tries to grasp about the analytical–interpretative process is the detective-like element of creativity and imagination that research needs in order to produce new insight (Danermark et al. 2002; Jensen 2002a). Abduction is thus a kind of empirically based quantum leap performed by the creative researcher who is capable, with an inspired insight, to reconceptualize a phenomenon in a new way:

> *Abduction is to move from a conception of something to a different, possibly more developed or deeper conception of it. This happens through our placing and interpreting the original ideas about the phenomenon in the frame of a new set of ideas. . . . all abduction builds on creativity and imagination. This is the essential difference between abduction and the other two modes of inference. . . .*[1]

(Danermark et al. 2002: 91ff.)

As an example from audience research, imagine a situation in which a researcher starts out with the simple, established conceptualization of TV viewers in terms of a division between 'heavy' and 'light' viewers, based on the simple quantitative measurement of time spent watching TV. A study by Jensen et al. (1994) was curious to explore the ostensible complexity of motivations underlying people's TV viewing, and conducted a small-scale family interview study in which people were asked about the role of television in their everyday lives: when they watched, what they watched, why they watched it, with whom, etc.

As the researchers analysed the transcripts and discussed possible groupings of families into meaningful viewer types, playing around with various potential criteria for setting up new categories, they suddenly realized that two criteria would make sense and exhaust the empirical material: the factors that appeared to determine people's TV viewing more than anything else, cutting across the heavy/light division, were (1) the attitude to TV as being

---

[1] Danermark et al. (2002) conceptualize abduction in close association with another analytical mode that they call 'retroduction', which we ignore here as it is not essential to our argument.

a waste of time or possibly even harmful, and (2) the extent to which they planned their TV viewing in advance.

Based on these two criteria it was possible to set up four viewer types: the Moralists (TV is harmful/a waste of time, and therefore must be carefully planned), the Hedonists (TV is a fact of life to be fully enjoyed, so no planning needed), the Pragmatists (TV is a fact of life to be fully enjoyed, but planning is necessary to make room for other activities), and the Laissez-Faire Viewers (TV is harmful/a waste of time, but lack of self-control makes planning impossible) (Schrøder 1999).

Thus a new conceptualization, or a new scientifically based 'version', of people's TV viewing had been invented through empirical analysis and abductive inferencing. Unlike deductive and inductive research, 'there are no fixed criteria from which it is possible to assess in a definite way the validity of an abductive conclusion' (Danermark et al. 2002: 81). In practical terms, what this absence of fixed criteria of assessment means is that the credibility and usefulness of the findings is a matter to be decided discursively by the community of scholars and other potential users of audience research, on the basis of the documentation offered by the researcher.

As far as we know, the division of viewers into the four types has on the whole been accepted by the academic community, at least as a fair description of the situation in Denmark in the early 1990s. Other studies of TV audiences have made reference to it without questioning its validity. On the other hand, however, the categorization has not been adopted by other researchers as a framework for their own investigations. Interestingly, the European broadcaster MTG, which runs commercial national TV channels in Scandinavia, found the division useful enough to fund an audience survey in which the categories were operationalized in a questionnaire and the survey results were used for programme-planning purposes.

We stated above that only research based on the abductive mode is capable of producing new knowledge. This should not be taken to mean, obviously, that the history of social research until the emergence of discursive realism has produced no new knowledge. What we do mean is that both the empiricist and interpretativist camps have included scholars who transcended the limitations of the deductive and inductive modes, and who succeeded through abduction in advancing the frontiers of human knowledge. As a case in point, the cultivation studies of Gerbner and his associates described in Chapter 2 were able to correlate studies of precisely heavy and light viewers of TV with other social variables, so as to produce intriguing findings about the socializing effects of television on the American population.

The point is that they have only been able to do so by violating the epistemological modes prescribed by their respective scientific communities. By rehabilitating abduction as a key inferential mode in social research, critical and discursive realism seeks to provide a systematic meta-theoretical foundation for research that transcends traditional criteria of scientific work.

## HOLISTIC AUDIENCE RESEARCH

The knowledge horizon of audience research as conceptualized from a discursive realist perspective is holistic. This means that although we focus on the meanings and activities of audiences as communicated to or with, we are interested in illuminating the whole communicative process from senders to receivers, and beyond this also in the larger sociocultural structures that circumscribe this process (Deacon 2003).

This is not just a matter of 'interest', an idiosyncratic whim of ours that makes us extend the boundaries of audience research far beyond the audience itself. We believe that this holistic aim is necessary if – inspired by Giddens' theory of structuration (Giddens 1984) – we wish to understand audiences as dialectically constituted. On the one hand, they are relatively autonomous agents in everyday life, whose meanings and behaviours affect both the close situational and the wider social contexts in which they move and act. On the other hand, they are social beings whose meanings and behaviours are constrained and shaped by the relatively powerful social forces, such media institutions, that have been constituted by the aggregate collective actions of previous generations through history.

The holistic perspective can be illustrated through a figure adapted from the critical discourse analyst Norman Fairclough (Fairclough 1995: 59). Figure 3.1 shows the ambit of communication research as such, comprising three dialectically related dimensions. The first dimension has to do with the *communication product* itself, whether conceived as a 'message', a multi-modal 'text' (relying for its meaning on the interweaving of multiple semiotic modes) or as the ensemble made up of a whole communicative genre or media.

**Figure 3.1**   Holistic audience research

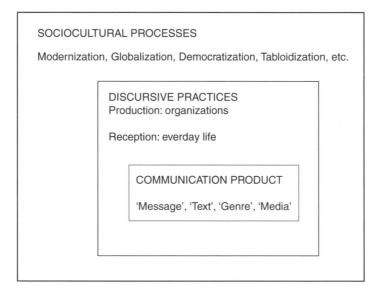

SOCIOCULTURAL PROCESSES

Modernization, Globalization, Democratization, Tabloidization, etc.

DISCURSIVE PRACTICES
Production: organizations

Reception: everday life

COMMUNICATION PRODUCT

'Message', 'Text', 'Genre', 'Media'

Source: based on Fairclough (1995: 59)

In the second dimension, this communication product is seen as the result of the *discursive practices* linking producers/senders and audiences/receivers, where the former operate mostly in the organizational contexts of the media while the latter are navigating mostly in contexts of everyday life. At this level, audience researchers should familiarize themselves in a general manner with the economic, political, social and cultural forces that structurally determine media production and distribution. They should also independently explore, to the extent made desirable by their concrete audience focus, the economic, political, social and cultural resources commanded by audiences as a prerequisite to their engagement with what the media have to offer.

Finally, in the third dimension, the communicative processes around the concrete communication product are understood as being inscribed in larger media-specific as well as *sociocultural processes* of (post)modernization, globalization, commercialization, democratization, tabloidization, etc. Like the institutional structures operating in the second dimension, the societal structures of the third dimension are seen by discursive realism as at the same time *enabling* and *constraining* with respect to the activities of media audiences. They are conditions and resources for sense-making and action, as well as limits on what is imaginable, thinkable and feasible, in and after the encounter with mediated communication (Deacon, Pickering et al. 1999: 10).

## HOW TO BE 'CRITICAL'

In this holistic perspective, audience research seeks to map the ways in which audiences navigate under modern, mediatized social conditions, for the enlightenment and benefit of commercial operators, political decision-makers and the citizenry at large. Some of the work required to fulfil this task is fairly descriptive, consisting for instance in registering behavioural patterns and taste preferences, using deductive and inductive research designs. But the academically and socially committed division of audience research, seeing itself as 'critical', orients itself more towards the theory-driven illumination of the opaque or latent relations operating around media audiences, seeking – by drawing on abductive modes of analytical creativity – to unravel the taken-for-granted assumptions about the social uses and consequences of media. This is because, as Deacon and his colleagues put it, 'there are social and cultural structures that shape people's options for action but exist independently of their awareness of them' (Deacon, Pickering et al. 1999: 10).

The purpose of such critical audience research is ultimately to provide a more enlightened – in discursive realist terms, more truthlike – foundation of knowledge for decision-makers concerned with social engineering in the field of media policy, or to empower audiences to better understand their own needs for and uses of media in everyday life.

As an example from the quantitative camp, the cultivation studies of Gerbner and his associates (see Chapter 2) have served to question the widespread common-sense assumption that the key effect of TV violence is to promote violent behaviour among the audience. Their unique research design enabled these researchers to delve underneath this surface assumption and to discover a surprising causal connection between a heavy dose of TV violence and increased audience expectations of meeting violence in everyday life, likely to lead to support of law-and-order policies. Their research thus provided an important input into the policy-making process, although subsequent violent events involving American youth have tended to confirm the common-sense beliefs about the TV/violence connection.

Critical or discursive realists thus have an explicit political agenda: 'By identifying the hidden springs of everyday action, critical realists hope to mobilise social knowledge in the interests of abolishing "unwanted and oppressive" constraints of social and personal choices and developing "needed, wanted and empowering" rules for social life' (Bhaskar, quoted in Deacon, Pickering et al. 1999: 13). As an authorial team we share this political commitment to human betterment, as is probably clear both from our theoretical discussions and many of the examples we use in this book. For us, therefore, audience research should ultimately serve the purpose of democratic empowerment of the modern hybrid personality of citizen-consumers.

But at the same time we wish to distance ourselves from the kind of self-congratulatory progressivism that presupposes that all sensible intellectuals are necessarily members of the same left-of-centre political congregation. We also wish to stress that there is nothing in the methods themselves we present that is partisan in a political sense. On the contrary, we wish to help remove the deep-rooted illusion in many circles that quantitative approaches are inherently more 'administrative' and conservative, while qualitative methods are inherently more 'critical' and progressive.

The history of communication and audience research is rich in cases that could support the myth, i.e. the research practices of the two paradigms have tended to be system-conserving and system-critical respectively. But there are many examples of quantitative studies with a critical or even radical edge, just as there are many examples – especially in the recent use of focus groups for commercial purposes in media organizations – of qualitative research being used with the narrow purpose of containing and controlling audience behaviour. We thus offer the four methodological approaches in the remainder of the book as tools at the disposal of anybody seeking knowledge about media audiences, for whatever purpose.

## AUDIENCE RESEARCH AND THE 'DOUBLE HERMENEUTIC' OF SOCIAL RESEARCH

The sequence in which we present the four methodological approaches is determined by the relative degree of openness and control with which they approach the empirical encounter between researcher and human subjects in the research situation.

We start out with the open approach of *media ethnography*, which proceeds by the least degree of intervention in situations of everyday life, stopping short of fly-on-the-wall illusions. Through participant observation, media ethnographers immerse themselves as 'naturalistically' as possible in the very contexts of everyday life with the media that they wish to understand, allowing subjects to act and speak as authentically as possible. We conclude, at the other end of the continuum from least to most situational control, with the closed approach of *the experimental tradition* that seeks to control as many contextual circumstances as possible, in order to be able to isolate and test the specific 'effect' of media.

In between these two poles of situational intrusion we present, as the second methodology, *reception research*, which intervenes moderately in the subject's everyday life by setting up the qualitative research interview as a speech event for the mediation of the media experience, but leaving ample room for informants to express their lifeworld-derived meanings and attitudes in their own discursive terms. As the third methodology we present *field survey research*, which resembles reception research in setting up a moderately intrusive elicitation situation, but which is discursively different in its imposition of the framework of strict questionnaire wordings for the elicitation of subjects' experiences.

In more theoretical terms, our methodological sequencing is governed by the methodologies' somewhat different relation to what Giddens terms the 'double hermeneutic' of social research (Giddens 1984: 374). By coining this term, Giddens tries to explain the fundamental difference between the natural sciences on the one hand, and the social sciences and humanities on the other, as originating in a different relationship between research discourses and discourses of everyday life.

In the social and human sciences, the concepts, classifications and categorizations used by researchers and those used by ordinary people are related in a mutual osmosis of meanings and, crucially, these frames of understanding are themselves the very phenomenon under study: 'the subjects of study in the social sciences and the humanities are concept-using beings, whose concepts of their actions enter in a constitutive manner into what those actions are' (Giddens 1987: 18). By contrast, the natural sciences operate according to a 'single hermeneutic', where lay understandings of natural phenomena may well intersect with those of natural scientists, but without affecting the natural phenomena studied by science. Therefore, natural scientists are able to conduct their research according to strict criteria of replication and control of variables in order to test their theories (Giddens 1987: 31).

All four methodological approaches we present in this book thus work according to the double hermeneutic of the social and human sciences, but they can be differentiated precisely by the manner in which, historically, each of them has handled this condition. As shown in Figure 3.2, media ethnography and reception research are founded on a common desire, although to different degrees, to approximate lay discourses about the media in everyday life, and to pursue this objective through a phenomenological hermeneutic of gathering and interpreting as many authentic accounts from lay voices as

**Figure 3.2** The positions of the four approaches in relation to the double hermeneutic of social and human research

| Lay frameworks of meaning | | | | Social science frameworks of meaning |
|---|---|---|---|---|
| | Media ethnography | Reception research | Field survey research | Experimental research |

possible. This very immersion in the complexities of the subjects' lifeworld has often made it difficult or undesirable for researchers from these traditions to generalize their findings and to make them useful for policy and commercial purposes.

On the other hand, field survey research and experimental research about media audiences share, to different degrees, the desire to maintain a certain distance through the research process between lay and scholarly frameworks of understanding, as they tend to make subjects conform to the discursive and situational frameworks of social research rather than the other way around. Because of their more standardized empirical tools, they have gained on generalizability what they have lost on affinity with respondent frameworks of meaning and interpretation.

While field survey research and experimental audience research are thus closer to the scientific modes of the natural sciences, this should not be taken to imply that the social scientists who practise these approaches from within discursive realism suffer from objectivist delusions about the insights they produce. This is because, as a consequence of the double hermeneutic, the social world as described and explained by social research inevitably becomes entangled in the struggles between different interest groups:

> *The social world is an internally contested one, in which dissensus between actors and groups of actors – in relation to divergent world-views or clashes of interest – is pervasive. The ties which connect the social sciences constitutively to the social world inevitably mean that these divisions tend to shape strongly the theoretical perspectives sociological observers assume (this is not merely a matter of deficiencies in their 'objectivity').*

(Giddens 1987: 31)

## EMPIRICAL RESEARCH IN THE SEA OF INTERPRETATION

Nor do the four approaches differ with respect to the way they conceptualize the basic stages of empirical audience research as an interpretative process of social inquiry. They share the following seven steps, which will receive a specific inflection when conceptualized within and adapted by each of the approaches, as elaborated in the toolbox chapters of our four main sections. All seven steps share an interpretative dimension, since 'science can never limit itself merely to observing, registering and reporting. . . . Reasoning, our ability to analyse, abstract, relate, interpret and draw conclusions, is a fundamental precondition for all knowledge and knowledge development' (Danermark et al. 2002: 79).

In practice, of course, the stages cannot and should not be kept in watertight compartments, as researchers, especially experienced ones, will often have quite specific ideas about many of the theoretical and methodological issues evoked by a research project. Moreover, in contexts of professional research, the securing of funding inevitably requires convincing preliminary planning of the first four stages. However, the stages as outlined in points 1–7 below may serve as a reminder of the dimensions that, irrespective of sequential order, are of vital importance for quality audience research.

1. *Formulating the general research interest.* An audience research project begins with curiosity about some aspect of audience behaviour that may have academic, commercial or political relevance, and is guided motivationally by a desire to make a difference through results that increase existing knowledge about audiences. The research interest is dependent on the researchers' interpretation of the surrounding social world and of the contribution that a study may make to fulfilling desirable goals. The research interest is thus always, directly or indirectly, a political interest.

2. *Building theoretical frameworks.* Any audience study requires the researcher to systematically familiarize him/herself with previous research – existing truths – in the same and related areas. Searching for, studying and interpreting existing research will alert the researcher to a range of theoretical frameworks for understanding the audience phenomenon in question, which may in turn inform decisions about specific research questions and help increase the validity of the study.

3. *Choosing the appropriate method(s).* The interpretative perusal of previous research about an audience question will have made the researcher aware of how different methods have illuminated different aspects of the phenomenon. This provides the foundation for the process of narrowing down one or more suitable methods for exploring the issues defined during the previous stages.

4. *Planning the fieldwork.* The interpretative reasoning of the previous stages must now continue by distilling the multiple issues raised so far into a finite set of assumptions and research questions, or in some cases (depending on the choice of method) operationalizing the theoretical and methodological issues into a set of specific variables and testable hypotheses. The discursive work of designing a questionnaire or an interview guide should be evaluated for relevance and comprehensibility, preferably in a pilot study, in order to secure validity and anticipate difficulties of data gathering. The logistics of fieldwork (respondent recruiting, selection of location, installation of equipment, etc.) should then be worked out.

5. *Executing the fieldwork.* The actual fieldwork can be seen as the interpretative implementation of all the preceding stages. Researcher–respondent interaction is managed verbally – in speech and/or writing – and is thus immersed in interpretative activity, irrespective of research method. Fieldwork is thus always what Willis calls 'a social relationship' (Willis 1980: 94).

6. *Analysing the data.* Fundamentally, data analysis and coding is an interpretative translation process, of respondents' words into researchers' words, or respondents' words into researchers' numbers (in the case of questionnaires sometimes accomplished by respondents themselves as they reply to each question by designating one of a set of multiple-reply choices), which are then interpretatively translated into researchers'

words. Analytical results should be checked for intersubjective agreement between coders. The data are interpretatively scrutinized for internally generalizable patterns and, if allowed by the sampling technique used, representative patterns, which may then be interpretatively reduced and converted into 'maps' of the audience phenomenon studied. The end product of data analysis is thus an interpretation of what the data mean, in relation to the social and political research interests formulated at the outset. This interpretation always includes an evaluation of what the data do *not mean*, i.e. a discussion of the possible errors or shortcomings of the study, the possible reasons for their occurrence and the implications for the results as well as for future research.

**7.** *Communicating the results.* Often labelled 'writing up' the research, the results (as interpreted by the researcher) are discursively encoded in the form of scientific publications for the scholarly community, action-oriented debriefs for commercial communicators, or popular science accounts for a smaller or wider section of the general public. Sometimes the results appear in the media as the radically compressed soundbite reinterpretation of the full academic report.

As we said at the beginning of this chapter, we regard the four approaches to audience research in this book as complementary and compatible. This view will be evident in the way we present each of them separately, because we make frequent reference to their co-application in specific research projects. The more detailed discussion of multi-methodological research designs will follow in Chapter 17, where we shall look at both side-by-side applications of quantitative and qualitative methods, often referred to as 'triangulation', and at the possibility of integrating quantitative and qualitative approaches into one research design.

# Section 2

# The Ethnographic Approach to Audiences

# Chapter Four

# Audience ethnography in □ practice: between talk, text and action

In 1991, a young Danish media scholar, Thomas Tufte, lived in three low-income urban communities of Brazil for two months carrying out empirical investigations of women's use of telenovelas – that is, long-running serials similar to soap operas, and a genre that is by far the most popular and the most exported TV genre in Latin America. Over the next seven years he made regular return visits to Brazil of up to a month's duration. Having previously lived in the country as an exchange student for a year and travelled it widely since, Tufte spoke Portuguese and knew of Brazil's social, ethnic and cultural diversities.

His research took place in three regions of Brazil: Vila Nitro Operaria in São Paulo, in the centre of the country; Santa Operaria in Canoas, in the southernmost region; and Calabar in Salvador, in the northeastern region. The study involved watching TV with groups of local women, talking to them during informal encounters and conducting more structured interviews with 13 women. In addition, he conducted a survey with 105 women on their TV habits in two of the three local communities, and he made a genre analysis of 12 episodes (out of a total of 177) of *The Rubbish Queen* (*Rainha do Sucata*), a then recently aired novela that was watched by about 80 million of Brazil's 110 million TV viewers (the total population is 160 million). In order to substantiate his genre analysis, Tufte also collected material documenting the institutional framework and development of novela production, and interviewed producers at the leading commercial TV networks, Rede Globo and Rede Manchete. The aim of his investigation was not so much to find out why novelas are so popular as to analyse more specifically and seek to understand ways in which the novelas play into the viewers' everyday lives, articulating personal problems as well as wider constellations of change in relation to gender and class, ethnicity and region. The resulting study is published in Tufte (2000).

Coming from a European context in which many of his contemporaries were steeped in postmodern theories and the related issues of personal identity formation and composite lifestyles, Tufte retained 'old-fashioned' notions of background variables, while going well beyond the empirical parameters chosen by most of his European colleagues. Rather, his choice of research agenda was informed by Latin American cultural theory, which has continuously stressed the political importance of culture, including media culture, and hence the necessary ethical, even politicized, role played by media research.

His main findings are as follows (summarized in Tufte 2000: 287). First, he demonstrates the crucial role played by television in general, and telenovelas in particular, in organizing everyday life and articulating forms of identity. Second, he shows how novelas serve as interpretative frameworks in users' definition of modernity and cultural citizenship. Third, he illuminates how television use acts as a catalyst in forming what is termed 'a hybrid sphere of signification' (Tufte 2000: 186): TV sets are placed in the homes so as to be watched also from outside, thus inviting and often creating a physical and symbolic blurring of private and public, female and male, boundaries of media interaction.

These findings serve to substantiate what the Latin American cultural theorist Jesus Martín-Barbero has termed mediation (Martín-Barbero 1987/1: 1993), that is, ways in which media intervene in people's everyday lives and transform articulations of popular culture. For our purposes, Tufte's concept of hybrid spheres is of particular significance since it is based on a processual form of data collection and analysis that allows for close investigation of the temporal and spatial aspects of TV in use. Moreover, to many European and North American readers, the concept is eye-opening in that it highlights how male and female spheres, public and private space, are cultural inscriptions rather than natural demarcations.

Tufte's study is an example of a media ethnography. The term denotes types of media investigation that focus on media uses as part of people's everyday lives and that apply the researcher's observation of and informal interaction with his and her informants as a major methodological tool. Media ethnography is not an approach that is reserved for studies of audiences alone, it may also be applied to studies of media production (see Helland 1993). Still, most major studies do have audiences as their point of departure and analytical focus. Like all other traditions of audience research, media ethnography harbours particular research perspectives and challenges the researcher with a plethora of choices – from designing the overall research framework to tackling the more mundane, but often equally important, restrictions imposed by time, money and personal resources. Let us look into some of the immediate issues raised by Tufte's study, issues that we shall describe more closely and systematically in Chapters 5 and 6.

The most obvious question raised by a study such as Tufte's could well be: 'Why make the effort of going to Brazil as a Dane, if you can study media cultures closer to home?' The answer is that media ethnographies can be conducted in your own backyard as well as in more unfamiliar cultural settings. The decisive aspect to keep in mind is that of *epistemological perspective*: in media ethnography, the researcher makes a point of being a stranger and makes the often cumbersome transition into familiarity by exchanging an outsider's view on the media culture under investigation for an insider's view. This perspective implies searching for and trusting media users' own actions, interpretations and world views, a trust that should not be mistaken for acceptance or truth. Rather, a media ethnographer is in search of how and why particular actions and articulations come to attain social meaning and significance as valid, relevant and truthful. This makes media ethnography part of a wider interpretative tradition in media studies, which has traditionally positioned itself in opposition to more hypothetical-deductive traditions. As we described in Chapter 3, this division has often served to obscure that all research traditions share epistemological and methodological issues of interpretation.

In moving between poles of strangeness and familiarity, the media ethnographer encounters and attempts to handle basic epistemological issues to do with boundaries of geographical place and cultural space. As Tufte's study demonstrates, these boundaries are invariably gendered. How is it possible to gain an insider's view of Brazilian women's novela cultures, which are so deeply embedded into gendered everyday spaces and forms of interaction and interpretation? Tufte touches on this issue when he describes how he has followed his informants on their daily routines, including shopping, cooking and washing, and he acknowledges the difficulty of accessing perceived female spheres of privacy: 'it was only on my own initiative that I would get access to the kitchens and backyards in my contact with the women' (Tufte 2000: 187). Following these difficulties, he states that he may have missed out on aspects of intimacy in his rapport with his informants.

Similarly, many novela narratives 'appear incredible' to him (Tufte 2000: 226) in their drawing so heavily upon the emotional intensities found in melodrama and on the magic realism found in much oral and written Latin American popular culture. Issues such as these point to basic epistemological issues of scientific interests and objects of research, of having the ethnographer stick to more well-known (same-sex) cultural domains, or conversely explore the stranger's position and perspective.

Following immediately from the problematics of epistemology, we may raise a number of questions that touch upon the issues of methodology that are our primary concern in this book. First, if we are interested in people's media uses, why not simply ask them, either by conducting a survey or a series of interviews? The answer here is rather complicated in that most media ethnography does, indeed, involve more or less structured interviews as did Tufte's study. But in media ethnography, these oral exchanges are only part of a research agenda that focuses upon media in use. These are processes of social communication and action. To study such processes as *processes* rather than as discursive claims or numerical statements, one has to apply a processual research design such as observation, which allows us to chart how people variously intervene into, draw back from and act upon the media.

The second methodological question to be asked is this: must a study of complex media cultures, such as the present one, be matched by complex research methodologies? Many media ethnographies assume an affirmative answer to that question in that they base their research on a combination of data and/or methodologies. Thus, Tufte's study involved the collection, coding and analysis of several types of data such as interviews, field-notes of observations made and analysis of media texts. It also encompassed several types of methodology such as textual and numerical analysis. Still, it may not be the case that the very application of several takes on our object of study guarantees our grasping of complexity. But it often nuances our answers.

Today, media are interlaced with other processes of our everyday lives on which they often imperceptibly impinge, and few processes of media interaction have clearly demarcated beginnings and endings. This makes an everyday perspective central to media ethnography, although several scholars choose to include other perspectives, too. (For example, Tufte's study involved an institutional genealogy, a survey and a genre history.) The blurring of boundaries between mediated and non-mediated activities makes it very hard to decide what it takes to fully and significantly observe processes of mediated meaning-making. So, we may ask a third methodological question: how long do you have to stay with informants in order to chart such processes? Tufte stayed in each of the local communities for 7–12 days and afterwards made intermittent returns to Brazil. Is this sufficient time? Too much, or too little? While researchers offer rather different answers to this question, actual decisions are often made on pragmatic grounds: money runs out, teaching obligations set in, informants move or Internet sites are closed down.

Not only are mediated and non-mediated activities increasingly entwined, the same is true of different media and types of expression. For example, many fiction formats traverse the terrain of film, computer games, Internet sites and TV; and it is increasingly difficult to follow John Fiske's neat notion of textual divisions (Fiske 1987: 108–27) and, for example, determine whether reality shows on TV are primary texts, the gossip columns in magazines secondary texts, and people's discussions about characters and plot developments tertiary texts. The complex flows of media expressions raise a fourth question of methodology: how may we define a media text with the precision that is necessary to carry out empirical investigations such as ethnographies? Tufte acknowledges the problem by emphasizing that his selection of a single medium (TV) and a single genre (the telenovela, and particularly selected episodes of *The Rubbish Queen*) is possible only because television has 'a massive presence' in Brazilian everyday cultures and because the novelas are serial manifestations of overwhelming social significance (Tufte 2000: 33). Still, particularly in processual studies such as ethnographies, attempting to define media texts is like trying to hit a moving target.

Among the more practical, yet decisive, methodological issues of ethnography is that of access: how may the ethnographer gain access to his or her chosen field of investigation? Answers to this fifth question often fill up a good part of methodology manuals, which comes as no surprise to anyone who has performed ethnographic studies. For behind this seemingly mundane issue lie the very central concerns of research perspective, the relevance of data to be had and claims to differentials of power. Tufte used people he knew beforehand to get access to local communities, and he is well aware of the importance played by these so-called gatekeepers for his study: Maria was chair of the local community organization, Servilho was an industrial worker and active trades unionist, and João Carlos was a young monk and active social worker. 'No matter who I chose they all had either religious, political or community organizational biases,' notes Tufte (2000: 45), thus pointing to the inevitable selectivity of perspective that the ethnographer has to take into account when entering the field.

Some cultural arenas are easier accessed than others. This is not merely a result of cultural (un)familiarity it is equally an indication of explicit status and power differentials. Thus; Tufte found it very difficult to gain access to, for example, Rede Globo, the world's largest producer of TV fiction in the 1980s and naturally a major player in novela production. 'Being a researcher from Denmark, with no substantial references within the TV networks, made it difficult to obtain the interviews I wanted' (Tufte 2000: 39). He had also planned to follow the production of one or more episodes but was allowed access to the studios only once, and outside the production schedule. Accessing high-powered people and high-status locales posed particular problems, many of which materialized as difficulties in gaining access and relevant information.

As is evident in Tufte's study, an ethical concern for particular groups of media users often underlies an ethnographic approach to media studies. But if you are interested in people in the first place, then why bother with integrating media in your investigation, we may ask. Is textual analysis at all relevant to media ethnography? Or, conversely, is an ethnographic approach part of media studies at all? This final question has caused much debate and controversy amongst media scholars, as we shall see in Chapter 5. Here we may note that the question raises crucial issues of the ways in which we define media and hence brings us back to the epistemological questions that Tufte's study raises. Are media separate entities that may be variously included or excluded according to research priorities and personal predilections? Or are they constitutive of our social and cultural meaning-making and inseparable from our social actions? Is the relative presence of textual analysis in particular studies a result of decisions made along a continuum of foci, or is it an absolute choice between yes and no?

Finally, we need to remember that an ethnographic approach is by no means limited to media studies. Within the academy, anthropologists and ethnographers have a long tradition of studying what have been labelled 'exotic Others', as we have seen. Today, ethnographic approaches impact also on disciplines such as education (Connell et al. 1982; McLaren 1986; Walkerdine 1989), medicine and sociology (Bertaux 1981; Smith 1987) and on interdisciplinary fields such as youth and gender studies (Ginsburg 1989; Fornäs et al. 1988/1: 1995; Skeggs 1997). Moreover, ethnographic perspectives, and the employment of anthropologists and other 'practising ethnographers' are increasingly part of applied studies made within organizational and commercial settings. The increasing interest in applying ethnography in a range of disciplines, fields and settings both within and beyond the academy testifies to a social and cultural situation in which we increasingly recognize that differences and divergences are part of a shared world and so cannot be conveniently ostracized to particular places, peoples or periods.

The application of ethnographic approaches, then, may be seen as an attempt to answer wider research problems than we encounter in media studies, problems that are thrown into relief by still more globalized and complex cultures. What constitute our objects of research? How may we as researchers relate to our topics of investigation? How do we communicate our findings so as to be properly understood, not only by our fellow researchers but equally by the wider community of multifaceted composition? We will return to these important questions in Chapters 5 and 6. But it would follow from the trajectory charted in the present chapter that we study not only how media scholars may learn from anthopology and ethnography, but equally to ask our colleagues within these disciplines how they have managed to study cultures without also including the media.

# Chapter Five

# Media ethnography: defining ☐ the field

Over the last two decades, contemporary societies have variously been defined as, for example, information societies, learning societies, knowledge societies and network societies (Masuda 1980; Husén 1986; Stehr 1994; Castells 1996/1: 1998). Irrespective of scientific traditions, these definitions focus on the crucial ways in which media and information and communication technologies (ICTs) are constitutive of the ways in which we make sense of ourselves and the world around us. Furthermore, the definitions point to the fundamental ways in which the mediated acquisition, articulation and exchange of information and entertainment are entwined into our social fabric in every way, shape and form: from our digital clock radio or favourite TV show pre-programmed to wake us up, to the video screens of shopping malls and airports – not to forget the macro-economic decisions made on Internet stock exchanges, by which entire economies are made and unmade overnight.

For the media researcher, this development has decisive implications. It is increasingly difficult to separate mediated and non-mediated cultures and forms of interaction. It is equally difficult to determine what are our units of study, since forms of expression and genres travel across media and locales with a speed that may only be rivalled by transborder media mergers and acquisitions.

In media-saturated and media-integrated societies, then, scholars are encouraged and enforced to seek routes of study that are geared to grasping how media interrelate as material objects and symbolic forms of expression, and how media are constitutive of people's sense-making processes and exchanges of experience in their everyday lives. In these complex developments lies the rationale of applying an ethnographic approach to media studies or, in short, media ethnography. It is an approach praised by many media scholars over the last two decades and practised by relatively few. It is part of the increasing influence made by the so-called 'interpretative paradigm' (Lindlof and Meyer 1987: 4) and a concomitant cross-fertilization between the humanistic and social science traditions of research that are described in Chapters 2, 3 and 17.

## ETHNOGRAPHIC TRADITIONS

The term ethnography derives from a combination of two Greek words: *ethnos* meaning people and *grafein* meaning to write or draw. Etymologically speaking, ethnography simply means description of (a) people, but application of the term is rather more complicated since the defintion immediately raises a number of fundamental questions: Who is in a position to make descriptions? How may people be defined and delimited? How can such descriptions be made?

The intricacies of finding neat answers to questions such as these are reflected in modern definitions of the term. The British sociologists Martyn Hammersley and Paul Atkinson, in a textbook on ethnography, specify ethnography as an interpretative research approach that involves a number of methodologies:

> *The ethnographer participates, overtly or covertly, in people's daily lives for an extended period of time, watching what happens, listening to what is said, asking questions; in fact collecting whatever data are available to throw light on the issues with which he or she is concerned.*

(Hammersley and Atkinson 1989: 2)

Participation, observation ('watching', 'listening'), interviewing ('asking questions') – in short, being in the field, as it is called, for quite some time: these are some of the methodologies applied by the ethnographer in his or her attempts to describe and interpret the daily lives of particular groups as experienced by the researcher and as seen from the researcher's priorities of relevance ('the issues with which he or she is concerned'). *Ethnography* is a particular research perspective that is characterized by an epistemological commitment to explicit and holistic interpretation from a bottom-up perspective, an empirical interest in first-hand exploration and an application of multiple, mainly qualitative but also quantitative, methodologies. As a term, ethnography covers both a particular process of research and the resulting product.

The characteristics of ethnography are shaped by and have impinged upon the two main traditions within which ethnography has developed, namely anthropology and micro-sociology. Both disciplines originated in the scientific climate of the late nineteenth century when academic institutionalizations emerged within major paradigmatic constestations over what counts as scientific truth. As discussed in Chapter 3, based on the rationalism of the Enlightenment, positivists strived to deduce universal laws via so-called *nomothetic research* whose results have predictive value, an approach that they saw perfected by the contemporary natural sciences. Conversely, hermeneutics sought to inductively understand concrete expressions (of human behaviour, culture, history) via so-called *ideographic research*, whose results have no direct predictive value. The German philosopher Wilhelm Dilthey (1833–1911) coined the phrase *Verstehen*, to understand (Dilthey 1944/1974), in order to distinguish the explicitly interpretativist stance from the positivist *Erklären*, or explain. Both anthropology and micro-sociology adhere to the interpretativist paradigm, which in Dilthey's definition encompassed objects of study that would later be separated out into the humanities and social sciences.

As processes of social and cultural modernity gain momentum in Europe and North America, and as economic modernization expands to colonies in, for example, Australia and Africa, Latin America and India, both academic and public interest come to centre on issues of Other-ness. These issues are defined in temporal terms as loss over time of traditions, social networks, material culture and language within one's own culture or neighbouring cultures. And they are defined in spatial terms as rituals, beliefs and language within cultures more distant from home.

The comparative study of domestic and neighbouring cultures, particularly in rural or historical settings, has become the professional domain of *ethnology*, a discipline that developed mostly in northern and eastern Europe. Its early emphasis on origins, and its conflation of cultural and geographical boundaries, is indicated by its German name, *Volkskunde* (knowledge about the people). Conversely, the study of contemporary societies and cultures, particularly in urban settings, has become the focus of *sociology*, a discipline that first flourishes in early industrialized countries such as the US, France and Great Britain. The systematic study of distant, or 'exotic', cultures has become the professional preserve of *anthropology*, whose early emphasis upon ethnic difference is indicated by the German term *Völkerkunde* (knowledge about peoples). Since ethnology has little international influence on the development of ethnography, we shall limit ourselves to outlining its legacies within anthropology and sociology.

The Polish-British anthropologist, Bronislaw Malinowski (1884–1942), is claimed as the founding father of ethnography, if not of anthropology. Based on two years of intensive and systematic study in the Trobriand Islands, he published *Argonauts of the Western Pacific: An Account of Native Enterprise and Adventure in the Archipelagoes of Melanesian New Guinea* in 1922. Here he defined ethnography as a scientific approach whose aim it is 'to grasp the native's point of view, his relation to life, to realize *his* vision of *his* world (Malinowski 1922: 25; emphasis in original). The ethnographer should study culture not just from a bottom-up perspective, but from an insider's perspective, an aim that demands committed, long-term immersion into a setting in order to understand how meaning is achieved and attained. Moreover, the ethnographer should study culture from a holistic perspective ('his world'), an aim that demands equally committed analysis of multiple views and often contradictory sources in order to understand how meaning is constituted as contextualized practices.

In Malinowski's definition, ethnography is not only a particular research perspective, it is also a perspective that presupposes what may be termed an *ontological and epistemological realism*: cultures are seen as bounded and unified entities, and it is possible for the scholar, and hence the reader, to reach a truthful understanding of a particular culture based on the scholar's description-cum-interpretation of its artefacts and symbolic processes. This realism should not be equated with a naïve naturalism, for Malinowski is well aware that the researcher does not enter the field as an intellectual *tabula rasa*. As he states in his introduction to *Argonauts*: 'Preconceived ideas are pernicious in any scientific work, but foreshadowed problems are the main endowment of a scientific thinker, and these problems are first revealed to the observer by his theoretical studies' (Malinowski 1922: 9).

From the outset, the interpretativism of ethnography implies a close integration of empirical description and analysis and theoretical conceptualization. This integration is found both within the tradition of social anthropology, which Malinowski developed around the London School of Economics between the two world wars, and within the tradition of cultural anthropology that has flourished, mainly in the US, starting with the work of Franz Boas (1858–1942). The interlacing of description and interpretation also characterizes the other main tradition of ethnography, namely micro-sociology.

*Micro-sociology* has developed as part of the larger discipline of sociology. It focuses on studying people's daily lives, interpersonal relations and informal modes of organization, while macro-sociology centres on the investigation of formal organizations and larger societal structures and developments. In 1892, the Department of Sociology at Chicago University was founded as the first sociology department in the US and in the immediate vicinity of a sprawling city, which illuminated issues of rapid urban development. From its inception, the department embraced a catholic range of research interests and topics; notably from the First World War on, a number of theories and empirical research areas developed that were all explicitly interpretativist in nature and that, to varying degrees, employed ethnography: urban studies (or social ecology), subcultural studies and deviance studies. Like most intellectual networks, scholars associated with the department rejected being seen as they are from the outside: as the Chicago School of sociology.

The theoretical underpinning of the interpretativist group of the Chicago School is, first and foremost, philosophical pragmatism as formulated by William James, John Dewey and Charles Sanders Peirce (who coined the phrase), and social psychology as formulated by W.I. Thomas and George Herbert Mead. The common core of pragmatism is its definition of meaning as constituted through social interaction. People are meaning-making creatures, but meaning is not an individual property, it is a social practice: meaning is part of doing.

In his book *Mind, Self and Society* (1934), Mead develops this line of thought into a theory of social psychology, which Herbert Blumer, one of the central figures at the Chicago School, in 1937 named symbolic interactionism (see Blumer 1969). For Mead, the self is constituted in continuous communicative action. In interpersonal communication we anticipate the response of the Other at the moment of address, and so we adjust our communication to our expectations of the Other's intentions. In 1928, W.I. Thomas radicalized Mead's interactionism by stating that 'if men [*sic*] define situations as real, they are real in their consequences' (in Rochberg-Halton 1986: 44). Human interaction is part of daily life and involves quite complex, practical abilities of role-taking, of seeing oneself from the perspectives of others and making continuous adjustments to the informal and formal rules of conduct within respective communities.

The Chicago School of sociology was pioneered by Robert E. Park and Ernest W. Burgess, both of whom advocated hands-on empirical research and had open minds to methodological diversity, including life histories, diaries and open-ended interviews, as well as participant observation and case studies. Park, who had been trained as a journalist before entering academia, urged his students to 'go get your pants dirty in real research', a remark that underscores the ideals found in much classical Chicago ethnography: the truth is 'out there' amongst 'ordinary' people in the 'real' world, and it may be found by the engaged researcher who looks long and hard enough.

After the Second World War, the central tenets of the Chicago School theories and empirical issues were carried on and developed by new generations of scholars, many of whom have impacted upon communications and media studies in general, and on ethnography in particular. The theory of role-taking has been systematized by Erving Goffman (1959), the description-cum-interpretation has been theorized by Barney Glaser and Anselm Strauss in grounded theory (1967, of which more below), and the verbal reasoning procedures ('methodologies') people use to uphold a sense of intersubjective understanding is the basis of ethnomethodology, as developed by Howard Garfinkel (1967).

## Box 5.1

Three aspects shared by the sociological and social-psychological adherents of the Chicago School are of particular relevance for ethnographic studies of communication and media.

- First, human beings are meaning-making creatures whose sense of self is constitutive of and constituted within communicative practices.
- Second, these communicative practices are forms of purposeful, yet taken-for-granted social actions.
- Third, these communicative actions illuminate how meaning comes to circulate and gain acceptance as much as which meanings are communicated.

Many scholars, not least between the two world wars, who have drawn their intellectual inspiration from the Chicago School, have related their work to issues of wider social significance such as social inequality and ethnic conflicts. For someone interested in media studies, it should be noted that this general social commitment goes hand in hand with an emphasis upon interpersonal communication as a conceptual axiom against which other forms of communication are measured. Moreover, it is the consensual, rather than the conflictual, aspects of communication that are studied, and empirical work is often carried out within geographically bounded cultures and communities.

From the 1970s on, a conflictual perspective begins to impinge on social and cultural theories themselves. The locus of this development has retrospectively been labelled *cultural studies*. It emerged as an interdisciplinary research perspective in countries as diverse as Australia, Brazil, Britain and Germany, under the combined theoretical influences of Marxism, structuralism and feminism. A catholic mixture of empirical studies on e.g. youth, gender, popular culture and sport is informed by theories of power and economic exploitation. Notably in Britain, where the term was coined, cultural studies was inspired by the Chicago School, and early researchers drew on ethnographic approaches (Willis 1977; Cohen 1972/1: 1980; Griffin 1980).

Within the discipline of anthropology, the American, Clifford Geertz, in 1973 stressed the constructivist nature of anthropology as an interpretative science by stating that 'anthropological writings are themselves interpretations, and second and third order ones to boot. (By definition, only a "native" makes first order ones: it's *his* culture). They are, thus, fictions' (Geertz 1973: 15). Spurred by feminist and, later, postcolonial scholars, many researchers have increasingly come to question the validity of the epistemological and ontological realism underlying classic anthropology. Instead of the researcher's distanced analysis, the subjective voices of informants and the scholar's partaking in the field are foregrounded.

The most radical version of this relativism is the so-called *postmodern ethnography* (Clifford and Marcus 1986; Marcus and Fischer 1986), which not only casts doubt upon the ontological realism of anthropology (our findings are highly selective and partial), but equally attempts to undermine the epistemological realism of anthropology (our analyses are not representations but constructions of the cultural interpretations under investigation). The *radical constructivism* demonstrates a 'textual turn' in ethnography that is heavily influenced by literary theories such as narratology, textual and discourse analysis, just as visual forms of analysis are being applied within so-called visual anthropology (Crawford and Turton 1992; Loizos 1993).

Through the 1990s, scholars – notably those with a good empirical grounding – have advocated a 'subtle realism' (Hammersley 1992: 50–4) or a more dialogical perspective within ethnography (Rosaldo 1980), in which ontological realism is combined with an epistemological constructivism (there actually exists an external reality that we as scholars may investigate, but it is a reality with which we are necessarily implicated, and we must be reflexive of the ways in which data are collected, analysed and communicated). In wider terms, the 'subtle realism' of more recent ethnography corresponds to the approach we discussed in Chapter 3 under the label of 'discursive realism'. Not surprisingly, the move from realism through relativism to reflexivity has also coloured the applications of ethnography within media studies.

## ETHNOGRAPHY ENTERS COMMUNICATION AND MEDIA STUDIES

Traditionally, communication research is divided into interpersonal and mediated forms of communication with organizational communication operating as a third category that includes both of the other two forms. Mastering the 'native' language is seminal, especially to American anthropology, which, from its inception, has spurred a sustained professional interest in interpersonal communication (Boas 1911; Sapir 1929; Whorf 1940). Interpersonal communication is also central to much micro-sociology, as we have noted. Both anthropologists and sociologists owe their theoretical axioms to the German philosopher Ludwig Wittgenstein, whose *Philosophical Investigations* (1953) states that language can only convey meaning in social use where its rules can be intersubjectively regulated and negotiated.

From the 1960s on, the *ethnography of communication* has developed as an academic under-current that draws on this general theoretical legacy. In its specific research interests it aims to develop comparative, empirical studies of socially situated language uses. Spurred by the American anthropologist Dell Hymes' paper, 'The Ethnograpy of Speaking' (Hymes 1962; Gumperz and Hymes 1964), the ethnography of communication develops under the influence of speech-act theory (Austin 1962) and sociolinguistics (Labov 1972a), both of which urge linguists to go beyond language structure and sentence units to look for patterned uses of speech. From ethnology and folklore studies, ethnography of com-munication is influenced by and impinges on cultural comparison and the aesthetic use of language as performance (Paredes and Bauman 1972). Hymes and his followers apply ethnography to study *in situ* the speech events of particular language communities, which are socially and linguistically diverse but geographically bounded units that share the same language. Being chiefly associated with the Annenberg School of Communication at the University of Pennsylvania, where Hymes was on the faculty, the ethnography of communication has been instrumental in widening linguists' units of analysis and their defintion of language to include, for example, song, sounds, kinesics – the study of human movement (Birdwhistell 1970) – and proxemics – the study of social distance (Hall 1959).

**THE FAR SIDE®    By GARY LARSON**

**"Anthropologists! Anthropologists!"**

The growing international interest in media ethnography from the 1980s on, may be seen as a scientific response to global shifts in the production and dissemination of culture and media.

Media studies has been somewhat slower in systematic applications of ethnography, and, not unnaturally, these applications have developed differently and in relation to prevalent research traditions in North America, Europe and Latin America, respectively. For example, a specific interest in ethnographic approaches appears in Australia (Hodge and Tripp 1986), Brazil (Leal 1986, 1990), Sweden (Fornäs et al. 1988/1: 1995) and Germany (Bausinger 1984; Baacke et al. 1990; Rogge 1991), often as part of a widening interest in the interdisciplinary approaches of research, such as is the case in cultural studies. Obviously, English publication dates are a poor guide to authors' publications in their own languages and their influences on a national level. This diversity is often ignored in debates on media ethnography (Lindlof 1987, 1995; Jankowski and Wester 1991; Jensen 1991a; Morley 1992: 173–97), but it is important to remember since it serves to stress that the growing interest in media ethnography, as noted in Chapter 4, is part of global shifts in the production and dissemination of culture and media, shifts that ethnography equally seeks to address.

As we saw, the interest in media ethnography in Britain is rooted in the cultural studies tradition. This tradition harbours wider sociopolitical aims that often result in particular analytical interest being paid to the relations between the ideological representations of media texts and audiences' various decodings and social uses of the media. Most British media scholars within the cultural studies tradition have focused on unravelling the social uses of the media, and some have done so by means of ethnographic methodologies such as participant observation, multiple research perspectives and several sets of data (Gray 1992; Gillespie 1995). In the Nordic countries of Europe, on the other hand, the human-ities form an important institutional frame for media studies, with semiology, historiogra-phy and linguistics as important theoretical frames. Here, several media ethnographies study media uses by combining textual analysis of particular media genres or formats with participant observation, diaries and ethnographic interviews (Rasmussen 1990; Drotner 1991; Helland 1993; Fuglesang 1994; Fornäs et al. 1988/1: 1995; Wulff 1995).

In North America, media ethnography is shaped in opposition to the positivist paradigm and the quantitative methodologies dominating the social sciences, including media studies. It builds on the interpretative traditions of anthropology and micro-sociology mentioned above (Bryce 1980; Lemish 1982; Lee and Cho 1995). Conversely, in Latin America, media ethnography is deeply embedded in wider discussions of the political role played by the media (Canclini 1988; Martín-Barbero 1987/1: 1993, 2000).

In retrospect, a good number of qualitative studies carried out within, for example, urban, youth or feminist studies from the early 1980s on, may be defined as media ethnographies without explicitly being labelled or acknowledged as such. It is worth noting that several of these are published within interdisciplinary fields of study that are often perceived as marginal to mainstream research at the time.

In the scientific community of media studies, the inception of media ethnography is asso-ciated with US media researcher James Lull's early work, which he undertook in the late 1970s. (Jennifer Bryce's dissertation (Bryce 1980), conducted at about the same time and applying a similar research design, is now virtually neglected.) Based on Lull's doctoral dissertation on 20 families and their negotiations over programme selection for joint TV-viewing in the home (Lull 1978), Lull designed a larger study that involved over 200 families of different social backgrounds in Wisconsin and Santa Barbara. They were contacted through girls' and boys' clubs, nursery schools and religious bodies, and the acceptance rate was about 30 per cent. Lull's research assistants spent from two to seven days in each home and were present from mid-afternoon until bedtime. Each observer had a preprinted log listing standardized items that enabled written documentation on the premises of the interaction taking place between family members (dominance strategies, talk patterns) including TV uses (programme selection procedures, viewing patterns). Each observer produced a written summary at the end of each day of observation. At the conclusion of the observational period, each family member was interviewed and was later asked to read the written report in order to confirm the validity of the observations.

Lull's main results showed that the social uses of television were of two primary types: structural and relational (Lull 1980). The structural uses were either environmental (e.g. background noise, companionship) or regulatory (e.g. dividing time and social activities). The relational uses were further divided into communication facilitation (e.g. agenda for talk, value clarification), affiliation/avoidance (e.g. physical or verbal contact/neglect, conflict reduction), social learning (e.g. problem-solving, social interaction roles) and com-petition/dominance (e.g. competence reinforcement, parental regulation). With a theoreti-cal background in ethnomethodology, Lull was interested in studying television as a social resource situated within informants' patterned everyday procedures and normative routines. Following that interest, he defined media ethnography as:

> *an integrated means for understanding the everyday world of social groups, their patterns of interpersonal communication, and their uses of the mass media. The intent of the ethnography of mass communication is to allow the researcher to grasp as completely as possible with minimal disturbance the 'native's perspective' on relevant communicative and sociocultural matters indigenous to him.*

(Lull 1980: 199)

Through the 1980s, media ethnography became 'an abused buzz word in our field' (Lull 1988: 242). The term has been invoked as a research perspective capable of overcoming the perceived impasse of audience studies (Ang 1990; Morley and Silverstone 1990); it has been equalled with reception research since both share the same 'general intentions' (Moores 1993: 4); and it has been proposed as an alternative to reception analysis (Drotner 1993). Conversely, media ethnography has been criticized as being an example of 'terminological usurpation' (Evans 1990) that is applied loosely as an equivalent of qualitative audience studies. It has also been denounced as a legitimating tool in order to claim political allegiance to the cultural studies tradition (Nightingale 1989), just as it has been said to make media scholars lose sight of their main object of investigation in a maze of social contextualizations (Schrøder 1993). Still, ethnographic methodologies, theories and perspectives continue to be applied within media studies, and the proliferation of Internet communication through the 1990s has served to further augment and complicate their uses, a fact that merits our continued analytical attention.

# DEFINING MEDIA ETHNOGRAPHY

Lull's definition resonates with the tradition of realist anthropology and micro-sociology, both of which have deeply influenced media ethnography, as we have seen.

## Box 5.2    Main characteristics of media ethnography

- Media are defined as *processes* of meaning-making that call upon processual empirical research approaches focusing upon ways in which media constitute experience in users' handling of mediated forms of communication.
- Media are defined as *symbolic* processes of meaning-making, processes that call upon explicit interpretative measures of analysis.
- Media are defined as socially *situated* processes of meaning-making, processes that call upon case studies of the actual practices of meaning-making and of the situations within which these practices unfold.
- Media are defined as *complex* processes of meaning-making, processes that call upon a holistic account and a combination of analytical measures in order to grasp these complexities.
- Media are defined as *articulations* of meaning-making, processes that call upon an attention to the ways in which these articulations are textually produced and made to make sense by somebody.

These characteristics raise a number of methodological and analytical issues that have been tackled in various ways by the relativist and reflexive developments of ethnography mentioned above. You have to address these issues before deciding whether or not your empirical research topic or theoretical interest fit an ethnographic approach. Let us look in more detail at some of these issues.

# DEFINING THE RESEARCH TOPIC

Suppose you want to investigate how players of computer games make sense of their activities: you cannnot limit yourself to making a textual analysis of the manuals at hand or the numerous literary traditions on which computer games often draw, for none of these are the media text that you want to study. Nor, indeed, is it enough to make interviews with a chosen number of players, trying to unravel how they play and what they think of it. You have to attend the actual activities of playing as they unfold, since the media text and the concomitant meaning-making is only shaped in practice – as the playing takes place. In addition, players will often form networks, seeking information in a nearby games shop, on the Internet or in the school playground, and so the contexts of use diversify.

In empirical terms, the majority of media investigations focus on a particular medium, such as television or the Internet, or on particular genres such as print news, action films or adventure games for the computer. But in media ethnography you will often start out with an interest in a particular group and the ways in which that group interacts with one or more media. The aim is to get a holistic and nuanced understanding of your informants' own sense-making processes.

Media ethnography raises epistemological questions about what the German sociologist Jürgen Habermas calls our knowledge interests (do I ultimately want to know about people or about media?) and about our research priorities (do I consider data culled *in situ* to be more valid or nuanced than data culled from a questionnaire or in a controlled laboratory setting?). Depending on your answers, you may choose to focus upon the social uses made of media and the ways in which viewing, listening and reading are integrated into people's daily lives, or you may also want to include analyses of media material – that is, what people watch, listen to and read.

For media ethnography also raises theoretical issues about the relations between media text and media context (are the computer players my text and the computer games my context, or vice versa) and about the location of sense-making (is meaning lodged within the computer game without it being played, or is meaning only generated when somebody realizes the text). Media scholars differ in their answers to these fundamental issues, and these differences will often materialize in their research design, in that some media ethnographies will emphasize textual analysis as part of their investigation (Fornäs et al. 1988/1: 1995; Bolin 1998; Tufte 2000), while others will focus on the social interactions (Bryce 1980; Lull 1980; Gray 1992).

Internet communication serves to complicate the relations between text and context even further. Imagine that you want to make a study of IRC (Internet relay chat) groups. What you have as your primary data pool for analysis are online, mostly textual representations of embodied identities that are often dispersed in vastly different geographical localities. This situation immediately calls into question a fundamental tenet of IRL (in real life) ethnography, namely the bounded physical nature of its units of analysis. In some cases, it is possible to contact and interview chatters offline, in which case we are able to compare the virtual and the IRL media uses and identity constructions (Correll 1995). This may, paradoxically, lessen the ethnographic perspective.

As the British media schola, Christine Hine, notes, the researcher's analysis of online textual interactions is in fact more real in an ethnographic sense than are his or her analyses of IRL interactions, since it mirrors the informant's position more closely (Hine 2000: 49). Hine reaches this conclusion on the basis of an ethnographic case study of the

Internet communication following the trial in the US of a young British nanny, Louise Woodward, charged with the murder of a child in her care (Hine 2000). Relying on Internet search tools, Hine documents and analyses online communication on the varied Louise Woodward sites (including news reports, video and sound files, discussion groups and support sites where people could register and lobby the judges). Hine's line of argument illuminates how online analysis serves to problematize ethnographers' traditional reliance on and prioritizing of face-to-face interaction within physical locales. Furthermore, online ethnographies serve to advance the application of various forms of textual and visual analysis such as semiology, linguistics and discourse analysis.

In addition to the issues thrown into relief by ethnographic approaches to the Internet as an object of study, there are numerous problems involved in applying the Internet as a methodological means when investigating topics unrelated to media (Mann and Stewart 2000). These we leave aside in the present context.

## DEFINING THE RESEARCH DESIGN

A hallmark of media ethnography is its explicit interpretative approach. This impacts on scholars' choice of research design, which must heed that ethnographies are all ideographic studies – that is, interpretative investigations of a culture based on the textual (rather than numerical) analysis of data culled from a small number of cases, at least when compared with survey design. The researcher focuses upon a holistic analysis of the variations found within the sample, unlike so-called nomothetic research, which is designed to examine law-like regularities with a predictive perspective.

In order to attain a holistic analysis, a combination of perspectives is required. So media ethnographies are designed as kaleidoscopes applying multiple sources. These can take the form of different investigators, various types of empirical data (e.g. informants), different methodologies or a combination of theories. The US sociologist, Norman Denzin, terms this combinatory design strategy *triangulation*, which he defines as:

> *comparison of data relating to the same phenomenon but deriving from different phases of the fieldwork, different points in the temporal cycles occurring in the setting, or, as in respondent validation, the accounts of different participants (including the ethnographer) in the setting.*

(Denzin 1970/1: 1978: 198)

In empirical studies, triangulation is primarily used to denote the researcher's multi-method approach. Participant observation is a mainstay that may be combined with so-called ethnographic interviews conducted in the field or in post-fieldwork interviews, as in Lull's study. To these may be added audio material and visual material in the form of photographs or video recordings of settings, diaries kept by informants and possibly media material. Furthermore, it is standard procedure for media ethnographers to keep an observer's diary noting reflections, ideas and personal reactions on ongoing activities.

Triangulation raises important questions on how to handle possible incongruence between different sources. Unlike most classical studies of ethnography, most scholars today acknowledge that 'unity in diversity' is an analytical asset: precisely when inconsistencies occur, when you become surprised or frustrated at not being able to find neat patterns, you should be on your analytical alert. The British youth researcher, Paul Willis, calls such moments of crisis 'a creative uncertainty' (Willis 1980: 93).

The truth of this statement was brought home to one of the authors during the late 1980s when she conducted an ethnographic study on young people's video production (Drotner 1989, 1991), with the aim of understanding the articulation and importance of informal media literacies. For a year, she made participant observations of a group of 14–17 year olds in a youth club; she had informal discussions with the teenagers; and she also conducted in-depth interviews with each of the participants in their homes at the beginning and end of the study. In addition, she analysed the group's videos, as well as a selection of their media products (books, magazines, films). During the initial interview, the informants all professed a near-negligence of their video-making activities. However, the extended observations illuminated an intense preoccupation with the process that often involved their cancelling of parties and important sports matches in order to be with the video group. During the final interview, the researcher probed into this inconsistency between what they said and what they did by asking them to narrate how they got their ideas, not what they thought they learned from it. Their radiant eyes and eager voices as they talked were a clear confirmation that the process was indeed profoundly important to them.

The triangulation method proved key to the conceptual analysis. It was precisely the perceived insignificance of a 'mere' leisure activity lodged outside the serious realm of schooling that enabled the informants' informal media literacy. Only the researcher's sustained presence with the group allowed her to discover, and subsequently use, the discrepancy between talk and action. Moreover, she realized that the discrepancy was epistemological more than empirical in nature. While she initially sought to explain the group's negative attitudes in terms of their ambivalent relations to schooling (the term 'learn' harbouring negative connotations for many young people), she ended up by realizing that the discrepancies were equally rooted in her own ways of asking (analytical why-questions vs descriptive how-questions). Since ethnography is an interpretative science, what we look for depends fundamentally on what we can see.

In this study, the researcher underestimated a fundamental issue that has to be tackled in designing a media ethnography, namely the very definition of media. In a holistic media ethnography, the researcher must theoretically acknowledge and empirically seek to analyse that media are at once material objects transporting messages and symbolic processes of meaning-making (Williams 1974/1: 1990; Carey 1989/1: 1992). Some media ethnographers have made this duality a particular focus of their research design in order to specify ways in which media technologies are appropriated by audiences and incorporated into their daily lives. In one such study, and as part of a multiple set of methodologies, British media researchers, David Morley and Roger Silverstone, let informants draw their domestic surroundings in order to play out the (lack of) importance they allocated to domestic technologies as material properties vis-à-vis their significance as meaning-making practices (Morley and Silverstone 1990, 1991).

In designing ethnographic studies on computer media, such as interactive games and Internet communication, the dual definition of media becomes an absolute necessity. In gaming, the software technology only emerges as artefact through use; and in Internet communication, the technology is not a material artefact but is basically a set of application programs such as email, the World Wide Web, videoconferencing and IRC. Studying the material aspects of these media is essentially the same as following the symbolic practices and discourses through which they are constituted by users. The dual definition of these media tends to be conflated in practice, while the processual character of these practices makes ethnographic approaches ever more central.

A final issue of central importance to the research design is whether or not to incorporate a 'sender' perspective (media organizations, programme producers, game designers and programmers) in an ethnographic study of media audiences. Most scholars refrain from such comprehensiveness, if less as a matter of principle than as a matter of feasibility. As we saw in Chapter 4, Thomas Tufte's (2000) study on telenovelas does include aspects of both media institutions and professional routines of production, in tandem with textual analysis of a selected corpus of novelas and their uses by audiences. Naturally, such inclusiveness serves to augment the holistic aims of the resulting ethnographic product.

## DEFINING THE RESEARCHER'S POSITION

A fundamental principle of media ethnography is to base one's empirical analysis and conceptual development on the informant's point of view. To fulfil this principle, you need a period of fieldwork where you are in the presence of the people you want to study for some time as a participant observer. How do you choose to position yourself while being in the field? This is a central question whose answers depend partly on the object of research, partly on ethical and practical issues. In Chapter 6, we return to the more practical ways of tackling these issues. For now, let us look into the general dilemmas involved in positioning oneself during the empirical research process.

The term participant observation is a clue to these dilemmas. To *participate* implies involvement, action and immersion in what is going on. It is a process of gaining insight that the realist tradition of ethnography underscores. To *observe* implies distance, rest and reflection on what is going on. It is a process of gaining an outlook that the more recent moves towards constructivism foreground. Both participation and observation are aspects of description as well as analysis – fieldwork is not about descriptive immersion and analytical distance. But media researchers wield these aspects in different ways. In Lull's study on the social uses of television, the student observers 'ate with the families, performed household chores with them, played with the children, and took part in group entertainment, particularly television viewing' (Lull 1980: 201). Unlike this active participation, in the study on video production mentioned above, the researcher adopted a more obser-

THE FAR SIDE® BY GARY LARSON

**"March 5, 1984: After several months, I now feel that these strange little rodents have finally accepted me as one of their own."**

Today, few media ethnographers harbour illusions about positioning themselves during fieldwork as unobstrusive flies on the wall.

vational position, which came fairly naturally since 'her' teenage informants were so involved with their projects and their more or less romantic entanglements.

No media ethnographer entertains any ideas about being an objective, uninvolved, fly-on-the-wall observer. To perform interpretative research is by necessity to be positioned as part of one's object of study, to adopt and acknowledge a perspective of analysis. Most ethnographies demonstrate a mixture of immersion and distance, a mixture that shows up as phases of more or less involvement. In his famous essay, 'The Stranger', the Austrian sociologist, Alfred Schutz, notes how the stranger coming to a new location is 'a marginal man' [*sic*], and because of this marginality:

> *the cultural pattern of the approached group is to the stranger not a shelter but a field of adventure, not a matter of course but a questionable topic of investigation, not an instrument for disentangling problematic situations but a problematic situation itself and one hard to master.*

(Schutz 1964: 104)

Schutz highlights how social and cultural marginality sharpens our senses and dislodges the obvious so that we simultaneously perceive our surroundings and ourselves in new ways. This is also what happens when performing partipant observation. It involves processes of destrangement (making the unknown known) as well as estrangement (making the known unknown). To manoeuvre within this terrain of familiarity and unfamiliarity involves tact, common sense and a capacity for continous reflexivity.

The concept of reflexivity has become a mantra in much methodological literature over the past two decades. Basically, it involves a systematic positing of alternative perspectives: How would this look from an outsider's point of view? How could this be otherwise? What if . . . ? Reflexivity is a strategy employed by the researcher, but it is not limited to self-reflexivity. It is a continuous process both when creating your research design, during data collection and analysis, and in the eventual creation of the ethnographic product. The highly complex nature of modern media cultures both enforces and enables reflexivity: you can only fathom and handle complex processes if you are able to take in multiple perspectives. If your perspective is unidirectional, you will see no complexity at all, and if you attempt to apply any number of perspectives (were that possible), you will see nothing but chaos.

## DEFINING THE RESEARCH LOCATION

An epitome of classical anthropology and micro-sociology is the focus on a particular location, be it a local culture or the social practices found in a particular group or community. These locales are the foci of fieldwork and the unquestioned boundaries of ethnography. Following this tradition, early media ethnographies focus on domestic media uses. But, spurred by media globalization, including the Internet, and the ubiquity and mobility of media, more recent work raises vital questions about the definition and empirical status of 'the field': Is it to be analysed and understood as one or more geographical places; or is it rather virtual spaces of communication – or perhaps both?

In her media ethnography on the ways in which media play into the identity formation of British Asians in the London suburb of Southall, Marie Gillespie followed a group of youngsters in diverse arenas (Gillespie 1995). Her study exemplifies the anthropologist George Marcus's call for ethnographic methodology being 'multi-sited' and its procedures geared towards tracking the routes of artefacts, symbols and ideas (Marcus 1998: 79–104). A diversification of spatial locales is clearly necessary for the ethnographer who wants to study what the American reception researcher, Janice Radway (1988), terms 'dispersed audiences and nomadic subjects', whose cultural universes are made up of transnational and mobile media output and transborder forms of communication as much as interpersonal interaction with neighbours and colleagues. For such multi-sited research, the field is not a bounded place but the range of places and spaces through which mediated forms of meaning-making take place.

Yet again, Internet communication serves to further complicate any neat definition of the ethnographic field even as a multi-sited field. By definition, the Internet researcher has no direct access to participants' spatial locales, but only to their intermittent constitution of virtual spaces through communication. Naturally, for Internet users, their IRL place and their virtual spaces are connected, but these connections are usually not accessible to the researcher. Rather than being an issue to be decided beforehand by research design, it becomes an empirical question in media ethnography to chart how such communicative spaces are enacted and disrupted, negotiated and possibly contested. And so in Internet ethnography, the definition and delimitation of space becomes not so much multi-sited as mobile, not so much interaction as flow (Hine 2000: 64).

## DEFINING THE DURATION OF RESEARCH

The researcher's sustained presence in the field is an important aspect of media ethnography. But how long should you be in the field? Answers range from Lull's two to seven days and on to the Norwegian anthropologists Odd Are Berkaak and Even Ruud, who spent nearly three years in participant observation for a study of music production performed by a group of young musicians (Berkaak and Ruud 1994; Ruud 1995). Let us enumerate some of the dilemmas that must be considered before deciding upon the exact duration of fieldwork.

The researcher's long-term commitment, which often includes repeat visits, is necessary to get into the processes of mutual destrangement and estrangement. Imagine that you go on a package tour to a distant country for a week. Upon your return, you can expound on local customs and cuisine, bus routes and beer labels. But what if you stay for, say, two months? Chances are that you will return with something to say about the locals and more to reflect on for yourself. Your own everyday routines and norms have been unsettled without a parallel formation of certainty about your host culture. In a similar fashion, media ethnography should proceed until you have reached a point of empirical saturation – that is, until a time when you are no longer surprised at what you learn in the field. Your informants have gone beyond 'performing' for the researcher, which often happens during the initial stages of fieldwork, and you have grasped your informants' often imperceptible routines and embodied regulations. But you still define yourself as a stranger, following Schutz. The very moment you feel naturalized, it is high time to leave, because you will have lost the analytical sensitivity that follows from being defined by your informants and yourself as a marginal existence (Hammersley and Atkinson 1989: 103–4).

In ethnographic Internet research, it is more difficult to delimit the duration of one's fieldwork. Because Internet research demands no physical travel, indeed it is most ethnographic when being performed intermittently in front of a computer, the question of familiarity and marginality does not emerge so clearly. Here, a rule of thumb is the concept of empirical saturation, which is closely related to concept-building (see below).

## DEFINING AUDIENCES

As we noted in the introduction to this chapter, media increasingly saturates and is integrated into our everyday lives, where it is ever more mobile and ubiquitous. The concomitant blurring of boundaries between mediated and non-mediated forms of communication and interaction makes it difficult to define our units of analysis, including our definitions of audiences. In our methodological discussion of defining the ethnographic field, we have already touched upon the audience as a multi-faceted concept. Let us look more into key problems arising from this conceptual difficulty.

In both qualitative and quantitative studies on audiences, sociodemographic variables, such as age, class, gender and ethnicity, are stable features in sampling and analysis. This material definition of audiences was also the point of departure in the study on video production discussed above. Since one of the aims was to unravel how well-known gendered genre and media preferences of reception are articulated and negotiated in processes of production, the researcher opted for a mixed-gender group. Other studies apply a more symbolic definition of audiences as being interpretative communities (Fish 1979), whose composition is defined though their joint cultural and media interpretations and uses rather than through their embodied features.

Suppose you want to make an ethnographic investigation of net-gaming, your definition of players will be decisive for the outcome of your study. If you opt for a material definition, you will most likely settle on studying gaming processes as they unfold in a cybercafé or in the domestic locales of a group of regular players. If you opt for a symbolic definition, you will most likely start with charting, and partaking in, particular games sessions as they are textually articulated on your computer screen.

In more general terms, audiences of computer media are the most dispersed. They materialize to each other through particular communicative uses. As an ethnographic researcher who wants to highlight the informant's point of view, you may focus on users' procedures of conduct, and their claims to authenticity and expression. But generally you have no, or very limited, access to also trace the material users (Turkle 1995). So, ethnographic Internet research implies a shift of interest from understanding who the net users are (and if they are what they say they are on the net) into an interest in studying how net users materialize and conduct their 'selves'.

Perhaps you noticed a shift in the preceding paragraph from speaking about audiences to speaking about users. This shift points to another pertinent problematic for the media ethnographer, which is rooted in the recent growth in the uses made of digital interactive media such as software programs for web design and music production, camcorders and digital cameras, not to mention MP3 players and the inception of more interactive forms of television. Today, people in large numbers and with limited technical skills or interests are able to explore how to make media, and this trend is very likely to increase in the future.

Together, these developments serve to question received notions of audiences in media studies. Mass-mediated and interpersonal forms of mediated communication increasingly merge (just think of group sms or mms messages), boundaries between material and symbolic audiences and between production and reception blur, as do the distinctions made between professionals and amateurs. It is increasingly evident that media audiences are also media users. So to perform a media ethnography involves analysis of a complex constellation of media, and of production and reception processes.

# BUILDING CONCEPTS

A major incentive and aim of fieldwork is to understand and analyse the object of research from the informants' or users' points of view. The ethnographic account should be structured from an *emic* perspective (Pike 1967), that is, it should employ categories that are meaningful to the informants. The emic perspective is part of an ideographic, case-based research design and can be distinguished from an *etic* perspective of nomothetic research in which categories are created from the analysts' point of view with the aim of reaching predictive patterns. A central task for the media ethnographer is to build on emic perspectives in order to form etic categories and concepts that acknowledge the existence of the researcher's 'foreshadowed problems' and analytical capacities when embarking upon fieldwork, and at the same time avoid taking informants' accounts at face value – what the US anthropologist, Clifford Geertz, wryly terms 'ethnographic ventriloquism' (Geertz 1989: 145).

A possible solution is to adopt a type of concept-building that is advocated by grounded theory. Based on the axiom that interpretative research moves between the analytic modes of induction and deduction, grounded theorists stress that concepts are formed from empirical data in an interlaced process of observation and analysis. Imagine that you were to perform your fieldwork through the lens of a camera and you will immediately realize that observation is performed from a particular perspective. No matter how open you attempt to be, how much you try to disband with your preconceptions and taken-for-grantedness, you cannot perceive everything. Perception always involves selection, and selection presupposes comparison with what you already know. Comparison is already germinating interpretation, analysis – and concept-building.

During fieldwork, through what we have called 'abductive inferencing' (Chapter 3), the researcher will continuously come up with new conceptual inklings and ideas of analysis that may be conceptual blind alleys or highways. In order to determine which is which, you proceed with your fieldwork in a dialectical process of description-cum-interpretation, matching existing data and categories against new data and analytical hunches, until no new ideas or surprises arise. This is the point that grounded theorists call *empirical saturation*, when it is time to leave the field.

Glaser and Strauss make an important distinction between substantive and formal theory-building:

> *By substantive theory, we mean that developed for a substantive, or empirical, area of sociological inquiry, such as patient care, race relations, professional education, delinquency, or research organizations. By formal theory, we mean that developed for a formal, or conceptual, area of sociological inquiry, such as stigma, deviant behaviour, formal organization, socialization, status incongruency, authority and power, reward systems, or social mobility.*

(Glaser and Strauss 1967: 34)

*Substantive theories* are closely related to and may evolve from empirical studies, while *formal theories* are related to more conceptual and hence abstract forms of investigation. In empirical analysis, the two may be combined so that substantive theories and concepts are formed first and often during the process of fieldwork and the early stages of analysis, while formal theories and concepts are developed at later stages (if at all) and build on the substantive foundations. Although formal categories are primarily formed during the processes of coding and systematic analysis, you may still need to go back to your data sets to enhance the validity of your analysis.

The simultaneity of data collection and analysis found in grounded theory underscores the epistemological constructivism of ethnography and should be set against a more realist (or functionalist) stance found in early folklore and ethnological studies in which, for example, the local schoolteacher would collect songs and narratives that were subsequently analysed by an academic scholar. This distinction presupposes a view of data as neutral items to be culled like flowers in a field.

## WRITING IT DOWN AND WRITING IT UP

The description-cum-interpretation of media ethnography highlights the necessity of having one and the same person perform an entire ethnography – that is, both the ethnographic process and product. Both of these aspects are based on textual, rather than numerical, forms of interpretation (texts may encompass both verbal and written, visual and audio materials). Media ethnographies are narratives about media reality – that is, they are articulations of and claims to particular realities, not reality itself. Neither are they fictional narratives inventing (possible) realities. The media ethnographer moves between 'this is' pronouncements and 'What if?' questions. The researcher is dependent upon and must be faithful to particular, empirical practices ('believing is seeing') well knowing that perception involves perspective ('seeing is believing').

Handling these dual demands of realism and constructivism is part of data collection, analysis and reporting, all of which involve interpretation of texts such as transcripts of informants' dialogues, the researcher's descriptions, memos and reflections, pictures of settings and scenes, and often media expressions too. Moreover, these texts are often very diverse, even contradictory, since triangulation is central to media ethnography. You should be aware of the status of different texts and be prepared to see systematic incongruences as potential analytical eye-openers, not just as faults or missing information. When coding and analysing field notes, you are already on the way to structuring your report. To be aware of the narrative stance and genre conventions you apply in the field-notes is therefore a good indication of how you balance on the tightrope of realism and constructivism. This awareness should guide you to adopt a position as author in your final report that suits your research objective.

Following Clifford Geertz, the ethnographic account should be a 'thick description' (Geertz 1973); that is, it should meet two aims: it should bear a blueprint of reality in the sense that readers will trust that the author has indeed been present and part of the practices being described; and these practices should be described in such a way that readers will get a feel for the practices in their richness and depth. Bearing this general requirement in mind, the media ethnographer may adopt several positions of authorship (see Box 5.3).

## Box 5.3   Four rhetorical strategies of ethnographic accounts

- the documentary or logos tale
- the confessional or pathos tale
- the realist or ethos tale
- the collage or polyphonic tale

The classical position, which is also the one adopted in most media ethnographies, is the *documentary* or *logos tale*. Here, the author explicitly addresses the audience in the first person, sets the scene and orchestrates the narrative. The demarcations between self and others are clear. At the other end of the rhetorical scale, we find the *confessional ethnography* or *pathos tale*. This is equally a first-person narrative, but the object of research is the researcher, not some external, empirical reality. Here the demarcations between self and others are conflated or irrelevant. In between these two positions, we find the *realist ethnography* or *ethos tale*. Written as a third-person narrative, the researcher recedes into the background as an omniscient author, whose invisible hand manoeuvres informants, settings and scenes. The demarcations between self and others are clear in as much as readers suspend their disbelief, as in reading fiction, that there are only 'others', so that the narrative is read as a self-organizing process. This is the genre that most easily invites 'thick description'.

As we noted, the radical constructivism emerging with postmodern ethnographers in the 1980s implied a textual turn in ethnography at large. This development has served to critique not least received modes of ethnographic representation in an attempt to empower informants by foregrounding voices of 'Other-ness' in the ethnographic accounts. Subsequently, a good deal of narrative experimentation followed, which might be called *collage ethnography* or the *polyphonic tale*. Disbanding with any claims to authorial authority, researchers present a medley of dialogues, visual and verbal accounts and descriptions, leaving it pretty much to the reader to find coherence. Even if no media ethnographers have adopted similar strategies, and even if their wisdom may be questioned, you should be aware of, and reflect on, the basic assumptions underlying postmodern ethnography, namely that any ethnographic tale is also a tale of self and other that involves and lays claims to particular positions of power. You will recognize that this division also informs the categorizing above of possible narrative strategies.

Finally, you should note that media ethnographies are situated texts of interpretation. The interpretative situatedness is of two kinds. First, like other studies within the social and human sciences, media ethnographies are interpretations of signifying processes – from financial transactions and sports to fine arts and swearing. As such they are second-order interpretations in Geertz's terms, as noted earlier in this chapter. Second, once written, and perhaps published, media ethnographies enter professional (and often popular) interpretative networks and locales of articulation, interpretation – and contestation. Spanning a diverse range of theoretical, empirical and methodological domains, such texts have no immediate and 'natural' routes of professional circulation and interpretation. As such, media ethnographies very often remain strangers in Schutz's sense – suspended between the familiar and the unfamiliar, the known and the unknown, within received disciplinary boundaries. This is one of the main reasons why several solid media ethnographies are relatively unknown to the scientific community of media scholars: they are labelled urban studies, youth studies or feminist studies. Conversely, media ethnographies often excite a substantial interest in popular venues of dissemination and discussion. In Chapter 6, we return to some of the more practical strategies you may adopt to handle these issues.

## SCIENTIFIC MERITS AND LIMITATIONS OF MEDIA ETHNOGRAPHY

As you will have learned having read so far, media ethnography offers no neat and easy approach to the media. Luckily, it is not the only one, nor even the best one in many cases. The main asset of the ethnographic perspective is also its main deficit: its endeavour to grasp and interpret the complexities of media culture. Let us first sum up some of the *assets of media ethnography* that have been described in this chapter, remembering that mediated meanings are both reflective and constitutive of users' social practices.

Seen from a perspective of social practices, the blurring of boundaries between processes of media production and reception serves to question many of the received notions of audience. By defining informants as media users, media ethnography enables a more holistic account of the intricate practices engendered by and through media.

The blurring of boundaries between mediated and non-mediated forms of communication, and the often seamless integration of ubiquitous and mobile media into everyday life, serve to question many of the received notions about public and private places, and between geographical place and virtual space. Through its processual methodologies, media ethnography enables accounts of the interrelations and combinations of space and place as they are enacted in concrete media practices.

Seen from a perspective of mediated meaning-making, the blurring of boundaries between different genres and the traversing of formats across different media, such as computer games, film and books, serve to question the classical focus in media studies upon a particular medium or genre with the unwitting result that certain patterns of production and reception tend to be over-emphasized. The interpretative depth of media ethnography enables analyses of how these intertextual and intermedia constellations translate into (selective) meaning-making for their users.

The emerging technological convergence between mass media, telecommunications and ICT shapes new foundations for media expressions and uses. The holistic perspective of media ethnography enables analysis of ways in which people appropriate convergence both in an aesthetic and social sense, forming new divergences, dialogues or convergences.

The *scientific limitations of media ethnography* are of two kinds. One is practical, the other more substantial in nature. As for the practical limitations, they are grounded in the difficulties in handling complex – that is, openly contradictory and multi-dimensional – elements of interpretation. 'Too much too soon, or too little too late' is the predicament facing the would-be ethnographer. Because ethnographic work is both extensive and intensive, it is often undertaken early in a scholar's academic career when there are fewer other professional obligations to fulfil than there may be later on. This is clearly at odds with the analytical demands made on the ethnographer, and the result may be poor ethnography and poor media science.

The substantive limitations of media ethnography have to do with its aim of grasping media complexity through explicit interpretation at all stages of research. This is an intellectually demanding cocktail. One strategy in handling the intellectual demands is to insist on the uniqueness of ethnography. Even if scholars deal with a limited number of cases, so the argument goes, they are from real life and hence the results assume a higher quality than, say, textual analyses or surveys. Such an insistence easily slides into an academic fundamentalism that has no methodological or theoretical grounding.

Another strategy in handling the interpretative complexities of media ethnography is to employ what we may call an ontological textualism. Because we cannot claim to represent reality, what we can do is to claim the veracity of the ethnographic narrative and explore formal experiments of writing. Adopting this strategy may advance the career of the would-be novelist or scriptwriter, but will easily trap the would-be academic; and it does very little to resolve the dilemmas inherent in media ethnography.

A final predicament of media ethnography, which may or may not turn out to be a limitation, has to do with the dispersion of both the ethnographic field and the material audiences in many forms of computer-mediated communication. For example, in studies of virtual communities it is difficult for the ethnographer to uphold the ontological realism of ethnography (I was there) even if narrative realism may still be achieved (this is what it would be to be present). In view of this dilemma, Christine Hine advocates what she calls an adaptive ethnography – that is, a mode of analysis that disbands with the holistic axiom of 'classical' ethnography in favour of a focus on the contestations between official discourses of what the Internet is like and users' particular discourses as they emerge in 'practising' the Internet.

Weighing assets against deficits in media ethnography, we may realize that ethnography harbours a research perspective that we may call *selective complexity*. Through media ethnography, we may trace the meanderings of contemporary mediated meaning-making in their depth and richness, but we cannot hope to simultaneously chart the full breadth of these processes – let alone predict how they will proceed. 'To generalise is to be an idiot,' said the English poet, William Blake, more than 200 years ago – maybe in an ironic attempt to address the contradictions inherent in his own dictum. The same could be said today about media ethnography. Because we cannot interpret media complexity in full, it does not follow that no interpretation is possible at all. As we have seen in this chapter, it is possible to opt for a venue of research that acknowledges and reflects upon the necessary selections and choices inherent in explicitly interpretative studies. In the next chapter, we shall spell out some of the practical questions you will need to tackle when you choose to follow that venue.

# Chapter Six

# The ethnographic toolbox: ☐
# participant observation

The ideographic approach and emic perspective of media ethnography, which we presented in Chapter 5, in many ways preclude giving guidelines on how to undertake empirical investigations. Since case-based studies are necessarily particular and specific, it may seem futile to offer general rules of thumb on how to go about performing them. Still, to be a researcher is to be on a quest for patterns, explanations and systematic accounts. Such an endeavour involves reducing the multi-faceted richness and colour of lived experience and live phenomena. You may think of and use the following toolbox as a framework that enables your own research process, while remembering that it is not a recipe book that you can consult to have all your methodological problems resolved. A toolbox is deceptively straightforward, logical and linear, unlike the muddled and multidimensional process of actual research.

## PLANNING YOUR RESEARCH

Before you even begin to think of, and possibly decide on, conducting a media ethnography, you need to answer two questions. First, what is it I want to know? Second, why do I want to know that? You need to start by choosing your research topic and determining your knowledge interests in that particular topic. To do empirical research is often a lengthy process that has its ups and downs. You must therefore be clear about your personal and professional reasons for embarking upon it. Basic curiosity and acumen will carry you a long way.

Next, you need to find out whether or not your chosen research objective is appropriate for an ethnographic study. Again, it is enabling to ask yourself a number of questions. Does my topic fit the epistemological axioms and methodological requirements of ethnography (as outlined in Chapter 5)? Do I want to carry out research that involves close and sustained encounters with other people? Do I have the practical possibilities of doing extensive fieldwork? It is your research topic and knowledge interests that should steer your methodological choices, not the other way round.

As for your personal predilections and proficiencies, you may probe these by giving yourself small 'tests'. For example, if you are in a supermarket or cinema queue, try to contact people and chat to them. Does this come easy to you, or do you feel embarrassed or annoyed? In order to carry out successful, ethnographic fieldwork, you need to professionalize and systematize social and cultural competences that we all use in our everyday encounters and interactions. The good ethnographer is able to handle, and enjoys handling, shifting perspectives, ambivalences and moments of indecision. If you are uncomfortable with these informal queries, the chances are that you would do a better research job in the lab or the library.

Suppose you have passed your personal 'feasibility test', you need to consider the practical circumstances of fieldwork. How can my empirical work be accomplished? Can I neglect other commitments? Do I have the necessary funds? What are the technical requirements for my study (e.g. video and audiotapes, cameras, other personnel)? Banal as these questions may seem, in practice the answers to them are often decisive for your research choices and design options. If you are new to the academic field, you will benefit from consulting a senior researcher who knows you as well as the craft, and can assess the economic and practical liabilities involved in ethnographic work.

## DESIGNING YOUR STUDY

Let us assume that you have answered the above questions on what, why and how to conduct your research, and that you have decided to do a media ethnography. Now you must draw up your empirical research design. Enabling questions for this endeavour are as follows. Which perspectives are relevant for my study? Who do I want to study? When and where can my empirical fieldwork be undertaken? Since ethnography aims at holistic analysis, it is necessary to answer the question of relevant perspectives. Particularly if you are not very experienced in doing fieldwork, you should invest a good deal of energy in considering the perspective or frame of your study, so that you are not overwhelmed by a maze of data whose analysis blurs your overall vision. The chart in Figure 6.1 can be used as a heuristic device for drawing up a research design that balances a holistic analysis of complex media practices with the exigencies of empirical data analysis.

Using the chart in Figure 6.1 as your basis will enable you to go beyond studying the structural and relational media uses that were central to Lull's early ethnographic work, as noted in Chapter 5, and to account also for mediated signification processses. The typology of the chart is developed from the dual definition of media as both material objects transporting messages and as symbolic, meaning-making processes (Carey 1989/1992; Williams 1974/1: 1990). But it nuances this definition by adding the user and media perspectives in an attempt to include spatial and temporal dimensions to the analysis that suit the processual and holistic aims of ethnography. The typology is meant as an analytical tool in your entire investigation as well as an aid to studying a single setting or situation of media use; and all four cells are aspects of a joint analytical process. Please note that the texts in each cell are merely examples to give you the drift of the typology.

The typology was applied in a student project on young Danes' uses of computer media in a public library that has implemented equal access to all information and entertainment media (print, audio, visual, computer, Internet), in accordance with Danish library law.

**Figure 6.1**   Analytical perspectives in media ethnography: a heuristic typology

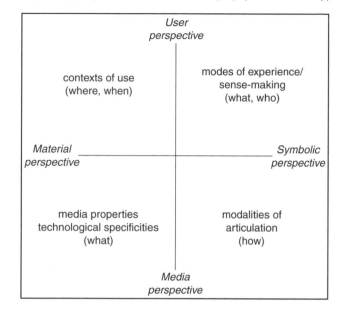

During one week's participant observation, the student used the chart shown in Figure 6.1 as a 'grid' for data collection, just as it was subsequently used in her first stages of analysis. For example, the *user-cum-material perspective* located ways in which users positioned themselves vis-à-vis computers, and their working rules of taking turns with the mouse. The *user-cum-symbolic perspective* attended users' choice of and discussions over various types of software and applications (games, search engines, Internet sites). The *media-cum-material perspective* focused on handling the contents of the interface (interpreting and evaluating site-specific information, guiding avatars, jumping between game levels). Finally, the *media-cum-symbolic perspective* clarified how the formal properties of the interface were applied and modified (learning to orient oneself spatially on a new site, locating signs of sms hyperlinks, changing program codes and rules of strength for game avatars).

As you may see from the examples given, the user perspective, when applied to an ethnography of computer media, focuses upon forms of social interaction while the media perspective locates forms of textual interactivity. In the student project, screen dumps made at regular intervals served as data material for the analysis of textual interactivity, while the analysis of social interaction was based on field-notes.

## BEFORE FIELDWORK

If you are not already familiar with the setting(s) within which you will conduct your fieldwork, you should prepare yourself well before going. You must learn about your research topic, including the relevant media, your informants' culture and locales. This knowledge can both be gleaned from library studies and by talking to other researchers who know about the particular topic or cultural settings. If your ethnographic study involves analysis of mediated expressions, it is a good idea to do a brief textual analysis at this stage, focusing on your own perceptions and predilections. In this way, you can specify your own perspective and so enhance your reflexive capabilities when encountering informants' takes on similar expressions.

If you are a member of the setting you want to study, the challenge before doing fieldwork is not so much to familiarize yourself with what you will meet as to defamiliarize yourself with what you take for granted about your setting. This distancing process is quite difficult to perform in advance, and you will need to draw in people who can take an outsider's perspective and play 'devil's advocate' in probing your ideas and 'foreshadowed problems'. Perhaps, paradoxically, it is often harder to study a culture with which one is intimately connected.

If you are to embark on fieldwork in a professional setting or amongst informants with a known higher status than yourself, you need to be especially aware of contacting and canvassing gatekeepers who can prepare you and ease your way into the field. If you have no previous experience with media ethnography, you should enter such settings only upon serious reflection, since the professional merits and 'yield' of your endeavours may be outweighed by the personal discomforts of sustained estrangement.

When you think you have a good understanding of your topic and setting, you write a guide for your fieldwork observations, noting the basic empirical properties that you want to study. The guide can usefully be based on Figure 6.1, where each cell can be seen as a three-dimensional 'grid' encompassing temporal, spatial and social dimensions (when, where, who, how). In the student project on computer uses in a library, the observation guide looked like that shown in Table 6.1.

Table 6.1   Observation guide for a media ethnography

|  | Time | Space | Relations |
|---|---|---|---|
| Material (social) user perspective |  |  |  |
| Symbolic (textual) user perspective |  |  |  |
| Material (social) media perspective |  |  |  |
| Symbolic (textual) media perspective |  |  |  |

In practice, depending on the breadth and duration of your fieldwork, you may expand each cell so as to allow for the insertion of your field-notes. Alternatively, you may list the analytical elements on separate sheets of paper (material user perspective – time; material user perspective – space; etc.). Do remember to date and number all your sheets. Fieldwork is a 'messy' business, and field-notes often bear the mark of severe time constraints, as you will see below.

# TIME IN THE FIELD

You need to plan your fieldwork with some temporal flexibility so that you are able to return with data that meet the basic demands of media ethnography: richness, multi-method perspectives, insight into the participants' perspective. It is vital that you get beyond the initial 'performing-for-the-researcher' stage, just as you should be in your chosen setting long enough to sense, and hence describe, the routine nature of what is going on and not just the peaks or highlights. If you do a pilot study as a first-time ethnographer, one week is usually enough to get into the basic flow and feel of the setting, to enter the dual process of estrangement and destrangement involved in participant observation, and to begin to see patterns in your informants' practices with and around media.

# BEING IN THE FIELD

Participant observation is central to fieldwork. If you have never performed it before, you may find it somewhat puzzling or unsettling at first. Even experienced fieldworkers sometimes feel that way, since each new study usually involves new settings. This puzzlement is part of the process, however. Use it positively, without forcing yourself or your informants into intensive engagements. Be available and show that you are open to being with your informants.

Often you will find that one or a few of the 'locals' will approach you early on, and they can act as your gatekeepers to the scene. In other cases, you may already be familiar with people within the arena that you want to study, and they will have a similar function. Often you will gradually acquire a more central position, talking to more informants and getting access to more sources. At this stage, you are in a position to probe with more incisive questions and to get your informants' views on issues that strike you as odd or inconsistent. But remember that your means of securing informants and establishing rapport with them are often still coloured by their perception of your initial gatekeepers, as we noted in Chapter 4 when describing Tufte's study.

The final stage in fieldwork is often the most difficult. Having gradually built up trust with your informants, you now have to regain a position of marginality so as to be able to leave with tact and without offending your informants, who have offered you their time and resources.

Remember that participant observation is a simultaneous process of immersion and distance. You will very likely experience fieldwork as a vacillation between chaos and order, between letting go, being surprised and finding insight. Remember also that fieldwork is a multidimensional task that involves an interlaced process of description and interpretation, recounting and accounting. At some stages, you will find that you have no clues to what is going on; at other times you will feel that everything is connected to everything else.

# FIELDWORK POSITIONS AND PERSPECTIVES

Doing fieldwork is a process, and often a lengthy one at that. You may think of yourself as an apprentice, who gradually learns the interpretative skills of your chosen area of research by applying a variety of ethnographic tools. You may use this position constructively to frame your observations and interpretations. Based on your observation guide, you can ask yourself seemingly stupid questions when encountering new textual items and social actors and events: what is going on at a textual and social level? When does the activity happen? What characterizes the symbolic and social spaces of the activity? Who are the actors and what are the relations between them? By answering such questions 'silently' in your field-notes, you are likely to grasp with liveliness and precision the processes you want to make sense of.

As you get more acquainted with your setting and with the interpretative rules and routines of your informants and their mediated expressions, you can position yourself differently, and are likely to be positioned differently by your informants. Thus, you can expect to modify your perspective and the focus of your enquiry as you go along. Following the American anthropologist, James P. Spradley (1980: 33–4), we may distinguish between three consecutive perspectives of empirical observation, namely:

- *descriptive observation*, where you ask yourself mainly general questions to get an overall feel for the scene

- *focused observation*, where you ask yourself more specific and structural questions, e.g. about the relations between specific textual expressions and social interactions (in more general terms, structural questions aim at relating the four cells found in Figure 6.1.)

- *selective observation*, where you ask yourself analytical questions – e.g. about specific textual expressions and social interactions, and why they relate the way they do.

As you may see, the relations between the three phases depend upon your time in the field, and their progression serves to narrow your analytical perspective as a way of getting more relevant and in-depth interpretations. It is important to note, however, that although you may gradually narrow your perspective to more selective observation, you should continue with your descriptive observations, if less intensively, in order to retain the holistic aim of your overall design. You reach the phase of selective observation by a constant vacillation between observation and interpretation of your chosen field of study, a vacillation that serves to raise new questions and issues of analytical interest. This vacillation is played out also in relation to your fieldwork material.

# FIELDWORK MATERIAL

Fieldwork texts can take many forms: oral and written, aural and visual. They can usefully be divided into on-stage texts and off-stage texts, which typically include those outlined in Box 6.1. Depending upon your topic and setting, you cannot always rely on being able to make extensive field-notes *in situ*. Train yourself in making mental notes of instances that you want to remember and record later on – preferably by going off in private as soon as possible (perhaps to the privacy of the toilet!). In many cases, you can also make haphazard, jotted notes in the field – for example, snippets of dialogue – and these notes are often only intelligible to yourself. Again, the extent to which this is possible depends on local circumstances and your position in the setting. For example, in a study on media uses in supermarkets and malls, some students encountered difficulties in writing field-notes while pretending to make shopping lists that seemed exceedingly long.

### Box 6.1   A list of typical fieldwork material

On-stage material

Written field-notes:
- your accounts of what is going on
- your descriptions of dialogues or exchanges beween informants.

Visual material:
- photographs of settings and people
- videotapes of informants' mediated reception and/or production practices.

Audio material:
- taped conversations with or amongst informants (to be transcribed and hence become print material)
- recordings of the 'aural tapestry' of settings.

Media material used by informants (e.g. film, TV programmes, screen dumps from computers).

Off-stage material
Your researcher's diary (e.g. reflections, comments, ideas for each day).
Sources about the field (e.g. maps, artefacts, press clippings).

To give you a flavour of the complexities involved in taking field-notes, let us look into a Danish PhD project on the linguistic and social patterns of youngsters' mobile phone communication (Rasmussen, in press). The researcher followed two groups of friends for a week, recording and collecting their mobile phone conversations in their everyday settings at school and with their friends in public and private spaces. Below (in Figure 6.2 and the subsequent translation) there are two versions of the researcher's field-notes, an *in situ* note (shown in the original and in an English translation in Figure 6.2) and a translation of the more elaborate field-note written at the end of the day's observation. Both record observations made during a Danish lesson in which Grades 8 and 9 are grouped together in order to choose a project theme with their Danish teachers, Helle and Gerd. The original version is shown in Figure 6.2.

**Figure 6.2**  Example of *in situ* and extensive field-notes based on a study of mobile phone use

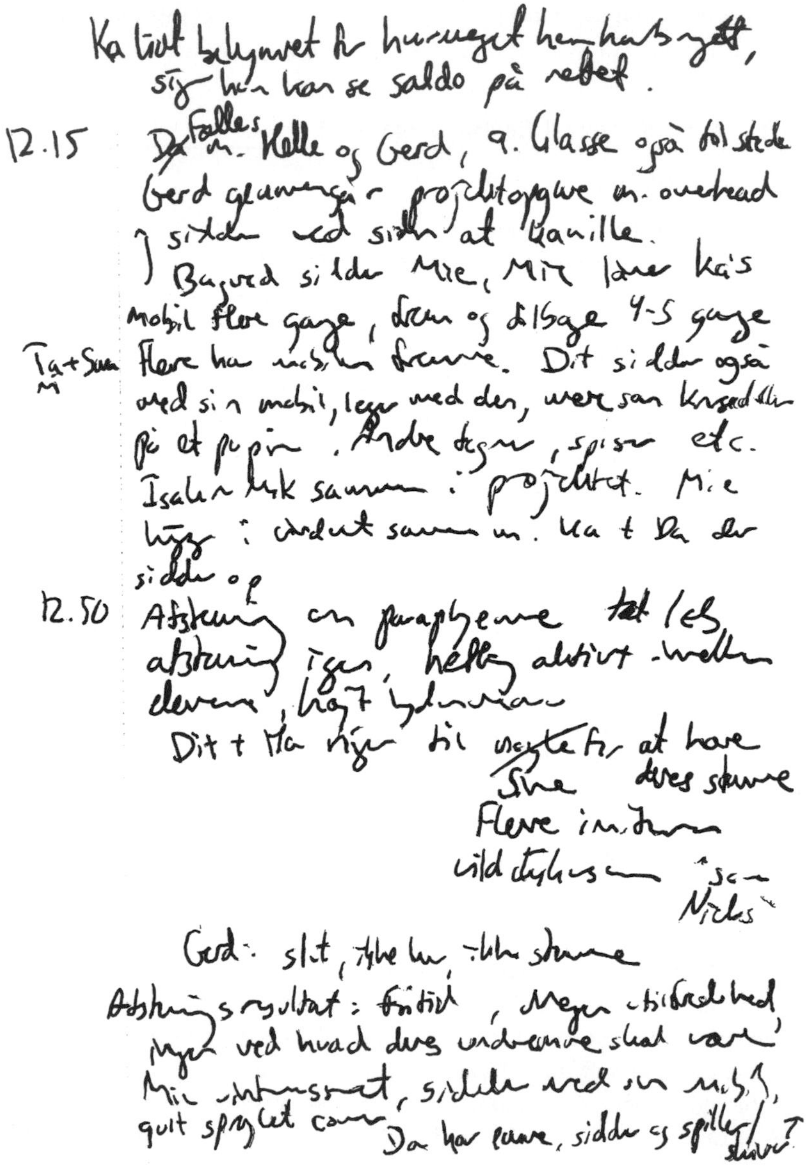

In translation, the *in situ* note shown in Figure 6.2 reads as follows.

| | |
|---|---|
| Ka | a little worried of how much she has phoned, says she can see account on the net. |
| 12.15 | ~~Da[nish]~~ Joint with Helle and Gerd, 9. grade also present<br>Gerd runs through project with overhead<br>I sit next to Kamille.<br>Behind is Mic. Mic borrows Ka's mobile several times, back and forth 4–5 times. |
| Ta+Suna | Several have the mobile at hand. Dit also sits with her mobile, plays with it, more like doodles on a paper. Others draw, eat etc.<br>Isak and Mic together in the project. Mic lies in the window sill with Ka + Da sitting up. |
| 12.50 | Closing project, close run, another vote. Intense activity among the pupils, high level of noise.<br>Dit and Ka phone ~~some~~ She to have their votes.<br>    Several imitate<br>    Wild discussion 'like Niels'<br>Gerd: Done, not hear more votes.<br>Closing – result: leisure, much grumping.<br>Nobody knows who their teacher is going to be.<br>Mic uninterested, sits with his mobile.<br>Yellow, loud cover.<br>    Da has [chosen his] theme and sits playing/writing. |

When comparing the researcher's *in situ* note with the field-note written after the event, you may easily detect a number of changes, amongst which aliases are the most evident:

08.01.02:  Danish lesson, joint lesson

Grades 8 and 9 have a joint Danish lesson. The two grades have collected in one classroom and many have found a place on the window sill, on the tables and the floor. The atmosphere is unrestrained; it is just after the long recess.

The eighth-graders' Danish teacher describes how they are now going to select an overall theme for their written projects. She brings an overhead and it shows examples of themes from previous years and themes that she has in mind, herself. There are themes such as the Future, Leisure, and Sex and Health. She runs through the various themes, giving examples on all sorts of concrete projects. The pupils are attentive, but not particularly engaged. Several do other things while they listen: one draws, one plays with the zipper on his pencil case, one eats an apple . . . several sit with mobile phones. Karen's mobile phone takes turns between Karen and Maja four to five times with less than a minute's pause. It looks as if they are playing a game. Dorte sits with her mobile phone, turns it in her hand, touches a few keys, takes the cover on and off, apparently without thought. Two girls sit close together. One keys her mobile and holds its display so that the other may see what is written.

Now they have to vote on the overall theme for the projects; but before the voting begins Nikolaj gets up saying that he has to go to the doctor and that he votes for Leisure. The teacher says OK and starts the voting. The result is a close run between three themes, and there is general agreement that they have to vote again, and this time they may vote for two of the three popular themes. Now Leisure and Sex and Health get an almost equal number of votes, and another round of voting is decided upon. There is intense talk, discussion and argumentation amongst the pupils – who will write together, what shall they vote on, and what could their concrete project be? In the middle of all of this, Henrik half-shouts to Dorte that she must call Siggi, who is absent, to find out what she votes for. Dorte rings her, briefly explains the situation and asks whether Siggi will also vote for Leisure. Dorte gets a yes and finishes the conversation. Meanwhile at least two others are phoning pupils who are absent. Other pupils protest, but one replies: *Nikolaj's vote counts, too, even if he has left.* Immediately, another says: *This is not the same thing.* Several more want to have a say, but then the Danish teacher cuts in: *Now finish it; if you are not here, you cannot vote, that's it. Who votes for Leisure?*

First, in a very basic way, the two versions offer a graphic demonstration of the unique character of ethnography: even people familiar with the Danish language are unable to decipher the scribblings of the *in situ* note that primarily serves as a memory prop for the researcher. Second, even if one could read the *in situ* note correctly, it only makes sense if contextualized, and this contextualization depends on the researcher's presence and particular perspective. Third, the more elaborate and extended field-note becomes a first and tentative interpretation of the situation as the researcher fills in the 'empty spaces' of the *in situ* note, thereby relating separate actions and snippets of dialogue.

In more general terms, the handling of fieldwork material illuminates the processual and interlaced character of performing ethnographic work. Based on your initial research questions and interests, you enter the field where you observe and describe what is going on, asking yourself questions and probing your informants. As you are yourself a participant and record the answers from a particular perspective, your records are also initial attempts at accounting for and seeking to understand what you experience. These accounts almost invariably raise new questions that guide your next steps of descriptions-cum-interpretation. The process may be delineated as shown in Figure 6.3.

Figure 6.3 demonstrates how questions asked and descriptions made at later stages in the ethnographic process illuminate and reflect back on earlier questions and descriptions, thus deepening the researcher's overall understanding. By following this spiral process, you may gradually focus your analytical attention during data collection in the field as described in the previous section. This spiral process, in turn, is continued in the more systematic analytical process following your time in the field.

**Figure 6.3** The process of description-cum-interpretation in ethnographic data collection and analysis

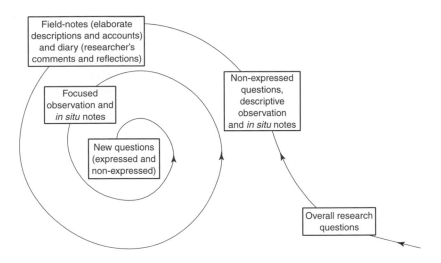

Extensive field-notes are the 'meat' of your empirical work. They are taken and recorded in a chronological manner in order to document the processual character of your data. Try to make notes immediately after the event you want to describe, or at least a few times a day. Be as specific and concrete as you can in your accounts. While your *in situ* notes are primarily descriptive in nature, your extensive field-notes may blend description and ideas and, gradually, more discriminating comments and conceptual hunches. Do not worry if you have no clues or conceptual ideas at first. It is wise to take seriously your position as a learner in the field in order to get into your informants' perspective, and you can suspend intellectual reasoning for a while.

It is in the extensive field-notes that you will mostly explore the blending of description-cum-interpretation that feeds into the final ethnographic product, and you should be aware of the possible genres of authorship available for such notes, as we described them in Chapter 5: the documentary, confessional, realist and collage ethnographies. In practice, you will probably mix these genres during fieldwork, but no later than in your systematic analysis of your data do you need to reflect on these choices.

## CODING AND ANALYSING DATA

You will very likely experience fieldwork as an intensive and exciting time after your initiation into the chosen setting(s). Conversely, the subsequent phase of coding and analysing a diversity of data is a lonely job and one that is often felt as an anticlimax to being in the field. It is useful to remind yourself that this is a phase of your research and a necessary time of retrenchment.

First you must transform your various types of material into a form that is amenable to coding and systematic analysis. Tapes must be transcribed, photographs chronologically numbered and possibly scanned into your computer (if you have not used a digital camera), and field-notes ordered. Since field-notes are the types of data that mostly distinguish media ethnography from the other methodological approaches documented and discussed in this book, we limit ourselves to describing the analytical procedures of field-note material.

Having ordered your material, and irrespective of your use of computerized software for coding and analysis, your next stage is to divide your field-notes. You may use the typology in Box 6.2 as a guideline.

## Box 6.2　Typology of coding fieldwork material

### On-stage data

Narratives:
- transcripts of recorded dialogues
- researcher's notes of dialogues
- researcher's notes of events, scenes and episodes.

Comments:
- informants' comments
- researcher's comments.

### Off-stage data
Researcher's reflections (fieldwork diary).
Other material about your setting(s).
Media material.

Your next move is crucial: coding. Codes serve to identify, classify and compare, sort and systematize your data so as to yield explanations. You start by coding your material according to type (as in Box 6.2) and then content. In coding the content of fieldwork material, you go through at least two rounds of coding procedures: topical coding and analytic coding. *Topical coding* is the first, and easiest, round. Here, you code occurrences in your text of people, events, settings, times, mediated and non-mediated forms of inter-action. Codes may be based on the units applied in your observation guide (see Table 6.1), so that each unit gets a number or letter(s). For example, in the study on teenagers' uses of mobile communication, the girls' recurrent sms messaging and brief calls (one ring) get a topical coding called SYUT (symbolic user perspective – time), and the messages of these brief contacts ('hi', 'c u') get the code MMR (material media perspective – relations).

This process should give you an intimate knowledge of your empirical material, which you will need for your next round: *analytic coding*. Here, you identify and code occurrences of concepts, beliefs and themes. In the study on mobile communication, the two topical codes mentioned above are combined into an analytical code ICY (for 'intimacy'). With ethnographic material, you will rarely need a degree of analytical detail that merits line-by-line coding. Rather, your coding units will be larger chunks of material that enable you to follow narratives, processes and practices. This also goes for the textual analysis you wish to make of media material and ethnographic interviews. These are less detailed than the analysis needed in, say, reception analysis.

As we discussed in Chapter 5, coding is an important part of analysis. Given the processual character of an ethnographic account, and the emphasis placed on emic perspectives, you must pay particular analytical attention in your analytic coding to recurring events and expressions, disruptions of routines, and the discursive schemata (including metaphors) and narrative formats that get taken up, appropriated or transformed by informants. In your final analysis, you should attempt to crystallize concepts and theoretical implications from your empirical data. These concepts and theories may be either of a substantive or a formal character, as described in Chapter 5. Do not regard a systematic, substantive account as poor ethnography: interpretative research also implies empirical patterning, and patterning necessitates reduction. As long as you respect the emic perspective of your ideographic account, chances are that you will balance empirical flavour and feel with intellectual reasoning and reflection.

## ETHICAL ASPECTS OF MEDIA ETHNOGRAPHY

The ethical aspects involved in all research are perhaps particularly pertinent in qualitative research, including media ethnography, since informants' anonymity is harder to guarantee than in quantitative research based on random selection and numerical analysis. Moreover, ethnography involves your sustained engagement with informants, and your data will often contain quite intimate aspects that informants have offered in trust. In handling the ethics of your research, you must attend to four aspects in relation to your informants, as listed in Box 6.3.

### Box 6.3   Ethical aspects of media ethnography

| | |
|---|---|
| Non-maleficence | Avoid harm to informants |
| Beneficence | Produce benefits for informants rather than research for the sake of research |
| Autonomy or self-determination | Respect the values and decisions of informants |
| Justice | Treat people equally who are equal in relevant respects |

Source: Beauchamp et al. (1982: 18–19)

The first two aspects are most topical for the ethnographic product, while the last two loom large during the ethnographic process. In conducting fieldwork, you must attempt to secure your informants' *autonomy* and self-determination in at least two ways: by protecting their anonymity to outsiders and by keeping your data confidential. Many ethnographers seek the written consent of informants before entering the field or very early on in doing fieldwork. If you conduct media ethnography involving minors, the written consent of parents is a statutory requirement in many countries (if not always the consent of the children themselves), and review boards and research councils may require documentation with grant applications.

Still, in media ethnographies it can be very difficult, if not impossible, to obtain the written consent of participants, since fieldwork is often performed in a variety of settings, as is the case in studies on the uses of mobile phones, or with shifting informants, as in studies on the uses of particular homepages. This puts an extra responsibility on you to strictly obey the general ethical rule in qualitative research of preserving the anonymity of participants' names and altering details of settings and scenes in writing your report, so as to minimize informants' risks of recognition. The responsibility of writing is augmented by the fact that your field-notes must be kept confidential, which deprives you of a standard academic proof of evidence in publishing your results. Unlike most scientific work, your reader has little to go on in checking the veracity of your account (see the section below, on authorship).

The ethical aspect of *justice* hinges on issues of human rights that are basic to western democracies. Depending on your setting, you must be prepared to widen your own preconceived notions of what the term implies to your informants. If you carry out ethnographic work in a culture very different from your own, you would be well advised to learn about the legal tradition pertaining to that culture before venturing into the field.

The ethical aspects of *non-maleficence* and *beneficence* are most relevant on publication of your results. Even if you have taken great care during writing in protecting the privacy and autonomy of informants, they may feel wronged, or even harmed, by your account. Particularly if you have done fieldwork within a local community or small group, your informants will not only recognize themselves in your account, but family members, friends and colleagues may also write 'revelations' about one another that cause problems and discomfort.

You must decide whether to return your finished ethnography to your informants for discussion and possible approval. If you do so, you should let your informants know, at best before terminating your fieldwork. Many professional ethnographers regard this approval as proof of the emic nature of their ultimate account. Still, such an approval must not be mistaken for a blueprint of ethnographic truth. The ethnographic account is a result of your perspective, your openness and limitations in both a professional and personal sense. Therefore, you must be prepared to bear the responsibility of authorship.

## THE MEDIA ETHNOGRAPHER AS AUTHOR

In writing and publishing a media ethnography, you engage in two types of dialogue that both harbour power relations. The first dialogue is the one you have with your informants, which is largely a matter of ethics, as discussed above. The second is the one you have with the scientific community and the public at large.

In writing your media ethnography, you must meet the demands made on academic work to be systematic, valid and trustworthy. You must balance this against the ethical demands made on the ethnographer, as described above. One way in which you can meet these dual demands is to choose your genre of authorship carefully. The easiest genre to choose is the documentary genre, since you are in a position to clearly mark yourself as author, and to make distinctions between the authorial and the informants' voices and perspectives. This gives your readers a fair chance to validate the academic merits of your account, which for ethical reasons usually cannot publicize fieldwork notes. In concrete terms, you may mix exemplary ('scenic') and analytical descriptions. Scenic descriptions are based on your field-notes and highlight central and relevant features of a topic or issue that you then go on to describe in more analytical fashion.

Another balance you have to keep in mind when writing up your media ethnography is that between epistemological constructivism and ontological realism, as discussed in Chapter 5. How do I balance the validity and trustworthiness of my analysis with an acknowledgment of multiple perspectives on 'my' field? Here you may use a distinction made by the British sociologist, Martyn Hammersley, in his advocacy of a 'subtle realism' of ethnography, as we mentioned in Chapter 5. The subtle realist strives for multiple, non-contradictory versions of reality – although they are different, they may all be true. Conversely, multiple, contradictory versions of reality are rejected – that is, contradictory versions of reality that cannot all be true (Hammersley 1992). You should endeavour to explicate your procedures of reasoning.

Once you publish (or publicize) your ethnography, your dialogue with the scientific communities and the public turns from being a consideration implicit in your writing process into an explicit dialogue. You must be aware that media ethnography moves between established disciplines and discourses, and you are not guaranteed a natural course of publication and dissemination. You must reflect upon that situation during your writing process, and decide whether or not to make strategic moves to highlight particular discourses or disciplinary issues that your results impinge upon. If you do media ethnography early on in your career, you would be well advised to seek counsel at this stage with one or more senior colleague(s) who may volunteer to read some of your report – if they are not your teachers and obliged to do so anyway.

Depending upon your object of research and the nature of your results, you must prepare yourself to tackle public debate. Once your report, article or book is out of your hands, you have only limited power over its fate. Particularly if you obey the wishes found in many university departments to make academic results accessible to a wider public, your way of doing so needs careful consideration: Which channels are amenable to my study? How can I frame my results? Which perspectives are most important for me to get across?

Many journalists harbour an interest in media studies because of its seeming relation to their own profession, and if your account covers a 'newsworthy' topic, you must reflect on the public agenda you want to address and impact on. If you do not, you will very likely end up reinforcing existing discourses, even if your study serves to reverse or question current assumptions. However, if you take care to prepare your strategies of dissemination, conducting and writing a media ethnography can be a most rewarding academic and personal experience.

# Section 3

**Audience Reception Research**

# Chapter Seven

# Reception research in practice: ☐ researching media meanings through talk

As the advertising copy in Box 7.1 shows, it has now come to be taken for granted in the western business community that a company has to be seen to behave as a responsible citizen locally, nationally and globally. This state of affairs has not arisen overnight, but has grown out of the often painful experiences of companies who did not pay sufficient attention to the environmental, social or political aspects of their business activities. One company that has particularly paid the price of ethical negligence has been the Dutch-British oil company, Shell, whose record in the 1990s included both the abortive attempt to dump one of its outdated oil rigs (the *Brent Spar*) in the North Sea in June 1995 and dubious business policies supporting the Nigerian dictatorship throughout the decade. In both cases, Shell had to face widespread political criticism and consumer boycotts, and was forced into face-losing ignominious defeats, tarnishing its image as a decent player in the business community.

### Box 7.1   An ethical advertisement from Volvo

A large step for our planet. A natural step for Volvo.

Our planet is hurt. Badly hurt. At a breathtaking pace mankind is exhausting all that makes survival on earth possible. Our world is being stripped bare and choked by pollution. The balance of nature has been upset.

   We all share responsibility for what is happening. Not least the automotive industry, which is why Volvo's top management has decided to act by agreeing upon a comprehensive environmental charter for the group. Systematically, efficiently and as quickly as possible, Volvo wants to clean up after itself.

. . .

Our position as a major international group with substantial operations in Europe and North America is a result of quality, safety, high ethics and showing care for people and the environment.

Source: Scandinavian Airlines' *Scanorama Magazine* (1990)

As these and other cases show, the 'ethical turn' in business practices has been the product of intense struggle. Across the world, from the Canadian forests to the sweatshops of Southeast Asia and the cosmetic counters of Britain, consumer activists, led by global and national activist organizations like Greenpeace, have fought against what they have seen as environmentally and socially irresponsible corporate behaviour, often exploiting the curiosity of the electronic and print media with great dexterity.

However, the demand for corporate responsibility towards the environment and social issues did not originate in the 1990s. Before that, in the 1980s, an observer in the advertising and public relations field noted that 'social responsibility in the last twenty years has moved from the status of optional extra to a built in component' (Bernstein 1984: 51). Most observers, however, seem to believe that the manifest demonstration of corporate responsibility in the communicative activities of business companies reached the point of critical mass around 1990. White (1991) thus observes that 'business organizations are now expected to meet social and political objectives as well as those of profit and employment' (1991: 181).

The reception study to be reported here was motivated by the researcher's curiosity, following unsystematic observation around 1990 of what seemed to be the apparent growth of a type of advertising that was closely related to the ethical turn in business. (Schrøder 1993, 1997). In the study, this kind of advertising was labelled 'corporate responsibility advertising', encompassing ads that proclaim a social ethos as they inform readers, or invite them to enter a dialogue about the company's commitment to environmental concerns, community relations or the future of mankind, without any overt attempt to promote a specific product.

## FOCUSING THE STUDY

The Volvo ad quoted in Box 7.1 is a typical example of this kind of advertising. The copy is placed under a two-page colour photo showing an orange sun setting (or rising?) over the hazy contours of a mountain sloping towards the sea, with part of a Volvo truck inserted at the right. No overt attempt is made to promote the truck, nor any other Volvo vehicle.

In order to capture more aspects of the ethical turn, it was decided also to explore a category of ad that falls between non-product, corporate responsibility ads and traditional consumer ads. The study therefore also included 'consumer responsibility ads', which promote a particular product, and do so by flagging an ethical, often environmental, concern.

Before launching the reception study, it was decided – in order to find out whether the study could serve as a kind of sociological seismograph – to ascertain whether the initial impression of the growth of ethical advertising was well founded in both a British and a Danish context, since the project was conceptualized as a cross-national comparative study. Therefore, an extensive quantitative content analysis of almost 7000 print ads, in British and Danish general-appeal publications (newspapers, magazines), was undertaken and found that a statistically significant increase in corporate responsibility advertising between 1981 and 1991 could be demonstrated for both countries. In this period, the proportion of traditional consumer advertising had dropped, while there had been a clear rise in both pure responsibility ads and the hybrid category of consumer responsibility ads.

The curiosity underlying the project's knowledge interest directed itself holistically, not just towards the readers' experience of such ads, but also towards the entire corporate communicative circuit, of which the ethical ads were one visible public manifestation, i.e. both senders, texts and recipients. Why would corporate communicators increasingly address such ads to the readers of newspapers and magazines? How similar or different were the ethical ads from ordinary consumer ads in terms of verbal and visual features? And, not least, how did the readers of the publications in question experience such ethical ads? This presentation of the project focuses on the last of these questions.

## THEORETICAL FOUNDATIONS

Theoretically, the project was located within the interdisciplinary field of discourse analysis, more specifically, the variant called critical discourse analysis, which has been developed mainly by the British linguist, Norman Fairclough (Fairclough 1992, 1995). While analysis of the media text stands at the core of this approach, Fairclough insists that any (media) text should always be seen as a product of 'discourse practices', i.e. as one link in the chain of communicative events that runs from the encoding processes within media organizations to the decoding processes accomplished by readers, listeners and viewers. Finally, media discourses are anchored firmly in the larger 'sociocultural practices' of the wider society.

The analytical practice of those who apply the framework of discourse analysis (including Fairclough himself) often falls short of this holistic ideal, as they leap directly from the micro-textual to the macro-social analysis, ignoring the intermediate level of discourse practices, which is precisely where reception belongs. However, when combined with reception theory (Hall 1973; Eco 1979), discourse theory provides an enabling framework within which it becomes possible to cross-fertilize the work of linguistic pragmatics, media analysis and recent social theory, such as Giddens' theorization of 'structure' vs 'agency' (Giddens 1984). This theoretical foundation makes it possible to see media and audience discourses as not unidirectionally determined by sociocultural forces but as a process of negotiation simultaneously constituted by and constitutive of such forces.

The project's emphasis was not business-oriented, but 'cultural' in a broad sense. This means that the project was not intended as an aid to business communicators, to help them communicate their ethical commitments more effectively to the general public, although its findings may well be used towards that end. Rather, the purpose was to explore corporate responsibility advertising as a social and cultural phenomenon, from the perspective of citizenship, public opinion, democracy and political power.

According to traditional political theory, a business company is simply an economic agent, whose activities take place in the market, which is conceptually separated from the political sphere (Habermas 1962). Its communicative relations with individuals frame them exclusively as 'consumers', as the company tries to affect their behaviour in the market-place. Consumers, for their part, take on the different role of 'citizens' when they enter the realm of politics, making their common will as political subjects known through parliamentary elections. In late modern society, however, these clear-cut roles have become transformed into more ambiguous ones.

Corporate responsibility advertising thus enables a company to enter the realm of politics in order to express its concerns as one responsible citizen to other citizens, not just about market affairs, but also about urgent social and political issues. Businesses thereby intervene directly in the public debate about international, national and local affairs, bypassing the journalistic gatekeepers of the media in order to get direct access to public opinion. The increased occurrence of such advertising, the project suggested, can therefore be seen as a symptom of a perceived greater need for corporate actors to legitimate their actions to the general public, and perhaps – from a long-term perspective – even as heralding a qualitatively new phase of capitalism in which the limits of democratic participation are being questioned and extended.

The need for businesses to communicate 'politically' as citizens about ethics in a wide sense was also seen as being related to a reverse extension of the political domain into the economic sphere of the market. Here, growing critical ferment among consumers has made itself heard more and more insistently, in the form of political consumption putting pressure on companies to live up to new standards of public accountability, a kind of 'social control of business via the market' (Smith 1990: ix). One question for the study was how far consumer sovereignty might extend, whether it had any real political potential. Along such lines, corporate responsibility advertising was seen in the project as a proactive move to anticipate the emergence of a popular consumer politics, an attempt by the individual company to immunize itself from the adverse effects of such a politics.

Ethical advertising was thus seen as one of the textual sites where the meaning of ongoing social and political change is crystallized, in the interplay of corporate intentions, textual messages and audience readings. The reception study therefore looked at the audiences' encounter with ads like the Volvo ad presented at the beginning of this chapter, asking what interpretative strategies people mobilize to make sense of such ads. Do readers identify them as different from ordinary consumer advertising and, if so, what connections do they make between this form of corporate communication and wider social and political processes in society?

## REVIEWING PREVIOUS RESEARCH: METHODOLOGICAL IMPLICATIONS

When the study was being planned in the early 1990s, reception research was characterized by a distinct predilection for the television medium and for the genres of news and serial fiction, especially soap operas. Only a handful of studies of advertising audiences had appeared on the research horizon (Mick and Politi 1989; Nava and Nava 1990), none of which dealt with corporate advertising.

The present study therefore aimed to remedy both of these gaps in qualitative research, and also to complement the large body of quantitative research about corporate advertising that had accumulated over the years. As can be expected of a reception study, the focus was on sense-making processes: How do readers make sense of corporate responsibility ads? Do they read them in the spirit in which the corporate communicators conceptualized them, or do they reject the claims made for corporate concern, invitations to dialogue, etc.?

The question that had received exclusive attention in all previous audience studies of corporate non-product advertising was effectiveness, most of the studies using questionnaire-based surveys that typically tested the respondents' awareness and memory of, attitudes to, or confidence in the company. Schumann et al. (1991) present an overview of 42 studies, all of which, bar two, used the survey approach. Most of these studies showed that corporate advertising campaigns were successful, although Schumann et al. had their reservations about many of these results, saying that in many cases 'it is difficult to determine the significance of the findings or to identify the influence of corporate advertising as the primary causal factor' (1991: 52). They concluded that 'it is still unclear how, when, and why corporate advertising works' (1991: 53).

The extent to which the studies of corporate advertising reviewed by Schumann et al. include ethical ads is unknown. Another research review (Finkelstein et al. 1994) analysed audience perceptions of a type of advertising that falls into the ethical category, namely environmental advertising. Their findings were ambiguous. One the one hand, they found studies saying that 'the majority of the public doubts the veracity of environmental advertising claims', but other studies seemed to indicate that people liked these ads and said 'that they were positively influenced by them' (Finkelstein et al. 1994).

However, the overall interest in 'effectiveness' explored through the survey studies runs the risk of falling into the 'hypodermic needle' trap of seeing communication effects as direct and immediate, instead of as being mediated and negotiated through the multiple face-to-face encounters and intertextualities of everyday life. Schrøder's project was based on the conviction that in order to answer fundamental questions about how the signs of ethical advertising live in society, it is necessary to adopt what could be called an ethno-semiotic approach, studying social meanings through qualitative fieldwork. Here, the basic premise is that the meaning of an ad cannot be taken for granted: it is not *in* the message, it is created in the reader's encounter with the ad; it depends on the cultural codes and communicative resources at the disposal of each individual reader; and it must be researched through qualitative empirical work.

The selection of ads for the study had to face a common problem of comparative research across cultural and linguistic borders: how to select stimulus texts that invite comparable responses. In rare cases the researcher may be able to use the same media material in the two communities, as when the objective is to study viewers' perceptions of, say, an

American soap opera that is broadcast in both (Liebes and Katz 1990). In many cases, however, this option is not available because the media material in focus is culturally and linguistically specific; this was the case in the seven-nation comparative study of news reception orchestrated by Jensen (1998). In such cases, the researcher has to use media material from each cultural context that, minimally, is homogeneous with respect to genre, and preferably also near-identical with respect to verbal and visual features, situation of use, cultural salience, etc. This solution was adopted for Schrøder's study, which used near-similar ethical ads from British and Danish print media.

Print ads were preferred to television ads for a number of those practical reasons that always play a part in research designs: TV ads tend to be more ephemeral than print ads, requiring the field interviews to follow immediately after the broadcasting of the ads (something that would be difficult to organize in practical fieldwork terms). Print ads, on the other hand, can be collected over a longer period of time without appearing obsolete, and can be presented to informants without the need for technical equipment like a video recorder. Last, but not least, it is much easier for a researcher not living in one of the communities in question to monitor and collect print advertising from a distance.

## FIELDWORK DESIGN

The fieldwork of this study was carried out in two rounds of individual depth-interviews with 16 British informants and 16 Danish informants in their homes in 1992–93. Depth-interviews were preferred over focus groups because the study wanted to analyse individual readings of and attitudes to ethical business communication, rather than to explore the consensus-forming negotiations that usually characterize group discussions. The informants were selected so as to represent a diversity of gender (eight men, eight women), of adult age groups (eight between 20 and 30, and eight between 40 and 50), of education (eight with higher, eight with lower education), and of political observation (eight labelling themselves 'Conservatives', eight 'Labour' or 'Liberal'). One informant was thus, for example, male, between 20 and 30, with high education, and Conservative; another was female but shared the other characteristics, and so on.

The British informants all lived in two London suburbs, a 45-minute drive from the city; the Danish informants lived in a similar sub-metropolitan area outside Copenhagen. For practical reasons, the following report from the fieldwork presents findings from the British study, but concludes with a comparison of results from the two countries.

On each occasion, the informant was given nine recent print ads from general-appeal national newspapers and magazines. Each set comprised both corporate responsibility ads, consumer responsibility ads and traditional consumer ads, so as to not artificially focus attention on the categories of ads that had an ethical element (see Box 7.2). During the first interview, the ads were handed to the informant and instructions were given to put the nine ads in the order in which he or she wanted to talk about them. The ordering principle – like/dislike, ethics, colourfulness, etc. – was up to the informant. They were also asked

**Box 7.2  The corporate advertising project: list of advertisements used in the second British interview series**

DishwashElectric  'Washing up needn't be a life sentence', a straight colour consumer ad for a dishwasher, talks about the advantages of having a dishwasher. *Telegraph Magazine*, Spring 1992.

Toshiba  'Not only do we help you clean up in the business world, we help clean up the world itself', a colour product ad for a portable computer, mentions its technical potential, and adds a 'green' touch. *Financial Times*, 25 September 1991.

Total  'To some this oil field is virtually empty, to Total it is more than half full', a black and white corporate ad emphasizing Total's leadership in oil extraction techniques. *Sunday Times*, 17 November 1991.

VW  'We put people in front of cars', a colour product ad that mentions VW's safety and environmental concern as good reasons for buying a VW. *Observer Magazine*, 10 November 1991.

Nokia  'Before. – NOKIA', a colour consumer ad for mobile phones. *Telegraph Magazine*, Spring 1992.

Zanussi  'Planets that are caring for your future', an environmental colour ad that stresses the caring image in connection with the entire Zanussi product range. *Green Magazine*, April 1992.

Vauxhall  'Drive the new Astra and help change the face of cycling', a colour consumer ad with a 'green touch': the Astra is recyclable, etc. *Sunday Mirror/News of the World*, 17 November 1991.

Midland Bank  'Midland's business banking charter', a black and white customer-oriented ad stressing the dialogic nature of Midland's communication. *Daily Mirror*, 23 October 1991.

BP  'Oil companies tend to invite criticism. At BP, we actively encourage it', a black and white corporate ad that stresses both environmental concern and the desire for dialogue with interested members of the public. *Green Magazine*, December 1991.

to respond to the visual and verbal characteristics of each ad, and to think about what kind of action the ad might want from them, but it was stressed that they were not expected to devote much more time to each ad than they would have done in a normal newspaper reading situation. Before the second interview, a set of nine colour-copied ads were mailed to informants and the instructions were repeated in the accompanying letter, which also served as a reminder of the appointment.

The type of interview conducted was of the semi-structured type, in which the informant was encouraged not to wait for the next question, but to speak freely about the ads, making associations from the advertisement to other aspects of their working and private lives. It was also made clear that the study was not 'after' anything in particular, except the informant's personal experience and impression of the ads. Every effort was made to create an atmosphere that was as informal and asymmetrical as possible (Spradley 1979), and small talk was not avoided.

The first of the two interviews was regarded purely as an encounter that served the purpose of establishing an open, dialogic relationship between interviewer and informant, i.e. to make the informant feel comfortable with the unfamiliar speech event of a research interview, and the first interview series was not used as data for the analysis. It was assumed that, due to this design, the second interview would give the researcher access to relatively unfiltered and spontaneous meanings from the informant's lifeworld, although absolute authenticity is obviously a phantom.

## ANALYSING THE DATA

During the analysis of the interview transcripts, the multidimensional character of the readers' signifying processes was registered (Schrøder 2000), noting the informants' *motivation* towards the ads, their individualized *understanding* of the ads, their *aesthetic awareness*, their *attitudes* to the ads and the companies behind them, and the extent to which the particular ads, together with other instances of ethical corporate communication, appeared to become a *communicative resource* for the informants – affecting their thinking and everyday practices in some small way.

During the analysis of the transcripts, two observations were made that hold general implications for reception analysis: one had to do with the inherently intertextual character of all signifying processes (O'Donohoe 1997), as the informants' perception of each ad in the set of nine was strongly dependent both on their perceptions of the other ads in the set, and on their associations with other advertising they had come across; the other had to do with the fact that informants' agendas may be quite different from the researcher's – for instance, people's motivation to read an ad may have very little to do with its 'message'. The following quotation from a male informant illustrates both these points: 'Another oil company, BP. Well, I don't know. When I first opened this, the first thing I did, the very first thing I did was that I went around and looked at all the people to see whether there are any good-looking women there to look at'. There is thus often an element of artificiality in confronting people with the requirements of a research agenda; however, we shall have to live with this if we want to explore signifying processes in people's lifeworlds.

## FINDINGS I: THE READERS' EXPERIENCE OF ETHICAL ADS

According to corporate communicators, ethical advertising 'is about reputation, about winning the benefit of the doubt' (BP's manager of corporate advertising, quoted in

Shepard 1993: 15), about getting across to the reading public that a company has objectives beyond profit and that the company has a sincere wish to engage in a dialogue with its significant publics. The field interviews were interpreted against these corporate communication objectives, because they are intimately related to the macro-social issues about politics and democracy that guided the theoretical knowledge interest of the study.

First of all, however, not wanting to take the researcher's division of ads into different categories for granted, the study looked for an answer to the question of whether people distinguish at all between different categories of advertisement. It was found that they do, although they don't use the categories used in academic research. The categories of ads used by informants should not, therefore, be regarded as belonging to a conscious, well-defined system, but rather as an informal ad hoc resource that resides in what Giddens calls 'practical consciousness', i.e. a subconscious framework that is activated whenever an everyday situation requires it, and which may become the subject of discursive, conscious reflection if necessary:

> *All human beings are knowledgeable agents. . . . Knowledgeability embedded in practical consciousness exhibits an extraordinary complexity. . . . for the most part these faculties are geared to the flow of day-to-day conduct. The rationalization of conduct becomes the discursive offering of reasons only if individuals are asked by others why they acted as they did.*

(Giddens 1984: 281)

All informants had some notion of ads with 'a green element' (Informant 10) or 'pollution ads' (Informant 1), and most did not hesitate to declare what the researcher categorized as an 'ethical ad' to be 'a concerned advert' (Informant 4) or 'going for the caring image' (Informant 7), or the like. Half the informants had clear labels that referred to different types of ad; one informant, for instance, had a system that included 'propaganda ads', 'green ads' and 'buy-our-shares ads', in addition to ordinary product ads (Informant 6). Another distinguished between 'environment' and 'product' ads (Informant 9), and a third distinguished 'PR ads' from ordinary ads (Informant 3).

In spite of their possession of such labels, however, pure corporate ads sometimes posed problems for informants. Faced with the Total non-product ad (see Box 7.2), one informant exclaimed, 'What are they trying to do? Nothing!' As this ad didn't describe a product or talk about investment, 'to me it's a page of nothing' (Informant 5). Another informant was similarly at a loss to understand the purpose of the Total ad: 'Didn't really know what to make of this one at all. . . . I can't see the point in that ad to be quite honest with you. I can't see what it is for' (Informant 1).

For these informants, an ad is a message that asks you, in one way or another, to buy something; they are puzzled by ads that appear not to do that, but rather to ask for respect, trust and dialogue. Their confusion about ethical ads may be related to their rejection of the idea that companies are genuinely becoming more socially responsible: they see nothing beyond a company's economic identity and interest, in its advertising or in its social behaviour.

They were thus found to apply what were called 'cynical' readings of ethical advertising. The two other types of reading, found through analysis of the transcripts, were labelled 'sympathetic' and 'agnostic'. All three types were defined according to the informants' willingness, or lack of willingness, to give the companies 'the benefit of the doubt' on the basis of the different ads.

- **Sympathetic readings** could be seen in those informant utterances that expressed trust in the corporate message of a particular ad; which accepted that the company was really as concerned, responsible, accountable, etc. as it claimed to be; and which believed that the company was prepared not simply to maximize profits, but to let ethical considerations enter into the picture.

- **Agnostic readings** occurred in informant utterances that expressed doubt about corporate motives and behaviours, and that found it difficult to know what to believe about contemporary business intentions – that one cannot know with any degree of certainty what business is really 'up to'. Another possible label would be 'sceptical'.

- **Cynical readings** were found in those utterances that rejected out of hand all corporate claims about concern and responsibility, and which believed that the professed ethic was nothing but empty rhetoric, and that corporate practice was completely unaffected by environmental or community considerations.

After generating these categories inductively from the data, it became clear that they corresponded with another set of labels that have frequently been used in reception analysis: dominant, negotiated and oppositional readings (Hall 1973). In this terminology, the sympathetic reading is one that simply takes over the ad's intended, 'dominant' meaning; the agnostic reading is one that struggles with, or 'negotiates', the intended meaning, ending up with a reading that is not totally antagonistic to it; whereas the cynical reading performs an 'oppositional' reading of the ad, in which the intended meaning is clearly understood, but vigorously resisted.

Hall's triad of readings often makes intuitive sense as a general descriptive framework for audience readings of factual media material. However, concrete studies will find it helpful to develop descriptive labels that are more directly related to their specific subject matter. The interview data from Schrøder's study found examples of all three types of reading.

Some informant statements were quite sympathetic to the corporate claims of responsibility. One female informant believed that companies were prepared to listen to criticism: 'They are ready to listen rather than to get on with it. . . . I think they have come round to thinking people are not being happy with the way things are being run. . . . And they are prepared to listen' (Informant 15). Another informant expressed a similar view in connection with the VW ad about safety and care for the environment: 'they actually . . . em . . . tell you in a way which makes you feel that it is credible, because they keep saying "we were the first to do this" . . .' (Informant 10). While she was critical of the 'green bandwagon' effect, she was nevertheless sympathetic to the view that business is fundamentally changing – 'Well, I would like to think it is' – continuing that companies 'wouldn't become responsible I'm sure if that meant that their profits were going to be cut dramatically' (Informant 10). At the level of manifest meaning she might seem to deny the possibility of businesses becoming more responsible, but at the more latent level of linguistic implicature she is actually granting that 'green' does have some power over profit maximization: businesses won't accept 'dramatic' cuts, but will apparently, accept moderate ones!

Such sympathetic statements were few and far between; most informants could readily be categorized as agnostics or cynics. One female informant expressed a certain ambivalence about the BP ad: on the one hand, she categorically denied the sincerity of the invitation to dialogue and the environmental concern – 'It is a propaganda thing, isn't it . . . in the end they have got shareholders and they want to make money, don't they. . . . I'm sure that they are still doing the same as they have always done' (Informant 9), but within the same argument she brought herself into a more open-minded stance: 'we as the public can change the system, by actually demanding, because if the demand is there, they will provide', seeing the BP ad as a response to such pressures, and concluding 'I am not sure . . . I don't know whether it is true' (Informant 9).

By far the majority of the informants were quite cynical about the ethical and dialogic claims of corporate responsibility advertisements. They simply didn't trust the promises and declarations made by the companies, and seemed to discern a gulf between corporate communication and corporate practice: 'to me it's all mouth and no do', as one informant put it (Informant 16). Another saw the Midland Bank's invitation to dialogue as 'icing on a rotten cake' (Informant 1). The BP ad triggered the cynicism of one female informant: 'It's all fine to invite criticism, but part of me says, "well, they'll listen and then they'll go through and bulldoze exactly what they want anyway"' (Informant 10). The BP ad was singled out for scathing comment by another informant, who was convinced that business responsibility is just a question of appearances, not substance: 'Well, businesses are having to be seen to be doing something about the environment and taking it into account in their products . . . I'm sure that they don't really want to do it at all' (Informant 12).

Many informants see only falsehood and hypocrisy in corporate responsibility claims: 'All these companies probably stick to speaking with a forked tongue . . ., they're saying one thing to the public, trying to convince the public that they're friendly. At the same time they're doing their utmost to make sure they don't have to,' one said (Informant 4), mentioning corporate lobbying at the Rio environmental summit in the summer of 1992.

# FINDINGS II: THE CHALLENGE OF QUALITATIVE GENERALIZATION

Some reception studies would stop here, satisfied to have discovered a diversity of readings of corporate responsibility ads, reluctant to embark on a further process of interpretative generalization of the data, because 'generalizations are necessarily violations to the concrete specificity of all unique micro-situations' (Ang 1991: 162). Others would start looking for possible patterns in the interview data, attempting to balance between qualitative depth on the one hand and the need to establish a systematic framework for generalizing the data on the other.

The ethical advertising study decided to opt for the latter strategy: first, because this was necessary in order to accomplish a systematic comparative analysis of the British and the Danish readings; second, in order to be able to offer its findings to various publics in a format that was readily comprehensible and useful for discussions about the power relations between business companies, sub-political movements and citizen-consumers, jointly moving towards a modernized democracy. Moreover, an interpretative reduction and 'mapping' of the data would also serve the purpose of facilitating a longitudinal study of the reception of ethical advertising, should someone wish to replicate the study at a future date.

With such an intention, it would be tempting to simply distribute the 16 British and 16 Danish informants among the three types of discourse outlined above, thereby producing a clear picture of which discourse was dominant among the two groups of informants in the early 1990s. However, a simple triadic categorization of informants turned out not to be possible – because the meaning processes in the modern world are complex and polysemous enough to allow an individual to hold ambivalent views on issues like corporate responsibility advertising. In other words, the three labels of cynical, agnostic and sympathetic readings are to be seen as descriptive of *types of reading*, not *types of reader*.

The first step in the generalizing process was therefore to categorize each informant's reading of *each responsibility ad* according to the three types of reading. Second, the *aggregate picture* of each informant's experience of the ads was determined on the basis of an interpretation that synthesized the readings of the individual ads into this respondent's overall experience of professed business ethics. As a result, an informant could be categorized as a pure inhabitant of one type of reading, or as a hybrid inhabitant of two or three types of reading. This ambivalence was illustrated by placing the informants' discourses in a model constructed from three intersecting circles (called a Venn diagram), on the basis of an analytical generalization of their readings (Figure 7.1; each number represents the aggregate reading of one informant). Realizing that past experiences of natural or social science diagrams might create an illusion of exactness, it was stressed that the figure should be regarded as an interpretative metaphor of the analytical findings, serving heuristic expediency, not mathematical accuracy.

Figure 7.1    Distribution of British and Danish informants' readings of ethical advertisements

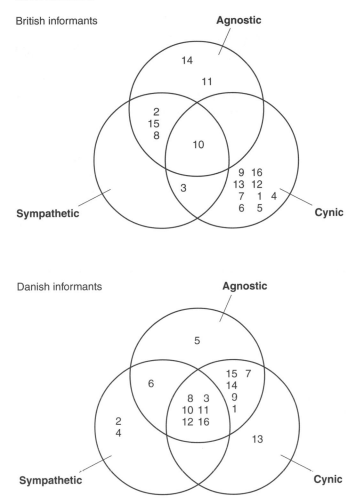

Using the British study to illustrate the complexity of audience responses, about half the informants could be placed fairly unequivocally in only one type of reading, as pure agnostics or cynics, but many informants were found to have a foot in several camps at the same time: one informant was thus predominantly cynic, but came out with a few isolated sympathetic responses; another was on the whole sympathetic, but leaned towards the agnostic; a third expressed views from all three types.

Addressing the question of the cross-national comparison of findings, the diagram illustrates the remarkable fact, contrary to the researcher's expectations, that none of the British informants fell into the pure sympathetic area of the diagram; most fell into the pure cynic area, a few in the sympathetic/agnostic area, one in the sympathetic/cynic area, and one in the area where all three circles overlap.

Just as remarkably, the Danish informants were almost completely absent from the pure cynic area, and indeed any other pure area, as they congregated in the hybrid areas near the middle of the figure, which represents mixed agnostic/cynic or sympathetic/agnostic/cynic readings.

The study thus concluded, first, that as regards *attitudes* to professed corporate ethics, the British informants were characterized by a clear preponderance of cynical responses, whereas the Danish informants expressed agnostic and sympathetic views. Second, as regards *resoluteness* of attitude, the study showed that the attitudes of the British informants are much more unequivocal – they are largely absent from the overlapping areas that denote ambivalence, whereas the attitudes of the Danish informants are predominantly ambivalent.

In other words, with the British informants, corporate responsibility ads were quite far from reaching the goal of 'winning the benefit of the doubt'; on the contrary, if these informants were typical, companies wishing to pursue an ethical line of conduct and communication appeared to be facing an uphill struggle of serious legitimation problems with the general public. The Danish informants, on the other hand, were just sceptical, not antagonistic. When asked to consider the sincerity of corporate claims of environmental and other kinds of social responsibility, they really don't know! Companies would therefore appear to have an easier task before them when they wish to persuade members of the general public in Denmark that they are responsible citizens.

This said, it should also be emphasized that the 16 informants of this study could not be claimed to be representative of the respective national populations. The issue of representativeness has always been the Achilles heel of qualitative research (see Chapter 2). The findings were therefore offered in the hope that they were, if not representative, then to some extent typical of the population groups used as informants. In order to corroborate this humbler claim, the study proceeded to make a theoretical argument that attempted to locate the nationally specific reader profiles in the social histories of the two countries.

Among the demographic variables included in the informant profiles (gender, education, age, political observation), the variable responsible for the difference between the two national groups appeared to be education: it was mainly the British informants with low education, presumably corresponding to a working-class background, who tended to be unequivocally negative towards the corporate claims of responsibility. No clear pattern emerged from any of the other variables in either of the two national groups.

This finding was tentatively explained by reference to the different histories of the two countries with respect to class structure. Class difference and antagonism are deeply rooted in British history, characterized by a dichotomous class structure that has given rise in the political realm to relatively clear-cut election victories by either the Conservative right wing or the Labour-rooted left wing, in a kind of swing-of-the-pendulum pattern.

Members of the British working class, therefore, tend to harbour a dichotomous consciousness of the social structure: a social map characterized by a deep-seated 'us' versus 'them' perspective, predisposing many working people to distrust or reject the ethical claims of business.

In Denmark, those with low education cannot be readily identified with a working-class background, because, historically, Denmark has been characterized by a class structure with a small industrial working class and a dominant agrarian class, based on the ownership of small and medium-sized farms, whose class loyalties have always been ambivalent. Politically, the country has not had one single-party majority government during the whole of the twentieth century, as a succession of alternating left- or right-inclined governments have always been based on coalitions and compromises with parties in the middle of the political spectrum. Many Danes with little education were therefore more likely to want to weigh the evidence for and against corporate responsibility in each individual case, instead of refusing to even consider the possibility of business 'going ethical'. Moreover, living in a welfare society with widespread protection of the weak, many Danish informants expressed the conviction that 'someone', such as an ombudsman for advertising, would have intervened if the claims made by the ads were false.

The different outlooks on responsibility advertising of the British and Danish informants were not matched by a similar difference in readiness to participate in consumer activism directed against companies that behave unethically. There was a clear willingness both among British and Danish informants to 'do something' if companies were caught cheating, i.e. if the rhetoric of responsibility turned out to be nothing but a thin veneer covering a reprehensible practice. But their motivations were somewhat different. In line with the argument about class consciousness above, the British informants believed that progress requires struggle: the companies are basically not to be trusted, therefore 'we' must be ready to fight in order to change things for the better (for interview documentation, see Schrøder 1997). By contrast, as a starting point the Danish informants believed that most companies acknowledged their obligation to be good citizens, but if they turned out not to be trustworthy after all they should be penalized and brought back to the path of ethical progress.

## CONCLUDING REMARKS

As described at the beginning of this chapter, one of the things that motivated the study reported here was the desire to explore the public's responses to the apparently growing need for businesses in the early 1990s to legitimate their activities in the eyes of the general public. Corporate responsibility ads were seen as one of the ways in which companies attempted to preserve or create a space within which they could navigate and fulfil their corporate goals, and, therefore, as closely related to the future social distribution of power between, on the one hand, the democratically elected legislators and executives at national and local levels, and the private interests of the corporate world on the other.

When addressing ethical ads of various types towards the public arena, or the public sphere (Habermas 1962), the corporate communicators thereby indicated that they would abide by the rules that apply in this sphere. Of particular importance here is the rule that the political actors in democratic societies have always had to follow, which holds that social power ultimately resides with the citizens and that only that which is sanctioned by the citizens can have legitimacy.

A couple of years after the fieldwork of this study was done, this was precisely the lesson learned by Shell management from the so-called *Brent Spar* affair in the summer of 1995. During a few weeks of intense media coverage, massive consumer pressure, spearheaded by Greenpeace, forced Shell to give up its seemingly well-prepared dumping of a scrapyard-ready oil rig in the North Atlantic. A couple of months after Shell's spectacular defeat, its UK director, John Wybrew, expressed his revised views about modern corporate management (quoted in the *Guardian*, 15 September 1995). The defeat, according to Wybrew, had happened because Shell had failed to understand public opinion and had underestimated the power of a campaigning organization like Greenpeace, as well as the international nature of the issue. He went on to conclude that, in the modern world, it is no longer sufficient for a corporation to rely on following the letter of the law and international regulations: 'We have constantly to earn trust and a licence to operate from the public.'

The reception study reported here showed that it is doubtful whether corporate responsibility advertising, addressing public opinion impersonally through the mass media, is an appropriate communicative strategy for achieving such a relationship of trust between corporate 'citizens' and increasingly politicized consumers.

# Chapter Eight

# Reception research: defining □ the field

In episode 105 of the 1980s American primetime soap, *Dynasty*, all the main characters have left for a global oil summit in Acapulco, among them, protagonist oil tycoon, Blake Carrington, and his former wife, Alexis, now a vengeful business enemy. Krystle, Blake's new, younger wife, has stayed at home in Denver, where she is being shadowed by a photo-spy of unknown identity, while she is having business meeting dates with horse-breeder, Daniel Reece (sounds like a classic soap opera . . .?). Meanwhile, in Acapulco, one of Blake Carrington's business allies, Ashley Mitchell, and his former wife, Alexis, of American and British origin respectively, are getting involved in a prolonged verbal duel about oil rights and emotional hang-ups. After a series of mutual accusations, with Ashley Mitchell being on the defensive, (British) Alexis gloats that 'Maybe I hit a nerve under that cool New England façade?' to which (American) Ashley replies, 'Don't go too far, Alexis; remember the Boston Tea Party!' (For the benefit of those not well versed in American history, the Boston Tea Party in 1773 is an event from the American War of Independence, and the first time the Americans gained the upper hand over the British.)

*Dynasty* episode 105 was used in a reception study of Danish viewers' readings of this imported and subtitled American serial (Schrøder 1988). Here follows a short passage from one of the interviews with a 50-year-old married couple. The identity of the above-mentioned photo-spy is being discussed, and the husband proposes an explanation that draws on something that happened 'years back, only we haven't been told about it'. His wife continues:

| | |
|---|---|
| **Wife:** | **And Ashley has something on Alexis, something from years back . . . something about a tea party . . .** |
| **Interviewer:** | **. . . something in the past?** |
| **Husband:** | **Yeah, and what the hell's that tea party supposed to mean, we didn't hear anything about that before!** |
| **Wife:** | **No, and she even mentioned where it took place . . . I forget . . .** |
| **Interviewer:** | **Boston.** |
| **Husband:** | **Yeah.** |

As this excerpt shows, viewers' understanding of a TV programme is something that cannot be taken for granted. Presumably American viewers would have had no problem in understanding Ashley's reference to the Boston Tea Party, as it is a major event both in official American history and in popular mythology. They are likely to possess the 'historical code' (or 'frame') necessary for understanding the reference. Whether they also possess the 'aesthetic code' necessary for understanding the utterance as a warning from an underdog American to an arrogant Englishwoman is more uncertain, but quite probable. Clearly, Danish viewers, lacking both of these codes, have to be creative if they want to make some sense of what they hear and see – which they clearly do. Thus, based on their intimate familiarity with the genre to which *Dynasty* belongs, they construct a perfectly plausible meaning to do with the often-encountered phenomenon of 'hidden events of the past' brought in to provide narrative resolution to an apparent fictional enigma.

The lesson to be learnt from this small tale from the field of reception research, therefore, is that when the viewers and other users of the media perform their – shared or idiosyncratic, 'correct' or 'misunderstood' – readings of the verbal and visual structures offered by the media in the context of their everyday lives, the outcome is often both unpredictable and uncontrollable. If we, as academic researchers, are interested in understanding how people experience media content, we have to use a research approach that enables us to explore the processes through which people actualize media meanings and incorporate them in meaningful ways into their daily lives.

Reception research is premised on the belief that neither the semiotic analysis of media texts nor questionnaire-based analysis of media gratifications is capable of grasping the complexities of the media experience. Consequently, the prescribed methodological approach to reception analysis is some kind of qualitative interview, in which viewers verbalize their experiences of media material (see Chapter 9).

## ESSENTIALS OF RECEPTION RESEARCH

It is a basic tenet of reception research that meaning is never just transferred from the media to their audiences. Meaning, in media as well as in face-to-face interaction (including verbalized research encounters), is generated according to the communicative repertoires, or codes, of the encoder(s) and interpreted according to the communicative repertoires of the decoder(s) – and there is no natural fit between the encoding and decoding (Hall 1973). Moreover, media/audience meaning processes are firmly embedded in the social contexts of everyday life in which people use the media.

Based on this premise, reception research has defined itself in dual opposition: on the one hand, to humanistic textual analysis, with its implied position that media meanings and ideologies are imposed on passive minds and may be brought to light by textual analysis alone; on the other hand, to the survey-based uses and gratifications (U+G) approach, whose analysis of media gratifications ignores the meanings that create these gratifications. Reception research is critical of both for neglecting to explore the everyday contexts in which meanings and uses arise in the first place, but does not go as far as media ethnography in assigning a primary role to the everyday itself.

Reception research can thus be seen as a cross-fertilization project, attempting to borrow from both of its predecessors as it 'draws its theory from the humanities and its methodology from the social sciences', as Jensen puts it, with 'a helpful overstatement' (Jensen 1991a: 135). It tries to understand audience meaning processes in accordance with hermeneutic theories underlying the humanistic traditions of semiotics and linguistic discourse analysis, and it explores these meaning processes through methods of empirical fieldwork, borrowed from the more phenomenological traditions in the social sciences (Schrøder 1987; Kvale 1996; Jensen 2002b).

The programmatic statements from the pioneers of reception research sometimes showed a close affinity with the concerns of the U+G tradition, even though they were also highly critical of its individualistic and rationalistic foundations. Thus Radway (1984) echoed the U+G platform when she criticized humanistic textual analysis because it 'discounts what readers *do* with texts', going on to call for an approach that 'focuses on the various ways human beings actively *make* sense of their surrounding world' of ubiquitous media messages (Radway 1984: 8; emphasis added).

When it came to the consideration of empirical methods for exploring cultural meaning processes, however, early reception researchers were highly critical of the prescribed methodology of U+G research: the survey questionnaire. The main objection had to do with validity – that is, the alleged distance between questionnaire wordings and the respondents' lived experience. As Lewis puts it, in quantitative surveys 'we have no way of telling if the respondents are comfortable with the ways of thinking that have been imposed upon them. . . . The ambiguities of language mean that it is difficult to explore the precise meaning of words or sentences without giving the respondent the opportunity to elaborate' (Lewis 1991: 78).

This is the reason why most reception researchers, from the pioneer days of the early 1980s until the present day, have – sometimes quite vehemently – distanced themselves from any trace of quantification and have insisted on the use of qualitative methods of data collection and analysis, such as the individual depth-interview or focus-group interviews. It is only recently that the possible benefits of quantifying some of the qualitative data have been opened up as a topic of discussion among reception researchers (Lewis 1997; Schrøder 1999).

Before leaving the subject of methodology for the time being, it is appropriate to issue a word of caution about the labels used by reception researchers over the years to designate their work in the overall field of audience research. During the early years of reception research in the 1980s, many of the scholars coming out of literary- or semiotic-type textual analysis of the media, in particular, were so thrilled that they had left their university offices and embarked on 'fieldwork' studies that they tended to delude themselves that they were now 'doing ethnography'. Therefore, in some reports readers will find the labels 'reception research' and 'media ethnography' used almost interchangeably.

## Box 8.1   The defining characteristics of reception research as an interdisciplinary area between the humanities and the social sciences

1. *Reception research explores the encounter of active audiences with media meanings.* The notion of 'active audiences' implies that reception research sees itself as continuing and redirecting the thrust of uses and gratifications research towards the empowerment of audiences in the cultural process. Audiences 'do' things with media messages, but what they do is not just to rationally expose themselves to media material likely to gratify this or that individual psychological 'need'. The activity of audiences is also a discursive activity that implicates audience members in the construction of social, political and cultural identities, and the collective production of social reality. It has been argued that the notion of 'active' audiences is self-evident and has little explanatory value (McQuail 2000); however, we wish to retain the concept, as there continues to be a need for an explicit antidote to the still widespread myth of television viewers as cultural dupes in front of the screen.

2. *Reception research regards meaning as a joint product of text and reader.* Contrary to the practice of critical textual analysis, which claims to be able to present the social meaning of the media text through an 'expert reading' of the text itself, reception research insists that the media text is merely an encoded meaning potential, which may constrain the readers' meaning production in various ways, but which remains to be actualized by readers in everyday life (as is demonstrated in a radical fashion by the Boston Tea Party example at the start of this chapter). The encoded textual constraint on audience members' meaning production has given rise to the notion of the media text having a 'preferred meaning' or 'preferred reading' that is, so to speak, naturally offered to and taken over by audience members, unless they are prompted to negotiate or oppose it (Hall 1973). The individual who encounters the media message is seen as someone who has been socialized into possessing a number of codes, or interpretative repertoires, acquired and developed in the social and cultural contexts experienced during the lifetime of the individual. These contexts being unique, the repertoirs at the disposal of an individual are ultimately unique, and consequently the production of meaning triggered by the media text will ultimately be unique to each individual.

3. *The situational and social contexts of reading affect the meanings actualized by audiences.* The radical individualism of meaning pro-

duction just outlined is tempered by situational and social constraints. The interpretative codes or repertoires are acquired by individuals interacting with other individuals in socially organized communicative structures of family, peer group, school, class, gender, ethnicity, etc. This means that the codes are also, to a large extent, shared and socially patterned – otherwise mutual intelligibility and social allegiances and communities would be impossible. The media meanings actualized by audience members are therefore also to some extent likely to be shared among the members of various social groupings (as was the case with the readings of the Madonna video largely following ethnic lines, as mentioned in Chapter 1). To these social constraints affecting the long-term constitution of interpretative repertoires must be added the immediate situational constraints affecting meaning production in the specific situation of media use, creating a difference of experience, for instance, between the same film being watched by a teenage girl with her family in the home and with her peer group on a night out at the cinema (Barker and Brooks 1998).

4. *The preferred methodological approach of reception research is the qualitative interview.* The combined phenomenological and hermeneutic pursuit of verbalized audience experiences that are as authentic as possible has caused reception researchers to adopt a method of inquiry that enables audience members to render their media readings in accordance with their own lifeworld categories. The qualitative interview has two main variants that serve different purposes, although the adoption of one rather than the other is sometimes simply a matter of convenience. One is the individual depth-interview, enabling the researcher to probe deeply into personal, possibly sensitive, perceptions and attitudes in connection with media experiences. The other is the focus-group interview, which enables the researcher to directly observe the social production of meaning as participants negotiate their readings of media material in an environment with strong consensual constraints.

Source: partly inspired by Hagen (1998a)

Recently it has been generally acknowledged that some measure of conceptual hygiene is necessary (Nightingale 1989). The term 'reception research' is thus being reserved for the interview-based study of how people make sense of specific media products like TV programmes, youth magazines or print ads. 'Media ethnography', as discussed in Chapters 4–6, is now usually reserved for studies defined both, methodologically, by their use of participant observation as the main approach, supplemented by interviews, and by taking their point of departure in the practices of everyday life in which people use the media. In practice, however, there are many borderline cases between these two approaches.

## THE TEXT/READER NEXUS

It has become conventional wisdom within reception research that one of its achievements has been to bring together two research enterprises that have traditionally been segregated: the analysis of media texts and the study of audience practices. 'Reception analysis submits that texts and their recipients are complementary elements of one area of inquiry which thus addresses both the discursive and the social aspects of communication. . . . reception analysis assumes that there can be no "effect" without "meaning"' (Jensen 1991a: 135).

It follows from this doctrine that one should expect any study that calls itself by the name of reception research to offer 'a systematic, comparative analysis of audience discourses and media discourses' (Jensen 1991a: 136). However, this expectation is often disappointed. Sometimes the fieldwork part of a reception study will indeed have been preceded by a close reading of the media text, which is just not reported, due to lack of space. At other times, deliberately, only a rudimentary textual analysis will have been done, with the sole purpose of preparing the researcher sufficiently for the role of interview facilitator.

In such cases, the researcher will usually intentionally have abstained from undertaking a detailed textual analysis of the media product, fearing that meeting the informant with a ready-made depth-analysis on his mind would impede a truly phenomenological exploration of the informant's lifeworld-based experience. Especially in students' reception projects, one often encounters interviews that have become rather like a structured check on the respondent's ability to discover the textual properties that the researcher found salient – turning the reception analysis into a kind of pointless 'are they as smart as me' exercise.

Naturally it can be perfectly legitimate to probe for the informants' readings of specific features of content or form. In the case of reception studies being carried out, experimental-style, as in the pre-testing stage of, say, a TV programme development or a public information campaign process, such exploration of aesthetic details will be the whole *raison d'être* of the study. But for broader purposes, such as academic reception research, interested in the role of TV news for democratic participation or the role of domestic TV fiction for the formation of national identity, it is often wiser to abstain from a detailed preliminary textual analysis, and just to familiarize oneself with the text sufficiently to be able to pursue the cultural or political research questions that motivate the project.

Another, and no less interesting, way to meet the requirement of doing a systematic comparison of audience and media discourses is to do them in reverse order. This can be done by taking the findings of a reception study of audience readings 'back to the text', looking systematically for the textual properties that seem to have triggered and shaped particular readings (Lewis 1983). This was the procedure chosen for Lewis's later study of the reception of British TV news (Lewis 1991).

In this study, Lewis found that informants' understanding of the news differed markedly from one news story to another. In some cases, viewers were able to establish clear connections between the elements of a news story; in others, 'the meaning the news producers intended to convey . . . often bore little relation to the meanings constructed by the viewers' (Lewis 1991: 132). Looking for a possible textual anchorage in the narrative structuring of the different stories, Lewis found that viewers' understanding was superficial when stories followed the traditional news format of 'giving away' the conclusion already in the anchor's 'headline', whereas viewers achieved a deeper understanding of stories that followed a more fiction-like format of building up suspense through the news item, requiring viewers to keep their attention focused on the whole story in order to get the resolution.

In a similar operation of tracing specific readings back to their textual anchorage, Lewis found that the agenda-setting element of a news story appeared to be not the studio anchor's verbal introduction, but the story's first 'main action sequence' (1991: 149). In a story intended by the journalist to inform viewers about the violent consequences of the Israelis' sacking of three Palestinian mayors on the West Bank, this causal element was lost on most viewers, in spite of its being mentioned in the verbal introduction. The decisive element for shaping the viewers' perception of the story as simply being about 'continued unrest in the Middle East' was the immediately following film footage of soldiers and civilians in street combat.

Lewis's analysis is thus an example of a reception study that set out to explore the broad issue of the power of TV news in the ideological reproduction of society, but that also ended up with an outline of a recipe for news that is easier for viewers to understand: 'If news adopted the conventions of narrative codes used in other cultural forms [i.e. fiction], it would be considerably more successful at communicating its message to people' (1991: 138). Lewis's study thus puts one foot in the product development camp within the larger community of reception research, where researchers seek to increase the communicative efficiency of commercial and public communicators.

## THEORETICAL DISCUSSIONS IN RECEPTION RESEARCH

### THE ENCODING/DECODING MODEL

We challenge our readers to find a single work from the empirical reception tradition that does not make a reference to Stuart Hall's article, 'Encoding and Decoding in the Television Discourse', first published in 1973 and later published in an edited version in Hall et al. (1980). Such has been the agenda-setting dominance of this seminal article that its whole conceptual framework, as well as its core theoretical concepts, have been canonical for a generation of reception researchers, far beyond what is warranted by the paper's modest intentions, its complete lack of an empirical foundation for its argument, and the political narrowness of its Marxist perspective (see Hall's retrospective and self-critical evaluation of the role of the paper for subsequent audience research in Lewis's interview with him in 1989 (Hall 1994)).

As its title clearly indicates, the paper was not intended to become the intellectual property of audience research alone. On the contrary, its aim was holistic as it tries to grasp mass communication as a complex, non-linear signifying process. In order to theorize this, Hall presents a model to constantly remind analysts that in analysing a media text, they are dealing not with a fixed structure of meaning, but with a volatile phenomenon resulting from the codes at the disposal of both the producers and the recipients of the text, all of whom are steeped in a sea of social meanings and ideologies.

When it comes to the understanding of audience decodings of media messages, Hall's argument makes no distinction between semiotic and ideological processes. This has contributed to considerable confusion in much subsequent empirical work because of the lack of a clear distinction between textual polysemy and ideological 'effect'. Briefly, this has meant that any occurrence of a variety of readings of, say, a newscast, has tended to be seen not just as simple divergence of meanings, but as evidence of the audience's ability to resist the programme's hegemonic thrust. With the wisdom of hindsight, therefore, it has become clear that the model's origin, as a direct product of left-wing political scholarship of the 1970s, makes it less suitable as a general foundation for the understanding of audience sense-making processes. Nevertheless, for years it has been immensely inspiring as a tool-to-think-with also for the authors of this book, and it is necessary to have a basic grasp of its conceptual universe in order to understand reception work from the last two decades.

Following Barthes' distinction between 'denotative' and 'connotative' codes, Hall argues that on the level of denotative codes (basic, literal meanings) there is a near-universal agreement between encoders' and decoders' meanings; the ideological work of the TV text, Hall argues, takes place on the connotative level (cultural, associative meanings):

> *So it is at the connotative level of the sign that situational ideologies alter and transform signification. At this level we can see more clearly the active intervention of ideologies in and on discourse: here, the sign is open to new accentuations and . . . enters fully into the struggle over meanings – the class struggle in language.*

(Hall 1973/1980: 133)

It is on this semiotic-ideological level that Hall finds it useful to distinguish between the three well-known hypothetical 'decoding positions': dominant, negotiated and oppositional (Hall 1980: 136). Before these could be defined, however, Hall had to set up a textual standard that the decoding positions engage in the sense-making process, leading him to suggest the notion of the *preferred reading*. This is the connotative meaning, inscribed in the text, which is produced by the hegemonic framework governing mass media production routines and which promotes socio-central taken-for-granted meanings that serve the interests of the dominant social groups. Within the terms of Hall's model, it is highly probable that the *meaning* 'preferred' by the ruling-class encoders will also become the preferred *reading* of the working-class decoders, because 'encoding will have the effect of constructing some of the limits and parameters within which decodings will operate' (Hall 1980: 135).

Having defined the hegemonic meaning inscribed in the media message as 'preferred' in this way, Hall can proceed to define the three possible decoding positions. The *dominant* reading occurs 'when the viewer takes the connoted meaning . . . full and straight', and is therefore ideologically dominated by the encoded meaning. The *negotiated* reading is an ambivalent reading with 'a mixture of adaptive and oppositional elements'. The *oppositional* reading is one in which the viewer makes sense of the TV message 'within some alterna- tive framework of reference' (Hall 1980: 136–8).

One of the first, and still most perceptive, critiques of the encoding/decoding model came from David Morley, one of the pioneers of empirical reception research, whose study of the audience of the British current affairs programme, *Nationwide* (Morley 1980), was a direct – and on the whole successful – attempt to try out Hall's model in practice. The study demonstrated that audience groups from different class backgrounds did to some extent decode the hegemonically encoded *Nationwide* programme in ways that could be meaningfully categorized as dominant, negotiated and oppositional, although 'class position . . . in no way directly correlates with' the three decoding positions (Morley 1992: 118).

Nevertheless, the *Nationwide* study also made it clear to Morley that the model suffered from a number of shortcomings (Morley 1981). One of these stems from the model's origin in the sociological theory of Parkin (1971), which was designed to explain different moral responses to class inequality in a capitalist society. The model is therefore narrowly concerned with the ideological processes of class struggle, to the exclusion of other equally relevant social categories like gender, ethnicity and age.

This leads to another shortcoming, because the model's stress on processes of ideological struggle biases it in favour of the more factual textual genres. It simply makes more sense intuitively to most people that news and current affairs programmes, as opposed to enter- tainment and fiction programmes, should have an overall preferred meaning that can be labelled according to ideological tendency. For a more extensive critique and a suggestion of an alternative model, see Schrøder (2000).

## THE CONCEPT OF 'POLYSEMY'

'Ambiguity', according to dictionary definitions, usually means that a word or a text can be understood in different ways depending on the textual context or the situation of use. The related concept of 'polysemy', Greek for 'many meanings', which incorporates the notion of ambiguity, is used in reception research in order to define the kind of textual openness that allows different readers to actualize different meanings from a text, as a result of *the readers'* differentially developed interpretative repertoires, or codes (Jensen 1990; Dahlgren 1998).

The notion has been developed as challenge to the implicit or explicit 'monosemic' ('one meaning') perspective that has dominated much literary and cultural analysis, assuming that the skilled analyst is capable of discovering *the* meaning (manifest as well as latent) of the text, and that this inscribed meaning is identical with the meaning actualized consciously or subconsciously by those who read it. By contrast, adherents of the polysemic perspective celebrate the unpredictability and diversity of meanings that audiences may come up with (as with the Boston Tea Party incident related at the start of this chapter).

In his numerous writings about television in particular, John Fiske (1987, 1989) has argued that television is an inherently polysemic medium that invites a diversity of audience readings. He has advanced the argument that within the basic social constraints of cultural production under capitalism, viewers do have a relative autonomy to act as members of a 'semiotic democracy' (Fiske 1989: 76).

One example, of an Australian soap opera set in a women's prison (which Fiske borrows from Hodge and Tripp 1986), shows how audiences may 'rewrite' a TV programme so as to generate their own point of identification with programme material. Reception research among school students found that they rewrote a number of narrative components and positions in the serial in order to construct a similarity between the women's prison experience and their own subordinate school experience. For instance, they focused on the fact that pupils would not be in school if they didn't have to be there; pupils have no rights, for instance, they have to suffer unfair teachers; and there are silly rules that everyone tries to break.

Although polysemy is basically defined in semiotic terms, it often turns out, in analytical practice, to slide into the realm of ideology, because the audiences' rewriting of the encoded message implies logically that they cannot completely be the victims of a hegemonic force inscribed in the message. In this sense, the polysemic perspective can be seen as a spin-off from Hall's model, which simply capitalizes on the negotiated and, particularly, the oppositional types of reading.

Theoretically, however, polysemy and opposition must be seen as two distinct processes. *Polysemy* means the multiplicity of meanings that arises all the time from encounters with media content, usually without the individuals' conscious awareness, simply as a result of the inherent diversity of social semiosis. *Opposition* to a textual position perceived to reside in media content is a less frequent occurrence, which cannot happen without the individuals' conscious awareness of difference. It necessarily occurs in the face of a position that one acknowledges and then rejects. An oppositional reading is thus what Corner calls 'an active, aware reading *against* the rhetorical grain of the text' (Corner 1980: 80).

Therefore, however oppositional the students may be towards the school system, their rewriting of the Australian prison soap mentioned above is just polysemic, not oppositional, since it clearly *follows* the rhetorical grain of the serial narrative.

# TOWARDS A SOCIAL SEMIOTICS OF RECEPTION

One of the most important theoretical tasks facing reception research in recent years has been to develop an adequate semiotic foundation for audience sense-making processes. Such a foundation must take us all the way back to the level of the sign and be able to explain signifying processes across different types of sign, and to situate meaning in a social context. In other words, we need a social semiotic of reception, which is part of a general social semiotic of communication (Halliday 1978; Hodge and Kress 1988; Jensen 1995). Such a theory is, in many ways, identical with a modern discourse theoretical approach to mediated communication (Fairclough 1995).

We believe that Peirce's theory of semiotics constitutes a promising starting point for such an endeavour. While there are considerable areas of overlap, Peirce's theory is in some ways in contrast with Saussure's binary definition of the sign as consisting of a 'signifier' and a 'signified', which locates the sign's meaning in the structural relations of the sign system, and which is based on linguistic foundations. Therefore, a reception theory based on Saussure's theory deals awkwardly with the social (as opposed to the systemic) production of meaning, and is less than ideal for understanding non-verbal meanings.

Peirce's semiotic is 'triadic' in two different ways. First of all, it distinguishes between three different types of sign, called 'icon', 'index' and 'symbol', which enables it to understand both verbal and visual sign systems. Second, it defines the individual sign as a triadic entity, arising from the interrelations of three labelled components: the physical entity that our senses recognize as 'the sign', the mental image triggered by this sign in the communicator's mind, and the object in the real world represented by the sign:

> *A sign, or representamen, is something which stands to somebody for something in some respect or capacity. It addresses somebody, that is, creates in the mind of that person an equivalent sign. . . . That sign which it creates I call the interpretant of the first sign. The sign stands for something, its object.*

(Peirce 1985: 5)

The attraction of this theory for reception studies is simply that by defining signs as being always *for somebody*, it ties mediated meaning processes insolubly to the social practices of audiences in contexts of everyday life. It also holds that all signs are inherently polysemic, since the 'interpretant' is conceived as a new sign, with a new triadic relationship, and so on. Therefore, the meaning of media content completely depends upon the users' actualization of the 'sign potential' offered to them.

The theory also enables us to understand reception processes as simultaneously individual and communal. On the one hand, the meanings actualized by the individual viewer are a unique product of the interpretative repertoires arising from his or her discursive socialization, with all its coincidental biographical factors. On the other hand, Peirce insists that the meanings of signs are to a high degree stabilized through the working of the *interpretative communities* we belong to, and which ensure a relative unity of interpretation under conditions of polysemy. For a more detailed discussion of the suitability of Peircean semiotics for reception theory, see Jensen (1991b).

With this conceptual apparatus in our analytical armoury, we are in a much better position to explain the unity in diversity that Hall and Morley label the 'preferred reading', as a property of the audience, not the text. Morley insists that 'while the message is not an object with one real meaning, there are within it signifying mechanisms, which promote certain meanings, even one privileged meaning, and suppress others' (Morley 1992: 21). The problem with this claim is an epistemological one. Even if there were such a thing as a preferred reading coming from 'within the text', how can we know it? Epistemologically, the attempt to discover one privileged textual meaning is bound to fail, for the simple reason that not even the most skilled textual analysts can arrive at a characterization of a media text without reading it. Consequently, any property ascribed to the text is always unavoidably a property of the analyst's reading of that text, and therefore a product of the analyst's interpretative repertoires, which are marginally or substantially divergent from all other readings.

Within the Peircean framework of understanding, any meaning is understood as a product of the communicators' signifying processes, not of the text. Therefore, the preferred reading becomes simply that reading which is shared by most members of the audience, and the explanation of the relative unity of reading need only resort to the empirical fact that apparently a large number of people possessed interpretative resources that made them understand a given text in a uniform manner. With an example drawn from the reception study of corporate responsibility advertising presented in the previous chapter (see Figure 7.1), we could say that the preferred reading of the British informants was the 'cynical' one, which rejected the ethical message as untrustworthy, whereas the preferred reading of the Danish informants was merely 'sceptical'. Both of these preferred readings were in contrast to the 'sympathetic' reading that the corporate communicators had attempted to promote through the textual design of their ads.

When reception research is used as a pre-testing tool in communication campaigns or for product development in media organizations, the question of preferred readings is not just an academic one: unless there is found to be a near-match between the sender's intended meaning and the recipients' preferred meanings arising from their engagement with the media content offered, the original textual incarnation of the sender's intention will have to be adapted until it meets the desired response. Also, under these circumstances, the Peircean doctrine will prevail: the preferred meaning is indeed an empirical question.

## THE COGNITIVE APPROACH TO RECEPTION

While semiotic theory in one form or another has been the hegemonic one in the battle of theoretical foundations in empirical reception research, there has been a consistent plea for at least one other theoretical approach, namely that offered by cognitive psychology. Starting out with relatively narrow studies of viewers' comprehension and memory of TV news (Findahl and Höijer 1984; Graber 1984), through the 1990s, a sustained argument has been advanced by a handful of scholars in favour of a cognitive approach to reception, which explores the viewers' media experiences in a broader social and cultural context (Livingstone 1990; Höijer 1992, 1998; Hagen 1998b).

The cognitive approach has its theoretical foundation in schema theory, according to which we accumulate our knowledge about and understanding of social reality, including the media, in accordance with cognitive schema, or interpretative frames:

> *Schemas are complex types of cognitive structures representing generic social experiences and cultural knowledge. They contain the common and characteristic features of similar phenomena, for example similar objects, events, situations or discourses. . . . Cognitive schemas exist in the minds of individual subjects as psychic structure, but they are linked to the socio-cultural and historical realities. Schemas are developed from daily life experiences which in their turn reflect socio-cultural circumstances at a certain point in history.*

(Höijer 1992: 287, 289)

Schemas serve for the individual as a vital means of economizing on mental energy in the execution of everyday routines, including the encounter with media content, because new situations are made sense of in accordance with existing schemas of perception and understanding, functioning as structured but adaptable recipes for appropriate perception, response and conduct in specific situations.

As an example, Höijer (1992) found that Swedish viewers had developed a repertoire of schemas for the effortless management of different TV genres. Basically, viewers met news programmes within a horizon of expectations made up of 'reality frames', whereas domestic drama and US soap serials were met respectively with a 'could-be-reality frame' and a 'pure-fantasy frame' (these labels are ours, not Höijer's). She also found that while 'the viewers had a tendency to use a mix of cognitive schemas from various experience spheres' (i.e. domestic, occupational, educational, media) across the genres, 'there were differences between different viewers, as well as between different genres, in how predominant the schemas originating from different experience spheres were' (Höijer 1992: 294).

Frames or schemas for understanding are socially produced throughout the individual's lifetime, as they vary from and intersect with the schemas possessed by other individuals. The following quotation stresses this point about the simultaneous uniqueness and sharedness of schemas, which was also made above in connection with the social-semiotic concept of 'codes'. While reading the quotation, readers may substitute 'codes' for 'schemas' in order to try out the similarity of the semiotic and the cognitive approach.

133

*In some cases, these models and schemas are intersubjectively shared among individuals in a society, in a socially constituted group, or among individuals otherwise forming an 'interpretative community' constituted by shared experiences. In other cases, the mental models or schemas are subjective in a more idiosyncratic sense.*

(Höijer 1992: 286)

The affinity between the semiotic and cognitive approaches is thus close, as is also borne out by the compatibility of the findings they have produced. The preference of one over the other is therefore largely a question of one's academic upbringing and sense of heuristic value.

Before leaving the subject we shall look at an analytical concept from reception research that may be said to bridge the gap between these two approaches. This is the concept of the 'super theme' suggested by Jensen (1991a), who is an adherent of the social-semiotic approach. In a news reception study, he found that a complex story about a hostage exchange between the warring parties in a Latin American civil war was simplified, or stereotyped, by viewers with short education, because one of the hostages exchanged happened to be the president's daughter. This led some viewers to read the news story according to a 'class privilege' super theme, according to which 'When it's people high up, things can always be arranged' (respondent quotation in Jensen 1991a: 142).

Jensen defines a *super theme* as 'a proposition entailed by a set of propositions summing up a news story . . . from the recipient's perspective', a cognitive process that establishes 'a meaningful relationship between the world of politics and the world of everyday life'. As he observes, the notion of super theme 'resembles the psychological schemata found by some other studies of news' (Jensen 1991a: 144–5). The frequent occurrence of such super themes may remind us that democratic empowerment of the audience does not consist in simply adapting news content to fit their existing schemas for understanding public affairs. Journalists should not try to accommodate the uneducated viewers by supplying news narratives easily reducible to super-theme format, but should explore alternative ways of preserving both complexity and digestibility.

## LITERARY APPROACHES TO RECEPTION

The literary approach to reception is mainly distinguished by is near-complete abstention from empirical fieldwork exploring actual reception processes. Nevertheless, it has supplied a number of useful theoretical concepts that have informed the understanding of the reading process among empirical researchers.

Literary scholars interested in reception have focused on the text/reader relationship, as opposed to the traditional focus in literary studies on the literary text as an aesthetic object in its own right or as a product of the author's imagination. Literary reception work is usually seen as belonging to two different traditions: the German 'reception aesthetic' tradition developed especially by Wolfgang Iser and Robert Jauss on the one hand (Holub 1984), and American 'reader-response criticism' on the other (Suleiman and Crosman 1980). They share the view that literary meaning is a product of the reading process but, with the exception of the work of Norbert Groeben (1977), their analyses are not anchored in empirical studies of the reading process.

Iser's work (1974, 1978) is especially associated with the view that the literary text has a shaping influence on the reading by virtue of the embodiment within its 'textual strategies' of an *implied reader* (Holub 1984: 84). This concept has many points in common with Hall's 'preferred reading', with the 'reading positions' of the *Screen* film-theoretical tradition in Britain (see Moores 1993: 12), and also with Eco's notion of the *model reader*, being the author's anticipation of 'the possible reader . . . supposedly able to deal interpretatively with the expressions in the same way as the author deals generatively with them' (Eco 1979: 7). Jauss's work (1975, 1982) is mainly associated with the concept of the *horizon of expectation*, already used above in connection with the concept of cognitive schemas, because they can be seen as differently rooted attempts to describe the same real-world phenomena. Never strictly defined by Jauss himself, Holub suggests that '"horizon of expectations" would appear to refer to an intersubjective system or structure of expectations, a "system of references" or a mind-set that a hypothetical individual might bring to any text' (Holub 1984: 59). The term is useful for talking about any kind of pre-understanding of a generic or thematic kind that readers bring to the experience of a media text. In discourse-theoretical terms, we may translate it as the 'intertextual predispositions' affecting the reading of a new text.

Both Iser and Jauss explicitly denied the need for empirical work, which, as hermeneuticians at heart, they saw as a sell-out to positivist illusions about objectively verifiable readings (for a similar argument, see Pateman 1983). Groeben (1977), however, as already mentioned, embraced empirical work wholeheartedly, subscribing to theoretical tenets very much like the four defining characteristics of reception research mentioned at the beginning of this chapter.

The American scholar, Stanley Fish, can be seen as a highly entertaining, polemical exponent of theoretical work on reception, whose radical theoretical argument is spiced with striking anecdotal evidence (see especially Fish 1979). With the interpretative battles within the sub-communities of literary criticism as his example, Fish's extreme argument is that the text itself can mean anything; what the text (for instance, a poem) ultimately comes to mean for its reader is solely a result of the interpretative constraints imposed by the *interpretative community* within whose perimeter the reading takes place and its meaning is negotiated.

To Umberto Eco, the text is 'an empty form to which various possible senses can be attributed' (Eco 1979: 5). The reading process, therefore, becomes of paramount importance, which Eco theorizes by developing a graphic model of reading as a complex hermeneutic process involving the encounter of textual signs and readers' codes. His explanatory focus is on micro-textual decoding processes like inferences and disambiguation of specific textual items and passages, rather than on their situational and social context.

135

Eco also proposes a binary classification of texts that divides them into the broad categories of *open and closed texts*. Ostensibly, these categories are derived from their textual properties, as well as from their respective 'model readers': a 'closed' text (such as a romance novel or a TV serial) typically comes out of popular culture and is read by 'an average reader', whereas an 'open' text (Eco gives Joyce's *Finnegans Wake* as an example) comes out of the literary avant-garde and is read by an aesthetically schooled person.

While he strives to deliver a theoretical account of reading that is unbiased by traditional judgements of cultural value, Eco's theory nevertheless ends up by elevating the literary works of good taste, by reserving for them the positively loaded term of 'open', and denigrating the works of popular culture as 'closed', despite the fact that a majority of the population actually hold the key to opening them.

Moreover, the definitions of open and closed texts are self-contradictory in a peculiarly oxymoronic manner. The difficult 'open' text, Eco says, is really closed, since 'you cannot use the text as you want, but only as the text wants you to use it' (Eco 1979: 11), and only if you have the educational key needed to open it, which most people do not. Conversely, a 'closed' text is 'in fact open to any possible "aberrant" decoding' (Eco 1979: 8)! The typology is therefore confusing and unhelpful as a way of conceptualizing the text/reader relationship. As we see it, the question of the relative openness or closedness of a media product can only be answered through empirical study of actual readings.

# THE USES OF RECEPTION RESEARCH

What can reception research be used for? If one takes a look at its historical record, it is hard to miss the fact that, until recently, almost all published reception research has been conducted within academic institutions in accordance with the general purposes of research in the humanities and social sciences. Generally speaking, reception research has mainly been used for the scholarly illumination of contemporary media cultures, as reception research since about 1980 has striven to fill a gap in the overall understanding of mass-mediated communication processes, due to the massive absence of empirical research into the ways in which audience members experience media content. Since the late 1980s, reception research has been moving into more policy-oriented and commercial research areas in the communication field, as focus groups have become a more respectable research tool in the related areas of sociology, political science and marketing. Below we shall present a necessarily brief outline of academic, policy-oriented and commercial reception research, with the emphasis on the first of these. For a more detailed critical discussion of academic reception research, see Moores (1993) or Tulloch (2000).

## ACADEMIC RECEPTION RESEARCH

The early beginnings of reception research around 1980, in a number of different countries, were uniformly motivated by one concern: the desire to empower media audience members, or rather to explore the ways in which audiences already possessed an empowering potential in a fundamentally class-divided, patriarchal, white-centric society. The news reception studies of Morley (1980), Dahlgren (1981) and Lewis (1983) took their point of departure in a social analysis according to which western societies were organized as class societies, to the detriment of the majority of working people, for the benefit of a ruling elite. Because the elite groups maintain ideological power in part through their successful handling of the media discourses, the subordinate classes come to accept the existing order of things as natural and inevitable. But since the notion of ideological *struggle* was central to the late-Marxist analysis of society, it followed that the consent of the subordinate classes had constantly to be won, not least through the dissemination via the media of distorting and passivizing ideologies.

Somewhat crudely put, perhaps, the early reception researchers set out to find the pockets of resistance, in which the common man and woman were *not* taking the televised news 'full and straight', but were engaging in processes of negotiation or direct opposition (see the critical discussion of Hall (1973) above). The insights coming out of this research were quite encouraging for political radicals, as they demonstrated that the cultural critics' idea of the 'misled masses' of capitalist society was at best only a half-truth, because ordinary people were, in many cases, able to exercise sound judgement in their encounters with mediated ideologies.

At about the same time, other researchers were pursuing reception analysis with a critical, but less radical intent. Researchers like Findahl and Höijer (1984) in Sweden, and Jensen (1986, 1988, 1990) in Denmark, criticized the news for being difficult to understand for non-elite individuals, who were thus barred from the full exercise of their democratic rights. The reformist perspective adopted by these researchers, and later on by Lewis (1991), Hagen (1994) and Gavin (1998), addressed their critique towards the broadcasters, who were called upon to change their news presentation strategies in accordance with non-educated viewers' and listeners' needs. In some cases, reception researchers were invited by broadcast organizations to participate in experimental projects designed to increase the comprehensibility of the news by adapting the level of linguistic complexity and adopting more narrative, fiction-like news formats (Jensen 1987; Poulsen 1992). The democratic potential of factual programming was also the focus of Livingstone and Lunt's (1994) study of studio audience discussion programmes that explored viewers' involvement in and empowerment from such programmes.

Reception studies of TV fiction, especially soap operas, have on the whole shared the radical political commitments of the news studies, taking sides with various non-elite groups of viewers. However, their focus has been not on the viewers' participation in the democratic process, but rather on the ways in which serial fiction affects the production of cultural identities.

Gender has been an overriding concern of many feminist reception researchers, who have studied the ways in which various groups of women acquiesce to or oppose patriarchal portrayals of gender relations. An early example is Radway's (1984) study of the readers of popular romance novels in the United States, recommending the use of her findings in concrete consciousness-raising educational projects for women. Similar concerns are seen in Hobson's (1982) study of British housewives' use of soap operas, Ang's (1985) study of the *Dallas* experience among Dutch middle-class women, Gray's (1992) study among British housewives of the use of VCRs for circumventing male definitions of appropriate cultural tastes, and Hermes' (1995) study of Dutch women's use and experience of glossy magazines.

In some European countries, in which fears of Americanization have been strong since the 1920s, reception studies have explored the possible contribution of American serial fiction to the formation of cultural identities. The most groundbreaking study in this area is probably that of Liebes and Katz (1990), which explored the experience of *Dallas* among five different cultural groups in Israel, concluding that the imported serial is, to a large extent, hybridized with elements of the indigenous culture. Similar results were obtained by researchers in Denmark (Hjort 1986; Schrøder 1988) and Belgium (Biltereyst 1991). Sometimes it was found, through a comparison of the experiences of domestic and imported American drama, that on the whole the viewers' preference was clearly towards the former (Hjort 1986).

Other researchers have been concerned with the televisual representation of ethnicity, and the ways in which white and black viewers negotiate ethnic identities and stereotypes from popular situation comedy (Jhally and Lewis 1992). Still others have focused on genera-tional issues as they have investigated children's and young people's media experiences, and their possible influence on the formation of cultural identities and critical skills (Drotner 1991; Buckingham 1993; Livingstone and Bovill 2001). More and more studies are beginning to explore children's use of Internet media (Turkle 1995). More often than not, these studies use their results to study the implications for media literacy and media pedagogy (Buckingham 1998; Tufte 1998).

A general tendency of much of this work has been the recurring emphasis on the ability of popular audiences to adopt a critical stance towards the products offered by the cultural industries. As an example, Nava and Nava (1990) asked whether young people as consumers of advertising are 'discriminating or duped'. Their answer, based on reception research, emphasizes 'the very considerable though untutored skills which young people bring to bear in their appreciation of advertisements and which they exercise individually and collectively . . . in millions of front rooms throughout the country – and indeed the world' (Nava and Nava 1990: 21).

Similarly, irrespective of their specific area of interest, many of the studies mentioned above have inscribed themselves into the general postmodern move to dismantle the tra-ditional divide between elite and popular culture, as they have argued for the rehabilita-tion of popular taste as expressed in the pleasurable enjoyment of romance novels, television serials or women's magazines (Schudson 1987). Along such lines, Schrøder (1992), based on a cross-cultural reception study of the primetime soap opera *Dynasty* in Denmark and the US, argued that we must abandon the traditional, universal idea of cultural quality as being the same for everyone. Instead he proposed that valid verdicts about cultural quality must be based on the audience experience of a cultural product, and be seen always as 'quality *for someone*' (Schrøder 1992: 211). It was therefore concluded that *Dynasty* held cultural quality for those audiences who took from it an ethically and aesthetically enriching, as well as pleasurable, experience.

## POLICY-ORIENTED RECEPTION RESEARCH

Many academic reception studies have used their findings not only to point to the need for further research (and few have abstained from the temptation to make this call!), but also to draw out important policy implications, for a country's provision of news to ensure a healthy democratic process, for the need to institute systematic media literacy education in the public school system, or for cultural policy in general. The studies of popular television serials mentioned above thus issued a call for cultural respect of all tastes, and therefore for the need to revise the Danish public service broadcaster's cultural policy, which for years had only grudgingly accepted the need to accommodate the popular audiences' preference for programmes with a light content and style:

> *To the extent that ordinary people are becoming, or coming to be seen as, aesthetically resourceful players in their cultural environment, a bit of populism might be quite an attractive proposition, a tribute – long overdue – to that majority of the population who have for years tolerated and paid for the consequences of paternal cultural elitism.*

(Schrøder 1992: 216)

On the whole, however, there have been few examples of genuine policy-oriented research into audience reception processes, in the sense of national or local government-commissioned research projects intended to function as a knowledge-building input to legislative or administrative processes. The single most important reason has been the lasting low credibility of qualitative research in political and administrative circles, which has been caused by an insufficient understanding on the part of policy-makers that the coin of qualitative research has both a strong and a weak side (see Chapter 2). However, there are indications that such understanding is now emerging, as focus groups have come into fashion as a tool for the fine-tuning of political as well as commercial strategic communication (Krueger 1994; Greenbaum 1998).

As an example, in 1994 the Danish government's Commission on the Media commissioned a series of reports, many of them based on existing reception work, others undertaking new empirical work, in order to map the Danish media landscape as a first step towards designing a new public media policy. One study carried out a large-scale reception study, with 27 family households each interviewed twice, of the ways Danish citizens used the entire range of media and programmes available as a resource both in everyday life and for political participation (Schrøder 1995; a summary in English is included in Schrøder 1999). It was the main objective of the study to explore the role of the media in the lives of democratically 'active' and 'passive' citizens.

Among the many findings of the study, a picture was drawn of the everyday media habits of one particularly information-weak group – citizens whose low level of information-seeking and non-participation in democratic organizations or movements positioned them on the margins of political and social life. This portrait was used for the proposal of media policy measures, including recommendations in the areas of the national media structure, as well as presentational formats, which would at least hold the potential to empower this group as future participants in public life, although obviously the role of the media in redressing sociostructural information weakness is necessarily a modest one.

## COMMERCIAL RECEPTION RESEARCH

Little is publicly known about the size, scope and results of commercial reception research, as indeed about other kinds of commercial research, which is, as a rule, classified as confidential for competitive reasons. There is no doubt, however, that a vast number of projects have been carried out in organizational and commercial settings, with the aim of pre-testing or fine-tuning the content of a communicative product (such as a campaign), following a procedure very much like that of reception research.

The main difference between academic and commercial research has to do with the quality and depth of analysis, as costs must usually be kept low. This difference is seen most clearly in respect of the analysis of focus-group data, which is often not based on full transcripts of recorded interviews, but on notes taken by a research assistant, either during the session or immediately afterwards, based on the tape (Bloor et al. 2001). Another difference concerns the more simplistic aim of much commercial research ('Should we use this picture for the ad or not?'), whereas academic research pursues more complex cultural issues with a high tolerance of discursive ambivalence in the data.

Sometimes quasi-commercial reception research is carried out by public institutions in order to assess their past performance and general standing with clients or customers. This was the case with a large-scale study done by the British broadcaster, the BBC, in 1995, which concluded that 'without a strong bond of understanding with our audience we run the risk of self-indulgence, elitism, and in the age of broadcasting choice, irrelevance' (BBC 1995).

The most frequent type of reception research within institutions of communications is caused by the need to reach increasingly recalcitrant and spoiled audiences, who are being flooded with a deluge of mediated communication. For instance, in the age of information clutter, it is vital for a national broadcaster to meet the interests and preferences of specific audience segments, not (as in the past) simply to broadcast supposedly edifying content to the general national audience. Therefore, a national broadcaster will pre-test, many, if not all, of its new programmes and monitor the continued success of its existing programmes.

Davidsen-Nielsen (1996) thus – in a rare published study of commercial research – reports on the pre-testing experience of a planned natural science magazine-format TV programme, at a time when programme-makers, not being used to this kind of critical feedback on their work, were still sceptical of the usefulness of focus groups as a programme development tool. With running TV programmes, a critical evaluation may be carried out with a combination of quantitative and qualitative methods, as when a qualitative study may seek to illuminate the reasons for low viewing figures among coveted audience segments delivered by TV-meter analysis.

Such studies are not error-proof. A major national broadcaster, which had produced an expensive and aesthetically advanced mini-series for a mainly youthful audience, aged 15 to 30, found through focus-group research that the series also held an appeal to older audience groups, and consequently placed it in a primetime slot in the programme schedule. When audience figures turned out to be disastrously low, the series had to be moved to a late-night slot known to be a niche for the young audience.

Communication students sometimes succeed in obtaining permission to carry out reception studies for advertisers, campaigners, publishers or broadcasters, which gives them a unique chance to work with real-world communication problems while getting credits for their degree. For instance, a student at Simon Fraser University in Vancouver carried out a focus-group study of current and potential donors' responses to a new campaign by the charity organization, The United Way (I. Roe 1996). Students at Roskilde University in Denmark did a reception study of a youth lifestyle magazine among three differently profiled youth groups, ending up with recommendations for the editorial content and visual style of a planned relaunch of the magazine (Olsen 2000).

## THE FUTURE OF RECEPTION RESEARCH

With more than 20 years' experience, reception research has now consolidated itself as an established research tradition, still developing but with a solid theoretical and methodological foundation, and an accumulating record of substantial findings. The immediate future of reception research appears to be characterized by three trends that can also be seen as ways of facing the new theoretical, methodological and analytical challenges that have emerged as a joint result of past omissions of a scholarly kind and emerging phenomena in the media landscape.

One trend has to do with the need for a holistic approach to audiences that considers the relationships between the main stages in the overall communication process: senders, texts and recipients. During its pioneering days, reception research found it necessary to, somewhat myopically, concentrate on audiences and fieldwork in an isolated way, usually with a glance at media content but almost never considering the senders. The holistic perspective is an obvious necessity for commercial reception research, for whom the whole purpose of communication is to 'get across'. But also in academic circles, it is again, in a return to Hall's (1973) dual emphasis on encoding and decoding, being realized that communication is a process running from encoding to decoding. The project of Deacon, Fenton and Bryman (1999) is a case in point, as its title shows: 'From inception to reception: the natural history of a news item'.

The second trend is towards more comparative work. Now that a number of studies have provided a knowledge base about reception processes in individual countries, the time has come to make comparisons across cultures. This tendency is also a natural consequence of current developments in economic, political and cultural relations, with the nations of Europe becoming more integrated within the EU and therefore inviting comparative studies, and with the overall process of globalization. The trend is witnessed in a number of existing studies, such as the Europe-wide study of children and the media, directed by Sonia Livingstone (Livingstone and Bovill 2001), and the parallel study of TV news in seven countries across the world, directed by Klaus Bruhn Jensen (Jensen 1998).

The third trend is caused by the increasing role of interactive communication media over the last decade, and leads to an orientation towards the uses and experiences of communication on the Internet. The main challenge facing reception research about interactive communication has to do with the bringing together of two modes of inquiry that are still, to some extent, leading segregated lives: on the one hand, the testing of technological communication systems known as 'usability research' (Nielsen 1993), which focuses on the navigational aspects of computerized communication; on the other hand, the more traditional kind of reception research that explores the users' meaning processes as they are anchored in situational and contextual circumstances in the users' cultural environment (Stald 1999).

Finally, reception research shares with other approaches to audience research the challenge of researching not just how people use and experience the Internet, but also how to use Internet communication itself as a research tool (Mann and Stewart 2000). Some of these issues will be taken up again in Chapter 18.

# Chapter Nine

# Reception research toolbox: the ☐ qualitative interview

Reception research methodology is predicated upon the qualitative research interview, which is used as a discursive generator for obtaining an insight into the interpretative repertoires at the disposal of the informants as they make sense of a specific media product. The interview is thus, ultimately, a vehicle for bringing forward the media-induced meanings of the informants' lifeworld, but in order to achieve this goal it is the first priority of the interview, in individual depth-interviews as well as in group interviews, to make the informants cooperate in the discursive production of meaning. Before starting on the thematic agenda of the interview guide, it is therefore the interviewer's job to make the informants feel at ease with the situation so they will pour freely from the discursive resources available to them in the area of study.

It is with this dual purpose in mind that the interviewer in the ethical advertising study (see Box 9.1; the study is discussed in Chapter 7) tries to frame the interview with a 40-year-old British school principal as a friendly conversation in which small talk and gossip may occur naturally. The interviewer has learnt that, by coincidence, this informant, Peter, knows another informant, Alan, who has a problem with his foot, and uses this topic as an ice-breaking device, before embarking on the interview proper (lines 1–7). At a later stage during the interview, which takes place at the school where Peter works, the interviewer realizes that the informant is very interested in bringing computers into the classroom, and asks a few questions about this – strictly irrelevant – issue, in order to stimulate and simulate the flow of natural conversation (lines 56–59).

Everyday conversations are characterized by many other features than *small talk* and *non-planned topic development*, such as *symmetrical turn-taking patterns* and the interlocutors' *reliance on shared knowledge*. The awareness of shared knowledge often enables people to anticipate the other person's reply in the very way they phrase their questions, often termed 'leading questions' in the research literature ('You didn't like the new Chinese restaurant, did you?'). One way to cast a research interview as a simulation of a natural conversation is for the interviewer to make a point of using the features routinely employed in everyday conversation, including the volunteering of personal observations and the asking of 'leading questions'. Indeed, the absence of such features will inevitably formalize the research interview, and possibly induce informants to mobilize more protective filters in their rendering of the media experience. Conversely, a research interview successfully cast as a symmetrical conversation will not deter interviewees from disagreeing with the implicit drift of the leading question, as lines 64–69 of the interview show, although – as always – the expression of disagreement is a delicate matter that may require the expression of initial agreement in order not to threaten the 'face' of the interlocutor.

The interview excerpt in Box 9.1 also demonstrates how the interview serves as a vehicle for the primary purpose of the interview, i.e. to obtain access to the informant's experience of and attitudes to the various ethical ads presented to him by the researcher, and thus to produce the insight that the study was designed to achieve. In the context of the interpretative framework produced by this study, his utterances show how his perceptions of the BP, Volkswagen and Toshiba ads can be categorized respectively as 'sympathetic', 'agnostic' and 'cynical'. The interviews were both intended to illuminate people's experience of examples of specific ads that invoked an ethical stance, and to address the more general question of increased business responsibility in environmental and community affairs. The excerpt shows how the informant's response to the BP ad is used as a natural pretext for moving from the particular to the general (lines 35–40).

Incidentally, one of the interview sequences (lines 26–30) shows how this interview is not in all details a perfect example of a qualitative reception interview – but also a guide to the avoidance of one of the frequent mistakes made by interviewers: forgetting to probe. After the interviewee has talked at some length about the Volkswagen ad, the interviewer lets him take complete control of the conversation as he proceeds to the next ad in his pile, the Vauxhall Astra ad, which he then puts aside almost immediately after two brief remarks. He thus leaves the study without any substantial data about the Vauxhall ad. A possible explanation of the interviewer's negligence here may be that, at this early stage of the interview, he is over-keen to preserve the conversational symmetry, and doesn't want to appear to intrude in the interviewee's train of thought. Perhaps he intended to return to the Vauxhall ad at a later stage – and then forgot.

This chapter will present some of the tools that together make up the toolbox of the qualitative reception interview. But, like the methodology chapter in the previous, ethnographic section of the book, it should not be seen as a 'recipe' for successful reception research, outlining the exact and necessary ingredients and processes that the prospective researcher *must* follow towards the perfect reception study. Rather the chapter is to be thought of as a 'traveller's guide' to a particular research territory, produced by previous, experienced travellers who know the consequences of following one path rather than another, but without being able to prescribe one route as inherently better than another. The best route for any traveller is that leading to the destination he or she desires to reach at the end of the day, and each journey has a different destination.

Through research design, the destination is reached by making endless methodological decisions, big and small, all of which entail gains and losses, and which therefore all involve trade-offs, a weighing of the pros and cons that will inevitably affect the outcome of your study. Thus individual interviews will enable you to illuminate aspects of meaning not likely to be illuminated by focus-group interviews, and vice versa, just as the choice of focus groups composed of members of a social network, who know each other, will illuminate different aspects than focus groups composed of strangers. The only prescriptive

**Box 9.1    Excerpt from reception interview from the ethical advertising study reported in Chapter 7 (Schrøder 1997) (for a short characterization of the ads mentioned see Box 7.2)**

*Interviewer*: So these ads were waiting for you when you got back?

*Interviewee*: Yes, yes, with a little card on top saying that you had been trying to get in contact (. . .)

*Ir*: Have you heard that Alan has broken his foot?

5 *Ie*: Yes, because I saw Jane, his wife, yesterday as well. He has only broken his toe or he has got gout, they're not really sure which it is [laughter]. So he's suffering a bit at the moment He is in quite a bit of pain.

- - -

*Ir*: Right, so you put that one first.

10 *Ie*: Yes, I .. I went through them, looking at the ones which appealed to me the most, and relevant to me the most. It was .. the first two were both about cars in fact, and both of them seem to offer, well, obviously cars, most people like cars [*Ir*: Yes], but it was just the .. I've had a few Volkswagens myself and I'm always inter-

15 ested in Volkswagen. And I think that was .. it struck me as being, you know, makes you read it. Quite poignant, sitting with a baby in front of it. I thought that was quite good. But basically when I read them all through, they actually said similar things. They were both offering similar things, which was actually that they had started to

20 think about the environment, I mean I think cars could do a lot more and the motor industry can do a lot more about the environment [unclear], but they're trying, which is quite relevant. And I thought again that was quite a striking ad .. the way it came across.

25 *Ir*: Yeah.

*Ie*: This one [going on to talk about the Vauxhall ad] is designed to make you think you know driving the new Astra makes you change the face of cycling, it is quite clever really. So that was the reason I chose that one. And the next one [taking up the DishwashElectric

30 ad] I chose purely because I liked the image of it . . .

- - -

*Ir*: BP's next?

*Ie*: BP's next .. em .. not for any reason in the ad .. but I think that out of all the oil companies BP do try and do something for the environment, I mean they are very conscious about it and their ads

35 always strike you as being **concerned** . . . I think they could do a lot more but .. I have always been *reasonably* impressed with what they do and what they offer as a service.

## Box 9.1 continued

*Ir*: Do you think they are an exception, or is business in general becoming quite a lot more responsible towards society than what they
40 used to be?

*Ie*: I think there *is* a trend towards becoming more responsible, but . . .

- - -

That one [talking about the Toshiba ad] I put in there basically .. well I .. it's neither here or there really. It says 'Not only do we help
45 clean up the business world, we help to clean up the world itself', and I really don't see how a computer does that a great deal. I mean it is offering to be environmentally friendly but it doesn't do very much at all [chuckle] . . .

*Ir*: So you think it's just a token gesture to the environment?
50 *Ie*: Yeah, how can a computer affect the environment, they're just trying to make you read it. I think it's just a clever trick. [*Ir*: Yeah] But .. obviously computers are one of the things that play a large part in anything that goes on these days. . .  You know, we have to, with the National Curriculum we have to incorporate them as much as
55 possible into the classroom as possible.

*Ir*: How has your school managed to get such a considerable number of computers?

*Ie*: Well, funding is difficult, just to have computers for one classroom is going to be 10,000 pounds . . .

- - -

60 [on the issue of consumer activism against industrial pollution]

*Ie*: Sewage pumped out to sea is not deemed the best way of doing things these days. When you think about it it's quite appalling. But in Victorian times they didn't even think about it, they just did it.

*Ir*: Yeah, that's, they didn't think about it, that's right. But then it
65 seems that in some ways, with some products British consumers are prepared to use their spending power to influence . . . producers?

*Ie*: Ehm in some ways, yeah, I mean, yes, you're right. But I mean if things like, as far as using gas and oil and coal and that, they don't worry so much, they just use it.

---

*Transcription conventions*

.. slight pause longer than a full stop

(. . .) short sequence of interview left out

- - - substantial sequence of interview left out

**Bold** word stress

advice one can really give in matters of research design, is to always be reflexive about the likely consequences for one's data of the decisions one has to make.

## THE EPISTEMOLOGY OF RECEPTION RESEARCH

Reception research is the empirical study of the social production of meaning in people's encounter with media discourses. Contrary to media ethnography, reception research does not study media use as it happens in the natural situations of everyday life. Contrary to the methodology of survey research, reception research does not expose people to a finite set of questions with pre-given response options. Instead, it explores media experiences through the medium of extended talk. It seeks to illuminate audience practices and experiences, by getting those involved to verbalize them in the non-natural but open situation of the qualitative research interview, in which informants have considerable power to influence the agenda. As with other methodologies in audience research, both the data and the findings of a reception study should therefore be seen as discursive constructions produced jointly by researchers and informants as they interact in the research encounter, and by the researcher interpreting the 'fossilized' discursive exchange that we call the interview transcript.

Reception research is as adamant about securing good data as any other methodological approach. Any study should therefore live up to the standard criteria of reliability, validity and generalization, as they are conventionally defined by the qualitative research community (see Frey et al. 1991; Lindlof 1995; Kvale 1996; Silverman 2000). Throughout this chapter we shall demonstrate how these credibility criteria may be fulfilled through multiple methodological decisions. Here we shall say but a few introductory words about each criterion.

The criterion of *reliability* means that the data gathering and interpretation should follow systematic procedures that strive to eliminate unwarranted subjective bias from the study, even as the data are jointly produced by the researcher and the informants in the interview encounter. In plain terms, the study should be conducted in such a manner as to convince readers that its findings report on the informants' media experiences, not on the researcher's preconceived notions of how people experience the media product. The research report should therefore, in a sense, enable readers to accompany the researcher into the field, in order to see what went on there as the data was jointly produced, and to 'read over the shoulder' as the researcher interprets the transcript. In short, the research process itself should be made transparent and adequately documented in the report.

*Validity* is an equally prominent concern, as it has to do with the faithfulness of the map drawn by the reception study to the real-world landscape of meaning that it claims to represent. As discussed in Chapter 3, more positivist-inclined researchers would phrase this as the *truth*fulness of the analysis, the extent to which the interview has been able to bring forward the informants' innermost experiences and evaluations of the media product.

147

In a discursive realist approach to social research like ours, which has abandoned the notion of essential and permanent truth in social and cultural affairs, we do not see the interview as a device for digging out the core of the informants' experience, but rather as a catalyst for activating the palette of discursive repertoires available to informants, in connection with a specific media product. These discursive repertoires, which represent what we just called the 'landscape of meaning', are constantly changing as people negotiate their inherent ambivalences under different situational and social circumstances.

Consequently, any 'map' drawn of such fluctuating landscapes, on the basis of an interview, can only be seen as a snapshot of flux. The quality of the resulting picture of the media experience depends on the extent to which the set-up and conduct of the interview induces informants to participate in a spirit of spontaneity and authenticity. It is the job of research design to ensure that these elements may unfold in the interview situation.

In qualitative research, *generalization* has nothing to do with representativeness, as no qualitative reception study has yet lived up to the sample-size requirements necessary to match this objective – for practical reasons of resources, or because they have had different, theory-generating objectives. This does not mean, however, that even very small-scale studies may not have wide-ranging, 'general' implications for how we think about media influences. One example is reception studies of popular fiction (Radway 1984; Schrøder 1992), which have countered prevalent myths about how individuals in mass society use entertainment media for nothing but 'amusing themselves to death' (Postman 1985).

In applied reception research, as it is carried out in media companies, which need guidance for strategic action, research findings are often given representative status when an advertising campaign is revised, or the components of a TV show are altered, in light of the verdicts of a handful (or even less than that) of focus groups. In academic reception research, the criterion of generalization takes two forms: one has to do with making *internal analytical generalizations* about the findings, as when the diversity of opinion found in a study of, say, 16 informants is interpretatively reduced to a small number of 'types' of reader (as was the case with the ethical advertising study); the other has to do with making *external analytical generalizations* about, for instance, news reception, on the basis of an interpretative comparison between one's own findings and those of other studies of the same kind of media product, in order to arrive at a more general picture of news reception as a sociocultural phenomenon.

# DESIGNING A RECEPTION STUDY

## THE FOCUS OF RECEPTION RESEARCH

A reception study aims to find out how people make sense of a particular media product, such as a news programme, an advertising campaign, a soap opera or a computer game. It may also extend its scope towards the exploration of not just the smallest unit of media fare, such as one TV programme or one campaign, but address the sense-making question towards higher-level units, like a whole genre (news, soap opera, magazine fashion pages) or a whole media outlet (a niche TV channel or a magazine publication). A few reception studies have extended the scope even further, encroaching on the territory of media ethnography in aiming to explore people's uses, taste preferences and experience of one media, such as television (Morley 1986), or even the whole range of media, as part of their daily, weekly and seasonal routines (Schrøder 1999). The difference from media ethnography proper lies in the exclusive use of one or two two-hour household interviews about media uses, as opposed to the extended time horizon of the participant observation method we described in Chapter 6. Here we shall be centrally concerned with the design of reception studies of individual media products, with sideways glances at other focuses when appropriate.

## THE RESEARCH INTERVIEW AS 'SPEECH EVENT'

As already emphasized, your first priority in planning a reception interview is to get people to speak from the depths of their hearts about their experience of the media product you are exploring. In order to accomplish this, it is necessary to conceptualize the reception interview in very practical terms as a 'speech event', i.e. a cultural occasion 'identified primarily by the kind of talking that takes place' (Spradley 1979: 55). Other kinds of speech event are a doctor–patient interview, a lecture, different kinds of telephone conversation, a job interview and a lunch conversation at work.

These, and a host of other speech events in daily life, are quite well-established 'genres', defined by rules and conventions that are both fixed and flexible: 'All speech events have cultural rules for beginning, ending, taking turns, asking questions, pausing, and even how close to stand to other people' (Spradley 1979: 55). A speech event can thus be said to follow a loose and largely subconscious script that the participants have internalized as a performative guide, which they may activate whenever they become involved in the particular kind of event.

What the prospective reception researcher has to bear in mind is that the people recruited as informants for a reception study have probably never had to perform in the speech event of the 'research interview' before, so they enter the interview setting as novices, but with more or less well-founded preconceptions of what is required of them, drawn from previous encounters with other types of event, which belong under the general label of 'interview'. It is therefore crucial that the researcher both defines the speech event of the interview explicitly to the informant, prior to the interview, and that, during the interview, he casts the informant conversationally in the participant role required by the study.

Although there is a range of possible roles that the researcher may choose for the reception interview, we believe, as a general recommendation – which one may deviate from if required by the circumstances – that the most productive way to conceptualize the reception interview is as a friendly conversation between strangers. This is the kind of speech event that sometimes occurs between fellow passengers on aeroplanes or trains, who get talking and take the opportunity to spend a few hours pleasantly in good company. In such a situation, one may achieve a remarkable degree of mutual openness and confidence, in spite of – or maybe because of – the fleetingness of the encounter. Long conversational sequences may cast one participant as the narrator of personal experiences, interspersed with encouraging interjections and questions from the other; at other times, the conversational turn-taking may be more symmetrical and take the form of an alternating dialogue.

Obviously there are also differences between the friendly conversation and the research interview, notably the explicit purpose of the latter, permanently present, to discover the cultural experiences of the informant. This leads to an inherent asymmetry, because the researcher has, to some extent, pre-planned the event and also needs to control the direction and progression of the encounter. While these differences remain, we believe that the framework of the friendly conversation is the one that should be presented to the informants, right from the recruiting stage and until the interview is over. One may even decide to completely avoid the word 'interview', as different informants are likely to derive undesirable performative scripts from this term, and consistently characterize the interview to informants simply as a 'talk' or a 'conversation' about the media product. A focus group may require further explicit directions that stress the desirability of having participants discuss the issues amongst themselves, without constant prompting by the moderator. Here a comparison with a lunch conversation at work may be the everyday script needed to produce the desired kind of interaction.

## CHOOSING THE LOCATION OF THE INTERVIEW

The concern with interactional symmetry means that in choosing the location of the interview, one should aim to find a setting in which informants are likely to minimize the normative controls easily mobilized in an unknown speech event, i.e. a place where the informant feels 'at home'. Evidently, for individual interviews, the most natural choice of such a setting is the informant's home – unless this solution is met with objections from the informant. Then one should try to find another location that may count as a kind of 'home turf', i.e. a place where the informant holds a kind of interactional power that may counterbalance that inherently held by the researcher, for instance, the informant's workplace after working hours.

For group interviews, the home solution is the natural choice if the family or household is chosen as the fieldwork unit. For other groups, an interview can often be arranged in a participant's home, if the group unit is small, i.e. from two to four people. In the case of 'network interviews', with people who know each other beforehand (such as two or three married couples) one may even succeed in getting one of the couples to host a group with up to six participants. For 'focus groups', composed of strangers, which sometimes include eight to ten people, one should try to find some kind of neutral ground for the interview.

A university setting should always be considered the second, or third, best solution, as many people are likely to feel awkward, overawed and inferior in the halls of scholarly excellence. In comparison, the choice of a meeting room in a community centre or non-luxurious hotel is likely to be more conducive to the creation of a relaxed interview atmosphere. In many cases, however, there will be practical limits (money, time, distance) to the choice of setting, and an institutional location may be the only feasible one. Many studies of young people's use of the media have had to conduct interviews in the school environment, even when the study aimed to explore their media uses and experiences outside of the school environment, thereby, to some extent, imposing a frame of mind on the youngsters that one might see as alien, and possibly counterproductive. The final adoption of such a solution, however, should only take place after more ideal venues have turned out to be impossible. And in the subsequent analysis of the interview data, one should be alert to and explicitly discuss the likely discursive consequences of the choice of setting for the validity of the findings.

## INDIVIDUAL VERSUS GROUP INTERVIEWS

Both individual interviews and group interviews are excellent ways of eliciting people's discursive repertoires for making sense of their media experiences. Much of the data that you would get out of doing a series of individual interviews and a series of focus-group interviews about the same media product would be quite similar. But there are also significant differences between the two approaches that make them suitable for different purposes. Sometimes it can be a good idea, resources permitting, to use both, one after the other, to reap the benefits of their respective strengths. In the following, we shall outline a few of the salient differences between the two, while referring the interested reader to more extensive presentations of their strengths and weaknesses, and the practical procedures of using them, in the research literature (Merton and Kendall 1946; McCracken 1988; Morgan 1988; Hansen et al. 1998; Bloor et al. 2001).

The first thing to bear in mind is that while the individual interview is always more or less the same kind of speech event, because it always involves just an interviewer and an interviewee, group interviews can be many different things, precisely because they can be many different sizes, and bring together people with many different kinds of background and relationship to each other. It thus makes a great difference, not least to the moderator, whether one convenes a group of four colleagues or a group of 12 strangers. In the former, there is no need to spend time breaking the ice, whereas in the other, one should allow for an introductory phase in which the participants get to know each other superficially. More substantially, with the group of colleagues, the moderator will have a harder time raising their extensive shared knowledge to the level of explicitness, while a group of strangers will automatically be a lot more explicit about their individual values and tastes, in order to be able to discuss the issues with each other at all. At the same time, in such a big group, the moderator will need a lot of experience in turn-taking management, in order to divide the talking time equally between the participants. For this reason, we recommend that student reception projects choose either individual interviews or small-group interviews of three or four participants, so that the situation does not get unwieldy.

The main difference between individual and group interviews lies in their producing, respectively, 'accounts *about* action' and 'accounts *in* action' (Halkier 2002). In the individual interview, the informant *reports* to the researcher about his or her negotiation of the meaning of a media product, as it normally happens, sometimes in the company of others, in the social contexts of daily life. In the group interview, informants collectively *enact* a negotiation of the meaning of a media product, which is designed to simulate, and thus to reflect, the way the social production of meaning normally takes place in interpersonal encounters, in more extended spans of time and contexts of space. This is the reason why some reception researchers, who may get perilously close to the illusion that groups can be a near-perfect replica of naturally occurring social interaction, have a preference for group interviews. In presenting their cross-cultural study of *Dallas*, the globally successful 1980s American soap opera, for which they used groups consisting of three married couples who knew each other beforehand, Liebes and Katz argue their case like this:

> *Group dynamics are such that opinion and participation are not equally weighted; some people have disproportionate influence. But real life is like that: opinions are not so much the property of individuals as public-opinion polling would have us think: Opinions arise out of interaction, and 'opinion leaders' have disproportionate influence.*

(Liebes and Katz 1990: 29)

As we see it, however, this characteristic does not make group interviews better than individual interviews. In spite of its pretensions to naturalism, the group interview is not a replica of any authentic social situation; in spite of their naturalistic composition and choice of location, Liebes and Katz's groups remain an artificially created, but fruitful situation for the social production of concentrated data about mediated meaning processes.

Conversely, the individual interview should not be seen as a method that is unable to capture the social production of meaning, just because it appears to celebrate uniquely individual media experiences. The meaning repertoire of any individual informant is a product of their lifelong immersion in multiple social discourses, which they bring with them into the reception interview, and which permeates and anchors anything they say about the media product and their use of it.

The group interview is a generator of diversity and consensus at the same time. As Bloor et al. put it,

> *In late-modern societies where identity is reflexive but behaviour remains normative, albeit subject to a widening range of influences, focus groups provide a valuable resource for documenting the complex and varying processes through which group norms and meanings are shaped, elaborated and applied.*

(Bloor et al. 2001: 17)

The very fact that the group interview brings together a considerable number of 'others' (as opposed to there being only one 'other' in the individual interview) makes for diversity, many different ways of doing and perceiving things being thrown on the table for comment, agreement, disagreement, negotiation: 'The hallmark of focus groups is the explicit use of the group interaction to produce data and insights that would be less accessible without the interaction found in the group' (Morgan 1988: 12). Groups are therefore always likely to produce the element of unpredictability that enriches the analysis, taking it beyond the limits of what the researcher was capable of anticipating as being of interest in the area of study.

But group interviews are equally characterized by being consensus machines, as they make participants conform to one of the general laws of human collectivity: to strive for harmony and agreement. This is not because humans are naturally peaceful and conflict-avoiding beings, but because the natural pursuit of self-respect and dignity in encounters with others makes us engage in complicated and subtle struggles, in which our first priority is not to lose face, and also to recognize and respect this priority in our fellow humans. It is important to realize that while group members do aim for a consensus of opinion and taste, they engage in sophisticated and continuous discursive struggles in order to make their own opinion and taste prevail. Focus groups may thus be deemed to be unsuccessful, both if they are too polarized and if they turn out to harbour too much conformity. It is especially at the recruiting stage that one has a chance to avoid either extreme.

Individual interviews are frequently called 'depth-interviews', a label that clearly singles out the advantage of interviewing people individually. The depth obtained is, first of all, due to the objective circumstance that an individual informant gets to say far more, and has greater opportunity to develop an argument or a narrative in an hour than any group member does in the same amount of time. More qualitatively, the one-to-one situation also enables the researcher to ask much more detailed questions that may be tailored to the specific circumstances divulged by the informant.

The individual interview also avoids the 'spiral of silence' effect that may prevent idiosyncratic or controversial views and experiences from being expressed in a group context. The individual interview may thus be the best choice for a researcher who wishes to illuminate a sensitive issue, located beyond the discursive range of the socially acceptable or the politically correct – or an issue that is felt by the individual to be too sensitive to talk about in the presence of others, other than a researcher who grants the informant full anonymity.

Studies of the reception of television serials will thus produce insights with somewhat different emphases, depending on the type of interview used. Group interviews about serials like *Friends*, *Survivor* or *The Osbournes* will mostly bring forward the diverse but normative discursive repertoires that people also draw on in everyday social conversations, about their narrative likes and dislikes. Individual interviews are more likely to enable researchers to illuminate more intimate aspects of people's appropriation of serial meanings. This is because they may probe into such matters as how the portrayal of fleeting and permanent relationships, infidelity, unexpected pregnancy, serious illness and homosexuality are experienced by and affect people personally. Similarly, reception studies of different types of website, such as Internet news services and dating sites, may call respectively for group and individual approaches, as they focus on experiences that relate respectively to people's public and personal selves.

Another reason for choosing individual interviews lies in the possibility they offer for holding informants individually accountable for specific discursive positions on an issue. This was the main reason why the ethical advertising study chose to interview its 16 informants individually, which enabled the study to end up with the graphic representation of the analysis shown in Figure 7.1. In group interviews, the role of the individual in the reporting of findings is often unclear. If you have conducted two focus groups of eight individuals each, can you really claim to have interviewed 16 people? Can you be sure that the apparent consensus produced has not been at the cost of silencing a number of participants who were too shy to argue their point? At least the individual interview eliminates the possibility of group pressure, although the possibility also remains here that some individuals may withhold their deepest feelings about a media product.

We shall end this brief discussion of the pros and cons of the two main tools of reception analysis, with the judicious assessment of Bloor et al. on the issue of methodological trade-offs; their advocacy of focus groups in no way blinds them to its shortcomings, or to the merits of rival methods:

> *[Focus groups] are superior to other methods only for the study of group norms and group understandings, and even here their superiority to ethnographic study is partly the superiority of convenience or accessibility (ethnographic work being difficult to undertake in increasingly private late-modern societies). When it comes to documenting behaviour, focus groups are less suitable than individual interviews: there is an understandable tendency for atypical behaviours to be unreported or under-reported in group settings.*

(Bloor et al. 2001: 8)

## PREPARING FOR FIELDWORK

### BUILDING UP A KNOWLEDGE BASE

Since reception research is defined as the interview-based empirical study of how people make sense of a media product, it follows that the researcher must have a certain amount of knowledge about this media product, in order to be able to conduct a meaningful and focused conversation with the informants about it. But this requirement has wider implications that go beyond the particular programme. This is because, in making sense of a particular media product, audience members are likely to draw extensively on their entire media environment, because other media experiences are likely to be relevant to their attempts to describe the experience of the particular product being researched.

For instance, a reception study of a television news programme should be prepared for, and possibly invite, informants' comments on other news formats on the same and competing channels, as well as on the comparisons being offered with alternative news sources, such as newspapers and web news sites. Similarly, a reception study of a 'reality' show like *Big Brother* will inevitably draw on informants' experiences of and attitudes to other contemporary and recent shows in the same and related genres (e.g. *Survivor*, *Temptation Island*).

Like all cultural sense-making, media experiences are relationally constituted so that what you like about one programme is related to what you dislike about another: a news presenter of one TV channel is *less* trustworthy than that of another, a protagonist in *Dawson's Creek* is *more* appealing than the equivalent character in *Beverly Hills 90210*, etc. Moreover an informant's experience of and verdict on any media product is always a discursive positioning of oneself in the taste landscape of the cultural community that one belongs to (Bourdieu 1984).

A reception study therefore requires the researcher to be capable of activating multiple media-related cultural repertoires, both in response to the views offered by informants, and strategically, in order to elicit the informant's experience of the media product. A lot of this knowledge comes naturally to any person who is alert to what goes on in his or her mediatized culture, but it should also be actively sought through familiarizing oneself with the aesthetic, generic and cultural analyses that media studies scholarship has provided over the years.

It goes without saying that before embarking on the fieldwork, one should also base one's work on what previous audience research in the area has to offer, so as to fine-tune one's own exploratory path as much as possible. Here we take a different stand from that of dogmatic 'grounded theory' approaches, which urge researchers to approach the fieldwork with as few preconceived notions as possible, and to postpone the orientation in previous research until the final report is to be written (Charmaz 1995).

For reception studies of print and electronic media, quantitative readership surveys, diary studies and TV-meter data should be consulted during the very first planning stages, in order to establish demographic and lifestyle-oriented patterns of exposure and use. In a study of the so-called 'tabloid' news formats of television, for instance, statistical data about the composition of the audience will enable you to decide who the core viewers are that you want to recruit for your interview study. Or if you are doing a commissioned reception study for a TV-channel wishing to extend the viewership for a particular programme, the statistics may help you find out who the once-in-a-while viewers are, so you can recruit some of them in order to explore what the dissatisfactions with the programme are that prevent them from becoming regular viewers.

Another valuable source of scholarly input to a reception study may be obtained from media ethnographic studies of how people fit media into the routines of everyday life, and vice versa. For instance, if you want to find out what people get out of listening to a particular radio programme, it will be helpful to know whether it is predominantly consumed from a stance of distracted or concentrated viewing.

Once you have decided on the media product that you want to base your interviews on, and that you may be going to show to people in the interview, it is necessary to obtain a detailed knowledge of its discursive content and aesthetic form as they are configured in different media and genres: social and cultural themes, narrative structure, main characters and their relations, visual features and style, editing, page design, sound, etc. As you develop a deep insight into the media product, there is a danger that the reception analysis may turn into a kind of test of whether the informants are clever enough to 'get' the meanings that the text seems to offer them. The best way to counteract this tendency, and to generate a valid account of the audience experience, consists in constructing an interview guide that asks as open and colloquial questions as possible, stays on the level of main themes, and uses vocabulary that takes into account that the everyday cultural expertise of the audience does not include the possession of a semiotic or aesthetic terminology.

## DESIGNING THE INTERVIEW GUIDE

Every research interview has an agenda, and since it can be difficult to memorize everything that you want to talk about in the interview, it is usually a good idea to prepare and bring a written interview guide. If you subscribe to the radical version of conversationalism mentioned above, however, you may be sceptical of the disturbing effect of bringing sheets of paper into what is designed to be a natural everyday situation – surely an interviewer who constantly buries his nose in typewritten papers will soon dispel any illusion of everyday conversation! Some reception researchers have therefore chosen to memorize their interview guide in, say, the car, prior to entering the informant's home, accepting the risk of forgetting important dimensions of the research agenda, as an unstructured interview may develop according to its own logic. We do not recommend that student projects adopt such a radical form for their interviews.

This said, many reception studies can do with a quite minimal interview guide, because the nature of the study makes for a simple and straightforward interview procedure, consisting of self-evident stages. This was the case with the ethical advertising study (Chapter 7), in which individual informants were asked to comment on nine different ads, one at a time. Here it was sufficient to ask two essential questions for each ad, in order to get the informant to talk about it: (1) Does this ad mean anything to you – if yes, what, if no, why not? (2) What do you think the company wanted to achieve with this ad? These questions would then be followed up by probing questions, for instance, asking informants to comment on aspects of the visual and verbal content of each ad. The interviewer would also be alert to the possibility of using the informant's comments on a specific ad as a launch pad for more general comments about other relevant issues concerning business ethics.

With less self-evident interview procedures, however, it is a good idea to develop a list of the issues one wishes to deal with, and possibly prepare a colloquially phrased entry question to each of the different topics. A good way to develop an interview guide is to conduct a brainstorming exercise with oneself or, in the case of a group project, with fellow students. Once the overall research purpose has been clarified, and the cardinal question(s) have been established, all the possible issues that one is curious to find out about should be written down. The next stage consists of clustering the different issues into a shorter list of major themes, for which the various issues then become the sub-themes. Finally, the interview guide is fine-tuned by discarding overlapping sub-themes and incorporating new themes that were overlooked in the first round.

The qualitative research literature recommends that an interview guide should include 'probes', i.e. follow-up questions about additional dimensions of the media experience in question. We feel that this can be difficult to do in a loosely structured interview, because in order to design a ready-made probe, you have to anticipate the informant's comments on an issue, and since these are not standardized, how can you design a probe in advance? In most cases, probes will emerge spontaneously as the interviewer feels that an informant's comment is not complete or perhaps obscure.

In Box 9.2 we present an interview guide, which was used for a student project about adolescents' news reception. This guide starts with getting informants to comment on their concrete experience of a specific news programme that the researcher has shown at the beginning of the interview. Another frequent way to begin an interview is to get informants to talk about a media phenomenon in general terms, i.e. starting with issues that in this interview are saved until the end: about the frequency of their watching TV news, other sources of news, etc. Both strategies are suitable for warming up the informants with relatively easy questions, while the more difficult, abstract questions to do with news credibility and objectivity should never be raised until informants seem to feel comfortable with their performance in this unfamiliar situation.

Some interview guides start by asking informants to *retell* the content of the programme to the interviewer. We generally advise against this strategy, unless it can be cast as a hypothetical task of how the respondent *would* enlighten an absent friend about the programme. This is because, from a conversational point of view, it simply makes no sense, except as a memory or knowledge test, for one person to retell another person a story they have just witnessed together. The same purpose – to get an impression of the informant's experience of the programme – can be served meaningfully by asking people to tell you what they found most and least interesting about the programme.

Lack of space prevents us from going into detail about many of the elicitation techniques interviewers may exploit in order to get to the heart of the informant's experience. While preparing the interview guide, researchers may consider three creative ways of getting people to draw on their discursive resources. They all require considerable interpretative reflection and skills of administration, and should therefore be used with caution.

One consists of the use of *indirect questioning*, which may be particularly suitable for eliciting their views about controversial issues. It works on the basis that 'people are more prepared

## Box 9.2   Interview guide for the study of news reception

(After a few minutes of small talk with the two to four group participants, a half-hour prime-time news programme was shown as the
point of departure for an interview about this particular programme
as well as TV news in general.)

### Content and presentation

Which news stories did you find most interesting? Why?
What do you think of the news programme as a whole – a good
    balance of stories? Informativeness? Entertainment?
There was also a story about X – what did you make of that?
Do you think that story X was relevant? Why do you think it was
    included in the programme?

### The news genre

Do you trust the news you saw in this programme?
Is TV news objective? What does it take for news to be objective?
Does television news give you the truth? Do you think it should?
Which of the main national news channels do you prefer to watch?
    Why?
How is the news produced by journalists? What are their aims? Are
    they constrained in any way in pursuing those aims? By political or
    commercial interests?

### The uses and effects of news

How often do you watch the news? What other sources of news do
    you have?
What do you get out of watching the news?
Do you think that your views are influenced by TV news?
Do you think people are capable of adopting a critical stance towards
    the news? What does it mean to be critical?

to reveal negative feelings if they can attribute them to other people' (Fielding 1993: 139).
Therefore, if you ask an informant who is reluctant to talk about his own viewing of a
socially stigmatized programme genre what he thinks the fans of such programmes get out
of watching them, he is likely to then report on his own gratifications, since he has little
way of knowing what others get out of them. This technique was used successfully with
male viewers of the soap opera *Dynasty* in the 1980s.

Another creative approach to the illumination of hard-to-express experiences is the use of
*projective techniques*. These rely on the fact that people's cultural tastes, intersecting with their
material and educational resources, follow similar patterns in different cultural areas, so
that regular readers of a particular type of popular magazine will often also share a taste
for particular types of TV show, have a preference for one type of holiday rather than

another, go out to certain kinds of restaurant rather than others, and so on. The technique consists of getting people to use their skills in cultural mapping by making a comparison between two such taste areas, one of which is easier to talk about than the other. A student project about core viewers' perception of a niche TV channel aimed at young viewers, thus asked informants to compare the channel to a car and to different types of restaurant. Interestingly, the car makes frequently mentioned were the new VW Beetle and small off-road vehicles, while the food taste that appeared to match the channel's presentational style best was Japanese sushi. With such knowledge about the channel's audience image and the way this image is anchored in particular programme features, programme managers can start to work on consolidating or changing the channel profile as they see fit.

Finally, one may explore non-verbal expressions of media experiences by getting informants to draw the typical situation in which they watch TV entertainment, or the typical situation in which they use their home computer. This technique is most often used for research about children's experience of media, because young children may not yet have acquired the conversational repertoires for fully verbalizing experiences (Stald 1999). While it may be hard to resist the temptation to interpret the drawings themselves, we advise against this unless the researcher is competent in both developmental psychology and visual analysis. A safer way to make use of children's drawings is to get them to verbalize their intentions in producing the drawing in the way they did, and then to draw one's analytical conclusions from their verbal account.

## RECRUITING INFORMANTS

When you start to think about who to interview for your reception study, you may as well forget everything you ever heard about random sampling. The sampling method used is often that of 'purposive sampling', in which informants 'are selected non-randomly because they possess a particular characteristic' (Frey et al. 1991: 135)

The notion of 'diversity' is central to how you think about the sample of informants for your study. But the complex nature of qualitative data, and the amount of time required in order to interpret it, means that the goal to aim for is qualitative rather than statistical diversity. The purpose being to map the discursive terrain of people's experience of a media product in great detail, there are three main issues to be dealt with in connection with the recruiting of informants: who to talk to, how many people to talk to and how to get hold of them.

### WHO TO SELECT AS INFORMANTS

Since a reception study always begins with curiosity about how people experience a media product, the answer to the question of who to recruit is almost given in advance: we want to interview people who are regularly exposed to the media product, most frequently because they take an active or a routinized interest in a TV programme, a newspaper or a film genre, but sometimes because they are inadvertently exposed to it, as in the case of most advertising. The relevant informants in a reception study are simply those who have something to say about the media product because they are familiar with it. An exception to this is when a reception study is designed to explore, in quasi-experimental style, how marginal audiences may be drawn into the regular audience by revising decisive elements of content or form. In studies with a pre-testing purpose for a media product that has not yet had an audience, the relevant informants are those people who are likely to be exposed to the media product in the normal course of events, because it conforms to their normal taste patterns.

Who these relevant informants are can usually be established by consulting the different kinds of media statistics that exist for both electronic and print media. If this information is not publicly available, it can often be obtained from the media producers in return for a copy of the report of the reception study. The default strategy for defining the relevant informants is simply to play it by ear, drawing on one's natural sense of the taste patterns in one's cultural environment.

## HOW MANY INFORMANTS?

The unavoidable quantitative challenge of even the most qualitative study is that of deciding on the number of informants. The standard recommendation in the literature is to aim for maximum diversity and continue one's series of interviews until the informant discourses start to resemble those of previous interviews. However, both professional and student projects rarely have the resources, time or patience to think about recruiting as a potentially infinite process. Therefore the rule of thumb is to operationalize the composition of the informant sample according to a fixed set of criteria, likely to ensure the occurrence of a diversity of discursive repertoires in the interviews.

In the ethical advertising study (Chapter 7), the social characteristics that were deemed likely to influence people's perception of the ads were those of gender, age, education and political observation. In order to include all possible combinations of these characteristics, 16 informants were recruited for individual interviews: eight men, divided equally between individuals aged 20–30 and 40–50, each age group divided equally between individuals with low and high education, and each educational group being divided into one Conservative and one Labour supporter; similarly for women.

Student projects for an audience course will often have to get by with far fewer informants, due to their status as a small-scale simulation of a real professional reception study. The same principles apply, though, so that in a study of, say, young people's experience of commercials on MTV, one should recruit informants according to a two-by-two, or two-by-three, systematic, with age and gender as the relevant variables for focusing the study within the relevant group of, say, 15–30-year-old individuals. Incidentally, the more narrowly one defines one's target group, the closer one may get to some kind of representativeness for the group in question: if one interviews, say, ten young teenagers, with different social backgrounds, about a youth programme, there will be as many representatives of this group as there are likely to be in a statistically representative sample of the whole population.

For group interviews the same considerations of being systematic apply, with the added issues of group size and how to compose the different groups. We have previously recommended that with inexperienced moderators, student projects should use relatively small groups of three or four, as opposed to the often much bigger groups of eight to twelve used in commercial research. In order to obtain this number, allowing for cancellations and unannounced absences, one should include one or two more informants over the desired number for each group.

The rule of thumb of group composition is to try to avoid too heterogeneous groups, because the flow of natural discussion is likely to be impeded if people cannot establish a modicum of common ground and a common wavelength. This is because cultural taste is still, to a large extent, an area characterized by segregation, in spite of the levelling developments of the postmodern age. In a study of different television news formats, therefore, ranging from the highbrow intellectualizing genres to the more tabloidized programmes, it is probably not a good idea to bring together individuals with very different amounts of educational capital. By keeping them in separate groups, one is still likely to witness extremely interesting cultural positionings being negotiated, as even homogeneously composed groups are likely to encompass sufficient idiosyncratic differences to trigger a lively discussion.

Academic reception research will usually hesitate to use fewer than six focus groups (Hansen et al. 1998), being sceptical of having achieved a sufficient degree of diversity with fewer groups. Paradoxically, commercial focus-group studies often stop at four, and sometimes as few as two groups, which is surprising considering that the resources saved on the number of groups may be lost tenfold if unwarranted conclusions are drawn from a too small-scale study and fed into a large-scale advertising campaign. A European national public broadcaster recently scheduled an aesthetically sophisticated horror serial, originally produced for a youth audience, into a prime-time family slot, on the basis of its favourable reception with just four focus groups. Viewing figures plunged dramatically, with potential long-term consequences for the channel's command of the time slot in question.

For the same reasons as with individual interviews above, for student projects of a non-dissertation kind, two or three groups will normally be considered sufficient. However, the norms may differ from country to country, and from institution to institution, so the safe strategy is always to consult one's supervisor before deciding on the number of groups required.

## FINDING INFORMANTS

How does one get hold of one's informants? If one has funding and wants to use groups of strangers, the usual procedure is to get a market research company to recruit informants with the profile needed. Without funding it is also possible to recruit informants oneself in this way. All it requires is a telephone directory and a knowledge of the area's cultural geography, since housing patterns usually follow the main social divisions in a community. Thus equipped, one can sometimes succeed in recruiting all the informants one needs in a day or two.

Much academic research being poorly funded, however, researchers often have to use other ways of recruiting. Sometimes this externally imposed need coincides with an independent wish to recruit informants in ways that are more sensitive to the everyday structures of the social fabric – for instance, in order to be able to interview 'network groups' composed of people who know each other in advance, as friends, workmates, neighbours or the like.

This approach, known as the 'snowball technique', usually starts out with contacting an acquaintance or a friend of a friend, who is then asked to bring together a specified number of other people, who live up to certain specified characteristics. In her study of consumers' use of mediated communication about food risks in everyday life, Halkier thus contacted six young couples, recommended by friends of hers, and got them to cooperate by each inviting two other couples to their home for the interview. Two families were anchored in each of three geographical locations: a big city, a provincial city and rural areas (Halkier 2001).

Another frequent technique used for student projects (and by some academic studies as well, cf. Gamson 1992) consists of approaching people in public areas like shopping malls, and asking them to participate in the study. It may work to the advantage of this approach to hand people a short questionnaire through which they may enable the researcher to ascertain whether they belong to the relevant audience group at all and to establish a few demographic facts about them. The questionnaire must also include the option of giving contact information if the respondent is willing to be approached again for focus-group participation.

A short questionnaire administered at the recruiting stage may also start the exploration of the informants' everyday categories in the area of research. If you are interested in finding out how people use news programmes, you may ask them to list their main preferences of TV news programmes and find that people with little cultural capital may mention programmes not standardly defined as 'news' by academic research. A student study of American teenagers' use and experience of horror movies asked prospective informants to list five horror movies as part of a short questionnaire. The movies mentioned enabled the researchers to see how the teenagers themselves defined the genre and to adjust their interview guide accordingly. The questionnaire also enabled them to detect a difference in boys' and girls' preferences within the genre.

It is often possible to persuade people to participate without giving them an incentive, apart from the refreshments usually offered during the interview. Irrespective of funding, conventions differ within the research community as to whether it is appropriate to include individuals who 'are only in it for the money'. If possible, researchers should try to give informants at least a token of their appreciation, such as a box of chocolates or a bottle of wine. Informants will usually understand that a student project cannot afford the kind of cash payment or gift voucher sometimes offered by professional research.

Once recruited, informants have to be carefully nurtured as informants. Soon afterwards one should confirm the appointment in writing, by sending informants a letter summarizing the aims and the conversational nature of the study, as well as stating the agreed time and place of the interview. It is also a good idea to remind informants by phone one or two days before the interview is to take place.

## IN THE FIELD

One should always start out with a pilot interview in order to test the research design. Two important foci of the pilot are the meaningfulness of the interview guide (including the media material shown to informants) and the researcher's skills in the art of discursive navigation in the interview situation – we therefore recommend that you listen through the taped interview in order to monitor your interviewing style. If the pilot is not hampered by grave shortcomings, it is sometimes possible to include it in the study proper as 'the first interview'.

It is impossible to overestimate the importance of the many practical aspects of an interview, although they may appear trivial at first sight and tend to be brushed aside during the planning, for later ad hoc solution. However, they are the lubricants that enable the interview machine to function smoothly, and should be carefully planned. The best way to signal a cosy social atmosphere is to offer different kinds of refreshment: soft drinks, chocolate, coffee, tea, biscuits, fruit or the like, which one should (offer to) take responsibility for even when the interview takes place at the informant's house. Taking a sip of coffee also gives informants something to do with their hands during awkward moments. If you plan to get informants to take notes, make sure you remember to hand out paper and pencils. Name cards will make it easier for group participants to avoid the awkwardness of forgetting each other's names during discussions.

Seating arrangements also matter, because they carry social and interactional meaning, and should be carefully thought about. The following suggestions may or may not offer the right solution to *your* interview design. For an individual interview in the informant's home, the armchairs around the coffee table may be a better choice than the upright chairs around the dining table, because armchairs signal a more relaxed attitude. During the interview, the interviewer should display a relaxed body attitude, sometimes leaning back in the sofa as people normally do, and not fold his arms over his chest. For a group interview, people (including the moderator) should be seated more like colleagues at lunch in the company canteen than like teacher and pupils in the school scenario. Commercial focus-group moderators often use recording aids such as flip charts to write down keywords. We advise against this because it will focus everybody's attention on you, instead of on the other participants and their views.

Important as they are, you should not worry too much if these practical aspects cannot be arranged exactly as you planned them. Be pragmatic about finding solutions and making compromises, if necessary. Sometimes an individual interview may end up as a pair interview, if a flatmate happens to be present and it would appear rude to ask him or her to leave the room.

When getting ready for the interview it is a good idea to start some small talk with informants, perhaps about the weather, transport difficulties or recent news events. The first stages should also include a short briefing in which the interviewer reiterates the purpose of the interview, goes through its main stages, defines the speech event in colloquial terms, assures informants of their anonymity, etc. (for a discussion of the ethical concerns involved in qualitative fieldwork, see Chapter 6). The need to record the interview should also be mentioned at this stage. For individual and small-group interviews, audio recording may be sufficient, while video recording is necessary to identify the speakers in larger groups.

During the bulk of the interview there are two pieces of advice that will help in securing good data. First, one should balance the need to cover all items in the interview guide with the need to allow informants to influence the agenda. Therefore one should follow informants down the side-roads they take, but also get back to the main street of one's interview guide. If informants start to talk about a topic you had planned for later, let them! Second, when you show informants a media product and ask for their experience of it, a good way to make them less susceptible to group pressure is to first invite them to write down their first impressions in keyword form on a piece of paper, and ask less talkative informants directly what they wrote. Another way to elicit the views of such informants is to nominate them explicitly, by referring to their having shaken their head or smiled in response to the views of another.

At the end of the interview one should conduct a short debriefing in which informants are invited to comment on aspects of the interview they found odd or interesting, things the interviewer could have done differently, etc. If interested, they should be offered a copy of the finished report, and contact information for reaching the researcher.

If you have no previous experience of conducting a reception interview, it is easy to devise a small-scale study in order to get the feel of it. If you follow the steps suggested in Box 9.3, such an exercise will take less than an hour.

## ANALYSING THE FIELDWORK MATERIAL

### APPROACHES TO THE REDUCTION OF QUALITATIVE DATA

It is when one is faced with the task of analysing pages and pages of interview transcript that one tends to find Lewis's observation that 'doing audience research is a messy and slippery business' (Lewis 1991: 73), particularly relevant: 'What do we do with these disorderly piles of data?' (Lewis 1991: 92). The task one is faced with involves reducing the massive amount of discursive data to manageable proportions, and creating an end product that has explanatory power with respect to the media experiences in question. There is no one tool that will make this interpretative task easy.

The overriding concern is to be systematic and explicit about the way one handles the interview data. It is with this goal in mind that the qualitative research literature often

## Box 9.3   Pairwork reception interview exercise

1. Team up with a partner in your class.
2. Each select a suitable one-page ad from a magazine whose target group includes you. Choose ads that have challenging verbal or visual elements.
3. Prepare an interview guide for interviewing your partner about his/her experience of 'your' ad.
4. Conduct your interview, then swap roles and become the interviewee for your partner's interview. Take notes during the interview.
5. Reflect individually on the interviewer and the interviewee experience, writing your thoughts down. What went well? What was difficult? Where could the interviewer have done better?
6. Discuss your reflections with your partner.

recommends a number of 'approaches' to the analysis of interview meaning. For instance, Kvale's (1996) guidelines suggest a choice between four different alternative methods.

- *Meaning condensation*: To 'condense' the meanings in an interview one looks for the natural meaning units in the interview (such as a couple of paragraphs) and rephrases each of them in a few words: 'Condensation entails an abridgement of the meanings expressed by the interviewees into shorter formulations' (Kvale 1996: 192). There is little 'interpretation' involved, as the analyst tries to be the informant's mouthpiece.

- *Categorization*: Here the analyst codes aspects of the interview text into a small number of dimensions or themes for quantification.

- *Narrative analysis*: This tool focuses on the stories told during interviews: their plot, interpersonal relations, good versus bad, and the point of the narrative. Alternatively, the analyst tries to 'create a coherent story out of the many happenings reported throughout an interview' (Kvale 1996: 192).

- *Interpretation*: Here the analyst undertakes a deeper analysis of the interviews, looking for latent meanings, going 'beyond a structuring of the manifest meanings of a text to deeper and more or less speculative interpretations' (Kvale 1996: 193). This may involve the analyst in working out the meaning of the everyday metaphors used and unpacking inferential meaning processes implied by the informants' utterances.

After demonstrating how these approaches can be used individually, however, Kvale (drawing on Miles and Huberman 1994) goes on to suggest that the pay-off of using a variety of analytical methods may be greater:

> *The most frequent form of interview analysis is probably an ad hoc use of different approaches and techniques for meaning generation . . . in this case no standard method is used for analysing the whole of the interview material. There is instead a free interplay of techniques during the analysis. Thus the researcher may read the interviews through and get an overall impression, then go back to specific passages, perhaps make some quantifications like counting statements indicating different attitudes to a phenomenon, make deeper interpretations of specific statements, cast parts of the interview into a narrative, work out metaphors to capture the material, attempt a visualization of the findings in flow diagrams, and so on.*

(Kvale 1996: 203–4)

We believe that to use any one interpretative tool is insufficient to deal with the richness of the interview data. In accordance with our overall principle of methodological pluralism, therefore, we recommend the ad hoc procedure, as long as it remains systematically structured and does not become idiosyncratic and impressionistic.

## INTERPRETATIVE TOOLS FOR INTERVIEW ANALYSIS

How does one do full justice to the richness of the spoken interview material? Since conversation, one way or the other, is the stuff that reception interviews are made of, the general recommendation is for reception researchers to familiarize themselves with discourse and conversation analysis. However, we realize that neither student nor professional reception studies are always done in an ideal world, and in the real world of university audience courses, supervisors are not expecting students to undertake the extra work required. Nevertheless, both disciplines have vastly increased our understanding of the verbal and non-verbal aspects of both ritualized and strategic forms of face-to-face interaction, such as turn-taking patterns, topic change strategies, and mechanisms of conversational dominance and symmetry. At least a cursory knowledge of such aspects will be a valuable tool for the interpreter of reception interviews, individual or group-based.

Inspiration may be found in general introductions to conversation analysis such as Nofsinger (1991) or Have (1999), or the summary account in Drew (1995). A small body of work is beginning to appear in which conversation analytical insights are applied directly to the analysis of research interviews. As an example, the work of Myers (1998) on how informants display their opinions as they negotiate topics and disagreements in focus groups, may serve to make interview analysts less rash in determining who agrees, how strongly, with whom about what. Myers shows that disagreements in focus groups should be recognized as such, even when they are indirect or hedged; this is because the pressure for consensus without loss of face is so great that the expression of blunt disagreement is quite rare. More generally, he demonstrates that researchers should look carefully at who is saying what, to whom and for what reason. Sometimes what appears at first sight to be the expression of personal opinion may turn out to have been a presentation of a view otherwise not represented in the group, or a view aired simply to impress the other participants.

The principles of conversation analysis may also inspire the reception researcher to respect *the interview transcript*, both as a whole and in its details. We recommend that interview tapes are transcribed *in toto*, and in sufficient detail to allow analysts (and readers) to pick up significant verbal as well as non-verbal meanings, but we do not require the kind of microscopic detail found in conversation analysis proper. The interview transcript shown in Box 9.1 may serve as a guide here, as we have transcribed all utterances verbatim, including the 'minimal responses' of the interviewer, and indicated the 'circumstances of utterance' such as laughter, significant tones of voice and, if video-recorded, significant gestures and facial expressions. During the analysis one should make a habit of going back to the tapes and checking one's interpretations against the tape's more faithful rendering of what was said and how.

By transcribing interviews in their entirety, one lives up to the non-dispensable requirement to 'soak oneself in the data', although this is often violated in commercial research, where a quick result may be given priority over a reliable one. To do a full transcription is also the best way to defeat faulty first impressions, as was the case in the ethical advertising study. Here the researcher left the British fieldwork stage with the general impression that informants, and especially female ones, were fairly positive in their assessment of the ethical credentials of the companies. When he immersed himself in the full transcripts, this turned out not to be the case at all.

Discourse analytical procedures can be extremely helpful during interview analysis. If we can be permitted to simplify a bit, while conversation analysis is mainly focused on the dynamic exchange of utterances, on the interview as *interaction*, discourse analysis is more focused on how people give accounts of the social world through language, on the interview as *representation* (Fairclough 1995; Van Dijk 1997; Schrøder 2002). A discourse analytical approach to interview analysis will therefore pay particular attention to the informants' 'lexicalization' of their media experience, i.e. the way they label individuals, institutions and processes through their choice of vocabulary, and the way they build taken-for-granted assumptions into their utterances through the verbal 'presuppositions' they use (Jensen 1989). For instance, by looking systematically at the way informants use descriptive nouns, including metaphorical expressions, about the political agents in the news, one may be able to draw a picture of their political sympathies and antipathies. The use of metaphors is always an important indicator of an informant's discursive representation of reality. When a female informant commented that to send the protagonists in a soap opera off to an exotic South American location was probably intended to 'add a bit of spice to the whole thing', the 'ingredient metaphor' became one indicator of her sophisticated understanding of the production principles of soap operas.

Another informant indirectly described her exhilarated state of mind during the watching of her favourite soap opera by telling the interviewer how, once the episode was over, 'then I'm just myself again'. This utterance was interpreted in the context to include the presupposition that, during the watching, she apparently did not think of herself as 'being just herself', leading to the conclusion (also based on other data) that during the viewing she saw herself as having been transported, carnival style, into a different realm in which it was possible to play with alternative roles and identities.

In the ethical advertising study (Chapter 7) we noted that while a female informant was critical of the 'green bandwagon' effect, she was nevertheless sympathetic to the view that business is fundamentally changing: 'Well, I would like to think it is,' she said, continuing that companies 'wouldn't become responsible I'm sure if that meant that their profits were going to be cut dramatically'. At the level of manifest meaning, she may seem to deny the possibility of businesses becoming more responsible, but at the more latent level of linguistic presupposition, she is actually granting that 'green' does have some power over profit maximization: businesses won't accept 'dramatic' cuts, but will apparently accept moderate ones.

## CODING THE TRANSCRIPTS

Our analytical premise in approaching the coding task in practical terms is akin to that prescribed by 'grounded theory' (Glaser and Strauss 1967), which exhorts qualitative analysts to let the data speak for themselves as it 'starts with the data and remains close to the data' (Charmaz 1995: 28). The analytical procedure should thus go inductively from the individual cases of each interview transcript, gradually develop conceptual categories and end up by identifying patterned relationships of media experiences. This said, we nevertheless distance ourselves from the *tabula rasa* illusions of hardcore grounded theory that prescribes an analytical procedure unpolluted by preconceived notions about the object of study.

When the analyst sits down to start the analysis, he or she is inspired by a multitude of pre-interpretations, originating in all the preceding stages of research. Therefore, 'the process of indexing then involves the analyst reading and re-reading the text and assigning index codes, which relate to the content of the data *and are of interest to the researcher's analytic framework*' (Bloor et al. 2001: 63; emphasis added). We suggest that the analysis starts from the guiding interests behind the study as they first materialized in the themes of the interview guide. The analysis is thus, to some extent, framed by a pre-given set of codes or categories, but proceeds with an open mind by adding new codes or categories as warranted by the transcript.

If the practical thematic indexing of the transcript discourse is done manually on paper, the page should be formatted as a text, with two columns of almost equal size, one consisting of the interview text, the other being gradually filled up with interpretative comments and preliminary themes. The analytical comparison of passages that have been given the same index may then be helped along by photocopying, cutting and pasting, followed by the formulation in writing of the interpretation of the data, theme by theme.

An alternative way to index the transcripts is to use one of the types of computer software available for this purpose, which can help by enabling easy storage and retrieval of the textual passages coded in the same way by the researcher, and which have a facility for attaching analytical memos to the indexed data. Whether to use such software or not is a matter of personal preference. As it always takes time to acquire the ability to use such aids, it may be easier for most student projects to use the conventional paper-based kind of analysis. As a partial implementation of computerized aids, you may find it possible to get an ordinary word-processing programme to perform some of the functions that these packages offer, such as doing wordsearches and exporting indexed blocks into separate documents. For further guidance on this matter, see Richards and Richards (1994) or Hansen et al. (1998) or, since software facilities are continuously being innovated, more recent presentations.

One can distinguish between two ways of generating analytical themes from the transcript. In analytical practice they are often mixed. One of them starts out with a set of guiding general categories, each of which may then be diversified by setting up subcategories as they suggest themselves to the analytical glance. The other procedure is the reverse of the first one. Here one starts out with establishing a multitude of lower-level themes, which may later be merged into the superordinate categories of those sub-themes that appear to be related to each other.

The interview analysis guide shown in Box 9.4 took its point of departure from the interview guide shown in Box 9.2, and used a mixture of the two procedures just mentioned. The student research project that it was based on dealt with adolescents' experience of and views on the social role of television news. A comparison of interview guide and analysis guide shows how the skeleton of the latter was clearly derived from the former, and was then expanded gradually during the course of the analytical process. It is

---

**Box 9.4    Interpretative guide for the analysis of news reception interview transcripts**

1. The character of television news: content and form
   - Between information and entertainment
   - The portrayal of protagonists: heroes and villains
   - Focus on conflicts

2. The production of news: behind the screen
   - Economic and political dependence of news media
   - The influence of the dominant climate of opinion/ideology
   - Journalism as selection of events and perspectives
   - Journalistic subjectivity and objectivity

3. The social influence of news media on viewer-citizens
   - Power of the media
   - Agenda-setting
   - The individual's impressionability: distance or immersion
   - News and democratic empowerment

thus clear how the interviewees' discourses have added several dimensions to the interview guide's three main categories, which have largely remained the same. Also it seems that a deeper familiarity with previous news research has refined the researcher's conceptualization of the discursive landscape and led to more precise scholarly terminology in the labelling of categories ('empowerment', 'agenda-setting').

The search for thematic patterns in one's data is the first and main concern in doing interview analysis. The second, and no less challenging, step consists of attempting to carry out an analytic generalization of one's material, by looking for use or user patterns in the discursive landscape, as mapped by the thematic analysis, answering questions like, 'Can the informants be meaningfully grouped into distinguishable types of viewer/listener/reader/user of the media in question?' By requiring such generalizations to be 'meaningful', we wish to stress that the generalizing interpretation should remain sensitive to the diversity and possible ambivalences of the data, while at the same time seeking to reduce this diversity to a form that may provide a platform for recommended action, of either the media producers, relevant policy-makers, or the informants themselves. We discussed this issue in some detail in connection with the ethical advertising study in Chapter 7. Third, one should always end up by generalizing one's findings externally, in the sense of comparing them to previous research in the area, pointing out whether existing knowledge has been corroborated or challenged by the new findings.

The first and last commandment of qualitative research is that one should be as systematic and exhaustive as possible, in the service of validity and reliability. One should thus strive to eliminate subjective bias from the analysis – which is not the same as eliminating one's subjectivity from the study, which is epistemologically impossible anyway, just as one has to grant that there may be more than one interpretation of the same interview passage. In presenting one's findings, after writing them up in a research report, one should therefore make it possible for readers to see how the interpretations were arrived at. This is mostly done by providing ample quotations from the transcripts, which anchor the interpretations in the data. If practically possible – as is the case with reception studies done by two or more people – one should build a devil's advocate perspective into the analysis and seek to reach intersubjective agreement about interpretations by having two people do the analysis independently, and then compare notes with the aim of negotiating a consensus about the points where they disagree about the interpretation.

Finally, let us conclude this chapter with a quotation from Giorgi (1975), which succinctly expresses what interpretative reliability is all about:

> *The chief point to be remembered with this type of research is not so much whether another position with respect to the data could be adopted . . . but whether a reader, adopting the same viewpoint as articulated by the researcher, can also see what the researcher saw, whether or not he agrees with it. That is the key criterion for qualitative research.*

(Giorgi 1975: 96, quoted in Kvale 1996: 209)

# Section 4

# Foundations of Quantitative Audience Research

# Introduction: the historical legacy of the philosophy of science

We have seen that qualitative researchers have been concerned with analysing the practice of 'audiencing' within the context of everyday life. Recall the observational 'diary' of a family at the start of their day in Chapter 1 (Box 1.1). How do we know this family's experience is representative of others? To determine this, we have to invent the ability to survey, that is to observe, find patterns, map and understand everyday use of various media, *in real time across a number of people in space*. We can then compare this family's experience to others, to find it typical or atypical. But perhaps we want to know the effect of a change in the morning media habit on the rhythm of the family audiences. To determine this we have to design an experiment, to determine causal influences, or model the relationships between family attention, family tasks and family member comprehension of the morning buzz of activity. In either mapping or modelling (audience surveys or experimental research) it is necessary – because we wish to obtain results that are generalizable to a larger population – to make decisions on how mathematical denotation will be used in quantitative observation.

Driven by the desire to survey the everyday practices of audiences, two researchers, Kubey and Csikszentmihalyi, invented a quantitative method called *experience sampling*, to collect observations systematically from a cross-section of people, armed with electronic pagers. Participants were randomly beeped throughout the day, asked what they were doing, and required to record their emotions and general feeling state at random times. The researchers' groundbreaking *Television and the Quality of Life* (1990a) sets out to compare different experiences of television by asking individuals about their emotions, activities and interests. By probing how people feel before, during and after watching television – beeped at intervals – the researchers set out to describe the patterns by which different people manage their moods by using television in diverse psychological and social circumstances. The Kubey and Csikszentmihalyi study counters arguments often levelled at quantitative studies of audiences, that they deny the importance of the agency of the subject, exclude the context and flatten the 'deep meaning' of television's effect. We raise this case, which is a hybrid survey and natural experiment, because it shows how quantitative modes of inquiry focus on ways of generalizing to broader patterns of behaviour in different populations, making comparisons between groups, and investigating the complex determinacies of media experience in everyday life. In short, the orientation of quantitative researchers is towards the mapping of diversity, comparing peoples across similar and different populations and modelling the processes by which media influence our lives.

Section 4 is intended to overview, as a prerequisite for students not familiar with the quantitative approach, the basic methodological and technical aspects of quantitative social science measurement, to explain its modes of inquiry, terminology and rules of evidence. But before we do so in Chapter 10, we shall take a brief look at, first, the historical origins of deductivism, inductivism and causality, as the basic concepts of empirical scientific work, second, at the nineteenth-century origins of a positivist social science, and third, at the positivist foundations of early audience research in the US.

We believe that the quantitative approach must be distinguished from positivism – a narrower philosophical movement, which has often been confused with all quantitative designs in the social science perspective. As discussed in Chapter 3, quantitative approaches to empirical inquiry rely no less on translation and interpretation than qualitative approaches. The data produced by quantitative researchers are constructs from start to finish, not facts. As constructs they are intended only as maps or models of everyday audience experience. Yet numbers can tell vivid stories. In some cases, they may even be able to explain why a story unfolds the way it does, or predict future ones.

Quantitative methodology can be thought of, then, as a set of formal techniques to 'reduce' the evidence derived through dialogue with subjects to numerical representation, and to describe it, map it, analyse it or model it, using mathematical models of relations. By mindfully analysing the patterns of data, quantitative research often provides a generalizable or predictable counterbalance to the contextual insights of particular audience interpretation.

## DIALECTICAL INDUCTIVISM AND DEDUCTIVISM

In many ways the key debates in communications studies are not new. Classical scholars also recognized many faculties for apprehending our world: intuition, introspection, faith, observation, dialogue and reason, creativity and imagination, aesthetics and appreciation, morality and feeling. They also believed in a law-ordered universe founded on an essential being or reality. The foundation of the modern social science approach to communication was, in fact, anticipated by Aristotle, who systematically connected the accumulation of knowledge to a reasoned discourse about nature – or 'science', seeing *dialectical reason* as the key method of science.

As a student of Plato, Aristotle admitted that all knowledge was just a representational scheme that 'refers' to reality in the form of propositions (a statement in which the subject is affirmed or denied by the predicate). So such knowledge in itself is neither true nor false: the truth or falsity of any proposition can only be determined by its agreement or disagreement with the facts and relations it represents. Propositional statements thus have a dual or ambiguous character, as logical relationships between ideas and as 'factual' references to reality.

Only through evaluating these arguments can any claim to knowledge of reality be upheld. Aristotle set out two tools for validating arguments: *deductive reasoning* proceeded with chains of inferences from a set of axioms, facts or first principles to specific conclusions on the model of classical geometers; *inductive reasoning* went in the other direction, from observations of specific events or facts to general laws and explanation, on the model of the clinical work of physicians of the time. Deductive and inductive reasoning provide the dialectic method at the heart of classical conceptions of scientific discourse.

Aristotle, especially, admired the way geometers based their deductive 'proofs' on systematic inferences that could be derived from a set of 'axioms'. Scientific argument, too, should develop in an orderly progression, from a set of simplified first principles to more complex explanations or interpretations based on syllogistic logic. The classic example of a syllogistic argument is as follows. All men are mortal; Socrates is a man; therefore, Socrates is mortal. Deductive arguments of this type are necessarily true because it is impossible to think of a disconfirming case when these propositions hold. And in certain logical conditions, deductivism may establish causality.

Similarly, a causal syllogism can be said to imply necessary outcomes concerning the temporal relationship between a specific determinant condition (X) and that of a consequent condition (Y), such that X regularly precedes Y (therefore X is sufficient to effect Y), and such that Y is unlikely in the absence of X (therefore X is necessary for Y). Aristotle claimed, under these circumstances, that it was possible to say that X 'causes' Y when the presence of X meets the necessary and sufficient condition for the occurrence of Y, so that the consequence Y only follows from the specified determinant X.

But Aristotle clearly did not believe that deductive reason alone was sufficient to establish a valid knowledge system. Arguments still had to be based on sound observations. Induction describes the kind of knowledge accumulated from specific observations of natural phenomena and grouped in general classifications. Inductive analysis proceeds through a process of observation, classification and comparison: to build generalizations (*genera*) out of the observations of specific cases (*species*). We cannot differentiate apples and oranges until we have both defined the category 'fruit', which allows for their comparison, and have completely specified the various observations that are included in that category. Inductive inferences could be made more sound, Aristotle argued, if the categories were mutually exclusive and carefully formed into hierarchical sets that had clear rules of inclusion. A rational classification system implies that all the members of that set have a defined feature or function in common, and that common attributes allow this set to be distinguished from other sets. Often called 'set theory' in mathematics, qualitative and quantitative sciences are equally founded on this principle of inductive classification.

## POSITIVIST TURN IN SOCIAL SCIENCE

Drawing on the advances in mathematics and probabilistic observation techniques of the eighteenth-century natural sciences, pioneering social scientists of the nineteenth and early twentieth centuries adapted them to the study of society and psychology. Sociologists Auguste Comte and, later, Emile Durkheim became advocates of a positive social science, theoretically grounded by empirical evidence in the nineteenth century. These self-styled 'social scientists' argued that social theory and philosophy must focus on social facts, i.e. on evidence that is carefully and rigorously gathered according to scientific principles. They assumed it was possible also to use numbers as representational schema for measuring social constructs. To do so meant translating social concepts into dimensional or numeric values. Once the measurable attributes of a phenomenon like class structure, for example, have been specified (i.e. wage, work process, number of hours, power over others, etc.) then each unique observation of an individual worker can be classified, counted, compared or contrasted with other observations of class across populations. Such assumptions not only standardized measurement, but enabled a statistical accounting and mapping across a whole population on the same construct.

Also during the early twentieth century, a group known as the Vienna Circle philosophers (Frank, Hahn, Neurath) argued that if you couldn't observe and measure something, you couldn't explain it. British philosophers (Moore, Russell and Wittgenstein), especially, championed a purely empirical mathematical language for scientific discourse. Only by stripping social theory down to its empirical content could social sciences become *impartial and objective*.

Psychologists embraced this idea of a scientific method for the study of human experience. To study the psyche empirically, we must be able to measure subjective experience and compare across the general population being studied. One example is the well-known IQ test developed by Alfred Binet, who argued that the scores of individuals on a standardized IQ test could be used to estimate the range and standard deviation in a population as a whole.

But under the surface of psychology's new-found empiricism rumbled a debate about what constituted the objective measurement of social behaviour. On one side stood American behaviourist psychologist, J.B. Watson, who argued that scientific observation should refer only to those acts that can be reliably observed firsthand by scientists in the laboratory, where it was possible to control the stimulus conditions. Similar to other natural sciences, behaviourists must restrict their measurements to 'the objective facts consisting of movements of the person's body or of any part of it'. Behaviourist psychology therefore refused to study, or even debate, mental events (intent, subjectivity, will, experience) because they could not be measured objectively. Their stimulus–response lexicon seemed to squeeze 'interpretation' out of the study of human transactions and implicitly denied agency to human subjects who were apprehended only as 'objects of study'. This union of positivist mathematical and behavioural theory became the modernist rallying cry for distinguishing social science from dogma. Yet, as Anthony Giddens notes, a cluster of philosophical ideas lay behind the emerging positivism of the social sciences:

- *phenomenalism* – the thesis that 'reality' consists of sense impressions;

- *an aversion to metaphysics*, the latter being condemned as sophistry or illusion;

- *the representation of philosophy* as a method of analysis, clearly separable from, yet at the same time parasitic upon, the findings of science;

- *the duality of fact and value* – the thesis that empirical knowledge is logically distinguished from the pursuit of moral aims or the implementation of ethical standards;

- *the notion of the 'unity of science'* – the idea that the natural and social sciences share a common logical and perhaps even methodological foundation.

(Giddens 1978: 237)

A different approach, sharing the growing interest in empiricism, inspired American sociologists of the Chicago School, who also proposed that sociology could be reconstituted by a natural experiment that could be documented and analysed (see Chapter 5). Robert E. Park's seminal essay 'The city', published in 1925, envisioned the city as a microcosm of human behaviour – an ecological nexus at the heart of modernization. Park states that the city, therefore, is like 'a laboratory or a clinic in which human nature and social process may be conveniently and profitably studied'. Inspired by demography and the census, Chicago School sociologists set out to gather all kinds of quantitative evidence by undertaking investigations of communities. Since human subjects also have language, it was also possible to study 'subjective experience' discursively, by enlisting 'the person himself as our observer'(Woodworth 1921: 9). These social psychological researchers believed that since thoughts and feelings were communicable through language, then interviews and questionnaires afforded another reliable way of observing and measuring mental life. A decisive rejection of naïve positivism, this methodological stance precipitated widening debates within the social sciences about the best way of studying subjective social experience on a broad scale.

## ORIGINS OF THE QUANTATIVE SCIENCE OF AUDIENCES

Throughout the twentieth century, American social researchers turned to statistical reasoning to assist in the process of analysing empirical evidence about social phenomena. The vast scale of mass society, the electronic technologies through which mass culture was transacted, and the uniquely 'modern phenomenon' of their impact on audiences, led this growing cadre of psychologists and sociologists to apply the same statistical tools to the exploration of communications. Most historians see Paul Lazarsfeld as the founding father of audience research because, during the 1940s, he became a leading proponent of quantitative surveys of preferences among the radio and TV audience. As we shall see in Chapter 14, practical concerns about media effects also galvanized a number of social psychologists to study Second World War propaganda, using experimental techniques to focus on the mass media's effects on military morale or public opinion. The statistical approach to populations quickly became the gold standard for the sale of audiences to advertisers and for predicting trends in voting.

Yet the empirical approach to audience research also became embroiled in the epistemological battles dividing the field of communications generally. The 'mindless' positivism of quantitative communications research was roundly condemned by scholars of the Frankfurt School (Chapter 3). Three arguments were especially central to the Frankfurt School's opposition to positivism. The first was the way audience sciences became tightly associated with the quantitative studies of mass persuasion. The second was the ideological criticisms of operationalism and quantification, and their ready application in the commodify processes of the cultural industries. Extension of control over audiences became conflated with science: once audiences and work processes could be measured, they could also be bought and sold, furthering the commercialization of the communications industries. Third, many argued that crude and reductionist behaviourism fails to provide an account of active audiences engaged in meaningful transactions. The positivist's arrogant claims to objectivity and truth were criticized as an attempt to legitimate and defend the banalities and commonplaces of their findings.

Yet the Frankfurt critics mostly had a rather superficial understanding of the working assumptions of quantitative empiricism. Karl Popper, a noted philosopher of science, has argued that the critics often fail to understand that the numerical procedures used to measure social and psychological constructs make no claims to absolute truth: indeed, the statistical analysis never claimed to prove anything absolutely, but rather to eliminate unlikely or improbable explanations or hypotheses. A hypothesis is a speculation that is accepted only in so far as it has 'not been disproven' by the data, and that is consistent with other evidence. The quantitative scientific method therefore claims only a qualified, contingent kind of 'validity' in mapping or modelling causes and effects.

Raymond Williams (1974) shared many of the Frankfurt critics' ideological concerns but, unlike them, he did not endorse a complete abandonment of all quantitative methods. He particularly did not want to confuse the rejection of the positivist philosophy with the abandonment of an empirical science for the field of communications. Williams felt that the problematic of cultural agency and determinacy required techniques of generalization and inference testing in order to advance the human sciences.

Our contemporary understanding of a cultural science shares many assumptions with Williams' conception. It can be derived from the strict sense of the Latin word *sciere*, which has the meaning 'to know'. The *OED* defines a modern science as 'a branch of study which is concerned either with a connected body of demonstrated truths or with observed facts systematically classified and more or less colligated (or tied together) by being brought under general laws and which includes trustworthy methods for the discovery of new truths within its own domain'. Implicit in this definition are two important ideas about the evolving rationality of the contemporary human sciences. The first is the idea that the observed facts must be demonstrated empirically. The second is the idea that the 'trustworthy methods' for establishing the certainty of the knowledge must be agreed upon by the community of scientists. Unlike everyday knowledge, the sciences are subject to a process of criticism by scientific peers. The development of scientific knowledge, therefore, is disciplined by the specified 'rules of evidence' and 'procedures for inquiry' established within any scientific community.

Quantitative audience research, like all kinds of research, can thus be understood as a self-regulating body of knowledge produced by and through scientific inquiry and debate. Scientific method is a sceptical and self-critical procedure for establishing consensual validity: scientists must clearly articulate their assumptions, and the methods and implications of their inquiry, as well as its contribution to previous theory and evidence, and show a willingness to debate the results of their investigations. Science's first principle of validity, therefore, is *consensual validity*, which refers to credence given to evidence that has resulted from peer review and criticism based on established criteria for gathering and assessing evidence in order to draw valid conclusions. The requirement of consensual validity is meant to ensure that the evidence is both reproducible and provides the best explanation of the observed results.

This basic principle has been extended to all forms of scientific discourse: when elements of an argument are clearly defined, coherent and consistent, it is said that the work has *internal validity* – that is, that the argument and conclusions are consistent with the assumptions and rules expected of logical argumentation within that body of knowledge. Equally important in discursive proof, however, is adducing evidence of *external validity*. This includes stating how the evidence gathered by the researcher contributes to, challenges or confirms other empirical explanations and theories accumulated within the body of knowledge.

As a body of social knowledge, any methodology is constantly being debated. Today, in practice if not in theory, the quantitative methods of contemporary social science exemplify, not rigid positivism, but rather a procedural oscillation between theory building and theory confirmation, inductive and deductive modes of reasoning, where reason and experimentation are the twin courts where scientists plead their case, following strict rules of evidence.

This is why naïve positivism is out of favour in the contemporary social sciences. Post-positivism or critical realism today holds that reality may be determined intersubjectively, rather than objectively, that value-freedom should be replaced with the self-reflexivity of the researcher, and that the search for 'laws' is less important than rigour in comparison and logical rules for generalization and discursive proof (Chapter 3). In retrospect, we shall argue in Chapters 12 and 15 that the early forays into audience measurement were of crucial importance to the overall development of communications research as it is practised today. Our claims are threefold: first, these quantitative researchers became leaders *in applying statistical reasoning to the study of diverse audiences*, which enabled comparisons across populations and over time; second, *they fostered a craft of question design and scaling* that resulted in more reliable techniques; third, *by routinizing the inquiry procedures* they contributed to the establishment of a methodological canon that had come to dominate scientific discourse and training in the US by the 1970s.

# Chapter Ten

## ☐ Towards a basic toolbox for quantitative researchers

We have defined quantitative research as a form of planned inquiry. No one will understand your arguments or accept your conclusions unless they see how the evidence justifies them. Researchers are generally expected to articulate clearly the steps taken to account for various interpretations of the evidence they gather. Prior to engaging in any investigation, researchers engage in an intensive process of formulating their questions, operationalizing their measures, and arranging for their evidence-gathering and analysis procedures (for the general stages of empirical social research, see Chapter 3, page 53).

Research design is the term we generally use to describe this complex decision-making process. Designing research can be fun because it combines creative problem-solving abilities with analytic rigour and insight. It is especially important to identify the key assumptions underlying the investigation and the ongoing explanations of evidence generated by other researchers. Both require acts of critical imagination. Although rarely recognized as such, the act of research design becomes a formative moment of theory building. The design phase is an excellent time to reflect on the assumptions and rules of evidence established within your own field of inquiry.

Quantitative researchers extend special attention to three tasks. The first is operationalization, to ensure that we are making the right observations. The second concerns a sampling strategy, so that we can generalize from the observed universe to the population (the total observable universe). The third concerns the application of inferential statistics, to manage the uncertainties that we face in explaining any phenomenon. They are defined as follows:

1. *operationalization*, the process of defining research questions, developing measurement instruments and gathering empirical evidence into a data set

2. *generalization*, the use of *basic sampling and statistical techniques* to estimate the likelihood of occurrence of a phenomenon in the general population; *generalization* involves developing a sampling frame, setting the sample size and estimating the sampling error in the data set

3. *inferential analysis*, which embodies a series of evaluative arguments concerning the relationships between the independent and dependent variables based on rigorous ways of comparing and testing data against hypothetical models of possible outcomes; inferential analysis uses the statistical tools of frequency distribution, measures of central tendency and measures of dispersion to describe variables as well as correlations, cross-tabulation and Chi-square to examine the patterned relationship between separate variables.

To illustrate the importance of these three tasks to quantitative research design, let's say we are investigating the topic of hypermaterialism, the seemingly excessive preoccupation of western society with material consumption and possessive individualism. What is the media's role in shaping our views on materialism? For fun, we turn to that bastion of marketing research, the *American Journal of Consumer Research*, and find a surprisingly critical piece in which researchers set out to discover whether TV programming depicting 'affluence' in the media world leads to an overestimation of affluence in the real world. Their rationale was that TV programming, especially game shows and soap operas, depicts a world of wealth. Therefore, the more people who watch TV (both in absolute terms and as a percentage), the more likely they are to believe that many families enjoy the affluence of a private home, luxury cars, swimming pools and wine collections. They start by stating their research question: Does television viewing distort people's estimates of affluence in the real world? The theoretical issue they identify is: Why do we think a relationship exists between TV viewing and estimates of affluence?

The remaining part of this chapter outlines a general inquiry process that provides the reader with a basic understanding of the application of these three keys to quantitative methodology. Box 10.1 presents a decision tree for a quantitative study (or a ten-step programme), intended as a guide.

## Box 10.1  A decision tree in a quantitative research study

### Step 1 in operationalization: state the research question
Does television viewing distort people's estimates of affluence in the real world?
*Theoretical issue*
Why do we think a relationship exists between TV viewing and estimates of affluence?
*Rationale*
TV programming, especially game-shows and soap operas, depicts a world of wealth. Therefore, the more people watch TV (both in absolute terms and as a percentage), the more likely they may be to believe many families are affluent.

### Step 2: identify the variables in the research question
*Variable i*  Amount of television viewing
*Variable ii*  Estimates of affluence

### Step 3: define the variables
*Variable i*
To measure the amount of television viewing, we may choose a diary of the number of hours per week or, as the authors did, survey people asking them to recall how much time, to the nearest hour, they spent watching TV in a specific time period. We may choose to get even more

## Box 10.1 continued

specific about the allocation of time to genres – especially game-shows and soap operas, which, content analysis suggests, depict affluence.
*Variable ii*
How to measure perceived affluence – estimates of the percentage of families in the American population thought to own a home, swimming pool or luxury car, go on holidays and have wine collections. These are "common sense" attributes of affluence, and reasonably well known to most people.

### Step 4: specify the independent and dependent variables
*Independent variable* TV viewing
*Dependent variable* Estimates of affluence

### Step 5: choose the level of measurement
Select nominal, ordinal or ratio level of measurement. Design mid-points or no-opinion-offered alternatives.

### Step 6: design the sample
Choose non-probability or probability sampling method. Decide the target population, how to locate the sample, sample size, and record non-response. Selection of the confidence limits and likely margin of error will allow you to set up basic rules for data mapping.

### Step 7: map and analyse the data
Look for general frequency distributions, measures of central tendency, measures of dispersion. Use Chi-square where appropriate. We may then look for patterns of relationships or measures of correlation. Data analysis can use statistical tests to assess whether the causal theory provides the best explanation of the observed relationship between the variables.

### Step 8: model the causal relationship
Dependent variable is 'estimates of affluence'. Independent variable is 'amount of TV watched'.

### Step 9: evaluate the causal relationship
Is it reasonable to assume the relationship between independent and dependent variables meets the following conditions?
  (i) Is it plausible to think TV viewing and perceptions of affluence are related?
 (ii) Is it plausible to presume that TV viewing occurs prior to our perceptions of worldly affluence?
(iii) Are there other variables that might cause both TV viewing and perceptions of affluence?

**Box 10.1 continued**

In this case, the type of programmes watched is important. Soaps and game-shows are more likely to feature consumption narratives than nature shows, and have a different impact on viewers. Conversely, education may have an effect. Those with more education are less likely to watch TV and less likely to over-estimate affluence. We revisit the links between variables to reframe the model. Levels of education influence the amount of TV viewing, which influence types of programming watched, which influences estimates of affluence.

Step 10: prepare and publish your argument
Write up the data to explain your research, debate and defend your findings before peers.

Source: adapted by George Gray and Neil Guppy from O'Guinn and Shrum (1997), in Gray and Guppy (1999: 41–3)

# STEP 1: PROPOSING A RESEARCH QUESTION

All quantitative audience research begins with the formulation of a research question. Whether it emerges from personal interest or from ongoing academic debates, developing a research question usually involves a review of the published commentary on the topic under investigation, as well as a deep reflection on one's own interest in this subject matter. To help frame the question, it is helpful to undertake a firsthand scoping of the circumstances surrounding the phenomenon to be studied, in one's own life as well as that of others. For example, if one wanted to survey where families located computers in their homes, it makes sense not only to look at one's own situation and that of friends, but also to informally examine a number of typical households.

Graham Murdock has argued that the human sciences only really pose four types of question: What is going on here? Why is it happening? What does it mean to those involved? Is it on balance a good or a bad thing? (Murdock 1997). He restates these general questions in terms of more analytic categories oriented to reportage, explanation, description and evaluation. Most research projects involve a combination of these various kinds of concerns, but it remains important to understand the fundamental orientation of the project – whether it is an exploratory, descriptive foray into a new topic or an attempt to adjudicate between different explanations of media effects.

Irrespective of the subject of the inquiry, quantitative researchers put special emphasis on the process leading up to the 'ask' – What do I need to know in order to answer my question? In exploratory descriptive research, a very general framing of the research question may be advised, leaving the process open to discovery of the language and experience of the subjects themselves. In Box 10.1, we see the researchers frame a general question about the role television plays in the construction of consumer perceptions of the 'reality' of affluence, based on some prior consumer research in the 'cultivation' tradition of Gerbner and his associates (see Chapter 3).

When explanation *and* evaluation are at stake, researchers often refine their questions into a series of hypotheses. A hypothesis is a carefully constructed and highly specific articulation of the key expectations of the research question – for example, that families with teenagers are more likely to locate their computers in children's rooms than those with young children. To make a question provable using the experimental method, quantitative researchers distinguish between the *null hypothesis*, where the question is stated in the form that the expected relationship does not exist, and the *alternate hypothesis*, where the question is stated that the relationship does exist.

Let us consider for a moment the research project where we are trying to determine whether viewers who watch gameshows are likely to perceive more affluence in their subsequent observations of peer behaviours. If this causal relationship explains the data, then we predict that shortly after watching a gameshow, but *not* after watching other kinds of programmes, the viewer will perceive a richer world.

*The expectation that there is no causal relationship between the dependent and independent variable is called the null hypothesis*, namely that people who watch a game show programme will be no different in their perceptions of social affluence than people who do not watch a gameshow:

- Hyp. 0: There is no causal relationship between TV game shows and perceptions of affluence
- Hyp. 1: There is a relationship between TV game shows and perceptions of affluence.

These two statements articulate the testable conditions that need to be observed in our study. The test is based on a quantitative comparison of the data under these two causal models, based on inferential statistics. We will discuss these statistical procedures in Chapter 16, but for now it should be clear that framing the study in terms of hypotheses helps the researcher to think systematically about the relevance and implications of their study. It also may force the researcher to consider fully the ethical and pragmatic implications of their topic, the assumptions behind their research, the resources and time available, and the methodological rules of evidence within which their contribution will be interpreted and evaluated. Once we have set out our research question (for survey work) or, by contrast, our hypotheses (for experimental audience inquiry), we can set about designing the study.

## STEPS 2 AND 3: IDENTIFYING AND DEFINING VARIABLES

Once settled on a topic, researchers must decide how they will define the key constructs so that they can be measured. Operationalization is the process of moving beyond questions and hypotheses to the instruments through which measurements can be recorded. In Chapter 13, we will examine more closely the scaling techniques used in audience research, but for now suffice it to say that there is no one superior way of measuring all phenomena. Inevitably, this process of operationalization is somewhat arbitrary because it is dependent on the formulation of the research question and the means available to the researcher to study that question (Babbie 1999).

The central methodological issue in operationalization is *construct validity*. Construct validity refers to the degree to which measurements actually measure what we say they do. The researcher must ask how well the operationalization of the variables in their study actually captures the processes, interrelationships or practices articulated in the hypothesis or causal explanation. The literature makes important distinctions between the levels of these observations, usually distinguishing between beliefs, attitudes, intentions and behaviour (perhaps even distinguishing bodily actions from heart rate to facial gesture).

The difficulties in establishing reliable and valid measures of our key constructs cannot be underestimated. Communication acts are very complex, varied and layered. We say this here as a challenge to young researchers, to remind them just how difficult it is to create valid accounts of audience behaviour. Clearly articulating one's own ideas about the variables is the first crucial step towards an operational definition. It is necessary because the construct's definition is what *enables* the researcher to make distinctions, whether it is based on direct observation by a researcher, or talk via interviews or questionnaires.

To explore their hunch in box 10.1 the researchers set out to measure two variables: the amount of TV viewing and the perception of affluence. How can we define and operationalize such muzzy concepts? The early stage of any project involves looking at the competing meanings of our key terms. A dictionary is not a bad place to start thinking about how to measure each term, because it provides a range of standardized usages of the terms.

At first, the amount of TV viewing seems a fairly simple concept to operationalize: observe the number of hours that each subject in the study watches TV. But there are different times and ways of watching, and different programmes and advertisements that will be viewed, depending on the subjects' media use habits. How much detail will we record? Moreover to measure the amount of television viewing, we may choose a diary of the number of hours per week, a people meter, or a questionnaire that asks subjects about their typical behaviours, preferences or allocations of time to TV watching. We may choose to specify the times or types of programmes watched, such as game shows and soap operas, which, content analysis suggests, depict different levels of affluence. In this case, the authors asked subjects simply to recall how much time, to the nearest hour, they spent watching TV in a specific day cycle over the last week.

The other key construct, affluence, is more problematic. First, we have to understand this construct in terms of its attributes, characteristics or qualities. Also asking a few friends to state what they think defines an 'affluent' person or country can be helpful. Don't be surprised if there is a wide range of answers. The task is to think about what these answers have in common. In this case, the researchers decided that the term not only refers to having lots of money, but to the possessions of the people who have it. For this reason, the researchers chose to measure the perception of affluence based on subjects' estimates of the percentage of families in the American population thought to own a home, swimming pool or luxury car, go on holidays and have wine collections.

But there is a deeper underlay to this process of definition. As we discussed in Chapter 1, designing questions is a matter of thinking about how to communicate with respondents (see Figure 1.1). The researcher/interviewer encodes meaning in the form of a question, and the respondents interpret or decode the intent and meaning of the question. They must then encode a response to that question, making a statement that the researcher must then decode. Because language is already ambiguous, researchers attempt to use clear statements that can be easily understood by their subjects. Depending on the project, it is possible to use open-ended questions where subjects generate their own categories in response to the question, or forced choice where subjects are requested to choose from a pre-defined range of possible answers. These options will be further examined in Chapter 13.

Finally, there is one additional step in quantitative analysis of this communication between researcher and subject: quantitative researchers must translate verbal responses into numbers, for the purposes of analysis. In the process of operationalizing variables, we then have to decide how we will code the responses we get as numbers, in such a way that each number means something specific, so that ultimately it can be translated back to words. Anyone speaking more than one language will be familiar with the possible errors that can also occur in translating from words to data and back to words. In Chapter 13, we will provide more detail on the techniques used to set up coding schemes for open and closed questions.

## STEP 4: SPECIFYING THE INDEPENDENT AND DEPENDENT VARIABLES

The researchers in our case chose just two variables to explore. Typically, we may choose to translate a concept into a set of variables or indicators. Whatever our definition, it will be important to decide what other variables influence it. In deciding whether one variable depends on another, we may be thinking descriptively (these types of people say this or that) or causally, stating that the independent variable causes, or is prior to, the other. We are not stating that one variable completely determines the other, only that it influences or has an effect on it. We set this up as an implied hypothesis or hunch about how the world of audiences works. We can reject this hypothesis, or partially confirm it. Generally, we think of demographic variables, or those that describe the innate unchangeable characteristics of a people (sex, age or ethnic origin) as independent variables. In this case, the researchers borrow from George Gerbner's cultivation model of research, and specify that TV viewing is the independent variable.

## STEP 5: CHOOSING THE LEVEL OF MEASUREMENT

In formulating our measures, we must also consider the 'levels of measurement'. Most importantly we must distinguish between nominal variables (based on categorical distinctions) or scaled variables (interval, ordinal or ratio) based on the intensity or magnitude of an attribute. If we decide on scalar variables, we need to work out the numeric system to denotation. The assumptions about these different ways of standardizing our measurement dictate the kinds of statistical tools available for later comparison and generalization.

The most frequently encountered form of measurement in social sciences is nominal. The *nominal variable* asks the respondent: 'Into which category would you fit yourself?' It must be classifiable into at least two categories, which are mutually exclusive, equivalent and exhaustive (Frey et al. 1991). For example, if it was possible to define a difficult concept like class, then why not operationalize class as a measurable nominal variable based on a self-defining coding scheme that equates each category with a number (blue collar = 1, white collar = 2, managerial = 3, etc.)? The only assumptions related to the reliability of nominal data concern the ability of respondents to understand the language and to assign themselves to a category. Once nominal variables are assembled into a data set, they can be used to provide a summary account of the distribution across populations as percentages of respondents that belong to a particular category.

*Scalar questions* ask the respondent: 'Where along this continuum do your perceptions fall?' (Fowler 1993). Ordering cases into a set of increasing or decreasing categories, the researcher assumes the subject can interpret a scalar relationship to represent relative magnitude of the construct. Generally speaking, scalar measurement in audience research can be constructed in ordinal, interval and ratio scales.

Any idea that is operationalized as an ordered set of terms is an *ordinal variable*. Ordinal scales assume that respondents have the ability to sort and rank a variable along a unifying dimension of judgement or experience. Ranking implies only that it makes sense to the respondent to compare those choices roughly along this dimension. Because there is no implied degree of difference between the categories, researchers who use ranking scales must use rudimentary descriptive statistics in assessing data sets constructed from ordinal scales.

By contrast, researchers may assume some equivalence in the intervals between the points on the scale. *Interval scales* imply a dimensional order of magnitude, but assume equal intensities between the value of 1 compared to 2 as between 3 and 4. There is no true zero on an interval scale, but it still allows inferences to be made about the order and distance between points. It is important to distinguish interval scales with a midpoint from those without one (or the use of even or odd numbers in answer categories). Midpoints are

187

favoured if you want an accurate reading of where people will place themselves in positive or negative orientation in answering your question. Even numbered scales (strongly support, support, oppose, strongly oppose) may skew to one side.

Although more points on the scale assume finer discriminations of judgement, researchers disagree about the optimum number of distinctions (3, 5, 7, 9) people can make on an experiential judgement of intensity. But most researchers accept the maximum number meaningful is probably 11 (or 0 to 10), and the fewer (3 or 5 range) the better.

*Ratio scales*, like that for income or time spent viewing TV, not only imply equal intervals between stated degrees on the scale, but have an absolute zero. They assume that it is meaningful that someone has nothing of the trait being measured. Examples of ratio scales would include the number of minutes spent watching television. In this case, absolute numbers may be expressed in relationship to each other. If older viewers spend over 30 hours watching television and teens about 15, we may say that seniors watch twice as much as teenagers as their preferred leisure activity. Indeed, time spent with the media has become a central variable studied in commercial and policy research. Quintiles, or top 20 per cent and bottom 20 per cent, of all audiences ranged in order or magnitude of their reported time spent viewing, are constantly compared in their viewing habits and carefully monitored for their spending patterns.

Because the ratio scales are anchored on zero, they can be used to compare the relative relationship between indicators – for example, income and amount of TV viewing. When two or more indicators are linked, these are called an index or data 'construct', most reliable when constructed with ratio scales.

## STEP 6: DESIGNING THE SAMPLE

Before we can gather data we need to decide who exactly we are going to communicate with in our study. Obviously, the best way to have valid observations of any phenomenon is to observe it around the clock and everywhere it happens. If we wanted to know when Danes were watching TV, and what exactly they watch, we might undertake a census or audit of TV watching in the whole country, by placing a researcher in every household, whose sole job was to record who was watching what. With multiple sets in many households a TV census might be difficult, not to mention a prohibitively expensive undertaking.

Designing for generalizable results turns the researcher's attention to the statistical procedures that help us ensure that sound or valid conclusions can be drawn from the observed evidence. In any sampling procedure, the researcher must think carefully about both the social and temporal dimensions of their measures and instruments. Another way of estimating the amount of time Danes devote to TV watching is to somehow draw a subset from the total population and observe them over the course of a day. This is called sampling from the population of Danes. Sampling is about taking a subset of a total population that is enough like it that valid generalization can be made to the total population.

Sampling assumes that we know how to select a representative group of individuals for the specified population. From the perspective of the need for generalization and the use of statistics, no decision is more important than the one about how to select this subset – it will determine how you may compare, contrast and generalize about how widespread your findings are in the general population.

In making generalizations, we must be assured that who we observe is not biased by the criteria of selection. The easiest way to do so is by selecting that sample randomly so that groups can be validly compared against each other and the total population, and the size of differences or correlations between them assessed (Sapsford 1999). To assess the selection, we can check the sample distributions against the tolerable margin of error assumed for the population.

There are four steps in framing the sample: defining the target population or universe for the sample, locating the sample frame, choosing a random probability or non-random sampling method, and deciding on the sample size.

The *target population* flows from the research question and literature review you have conducted. In the affluence study, the researchers chose adult TV viewers. There are many ways to define a target population, and students are encouraged initially to think through the basic demographic or behavioural characteristics that may affect their research question.

A *sample frame* is as complete a list of your total population as possible. Voters lists, directories or other compilations of people may be used. It is important to understand how exhaustive the list is. Telephone directories, for example, are notorious for excluding the homeless, the poor or the very rich in most western societies, but they are often used as a sample frame in surveys.

When it comes to sampling methods, you may decide to use probability sampling methods or not – one of the best-known leading non-probability samples is the *TV and Everyday Life* study. But if you choose a non-probability sample, you are severely restricted by the statistical tests you may use to help in your data analysis.

Probability sampling involves selecting individuals in such a way that their chances of selection are known. A systematic random sample allows each person listed an equal chance to be selected for participation. For example, the census provides very accurate estimates for the demographic composition of a sample. If one randomly knocks on 100 doors throughout the country, one would expect to encounter the same demographic composition in the sample as in the whole population (for example, 50 per cent female; 25 per cent under 18 years of age) – within known margins of error. A probability is a projection, or estimation, expressed as the number of chances (one in four) or as a percentage of times the outcome will be observed (.25) by chance if randomly sampled.

The simplest way to find those 100 doors is to use an 'n select'. Count the number in the sample frame, and divide it by the sample size you want to obtain. This number (n) allows you to use a fixed interval in selecting names from the list. If you have 1000 in your sample frame, and need only 100 subjects, then you choose every tenth name. You choose a random number between 1 and 10 (7, in this case) and move through the list by tens. Some researchers alternate selections from the top and bottom of the list, to ensure they cover the universe. In general, such a simple method works unless there is systematic bias in the underlying list. This method is a systematic random sample, and is often easier than pure random samples (where each respondent is chosen from a random number generator, in any off-the-shelf statistical package).

Occasionally it is important to carefully identify certain (mutually exclusive) subgroups or strata. For example, it might be necessary to ensure different socio-economic levels are adequately represented. *Stratified random sampling* is a useful tool in communities with complex linguistic, ethnic or regional sub-populations, to ensure large enough sample sizes to allow within- and across-group comparisons equally. In the affluent study, you may wish to ensure you select equally from known rich, middle-class or poor communities, but in greater proportion than is expected from the population, in order to be able to compare across subgroups.

Much early survey work in the community sociology tradition (underpinning the *Everyday Cultures Project* described in Chapter 11) relies upon a final variation of this stratified random sample, called the *multi-stage stratified area sample*. These are the most rigorous and representative, and usually the basis for each nation's census. In the case of the Australian *Everyday Cultures Project*, a sample total of 5000 adults was drawn, and stratified to be representative by state and territory. Respondents were systematically drawn randomly from within these strata. An alternative stratification method might be by language. Stratification is possible because the incidence of the area population in the total universe is known: if over-sampling, or drawing proportionately more respondents from a subgroup than might be expected is done in order to allow more within-group and across-group comparisons, a multi-stage stratified sample (by region within ethnic enclave, for example) can then be brought back into balance with the total population.

In any sample, it is inevitable that an individual will be unable to be contacted, unable to participate or will refuse. In both systematic and simple random samples, there are strict rules for 'replacing' the originally selected individual. The 'replacement' is also randomly selected, and careful records kept both of refusal rates and sources of substitution (from what may be called secondary or tertiary random sample replicates).

## SAMPLING ERROR AND CONFIDENCE LEVELS

How well does the mean of the sample match the mean of the parent population (Sapsford 1999)? The statistic most often used to describe sampling error is the standard error of a mean. Underpinning this idea is the likelihood that our sample follows a normal distribution. If you were to replicate the study with 100 different random samples, we would normally expect 66 per cent of them to fall within one standard error of the population mean, and 95 per cent to be within two standard deviations of the mean of the parent population. A calculation called the sampling error estimates the extent to which the sample differs from the 'universe' or population from which it was selected. The formula for calculating sampling error will not be presented here, but it is based on the sample size and the extent of homogeneity or diversity of the population. In general, the larger the sampling size, the smaller the sampling error. The sample with high homogeneity will have a smaller sampling error (Neuman 2000). Sampling error is also related to confidence levels. You often hear of polling results being reported with the proviso that they are accurate '19 times in 20' (or 95 per cent) of the time, were the same study to be replicated over and over, based on probability theory (Gray and Guppy 1999).

## SAMPLE SIZE AND MARGIN OF ERROR

Sample size is one of the most important final decisions an audience researcher can make. Interestingly, the relationship between sample size and sampling error is not direct. While there are complex statistical formulae for choosing sample sizes, most depend on the confidence level wanted (usually not less than 95 per cent). We call this the 'margin of error'. A customary sample size for academic study is 100 – at the 95 per cent level of confidence, we would expect an estimate from our population to lie within a range + or −10 per cent (De Vaus 1995). This means, if we find that 57 per cent of our sample report use the Internet, then, based on a sample of 100, with a margin of error of + or −10 per cent, a 'true' estimate may range anywhere between 47 and 67 per cent. The larger the sample, the smaller the margin of error in estimates. After a sample is greater than .0001 of the total population, its size has very little impact on confidence levels for generalization. Accordingly, Canadian pollsters often use a sample of 1500, with confidence limits of + or −2.5 per cent, the same as their American counterparts, despite a population one-tenth the size. The major concern in constructing samples is more practically related to the subgroups you are interested in analysing. The greater the number of subgroups, the larger the sample size needed. Sample sizes are often smaller in academic study, unless it is subsidized; 30 to 50 cases, however, is frequently the floor for small-sample statistical testing, and is usually the minimum for exploratory quantitative studies. Precision increases steadily for samples up to 200 in size, but after that point there is a more modest gain in the margin of error.

## STEP 7: MAPPING AND ANALYSING THE DATA

The purpose of standardized codes or numbered variables in our deployment of measurement scales is to help us compare the same variables between different subjects within a sample. Probability theory and statistics provide us with useful ways of describing our results, looking for patterns by comparing within and across different sub-populations, examining relationships between variables, and ultimately testing our hypotheses. The selection of various tools of statistical data analysis depends on many factors over and above whether we set out to describe, explain, evaluate or predict outcomes for a general population. These include the size of the sample, the number of variables and the level of measurement.

If a survey and sample are small, researchers may be able to track each subject's responses and make comparisons without recourse to quantitative tools. To cope with large data sets, however, the researcher relies on statistical procedures and computer-based probability tools to map, analyse and generalize from the data patterns. Computer programs are designed to help the researcher map the complex relationships between variables when large numbers of respondents are asked multiple questions. Many researchers find these programs extend the scale and scope of their initial analysis and help them reveal the pattern of relations underlying the data. They are also useful in the second stage of data analysis, because off-the-rack programmes enable researchers to explore and test for the correlations between variables and by cross-tabulating results in ways that reveal statistically significant differences quickly.

The first task in discovering what stories our data tell is to explore the basic patterning in the data. Descriptive statistics are useful to provide us with numeric maps of the data set. Mapping is aided by visual representation of patterns in the form of charts and graphs, as well as statistical summaries that indicate central tendency (means, frequencies and medians) and the kinds of dispersion of responses (variance, clusters). But researchers need first to understand what these descriptive statistics refer to. So let's begin our foray into data analysis by thinking about just one variable: how much time did a random sample of 100 respondents spend yesterday using a computer? In what follows, we will outline the spatial metaphors that statistics uses for mapping or describing such data in terms of central tendency (mean) and dispersion (variance from the mean).

## MEASURES OF CENTRAL TENDENCY

Central tendency is based on the probability that responses will be randomly scattered around a 'centre' cluster, evident when all data is graphed. We know that people differ considerably in the amount of time they use a computer: some people don't use one while others spend most of their waking time in front of one. So in our survey we will use a random scale of 0–5 representing time spent, where '5' represents 5 hours or more. Figure 10.1 represents a possible distribution of responses by a frequency distribution, which shows what percentage of respondents answered in each time slot offered.

We may describe our result in a number of different ways. The simplest is a frequency chart, which displays the distribution by plotting the number of times various answer categories are used. Another way to think about this result is to identify which answer category occurs most often. Among our sample users, between two and three hours is by far the most frequent time spent with computers. This number describes the *mode of our distribution*. In measurements where the numbers really imply no conceptual distance or intensity (say, in a nominal scale), this is the only meaningful summary measure.

Another way of describing this distribution is the *median*, the *middle case*, which is relevant in analysing ordinal or ratio scales. Or you can add up all the answer categories, divide

**Figure 10.1**   Time spent with the computer last week from home (hours) (base: users)

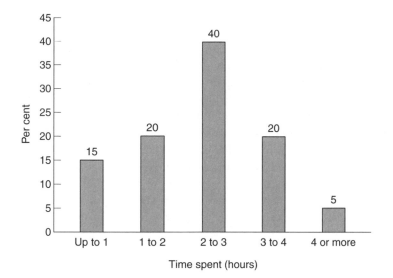

Note: most scales are careful to specify terms under which rounding up or down are important for coding, or defining categories in such a way that they are not overlapping (1–59 minutes, 60–119 minutes, and so on); hypothetical example

them by the total sample size and calculate an *average* or *mean* number of hours. Researchers often like to record raw numbers (that is, estimated time to the nearest quarter-hour), as actually reported by the respondent, in a relatively open-ended manner, rather than use pre-set numerical categorics, to improve the quality of the mean calculation. The mean for any scalar variable represents the total of all scores on a variable divided by the number of cases. The more closely clustered the reported times are – or symmetrical the distribution of answers – the more substitutable are the mean and the medians. Means, however, are vulnerable to distortions from outliers – the one or two respondents who may report that their computer use is well over 50 hours a week, perhaps because they work from home on a computer. The further the mean is from the median, the less reliable it is.

## MEASURES OF DISPERSION

To describe how cases are dispersed around the mean, mathematicians have developed the *standard deviation* (a useful concept, we have seen, when thinking about confidence limits in sampling). What the standard deviation calculates, in fact, is square or weight numbers far from the mean; sum them, and then express this as the square root of the sum divided by the sample size (for the formula, see Deacon, Pickering et al. 1999). The standard deviation thus expresses the variance or dispersion of answers from the centre in a single number. A high number suggests the values are widely dispersed. A low number suggests they are grouped closely around the mean (Deacon, Pickering et al. 1999: 87). This formula standardizes the distribution by assuming that 95 per cent of all samples will fall within (plus or minus) *two* standard deviations or a certain space from the expected value.

Imagine samples of individual opinions from two communities and the distribution of those opinions within each community arrayed along a scale from 'strongly agree' to 'strongly disagree' with the question, say, of regulating offensive content found on the Internet. Profound polarization of attitudes within one community would plot a map of responses as a U-shaped distribution of individual views, in which about half the people are strongly opposed and nearly as many are strongly in favour, with next to no one in the middle. A state of consensus in the second community, on the other hand, might be mapped as a bell-shaped or bell-curved distribution, with a strong central tendency and relatively few people at the extremes of the scale. We would probably not want to speak of these two communities as being alike in the formation of their public opinion, even though the median or average positions could very well be similar (Price 1992). Caution is needed in applying these measures of central tendency and dispersion in interpreting raw data. Their prime benefit is that, by standardizing dispersion, they enable us to compare similarities and differences in distribution for scalar variables across subgroups.

## ANALYSING DATA RELATIONSHIPS: THE CROSS-TABULATION OF NOMINAL VARIABLES

After we have mapped the responses to every variable, reporting both the number who selected that category and the percentage answering, and means and standard deviations where appropriate, then the fun begins, for now we can start to explore how our variables interact. For example, consider two nominal variables from an actual survey of Canadian individuals aged 15 and over. Statistics Canada chose gender, which is nominal (1=male; 2=female), and a yes/no answer to Internet use in the past year, as Figure 10.2 shows. Let's start by suggesting (perhaps from a hunch drawn from other studies we have read) that gender is related to computer use. We are testing whether males are more likely to use computers than females, speculating about a correlation or a probable causal relationship.

Our first concern might be to check to see if our sampling of gender was similar to that of the known general population. Perhaps we have skewed the sample and more women than men answered the questionnaire. From the census we know that a random procedure should result in a sample that is 51 per cent female, which Statistics Canada reports was the case.

We can now examine our data in Table 10.1 in a simple bivariate, or two-way, cross-tabulation, showing the independent variable, gender, in the vertical column and the dependent variable, computer use, in rows. Incidence of Internet use in 2000 overall was reported by 53 per cent of Canadians. Often such summary or basic frequency distribution data is presented graphically, perhaps as bar charts (Figure 10.2). Note that both the table and figure presents the independent variable – that is, the factor we believe influences computer use – as a column, a vertical total adding up to 100 per cent.

Table 10.2    Internet use in past year by age within sex (2000)

| Age group | Total % | Male % | Female % |
|---|---|---|---|
| Canada | 53 | 56 | 50 |
| 15 to 24 | 85 | 86 | 83 |
| 25 to 34 | 66 | 68 | 64 |
| 35 to 44 | 60 | 62 | 58 |
| 45 to 54 | 51 | 53 | 49 |
| 55 and over | 19 | 23 | 15 |

Source: Statistics Canada; this is an example of a column percentaged table; it does not add to 100 per cent because 'no' responses (or non-users) are not shown

**Figure 10.2**    Incidence of internet use in the past year by gender (2000)

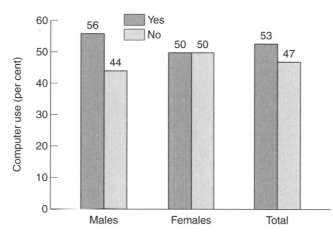

Source: Statistics Canada, Access to and use of information communication technology. *General Social Survey*, Cycle 14, Catalogue 56-505.XIE; this is an example of a vertical or column percentaged table

We can see that 56 per cent of the men sampled indicated they had used the Internet in the last year, compared to 50 per cent of women. On the face of it, men would seem to be more likely to be Internet users than women. By how much? Is this difference significant or not?

To answer this question we refer to the application of the Chi-square statistic in Box 10.2, which, because of its availability, most students can use 'off the shelf' if they understand its basic logic of assessing the expected and reported results for nominal variables like those examined here.

## Box 10.2  Using Chi to test actual versus expected data relationships

Chi-square ($\chi^2$) is used to test the relationship between two variables. The test is based on a 'null hypothesis' — that is, a working assumption that a statistically significant relationship between an independent variable and a dependent variable does *not* exist. In this example we will look at gender as the independent variable and computer usage as the dependent variable. As researchers, we ask ourselves: 'What is the probability that an observed difference between men and women, with respect to computer usage, is due to randomness?' If $\chi^2$ gives us a low probability, we can reject the null hypothesis and conclude that a statistically significant relationship does indeed exist.

The first step is to calculate 'expected values' for men and women, based on the null hypothesis assumption in our hypothetical data set.

|         | Total | Use computer | Do not use |
|---------|-------|--------------|------------|
| Gender  | 200   | 120          | 80         |
| Men     | 100   | 45           | 55         |
| Women   | 100   | 75           | 25         |

Assuming gender to be a non-factor, we would expect the composition of computer users to be 60 men plus 60 women. This intuitive calculation can be expressed as:

Row total  $\times$  Column Total  /  Grand Total
100        $\times$  120           /  200          = 60

The expected value calculation for the entire table is:

|              |     | Use computer | Do not use |
|--------------|-----|--------------|------------|
| Total sample | 200 | 120          | 80         |
| Men          | 100 | 60           | 40         |
| Women        | 100 | 60           | 40         |

We then calculate the differences between observed and expected values:

|              |     | Use computer | Do not use |
|--------------|-----|--------------|------------|
| Total sample | 200 | 120          | 80         |
| Men          | 100 | −15          | +15        |
| Women        | 100 | +15          | −15        |

We need to measure how different our observed results are from the null hypothesis, whether we can reject the null hypothesis, and with what degree of confidence we are not making a mistake in generalizing from our sample results to the larger population.

The next step is to calculate the $\chi^2$ value for each table cell. Difference squared divided by the expected value:
$15 \times 15 / 60 = 3.75$

|  |  | Use computer | Do not use |
|---|---|---|---|
| Total sample | 200 | 120 | 80 |
| Men | 100 | 3.75 | 5.625 |
| Women | 100 | 3.75 | 5.625 |

The table $\chi^2$ value is the sum of the table cell $\chi^2$ values.
$3.75 + 3.75 + 5.625 + 5.625 = 18.75$

The interpretation of our $\chi$ value (18.75) can be obtained by referring to the appendix of a statistics textbook (or using statistics software), where the probabilities of getting $\chi$ values for tables of various sizes are listed. Table sizes are referred to as 'degrees of freedom'. Our example table has two categories in each variable so there are four degrees of freedom (or cells in the table).

Expressed mathematically, DF = (rows $-1$) $\times$ (columns $-1$).

Looking up an $\chi$ value of 18.75 for four degrees of freedom, the appendix tells us that the probability of this value occurring due to randomness is 1 per cent. Therefore we could reject the null hypothesis with a confidence level of 99 per cent.

Statistical significance does not ensure substantive significance. An actual relationship between variables may be trivially weak or may not exist at all. Statistical significance means only that the data patterns or variable relationships can be confidently generalized to the larger population from which the sample is drawn.

Note: $\chi$ can be used for all levels of measurement scales.

Source: adapted from Neuman, (2000: 340–1); see Deacon, Pickering et al. (1999: 104–9) for a fuller explanation

The logic of Chi asks: How many users are women? If computer use is randomly distributed, proportionate to gender, we might expect 51 per cent. Is the actual number or percentage obtained higher or lower than expected? By how much? Is this difference significant or not? As Box 10.2 demonstrates, the Chi-square value of 18.75 suggests that there *is* a relationship between gender and computer usage. The calculation has been done using the confidence limits from the reported sample size, which established a margin of error that is + or −2.2 per cent, so the gap of 6 per cent is not likely to be due just to random error.

We discuss the Chi statistic fully in Box 10.2 because it is perhaps the most versatile statistic and can be used for both nominal and ordinal measurement scales. If our measure of computer use had been a ratio scale, for example, the number of hours spent using computers in the last week, an alternative and more robust statistical test for comparisons is the T-test or ANOVA, or (analysis of variance), which will be presented in more detail in Chapter 16.

## EXPLORING ASSOCIATIONS OF VARIABLES

In many studies we are also interested in thinking about the relationships between more than two scalar variables. Let us take, for example, the question of links between the amount of time spent using computers, age and gender from our recent Canadian survey of media use. We have already seen that there is a slight variation in computer use by gender. Is there a similar variation by age? Table 10.1 illustrates an even larger range of computer use – from a low participation of 19 per cent over the past year, among those aged 55 and over, to 85 per cent among those aged 15–24. This suggests that there may be stronger cultural variations in use by age than gender. So let's look to see if similar patterns of gender variation hold *within* the various age groups (Table 10.2). In non-experimental research, you can introduce a third variable in statistical analysis (and many more in series) to see if the bivariate relationship persists within categories of the control variable (in this case, sex). If the relationship between gender and computer use is weakened or disappears after age is introduced, this suggests that the third variable, age, may be a more important predictor of Internet use. Table 10.2 introduces a trivariate, or three-way, table, the easiest way to display the data using a basic control.

Table 10.2 illustrates that among those aged 15–24 who are most likely (85 per cent) to use a computer, there is little (3 per cent) variation between males and females. This data suggest that it is erroneous to speak of a gender gap in computer use among Canadian youth. But the gender gap increases somewhat after age 25 and is largest over 55. Had we used a more sensitive measure of use, perhaps time spent on the computer that may have led to a broader distribution of reported minutes (ratio level data), then we may further strengthen our powers of mapping data.

Looking for greater detail helps us determine that men not only use computers more, but spend twice as long on them as women (an average of 3.2 hours a week compared to women, who report spending 1.6 hours (Table 10.3). How does time usage interact with age? If older people report using the computer less often than their younger counterparts, we may reasonably suspect that the time reported on the computer will decline with age.

This alternate hypothesis states that if there is a linear relationship then, on average, we would expect that for every year older, there is a unit decrease in time spent using the Internet (from a reported 5.6 hours a week to .5 hours a week across all age groups. This relationship can be represented by drawing a straight line $y = mx + b$ through the average

Table 10.3   Mean time spent with computers in an average week

| Age group | Total hours<br>X | Male<br>X | Female<br>X |
|---|---|---|---|
| Canada | 2.1 | 3.2 | 1.6 |
| Age group | | | |
| 15–24 | 5.6 | 8.4 | 4.2 |
| 25–34 | 4.4 | 6.6 | 3.3 |
| 35–44 | 2.5 | 3.8 | 1,9 |
| 45–54 | 1.1 | 1.7 | 0.8 |
| 55 and over | 0.5 | 0.8 | 0.4 |

| | Male | Female |
|---|---|---|
| % users | 56 | 50 |
| Mean or X | 3.2 hours | 1.6 hours |

Source: Hypothetical example

weekly use for each age group, where y is computer use, x is age and m (slope) represents the unit increase in use time for every additional year of age. b is the y intercept, which signifies the minimum time spent on computers, which in this case is 0. The question, then, is how can we establish whether this hypothetical linear relationship is a useful model of the actual relationship between these variables in our data sets?

Since there is variability in computer use, we expect that some people in each age group will use computers more than others and that some young people may not use them at all. Despite the variation, by plotting each data point in our hypothetical data set, we can see that, on average, there is a consistent tendency for older people to use computers for shorter periods of time. Using the standard deviation method for plotting divergence, mentioned earlier, we can estimate the dispersion of our data around the mean for each age level, using the formula sd = root sum x-x1/n-1 and in fact derive an equation for the straight line that best fits this particular data set. Often data sets contain contrary outcomes (perhaps a dip in use for those aged 35 to 44 and then a rise) and it is not possible to say a linear relationship exists between age and use.

A *correlation coefficient* is the statistic we use for testing any linear equation between two variables. There are a number of ways of calculating a correlation, but perhaps the best known is Pearson's r, which is readily available in a number of statistical software packages. Pearson's r calculates the correlation coefficient by first standardizing both variables so that their variance can be compared. The calculation itself expresses the square root of the sum of squares for every data point's deviation from the expected distribution under the assumption that there is a linear relationship. The formula and standard dispersion charts may be found in any basic statistics text (De Vaus 1995).

Correlation analysis tells us two important stories about how these values are associated across the sample (Deacon, Pickering et al. 1999). The first concerns the 'goodness of fit' between the expected linear model and the actual data points expressed as the magnitude of the r value. The r value only varies between $+1$ and $-1$: under the assumption that both variables are normally distributed around the mean, this number indicates whether the variation in the dependent variable can be explained by positing a straight line relationship with an independent variable (Sapsford 1999). The confidence we have in any particular value of r depends on the total variation within the sample as a whole, but generally speaking we know that the closer its absolute value is to $+/-1$, the stronger the relationship. The direction of the relationship between the variables is represented by the $+$ or $-$ sign. These are easy to interpret too: when both variables increase together, then the relationship is positive. But if older people used computers less than younger people, then we would expect the slope to be negative, as is suggested by Table 10.3.

If we are interested in examining the possible relationships between even more variables in our data set (let's say a number of reported cultural practices), then a correlation matrix is a useful diagnostic technique. For example, the *Canadian Arts Consumers Profile* conducted in 1992 by a joint federal–provincial government task force asked 11,000 Canadians which of 15 different cultural activities they had done recently. The results for each of the 15 sectors of the arts (pop concerts, opera, and so on) they had attended were plotted against each other (Table 10.4).

In Table 10.4 we may see relatively moderate correlations between Q12 Plays and Q11 Musicals; Q11 Musicals and Q10 Modern Dance; Q2 Pop Concerts and Q3 Jazz; Q12 Theatre and Q6 Classical Music Concerts. A high correlation, if you will remember, suggests the more you go to plays, the more you go to musicals. Given assumptions about the gulf between 'high' art tastes and 'popular' art tastes, the surprise found among popular music concert-goers was the correlation with jazz attendance, calling into question any assumed mutually exclusive relationship between these so-called 'high' cultural and 'popular' forms (as we will explore further in Chapter 11). It is easy to see how correlations provide a convenient first reading of the various associations underlying a complex data set where there are two or more interacting dimensions.

## STEP 9: EVALUATING CAUSAL RELATIONSHIPS

We are nearing the end of the data mapping stage. By now, patterns connecting data, and hunches about relative associations (perhaps even measures of the strength of association between the independent and dependent data) may be calculated. In Box 10.1, we saw the researchers were forced to refine their model of the independent and dependent variable. They learned that levels of education influence the amount of TV viewing, so education became the independent variable and TV viewing the intervening variable (and especially

Table 10.4  Correlation matrix between all attendance variables from the BC Arts Consumer Study (1994)

|      | Q2 | Q3 | Q4 | Q5 | Q6 | Q7 | Q8 | Q9 | Q10 | Q11 | Q12 | Q13 | Q14 | Q15 |
|------|----|----|----|----|----|----|----|----|-----|-----|-----|-----|-----|-----|
| Q2   |    |    |    |    |    |    |    |    |     |     |     |     |     |     |
| Q3   | .38 |    |    |    |    |    |    |    |     |     |     |     |     |     |
| Q4   | .19 | .18 |    |    |    |    |    |    |     |     |     |     |     |     |
| Q5   | .08 | .07 | .07 |    |    |    |    |    |     |     |     |     |     |     |
| Q6   | .06 | .22 | .01 | .12 |    |    |    |    |     |     |     |     |     |     |
| Q7   | .06 | .10 | .62 | .08 | .32 |    |    |    |     |     |     |     |     |     |
| Q8   | .21 | .19 | .09 | .17 | .24 | .14 |    |    |     |     |     |     |     |     |
| Q9   | .14 | .16 | .06 | .19 | .31 | .27 | .21 |    |     |     |     |     |     |     |
| Q10  | .21 | .19 | .09 | .19 | .11 | .11 | .25 | .20 |     |     |     |     |     |     |
| Q11  | .15 | .15 | .20 | .20 | .29 | .25 | .28 | .22 | .42 |     |     |     |     |     |
| Q12  | .23 | .26 | .09 | .17 | .35 | .23 | .26 | .28 | .22 | .42 |     |     |     |     |
| Q13  | .27 | .16 | .18 | .14 | −.01 | .03 | .12 | .04 | .11 | .15 | .12 |     |     |     |
| Q14  | .29 | .17 | .03 | .08 | .06 | .09 | .14 | .09 | .12 | .16 | .22 | .22 |     |     |
| Q15  | .20 | .25 | .05 | .16 | .23 | .13 | .23 | .17 | .13 | .16 | .27 | .06 | .17 |     |
| Q16  | .14 | .19 | .04 | .19 | .19 | .10 | .25 | .14 | .11 | .19 | .24 | .08 | .12 | .40 |

Index: Q2 = Pop Concerts; Q3 = Jazz; Q4 = Country; Q5 = Children's; Q6 = Classical; Q7 = Opera; Q8 = Ethnic; Q9 = Ballet; Q10 = Modern Dance; Q11 = Musical; Q12 = Theatre; Q13 = Sports; Q14 = Movie; Q15 = Art Gallery; Q16 = Museum.

Source: derived from Murray (1994), 80–8 correlation matrix

genre of TV watched). Fuller discussion of how to 'test' causal relationships with more advanced inferential statistics can be found in the experimental toolbox (Chapter 16). Such re-evaluation of the causal models in data is not enough to provide 'proof' for your study; you must now design public communication of it.

## STEP 10: REPORTING FINDINGS

Every quantitative research report tells its story in a manner that allows the reader to understand the whole research process – how the researcher translated questions into data sets and went from evidence to conclusions. When we write about empirical quantitative research, we must develop three arguments about:

- the validity and reliability of our evidence

- the meaning or interpretation of that evidence

- the relationships between our concepts (Sumser 2001).

The research report thus provides a 'thought map' of the research process as a whole, outlining each step (operationalization, generalization and inferential analysis) in the inquiry process in sequence.

It usually starts with an *Introduction*, which states the framing of the research question and justifies why it is important to investigate it. In doing so, writers often review what other people have said about the topic, to help articulate the specific questions that have emerged in the literature. It goes on to explain how the researcher defined and operation-alized the concepts under investigation. In the *Method* section, the author explains the rationale for the design of the study, justifying the research method (survey, experiments) used. The quantitative audience study goes on to define the sample frame, and notes how subjects were selected and approached. In experimental studies, it also articulates a rationale for the controls and treatments that were used.

The *Results* section reports on the data findings, usually by providing charts and tables that map the data set. It also sets out the analytic procedures that were used to address partic-ular arguments, and articulates what the research believes the findings mean and the con-fidence they have in these inferences. Beyond summarizing the results, and explaining our conclusions, the *Discussion* or *Findings* section usually explores the implications of the main findings, explaining how they relate to the original research question (Sumser 2001). Most survey research stops just before causal determinations are made. In experimental research, it will be necessary to build the argument about effects, or causality, and the directional relationship between independent variables and dependent ones in a complex world. Most researchers are also likely to provide some comment on the validity and reliability of their methods, and to refer to external studies that may confirm or refute their argument.

Put another way, the research report describes each of the steps in the decision tree in Box 10.1. Here is my research question. This is why it is important. Here is what other people have said. These are the likely hypotheses that have emerged from secondary literature examining similar questions. This is how I defined and operationalized the concepts. Here is how I designed my study, and what research method (survey or experiments) I used. This is who I spoke to, and how I selected them. Here are my data findings (data mapping). This is what the findings mean (data analysis). This is how what I found relates to my original research question. Here are the limitations. Here are the implications and recommendations for further research.

Every quantitative research report tells a story about translating ideas to numbers, and interpreting numbers as ideas. If you remember this double hermeneutic, introduced in Chapter 1, you are well on the way to becoming a self-reflexive and critical quantitative audience researcher.

# Section 5

## Survey Research on Audiences

# Chapter Eleven

# Audience surveys in practice: from social context to numbers and back again

Are cultural tastes today so chaotic and idiosyncratic they defy mapping? Despite a popular postmodern shrug that 'there's no accounting for taste', a group of Australian cultural researchers decided to do a large-scale survey in 1995, to produce a richly textured social cartography. Based on their research, they argued that likes and dislikes have a definite pattern in which social class, age, gender, education and ethnicity combine to distribute cultural interests and abilities differently across the Australian population.

This chapter presents the study by Tony Bennett, Michael Emmison and John Frow, *Accounting for Tastes: Australian Everyday Cultures*, a single cross-sectional survey of 2756 adults, published in 1999. Financially supported by the Australian Research Council, and relying on the Australian Bureau of Statistics for a sophisticated probability sample frame drawn from electoral lists, *Accounting for Tastes* is a typical policy-inspired survey. The goals of their Everyday Cultures Project were to map as comprehensively as possible the full range of Australian cultural practices, understand the aesthetic principles underlying patterns of cultural activity and explore how tastes are social in their organization and character. The authors wanted to contribute to the international policy debate over the development of 'cultural life chance' indicators that can assist in evaluating the equity objectives of national cultural policy (Bennett et al. 1999).[1]

The Everyday Cultures Project is interesting for audience researchers for the way it situates media consumption in everyday life and deliberately bridges the methodological divide. Qualitative and quantitative findings are interwoven throughout. Qualitative data are used to study individual style and identity issues, quantitative data to isolate and generalize about cultural patterns of similarity and differences. Developed after an exploratory phase of 12 focus groups, the survey was followed by 34 individual depth-interviews, so the more open oral testimony could help make sense of the statistics and 'give a more vivid sense of the lived texture of cultural practices'.

---

[1] The *National Everyday Cultures Programme* continues at the Pavis Centre, affiliated with the Open University in the UK, under the direction of a steering committee that includes Richard Collins, Angela McRobbie and Roger Silverstone, among others (see www.open.ac.uk.socialsciences/sociology).

## Box 11.1  Research themes of the Everyday Cultures Project

- Access to cultural infrastructure and opportunities for participation.
- Capacity for cultural participation (learning of codes or TV visual practices to allow enjoyment of or participation in popular education and entertainment).
- Patterns of cultural participation, particularly the relationship between mediated forms of culture and performing arts, museums, libraries or other venues.
- Cultural mobility, or patterns of access contrasted to use in relation to sociocultural inequalities.

Such surveys of everyday life consciously set out to plot the meaning of the changing media environment for audiences and the way media practices adapt in the context of overall work/leisure lifestyles. The Project's research questions define the study as:

- *exploratory* (just how rapid/diffuse is the change in media use?)

- *descriptive* in its accounting for change (how many/how extensive?)

- *directional* (what happens over time?)

- *comparative* (how do those without access to the Internet compare to those with?)

- *contextual* (where do media fit in everyday life, and what space is left for public, non-commercial cultural practices?).

Implicit in the authors' agenda is also a normative position: that cultural participation should be widely available to citizens in a democratic society. For audience researchers, the challenge is to find a research method that offers sufficient scale, defined as the capacity to have enough cases in various demographic groups, to be able to compare and contrast among them and search for similarities and differences. We are talking, then, about using quantitative social scientific conventions of larger sample sizes, use of measurement theory and denotation with numbers to map patterns of cultural activities and media use/non-use. We thus use quantitative measurement in order to:

- 'represent something' within known probabilities

- compare and contrast audience practice in everyday life across regions or countries of demographic groups using known statistical conventions

- present evidence in terrains of discourse in policy, market and academic spheres, which may be examined for reliability, validity or other comparative confirmation.

Audience researchers choose the survey method if they wish to ask questions of people in a similar way across a wide variety of potential settings.[2] Yet such a choice involves trade-offs between greater 'standardization' and flexibility of interviews. Surveys are unlike ethnographies, which use more non-directive or open-ended conversation, but the benefits of relative standardization afford easier operationalization across very different populations (Livingstone and Bovill 2001) since they streamline talk. They also incorporate rules of evidence (estimates of error, statistical tools to measure association or dispersion) that allow policy-makers to weigh them in debates, as discursive constructs, or use them as aids to mapping discursive repertoires on issues. Justin Lewis (2001) argues convincingly that in many cases, surveys are themselves historical moments of ideological reproduction. In using surveys for policy interventions, this kind of discursive self-awareness of dominant and minority cultural interests is critical.

Deciding the scope of subject matter to be covered in surveys is very important. A strong argument can be made in contemporary media environments that researchers must examine a broad scope of subject matter – that is, media use in the full context of cultural practices. There are several reasons for avoiding media-centrism, as the Australian Everyday Cultures Project seeks to do. First, while we know TV occupies most leisure time, it does not occupy all of that time, and most TV time carries only inattentive or partial processing of viewing. TV may supplant other cultural activities, especially attending a festival, theatrical or movie event. Second, while there has been only one generation since the advent of the medium, some data suggests that TV habits are intergenerational and related to class replication of 'high or low' cultural capacity. Finally, as suggested by the 'cultural studies' perspective, if leisure and work in contemporary societies increasingly revolve around media and media cultures, it is important to understand the contexts of media use (Livingstone and Bovill 2001). Placing media or arts experience in the total range of human activities is a de facto rejection of the segregation of media from everyday life, which is often characteristic of bad surveys done in the policy or marketing worlds.

The Australian survey posed some 140 questions, covering a wide array of subjects, from decoration of the household, domestic leisure and social activities, personal tastes and preferences, recreational activities, family and friends, and individual characteristics, to broader social and political attitudes (see Box 11.2). The questionnaire designers were directly inspired by Pierre Bourdieu's (1984) seminal study of the origins, production, meaning and function of taste in French society in the 1960s. Heavily influenced by his creative questionnaire approach, there is a section on cultural judgement across a number of arts and media (how subjects for a photograph may be classified, as clichéd or interesting, and so

---

[2] For his book *Cultural Distinction*, Pierre Bourdieu administered a comprehensive survey, door to door, to 1200 people in Paris and Lille, a nearby medium-sized town. Bourdieu would not have been able to conduct his study without the patronage of the opinion research arm of the French public broadcaster ORTF. A similar random probability study, the *Canadian Arts Consumer Profile*, published in 1992, surveyed 11,106 Canadians over the age of 18 via telephone, with a follow-up mail survey among 5400.

## Box 11.2: The Australian Everyday Cultures Questionnaire (selected questions)

### Section A. Your Household

A.12  Do you have any of the following in your home?

Original paintings/drawings _____      Pottery or ceramics _____

Signed limited edition prints _____      Sculpture _____

Rock music posters _____      Nature posters _____

Art posters _____      Political posters _____

A.13  Do you have a musical instrument(s) in your household? (Please specify)

_____

### Section B. Domestic Leisure

B.2  Which of the following do you *mostly* look for in your domestic leisure?

Relaxation _____      Intellectual stimulation _____

Escape from work _____      Developing new interests _____

Doing something useful _____      Just passing time _____

B.5  How many hours of TV do you think you watch over the course of a week?

30 hours or more _____      9 hours or fewer _____

Between 20 and 29 _____      I don't watch TV at all _____

Between 10 and 19 _____

### Section C. Your Social Activities

C.2  When you have guests for a meal, what kind of food do you prefer to serve?

Your usual cooking _____      Innovative or exotic recipes _____

Health food _____      Whatever is going _____

Simple but tasty food _____      Takeaways _____

Something special _____      I don't entertain _____

### Section D. Tastes and Preferences

D.8  Here is a further list of musical works. Put a tick against those you know and name either the composer or performer with whom you usually associate these works.

Unchained Melody _____      November Rain _____

Jailhouse Rock _____      Hotel California _____

Dark Side of the Moon _____      Cabaret _____

Tip of my Tongue _____      Stardust _____

Nessun Dorma _____      Stand by Your Man _____

My Fair Lady _____      Predator _____

Piano Man _____      Burning Down the House _____

Smells Like Teen Spirit _____      I'm Your Kind _____

Orinoco Flow ('Sail Away') _____

D.23    How would you characterize the following subjects for a photograph?

|  | Beautiful | Interesting | Cliched | Unattractive |
|---|---|---|---|---|
| A landscape | ____ | ____ | ____ | ____ |
| A car crash | ____ | ____ | ____ | ____ |
| A pregnant woman | ____ | ____ | ____ | ____ |
| A vase of flowers | ____ | ____ | ____ | ____ |
| Homeless people fighting | ____ | ____ | ____ | ____ |
| A sunset over the sea | ____ | ____ | ____ | ____ |
| A tackle in a football match | ____ | ____ | ____ | ____ |

D.24    Could you indicate in a few words what you think 'good taste' and 'bad taste' entail?

## Section H. Social and Political Attitudes

H.3    Which one of the following do you think *most* helps people to get on in life?

| | |
|---|---|
| Natural ability ____ | Who you know ____ |
| Education ____ | Ambition ____ |
| Hard work ____ | Determination ____ |
| Social background ____ | Inherited wealth ____ |

H.4    Do you think there should be more or less public money given to . . . ?

|  | More Funding | Less Funding | About Right |
|---|---|---|---|
| Sport | ____ | ____ | ____ |
| The Arts | ____ | ____ | ____ |
| Heritage and the Environment | ____ | ____ | ____ |

on), and on cultural knowledge (whether a list of musical works is known, and if the composer of a given work can be named). Like Bourdieu's survey, the questions probe aesthetic preferences, tastes in music and reading, and political views. Unlike *Distinction*, the study does not explore food passions, but substitutes a section on the care of body and self (arguably an equivalently powerful indicator of class), adding work and extensive popular culture and media sections (Bennett et al. 1999: 6). Most importantly, gender, race and ethnicity are added to the analysis.

Both the French and Australian cultural surveys share three characteristics:

**1.** they focus on questions about parents and children in order to understand 'cultural mobility' across generations, within the constraints of a cross-sectional or single-point-in-time survey

**2.** they explore a wide ambit of activities

**3.** they include questions probing actual knowledge of categories of cultural practice, and affective or evaluative questions about intensity of cultural practice.

Unlike Bourdieu, Bennett, Emmison and Frow administered their study independently of their Bureau of Statistics, while relying on it for assistance in sampling. The scope of their undertaking necessitated trade-offs in the strategy of their data collection. They decided to use a mail survey, since the questionnaire was too complex for the telephone and too potentially intimidating to conduct face to face. They were prepared to live with the known weaknesses of their mail survey instrument. Self-administered data collection places more of a burden on the reading and writing skills of the respondent than do interviewer procedures. Another problem is getting people to return the completed questionnaire. To ensure cooperation, the mailed questionnaire included a letter from the sponsoring Australian University. It attracted a 61.9 per cent response rate (that is, more than six in ten agreed, after being approached, to participate), considered quite robust by social science standards. But there were systematic under-representations among those who cooperated: men and those with less formal education did not return the surveys as often. As a consequence, the sample answers had to be adjusted (sometimes called 'weighting up') for these subgroups, to be representative of the population. It is curious that in their published study, the authors do not explicitly defend these biases or test them experimentally via a non-response comparison, for example (perhaps by calling back those who did not reply).

## THEORETICAL BACKGROUND

Indebted to Raymond Williams' conception of culture as ordinary, *Accounting for Taste* follows Bourdieu's study closely. *Distinction* remains the most rigorous theoretical exploration of cultural preference:

> *In* Distinction *. . . Bourdieu effects a Copernican revolution in the study of taste. He abolishes the sacred frontier that makes legitimate culture a separate realm and repatriates aesthetic consumption into everyday consumptions. He demonstrates that aesthetic judgement is a social ability by virtue of both its genesis and its functioning. In so doing, Bourdieu offers not only a radical 'critique of judgement'. He also delivers a graphic account of the workings of culture and power in contemporary society.*
>
> (Wacquant, in Fowler 2000: 114)

Bourdieu asks, 'How is culture differentially distributed and what statistical regularities can be observed in this distinction?' In his view, social class is the major dimension of social inequality structuring cultural preference: 'culture is a class signal that helps maintain class domination and to shape individual life chances as much as economic capital does'. Translated into English in 1984, Bourdieu's work has been influential in cultural studies for its call to 'get hands dirty in the kitchens of empirical research' (Bennett 1997). The focus of his study is the uses to which culture is put – not just its intrinsic value.

The Australian researchers take what they see as a departure from Bourdieu in their self-defined stance of epistemological pragmatism, which Tony Bennett has called a 'concern with practical consequences or values, with matters pertaining to the affairs of a state or community'. In particular, Bennett calls for:

*a shift in the 'command metaphors' of cultural studies . . . away from the rhetorics of resistance, oppositionalism and anti-commercialism on the one hand and populism on the other, towards those of access, equity and empowerment and the divination of opportunities to exercise appropriate cultural leadership. Access and equity aspirations in policy require more detailed forms of statistical monitoring . . .*

(Bennett 1997: 20)

Although later in his life Bourdieu's interventions as a public intellectual in France were increasingly political, *Distinction* is not noted for its exploration of the more mundane policy implications of its findings. Others have described it as a charmingly dated social portrait of its time, noted (unfairly) more for its focus on structural determinacy than agency, epistemological idealism rather than pragmatism (Moores 1993). Indeed, the Australian authors argue that it may reflect a 'modernist' structure of social power that is no longer fully applicable to the mass-mediated, weakly taxonomized social formations at the end of the twentieth century (Bennett et al. 1999: 12). Like others, they speculate that we are entering a period of cultural declassification, with the advent of a widespread commodification of culture. Producers and distributors seek extensive and weakly differentiated markets in order to achieve economies of scale. In such a milieu, ritual differentiations between status groups are hypothesized to decline.

The researchers also share a concern about the limitations of the ethnographic and reception direction in audience research. Jim McGuigan has pointed out the strong correlation between the rise of 'reception theory', the active audience and the politics of cultural consumption today, and the theoretical deepening of cultural populism (McGuigan 1992). Unfortunately, in his view, this one-sided occupation with consumption and production of meaning by audiences has not left enough attention to the institutional context or 'political economy' or policy framework of the cultural industries.

## PROBLEMS IN OPERATIONALIZATION

The first challenge facing the Australian researchers was to adapt Bourdieu's design across cultures and cultural epochs. They retained his central concept – cultural capital. In Bourdieu's work, cultural capital refers to cultivated competence, knowledge of classificatory schemes, codes and conventions, and the ability to display such knowledge to social advantage with a kind of game-playing confidence. What is at stake, for Bourdieu, is not simply differences in taste, but the ability of the dominant class to impose some differences as 'legitimate' and others not (Bennett et al. 1999: 10). Cultural capital is reproduced across generations by family and schooling.

The Everyday Cultures Project researchers define cultural capital more simply as skill in making cultural distinctions, later expanding their definition to include skill in making *social* distinctions:

> *Cultural choice positions us: it tells us and others who we are. And it defines for us and for others who we are not. It sorts us into 'kinds' of people . . . that sorting is done by us as we shape and elaborate a social place that is partly given and partly chosen in the open-ended formation of our lives. The choices are always constrained.*

(Bennett et al. 1999: 8)

In Bourdieu's work, distinction also involves policing the realms of vulgar taste, and one of his funnier stories tells of the provincial bourgeoisie banning the placement of gnomes on lawns. State the *Accounting for Taste* authors, 'Cultural taste is clearly linked with feelings of distaste, disgust and embarrassment.' Their depth interviews reveal 'distinctions of social exclusion' among Australian working-class youth. Peer pressure and fear of ridicule contribute to a decided antipathy to art galleries and a decision not to visit them as a point of principle.

To explore some of the dimensions of this distaste in the mail survey, the researchers develop batteries of more indirect questions, such as 'Which type of music do you most *dislike*?' or 'Could you indicate in few words what good and *bad* taste entail?'

The second challenge was to develop a model of social class for which Bourdieu left little instruction. He argued that statistics are much better than capital at measuring consumption and income and property, but he went a long way in pioneering social scientific methods by designing a culturally specific version of class (16 categories in a typology) that was reflective of France in the 1960s (Bourdieu 1984). What was remarkable at the time were findings such as a child of upper-class parents had 80 times the chance of entering tertiary education as the child of an agricultural labourer, 40 times that of the child of a worker, and twice that of the child of middle-class parents (Bennett et al. 1999: 10).

The Project employed an occupational model, but found Bourdieu's of little value in the 1990s in Australia. The researchers turned to later theorists, who introduce the elements of income, security and degree of autonomy in occupational classification, to model nine categories. These range from employers to the self-employed, to managers, professionals, supervisors, sales and clerical, and then manual classes (Bennett et al. 1999: 18–20). They acknowledge their class model, like Bourdieu's, is heavily weighted to occupation, but expand upon it to include a subjective sense of class belonging – self-placement on a class scale. Two-thirds of their respondents were able to place themselves in a class without hesitation, unprompted, and 29 per cent of the remaining 33 per cent could place themselves after the list (working, middle, upper middle and upper) was read.

The third challenge was to decide how to look for intergenerational class assimilation – without the luxury of a longitudinal, or rolling periodic, study like the Media Panel Project directed by Karl Rosengren and colleagues in Sweden (Rosengren 1994). Like Bourdieu, the Everyday Cultures Project researchers relied heavily on the respondent's account of his or her parent's occupation and education to look at upward or downward social mobility. They also rely on questions about where children are sent to school (private or public systems) and how much emphasis their children's school places on art and musical training as passports to distinction (Bennett et al. 1999: 265). Despite their methodological contribution, the authors acknowledge that such a class schema fails to indicate the process by which gender, age and education influence the recruitment of agents to their class locations. They make a point of examining how many women inhabit each of their classes, but their sample size is too small to explore how gender influences cultural practices or the exercise of distinction among employers, for example. Bourdieu spends extensive time in this area of within-class variations.

## KEY FINDINGS: CULTURAL MOBILITY

The paradox that cultural competence is concentrated in the most educated classes but not the richest (or those with the most economic capital) raises questions of whether cultural capital is directly tied to the reproduction of class inequality. The Australian study assigns a weaker, less exclusionary role to cultural capital than the French study three decades earlier. Social networks play a stronger role than cultural capital in the maintenance of social position. It is worth remembering that Bourdieu's surveys established that all cultural practices and preferences are closely linked, first to educational level and second to social origin, and that the selective weight that education wields varies according to which cultural practices are recognized and taught. He clearly read school as a social class sorter:

> *Education is the means by which we acquire a practical command of the master patterns of culture and the codes required to read and make sense out of cultural products, and also the means by which disposition and the propensity to appropriate cultural distinction are acquired.*

(Quoted in Roe 1994: 189).

Bourdieu also found that educational influence and origin are strongest in what he called the 'extra-curricular' or avant-garde culture. The Project finds that the working classes, and especially manual workers, have a clear cultural disadvantage, but it stems less from their exclusion from 'high' culture than from the relatively more restricted ambit of their cultural practice overall (Bennett et al. 1999: 268).

*Accounting for Taste* rejects Bourdieu's classic modernist dichotomy of 'high' and 'low' culture, arguing that there is no single powerful, universally binding scale of cultural legitimacy that produces the effects of social status in Australia, or endows those without capital with a sense of their own inferiority. Instead, cultural authority and prestige are dispersed across a range of incommensurable regimes of value, but *may best be conceptualized as a general cultural dichotomization between restricted (or limited) and inclusive (or widely shared) forms of cultural practice* (Bennett et al. 1999: 269).

The authors argue that taste cultures of contemporary society have shifted from elite to mass, to an urban landscape more adequately contrasted as omnivore and univore (Bennett et al. 1999: 187). High-status people no longer confine their cultural tastes and practices to foraging for traditional forms, but gain their prestige from knowing about a much wider repertoire of interests – even if they do not personally like them. Originally applied to characterize omnivores' appetites in music (Roe 1994), the concept has much wider relevance. *Accounting for Taste* found the statistical anomaly that professionals were less likely to fit the ideal of the cultural omnivore, contrary to the expectation that they would be more concerned to display markers of cultural mobility. Not until the analysis separated knowledge and musical affinity were professionals found to be the most likely to be musical omnivores. By contrast, lower-class and manual workers traditionally confine their activities to the most popular, and demonstrate a narrower ambit of cultural experimentation, tourism or openness to different cultural experiences.

The Everyday Cultures Project relies on a weaker measure than the rolling longitudinal media panel studies in Sweden, which explored children's transition from one social position to another, horizontally or vertically, with the creation of upwardly or downwardly mobile cultural tastes (Roe 1994). The researchers do not operationalize class origin as Bourdieu did, but class aspiration. They ask Australians specifically how much emphasis their children's school places on art and musical training, on a four-point scale from 'a great deal' to 'none at all'. Figure 11.1 shows that 57 per cent of professionals believe that their children's school places a great deal or quite a bit of emphasis on art and musical training,

**Figure 11.1**　Children's schools' emphasis on art and musical training by class

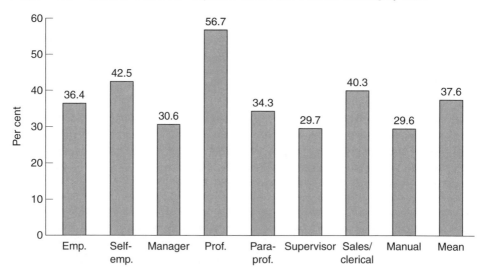

Note: combines the responses 'a great deal' and 'quite a bit'
Source: Bennett et al. (1999: 265)

contrasted with about 30 per cent of managers, supervisors or manual workers. The researchers found that the primary mode of status distinction in the Australian social order is less display of good cultural taste than conspicuous consumption:

> *This question of course allows considerable scope for interpretation, and it may be part of what the figures indicate is not just class based variations in kinds of schooling, but also variations in what parents expect of their children's schools, or indeed, variable understandings of what would constitute a strong emphasis on art and musical training.*

(Bennett et al. 1999: 265)

Contrary to expectation, the two classes with the strongest relation to economic capital (employers and managers) are below the mean (38 per cent) on the question, while professionals, self-employed and sales or clerical staff have the highest cultural aspirations. To gain a clearer picture of such aspirations, the researchers additionally tested 'rate of private education', calculated as a ratio between attendance at private versus public schools (Table 11.1). They compared the adult and child in the household for comparative social mobility through the private school system, to explore the extent to which each class values private education as an instrument of class improvement and has the capacity to invest in it.

Table 11.1    Ratios of all private schooling to state schooling, by class, and percentage shift to private schooling from respondents' generation to their children's generation

|  | Self | Children | Percentage increase/decrease |
|---|---|---|---|
| Employers | 0.50 | 1.23 | 247 |
| Self-employed | 0.42 | 0.36 | 86 |
| Managers | 0.53 | 0.53 | 100 |
| Professionals | 0.56 | 0.79 | 140 |
| Para-professionals | 0.38 | 0.32 | 85 |
| Supervisors | 0.24 | 0.39 | 160 |
| Sales and clerical | 0.43 | 0.34 | 78 |
| Manual | 0.18 | 0.20 | 108 |

Source: Bennett et al. (1999: 267)

Employers and supervisors are found to increase upward mobility across generations (employers' children are more than two times, or 247 per cent, more likely to have switched to private schooling from their parent's state schooling). The juxtaposition of these two dimensions of analysis allows the analysts to conclude that what Australian parents want for their children from private schooling is not cultural capital, but the acquisition of what Bourdieu calls 'social capital', or access to the social networks that play a strong role in the maintenance or mobility of social position. In general, they hypothesize, it is economic capital and social capital that play the major role in transmitting advantage to the next generation and reproduce class inequality in Australia (Bennett et al. 1999: 268).

Next, Everyday Cultures finds that publicly subsidized forms of art recruit audiences more evenly than do private. The current tendencies towards increased privatization of both culture and education are likely to result in more unequal distribution of life chances. The authors address Bourdieu's argument that the nineteenth-century forms of publicly funded culture (art galleries, museums, operas, theatres) are restrictive – conserving symbolic goods and delivering a selective benefit of distinction to those equipped to make use of them. To identify different patterns of social participation, the authors worked from a list of over 40 different reported activities and conducted a factor analysis to identify a typology consisting of three principal groups, later adding a fourth. One group of activities is called subsidized culture, defined to mimic Bourdieu's sphere of cultural consumption outside the home with a heavy user-pay component (see Box 11.3). The second is public culture, featuring participation in arts events or experiences outside the home, such as art galleries, botanic gardens or libraries, supported by a mostly public tax base. The third group is private cultural activities, which feature private consumption, usually centred on the home and privately funded, including the ownership of books, sculpture and so on. The final sphere, public television, is a hybrid cultural practice where public

## Box 11.3  Typology of public/private culture

| Group 1 Subsidized culture | Group 2 Public culture | Group 3 Private culture | Group 4 Public broadcasting (television) |
|---|---|---|---|
| *Participation, often or sometimes, in:* | *Visiting often or sometimes:* | *Ownership of:* | *Watch mainly or regularly:* |
| Public musical performances | Art galleries | Signed limited-edition prints | ABC |
| Public lectures | Museums | Sculpture | SBS |
| Orchestral concerts | Botanic gardens | Art posters | |
| Chamber music concerts | Public libraries | 500+ books | |
| Ballet | Special exhibits at museums or art galleries charging entry fees | Literary classics | |
| Musicals | | Art books | |
| Opera | | Piano | |
| Theatre | | | |
| Cultural festivals | | | |

Source: Bennett et al. (1999: 265)

tax money subsidizes private consumption in the home. The object is to study the aggregate patterns of involvement in each of these groups, and differences between them. Once the analysts have found a group of 'factors' of similar 'activities', they have to group respondents according to this data construct.

Any respondents who answer, for example, that they participate often or sometimes in one or more of the listed activities characteristic of the type is exclusively assigned to one of the four types. How this works is that an additive index is created: each individual's activities are summed by type, and the respondent assigned to represent a predisposition to the type of cultural practice based on his/her highest score. The researchers then analyse a cross-tabulation of education against the typology.

Table 11.2   Participation in public/private culture by education

|  | Primary | Some sec. | Comp. sec. | Voc./ appr. | Part. tert. | Comp. tert. | Tert. as % of primary |
|---|---|---|---|---|---|---|---|
| Group 1: | | | | | | | |
| Subsidized culture | 12.4 | 14.5 | 16.8 | 14.7 | 16.6 | 24.1 | 194 |
| Group 2: | | | | | | | |
| Public culture | 22.6 | 29.7 | 33.2 | 25.9 | 34.6 | 46.0 | 204 |
| Group 3: | | | | | | | |
| Private culture | 8.2 | 14.4 | 18.2 | 17.6 | 27.9 | 36.1 | 440 |
| Group 4: | | | | | | | |
| Public broadcasting | 30.7 | 19.8 | 25.7 | 28.1 | 23.3 | 38.5 | 125 |

Source: Bennett, et al. (1999: 233)

To present the data simply, Bennett, Emmison and Frow use another index, summarized by expressing the rate of participation for those with tertiary education as a percentage of the participation rate for those with primary education (Table 11.2) The steeper the gradient, the more educationally selective the group of activities in question (Bennett et al. 1999: 233). The lower the gradient, the more open the sphere of cultural activities. As Table 11.2 illustrates, the average participation rate in private culture is quite low (8.2 per cent) among Australians with primary education, but relatively high (36.1 per cent) among those who have completed tertiary education. When expressed as an index, with primary participation rates as the denominator and tertiary rates as the numerator, the product is 440 – the steepest of the four types. The effects of more formal education, then, are more pronounced for private patterns of cultural consumption than any other. Second ranked in exclusivity is public culture – museums, libraries or galleries – and third is subsidized culture. By contrast, public broadcasting proves the most open and accessible of all – even though only 31 per cent of those with primary education report SBS (Special Broadcasting Services) or ABC (the Australian Broadcasting Commission) as their main or their regular channel (Bennett et al. 1999: 233).

The authors go on to test this finding by further analysis of class, schooling and income (Table 11.3). As other studies have found (Beale 1999), women are also more likely to be involved in subsidized and public culture in Australia. Involvement in all cultural spheres appears to increase with age, but as Table 11.3 shows, the highest proportion of under-25s compared to over-60s is found in the realm of private culture, suggesting a preference for private consumption patterns among the young. The effects of income are also more marked in private and subsidized cultural realms. Professionals, or symbolic analysts, outnumber manual workers, as do employers in these two realms, showing pronounced class selection. The realm of public culture, by contrast, is less stratified by class and income.

Table 11.3   Public/private culture – summary of patterns of participation

|  | Group 1 Subsidized culture | Group 2 Public culture | Group 3 Private culture | Group 4 Public broadcasting |
|---|---|---|---|---|
| Female as % of male | 149 | 138 | 119 | 99 |
| Tertiary as % of primary educated | 194 | 204 | 440 | 125 |
| Private as % of state schooling | 151 | 113 | 173 | 124 |
| Highest as % of lowest income | 179 | 135 | 283 | 166 |
| Professionals as % of manual workers | 259 | 232 | 293 | 195 |
| Employers as % of professionals | 73 | 53 | 63 | 74 |
| Employers as % of manual workers | 189 | 123 | 184 | 145 |
| Under-25s as % of over-60s | 70 | 58 | 127 | 27 |
| Inner city as % of rural | 208 | 192 | 148 | 135 |
| Australia as % of N. Europe | 54 | 78 | 88 | 67 |

Source: Bennett et al. (1999: 240)

The authors conclude that the data suggest there is a 'publicness' to public culture, if we use egalitarian tests of participation. The social exclusiveness of art galleries, a cause for concern on the part of economic rationalists in cultural policy analysis today, like high art music, remains an unusually sensitive barometer of social distinctions (Bennett et al. 1999: 241). Bennett, Emmison and Frow critically unravel apparently 'populist' cultural policy recommendations to develop audiences in the private and subsidized sectors, suggesting that they are likely to reduce rather than increase social reach. Why should societies provide a wider range of positional goods for the employing, managerial and professional classes, based on the bourgeois strategies of distinction in the nineteenth century?

## KEY FINDINGS: ACCESS, YOUTH AND GLOBAL ACCULTURATION – THE UNITED TASTES OF AUSTRALIA?

Many countries share a concern about the creeping commercialization of youth media realms (video games, Internet, new speciality youth channels) and their implications for cultivating cultural practices and building cultural citizenship.

In measuring capacity for cultural identification, the Everyday Cultures Project researchers used open-ended questions to identify respondents' favourite films, TV programmes or books. The widespread use of such open-ended questions in the study is an important sign of the commitment to quasi-qualitative concerns. By asking 'Who are your three favourite authors?' analysts embark upon an intensive coding task, which is costly in time. Categories of authors must be established according to an analytic protocol. Researchers may be interested in a bipolar code (fiction or non-fiction), a code of national origin (Australian or other) or, conversely, twentieth-century versus nineteenth-century authors. The point is that each title nominated by the survey participants will have to be searched for its provenance, in order to be catalogued and coded (1 for Australian, 2 for other, 9 for unknown).

One way to operationalize this sort of information for its relationship to a 'popular commercial agenda' is to look at book publishing statistics on titles most often sold, for example, to determine if the titles mentioned are widely marketed. In simple terms, correspondence to such a list marks a kind of 'popular' taste, where scope or appeal is measured for its prevalence or ability to cross over different regional, gender or other demographic boundaries. By assigning a country of origin category to such spontaneous answers, the researchers have a quick yardstick by which to assess the extent of foreign cultural influence within Australia's mediascapes (Bennett et al. 1999: 205). While they are quick to agree that this is an imperfect way to ascertain any kind of cultural value except the pattern of national influence, they note that even this cursory an examination is a remarkable extension of Bourdieu's work in the 1960s, where insularity of cultural preferences was marked. Bourdieu ignored the terrain of global popular culture in *Distinction*, a shortcoming these researchers find serious.

In three major areas of consumption (TV, music and literature) the Everyday Cultures Project finds that younger Australians prefer US programmes, musicians and authors. No demographic factor accounts for as much overall variation in tastes as age (Bennett et al. 1999: 217). Only in film is there an exception, prompting the authors to speculate that there are deep lessons for cultural development policy in constructing the appropriate financial and cultural circumstances for producing films that attract local and international attention.

Television showed the highest convergence of tastes in a top 30 list. About half of the TV schedules available show imports, and 53 per cent of the top 30 cited by Australians

**Figure 11.2** Country of origin of top 30 television programmes by age

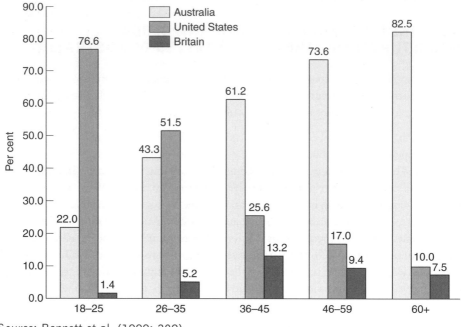

Source: Bennett et al. (1999: 209)

surveyed are Australian in origin. The rest are mostly from the US or UK. When age is introduced into the analysis, however, the incidence of preference for US TV grows to 77 per cent among those aged 18–25 (Figure 11.2).

Because of the gendered pattern of programmes – sports and factual programmes preferred by men are more often indigenous in orientation – it is women who are more likely to select genres and series from the US. In books, the youngest cohort (18–25 years) identifies 63 per cent of its authors as American; the equivalent figure in music is 55 per cent. This is quite different from trends in Europe (Drotner 2001: 289) but similar to Canada (Murray et al. 2001). Compared with the other media, however, music shows a greater dispersion in national origin among nominated choices. Dispersion is interpreted as a sign of cultural relevance (or interest) and acquired cultural knowledge. Quite unexpectedly, the data show more Australian films nominated among the young than among those over 25. The data suggest not only that young Australians inhabit cultural worlds saturated by American materials, but that they are more likely to prefer this material (Bennett et al. 1999: 221). The authors' definition of 'youth', however, revolves around the young adult in the making, not the 'tween'. Other studies of Internet usage suggest that six- to seven-year-old boys are the most international in orientation (Drotner 2001).

Without longitudinal data, however, the researchers cannot speculate if this is a life-cycle phenomenon – conditioned by age or family status – or one in which we may see a trajectory of cultural taste, entailing movement from the active, spectacular, physical and entertainment-oriented cultural pursuits to the more contemplative, informative or cerebral (Bennett et al. 1999: 222). While they concur that 'choice between domestic and international media output implies more or less explicit symbolic negotiations between known and unknown narrative repertoires and formal signs, social conventions and world views' (Drotner 2001), the researchers cannot offer much ethnographic observation, beyond some idiosyncratic reservations about Americanization expressed by respondents in the individual depth-interviews (which notice the American vernacular reference to railway stations as train stations, for example). How we understand this recognition of traits of 'Otherness' and similarity in global media reception is a major challenge in cultural studies.

Certainly, the Everyday Cultures study did not conclude that such widespread preferences indicate that young Australians are turning into Americans. Asked 'Which country was the most important in making you the person you are today', an overwhelming majority of youths aged between 18 and 25 said 'Australia'. Most also agreed that a distinctively Australian culture exists, with more young people citing a 'multicultural heritage' as a more important defining Australian cultural characteristic than their older cohorts. Methodologically, the researchers are vulnerable because the other side of 'global village' identification is not posed. How can we theoretically reconcile such seemingly contradictory but concurrent taste and belief systems among young people? Is the thesis of cultural imperialism borne out by the youth data in this study? Or is it 'multiculturality' that bridges to the more complex process of intermixing of identities and hybridity today? The Everyday Cultures Project, despite asking about trends in immigration, personal and collective identification with ethnic groups, and so on, does not foreground this kind of analysis. Arguably, such work may be better developed in ethnographic venues (Greenhouse and Kheshti 1998) before it can translate into the more standardized forms of questioning and comparison of more 'informational or educative' genres and entertainment sources of practical reasoning. Understanding these processes is key to public debates about the changing nature of national and civic identities and future global media institutions (Drotner 2001).

## POLICY IMPLICATIONS

Cynics may question why such policy-driven surveys legitimate a broad ambit of popular participation in the arts and services of the cultural industries, but correspond to a contraction in state cultural spending in neo-liberal times:

> *What might follow from findings of this kind depends on the angle and political and policy vision that is applied in interpreting them. Looked at from one perspective, the predominance of urban, well educated, mainly female, middle class professionals from a northern European background across this whole field of activities might seem good reason for reducing the*

*level of government support for the publicly funded or subsidized components of the field . . . The degree to which such groups derive a disproportionate benefit has been a thorny policy question throughout the 80s and 90s . . . The primary policy consequence flowing from the influence of (such) economic rationalism in Australia . . . has been an increased emphasis on audience development . . . [which runs the risk of] increasing the rates of participation of existing users rather than attracting new ones . . . [and reducing] social reach.*

(Bennett et al. 1999: 239–41)

Australian voters' political views on the policy question of whether the arts should receive more state funding are analysed against patterns of participation and class. Only professionals, or those who have completed a tertiary level of education, favour public subsidy for the arts. Manual workers and those with primary education are less likely to support state funding (and less likely to use state-funded arts). Nonetheless, some groups of Australians with less formal education do indeed participate in forms of public culture, and the possibility of converting these 'light users' of public culture to supporters of public arts spending is not explored.

The researchers argue, however, that their findings offer confirmation of the role public funding has played in equalizing access and participation in comparison with the operation of private cultural markets: *the participant profile of public culture is considerably more democratic than that of subsidized culture.* Public cultural sites offer an important basis for cross-class forms of social mingling, involving the employer, managerial and professional classes, but much less so the working classes. More importantly, the most democratic of subsidized cultural forms tend to revolve around documentary (museums, festivals, and so on) rather than aesthetic culture (art galleries and operas). Documentary cultural practices offer a greater degree of bodily involvement: walking and seeing and direct experience, rather than sitting and listening and spectatorship (Bennett et al. 1999: 242). Teachers are far more involved in these participatory/documentary realms of public culture, generating benefits whose public effects are multiplied as they are relayed, via the classroom, more widely through the public education system. The institutions of public culture, then, present a stronger case for government support than do those of subsidized culture, where the authors conclude openness may mask social closure.

Because education serves as a gateway to virtually all forms of cultural participation, the authors conclude that public investment in education of a kind and level capable of offsetting the effects of different social backgrounds is crucial to any government concerned with enhancing the cultural life chances of its citizens. Of all realms of public culture, public broadcasting achieves the best social mix, with the exception of age, doing a 'passable job at meeting the requirements of a mass-mediated public sphere in regularly involving a heterogenous public in the major affairs – political, intellectual, and cultural – of the day' (Bennett et al. 1999: 247). Following this reasoning, public broadcasting may deserve a central role in cultural policy, but there is a large caveat: the Australian Broadcasting Commission, like other public broadcasters around the world, is less and less relevant to youth.

## THE VALUE OF SURVEYS

Finally, the Everyday Cultures Project aggressively defends the use of survey technology in the study of culture. Shaun Moores (1993) asks if the large-scale questionnaire survey of the sort used by Bourdieu (and, by implication, that of Bennett, Emmison and Frow) can cope on its own with the significance of cultural consumption activities in everyday life:

> *There are . . . real advantages to be gained from the use of this method, enabling the researcher to map out broad cultural patterns of identity and difference . . . but the modalities of practices are left out. So whilst the survey presents a valuable general picture, it is less fruitful for our understanding of the complex meanings which underpin instances of consumption in specific situational contexts.*

(Moores 1993: 124)

Graham Murdock underlines this view:

> *There is . . . a strong case for incorporating the results of large-scale surveys of cultural activities into the project of cultural studies. Given the distribution of funding for research, official statistics and commercially sponsored probes are the only sources of systematic national and international data on the social bases of cultural practice that we have. They have to be read and used with care and in the full knowledge of the way materials have been obtained and put together. But, as Pierre Bourdieu demonstrates so forcefully in* Distinction *(1984), if the results are seen as posing puzzles and cues for further inquiry and interpretation, rather than offering accomplished facts, they can play a vital role in extending the scope of cultural analysis. As he points out, a 'statistical relationship, however precisely it can be determined numerically, remains a pure datum, devoid of meaning until it is interpreted'. Certainly, his own, very influential model of the ties binding cultural practices to social locations consistently uses other people's often crude surveys as a jumping off point . . . it is useful to refer to available statistics alongside fieldwork materials . . .*

(Murdock 1977: 191)

The Everyday Cultures researchers are concerned not to reify quantitative audience research technologies. While they concede the figures do not imply exact counts, but estimates, these constructs are found useful precisely because they produce regularities or patterns of repetition (Bennett et al. 1999: 15). If the patterns of public taste revealed are not 'exact' counts, their effects are none the less real:

> . . . *we must step back for a moment to reflect upon a fundamental deficiency in this profiling of social groups conceived as more or less autonomous social agents . . . It is important to avoid a naïve representationalism which would endow the categories of our analysis with an existence outside and prior to the two sets of relations from which they emerge: on the one hand, the multi-variate relationality of social life . . . and on the other, their formation within the frameworks of interest and knowledge that have governed our research. This is not to argue that these categories have nothing to do with reality. But their logic is stochastic rather than representational: they build a reality on the basis of probabilities and statistical trends.*

(Bennett et al. 1999: 257)

Surveys allow us to quantify and interpret rather abstract patterns of culture, serving as a map against which the dynamic character of an individual taste culture or lifestyle may be brought alive.

Surveys represent the drive in the human sciences to categorize or generalize social phenomena, the will to find unity out of the buzzing confusion and diversity of everyday life. As long as we remember the macro-pattern of a statistical map is just one dialectic of the human sciences, the other being the will to find diversity in unity, to particularize human experience, surveys may aspire to 'deep description', offering a strong tool in critical audience research. To quote Justin Lewis: 'All research into the way people think or say they act is a contrivance in some way: the issue is how we respect and interpret the limits of that contrivance' (Lewis 2001).

Methodologically, the challenge facing surveys is to use them in cross-cultural comparison, and to further perfect the operationalization of key measures to do with class, cultural capital and cultural mobility over time. There is as yet insufficient critical mass of surveys that blend numbers and context in a practical way to contribute persuasively to democratic debates over 'cultural life chance' indicators and evaluate equity in cultural policy.

# Chapter Twelve

# Audience surveys: defining □ the field

*Survey: (verb) Latin:* videre, *to see;* sur*: over; to determine and delineate the form, extent, position of a tract of land by taking linear and angular measurements; (noun) a critical inspection, often official, to provide exact information; a comprehensive view; a measured plan or description*

(Webster's New English Dictionary)

Surveys gather information from people by asking them questions about themselves. Surveying implies space – viewing a whole, such as a social landscape, from a particular vantage point. Scale and scope are important theoretical and methodological metaphors to describe the place survey work occupies in the terrain of audience studies.

*Scale* can refer to territorial span, or size. Surveys are often rooted in geography, describing characteristics of people in some spatial location. Scale also implies sampling, or representative rules for generalizing from the part to the whole. *Scope* of survey work is important, for scope measures breadth. Surveys tend to examine a range of questions, units of observation, or *variables,* to see possible patterns of convergence or divergence in audience practices.

## ADVANTAGES AND DISADVANTAGES OF SURVEYS

Surveys have the advantage of flexibility. They are conducted in relatively natural settings, collect large amounts of data over large samples, standardize measurement protocols to enable comparison across very different sub-populations, and are thus relatively cost-effective. If your goal is to determine a single value, describe a variable with more than one value, describe a relationship between variables, explain a relationship among variables, or influence something, then a survey is a useful research design (Gray and Guppy 1999). Survey research is high in reliability and, due to ease of replicability, contributes to the advance of debate over scientific discourse (Sumser 2001).

As we will explore, however, the fact that independent variables cannot be manipulated in natural settings means surveys are weaker tools than experiments when causal models are sought. The standardization of measurement, while high in reliability, may be weak in validity, flattening qualitative ambiguity or interpretation of the contexts of meaning. The biggest weakness inherent in survey design, which it shares with all verbal methodologies, is the gap between what people say and what they do. Surveys can find out what people are thinking, but the link between what they think and what they will do is not necessarily strong. That is why some researchers argue that surveys are not useful in understanding behaviour, and observational or experimental techniques may be better. Surveys tend to be cross-sectional – providing snapshots at a particular point of time – so they are not a good way to examine audience changes over time. Finally, survey work in the academic realm is often expensive. As a consequence, surveys have often been funded by government or academic agencies, and have therefore received extensive peer review. They may represent the lowest common denominator of consensus on research aims, or reflect the dominant ideology, critics allege.

## WHY USE SURVEYS?

Policy, market and academic terrains of audience research share a preoccupation with developing survey methods to map and analyse audience trends with ever-greater economies of scale and scope. In a time of rapid social upheaval, it is not surprising to find students of audience studies turning to quantitative social science methods to explain risks associated with uncertainty. They are the dominant tool in the uses and gratifications (U+G) school within audience research, to be discussed in the last part of this chapter.

This chapter will set out the three main problems in mapping audiences, which cut across policy, market and academic terrains of quantitative studies. The first, as we saw in the Australian Everyday Cultures Project (Chapter 11), is *how to measure access to media*. Policy-makers may subsidize access to new computer technologies, for example, as a social policy measure to aid lower-income families in education, or study how technologies may supplant other cultural practices (like reading). But access may not imply exposure. Media businesses need measure exposure, or opportunity to view advertising, to determine the effectiveness of their promotions.

The second problem is *how to define use*, which is different from both access and exposure (or what some analysts call the difference between watching and seeing or interpreting meaning). Academic studies are interested in patterns of audience activity and effects of specific media contents.

The third problem is *how to place media consumption in the context of everyday life*, comparing and contrasting mediated versus unmediated patterns of cultural practice and meaning within and across cultures. It is here that we collide with the limits of standardization in quantitative measurement. In the relatively young field of quantitative audience studies, there have been few systematic studies within cultures over generations, and few cross-cultural comparisons to identify the important relative effects of institutional media contexts and audience agency or activity.

Why have surveys become so central to the workings of culture and power in the study of audiences? Privatization, individualization and globalization of the TV experience have escalated for northern audiences in the past decade, with important consequences for how we understand social identity, cultural tastes and cultural influences on the audience.

*Privatization* refers to three related phenomena:

- the changing political economy of entertainment, where commodified, deregulated entertainment forms are growing

- the changing practices of consumption, where consumers are increasing entertainment spending and directing it to new media

- the deepening ideology promoting consumption, in which audiences are conceived of primarily as 'buyers' or 'target markets' (Livingstone and Bovill 2001).

*Individualization* refers to the decontextualization of the social experience of TV viewing. This may mean the trend to 'special interest' or niche or 'fragmented' viewing of thematically related TV channels (gay TV, for example), like the magazines of print culture, or it may refer to the trend towards what US social theorist, Robert Putnam, has called 'bowling alone', with individual sets, customized recording or time-shifting of TV consumption (me-TV scheduling). Individualization affords even more opportunity for erecting 'walled media gardens'. The appearance of 'bedroom TV cultures', as seen in Europe and North America, is key to the emergence of teen autonomy, self-image and gender identities (Livingstone and Bovill 2001).

Finally, *globalization* of the TV experience refers to the flow of 'peoplescapes', with increasing immigration, as it does to 'screenscapes', with growing imports and exports of TV products and services. TV has been considered an important public good in most national cultural policies, conveniently employing a technology which by its form (use of the electromagnetic spectrum) was initially conceived as subject in international law to the doctrine of national sovereignty, and thereby necessitating intergovernmental spectrum sharing and a high degree of autonomy in cultural regulation. Most nations have treated TV as an important cultural practice, devoted a large share of their cultural spending to it, and protected their public national television ventures from commercial or international competition (Baeker 2000).

All this has been changing since the 1980s, with the increasing international flow of media. Domestic protectionism is out of favour, with policy-makers instead championing free trade in audiovisual services. Not only have nations universally introduced commercial TV; in many cases, introduction of cable and satellite distribution has meant a shift to a more hybrid form of advertising and subscription support, challenging the tax base of public ventures, and importing more foreign channels and foreign programmes (Buonanno 2001). While some nations are pushing for increased access to markets and freer trade in audiovisual and cultural services (US and India), many are now considering alternatives to maintain some cultural exemptions to free trade (see www.incp-ripc.org).

Monitoring how national audiences gain access to domestic and international television channels, which forms of cultural TV fare they prefer, and the citizen's capacity for

227

cultural learning has increased in importance on policy agendas. Audience surveys can supply many of these policy information needs.

## STATE-PRODUCED AUDIENCE STATISTICS

One way of finding out about a group of people is to collect information from everyone, via a *census* (from the Latin word *censere,* to assess). Some constitutional legitimacy is usually required, as well as some coercive power in order to obtain compliance from everyone. Censuses, usually conducted every ten years or so, establish general-purpose data sets that are invaluable in secondary research about audiences.

The most important use of the census, or other official registers of national populations, is in mapping the major characteristics of a people: age, gender, race, family structure, working status, patterns of emigration or immigration, life cycle, education or income. This information is then used as the *sampling frame* to guide later sampling in many audience surveys, panels or polls. Census data thus helps the design of the sample before a survey, and helps validate it after responses are obtained.

Other well-established rolling national surveys have been designed to cover a wide range of topics. For example, Canada, Britain, Australia and the US have conducted General Social Science Surveys since the early 1970s. In the Nordic countries of Europe, state-organized media statistics are assembled by Nordicom, the Nordic Information Centre for Media and Communication Research (Carlsson and Harrie 2001). For the EU, media statistics are gathered by the Audiovisual Observatory (see http://www.obs.coe.int/). Although development of specific communication or cultural questions has been relatively slow, there has been improvement in the last 20 years in the way these comprehensive databases map media practices in everyday life.

There are four central axes in audience mapping by states. The first traces the diffusion of *social access to media technology* across space and time. How many citizens have media technologies in their home? How many receive media services? Many countries place a high normative value on making diverse media sources available to their citizens. Governments track the penetration of various media technologies in the home over time and describe patterns of media ubiquity, substitution or complementary use. Analysis of this type of data has allowed historians to predict a general pattern of increasing rates of social diffusion of new media technologies and specialization in media use across three stages: elites, mass, fragmented audiences (Defleur and Ball-Rokeach 1982). The final trend observed in large-scale state surveys is towards privatization or payment of fees for service and individualization of media use (Webster and Phalen 1997: 41).

The second axis is *time use*, to better map work/leisure practices over the life cycle. Work still structures time available for TV viewing: most prime-time or peak viewing occurs after the work day. Gender and age are important variables affecting TV consumption and relationship with work. Television viewing continues to account for most leisure time, but actual time spent viewing is declining for those under 25, in many advanced industrial countries, replaced by video game and computer use. The increased number and types of programme and station options in most media markets have redirected adult viewing, but time spent viewing has not increased substantially. The trend is towards increasingly mobile communication technology use outside the home. TVs are increasingly penetrating public spaces (at the luggage carousels in airports, for example) and family vans in North America.

The third axis where government statistical agencies produce data compendiums is in monitoring *consumer patterns of spending* on reading, education, communications and entertainment. The proportion of discretionary income directed to media and culture, elasticity of demand and changing patterns of consumption, are all important in monitoring growth of media markets, identifying mature markets and predicting when mergers and acquisitions may occur in the private sector to grow revenues.

The final area monitored is *cultural participation*, as we saw in the Australian Everyday Cultures Project (Chapter 11). Higher education leads to more diversification of cultural activities and less TV consumption. Many countries are concerned with the relationship between mediated culture and viability of non-mediated (or non-commodified) cultural practices (such as the amateur performing arts).

## COMMERCIAL AUDIENCE MEASUREMENT

While the data that states collect will help businesses develop a long-term planning horizon, they are not sufficient for most of the day-to-day business needs, which explains why advertisers pressed their media suppliers to develop or outsource their own regular ratings services in most countries by the 1950s. Media businesses are necessarily keen to chart changing audience tastes and map new taste communities. Businesses need to segment markets, first, geodemographically and, second, by lifestyle or potential psychographic type. Their second business priority is to monitor market change: access to audiences may rise or fall, as they are diverted either to new competitive services or to new media. Audiences are typically then anchored in the wider consumption economy as various similar or different groups.

Audience segmentation divides the 'target' audience for advertising into meaningful subgroups with shared characteristics. Those within the segment are assumed to be as homogenous as possible, and thus merit a separate marketing approach. Segmentation can be a priori – that is, defined by marketers in advance to be relevant to their consumer group – or post hoc, arising out of analysis. If it is a priori, it usually flows out of the researcher's study objectives, or remains in the descriptive demographic realm. If it is post hoc, it is constructed out of the data of a study, using advanced statistical methods (such as cluster analysis) to identify mutually exclusive, non-overlapping 'types' or 'subgroups' within the audience. Segments are formed by grouping respondents who respond similarly to sets of classification questions, which may cover media and product usage, attitudes toward media consumption, frequency of consumption, brand switching or other variables. Subgroups thus may be defined by different types of variables: demographic, attitudinal or lifestyle, and psychographic (the classification of people according to their attitudes or aspirations).

Advertisers are particularly interested in segmentation methods in order to help guide the relative informational, emotional or style appeals to their ad campaigns (Gunter and Furnham 1992). They may want to reach only the age group most likely to buy, or go out, or consume their service, or conversely, they may be interested in those that may be taste-makers, if launching a new brand. Increasingly, consumer retention is a large part of the strategy in direct marketing, so advertisers are interested in developing 'loyalty' clubs or repeat purchasers.

One commercial – and private – segmentation model of information technology consumers, according to their motivation, desire or ability to invest in technological products, is typical of this type of corporate research. In the US, Forrester Research Inc. produced an influential report for its customers entitled 'Why consumers buy', in a review of people and technology, dubbing its model 'technographic', not 'psychographic'. To create the segments, consumers were asked how they would spend a $1000 technology gift certificate. They were asked if they believe that technology will benefit their lives (and were further typed into those sharing 'technological optimist' or 'technological pessimist' outlooks). Finally, disposable income was used, in the context of ecological data from the US Bureau of Census and other rolling lifestyle market studies.

Four general motivators for the adoption of new information and communications technologies were found: family, career, entertainment and status. The two largest segments found were the 'technology loving, family focused, Neo-hearthminders', accounting for 24 per cent, and the 'technophobic Sidelined Citizens', accounting for 36 per cent of adult Americans. Women proved to be the drivers of the family segment, concerned about their kids' skills in the wired future. Sidelined Citizens are, to quote the report, 'hard to motivate, at the bottom of the technology marketing bucket, with low incomes'. Interestingly, just 14 per cent of all Americans were found to demonstrate primary entertainment motivation (with DVDs, or high appetites for video on demand). Students and men under the age of 44 were found more often to claim a technological optimism, with scepticism rising with age. Such segmentation models are important in market scanning for entertainment and information service providers. The report proved a stroke of clever marketing, just before the boom of heavy investment in high-tech stocks in 1998, rise in merger and acquisitions (AOL Time Warner) and a hyper-inflated speculation in information technology just around the corner (since corrected in the market).

## NEW MEDIA MONITORING

New technologies in the TV market (satellite, cable or Internet) may divert media audiences, causing a potential erosion of commercial revenue, which may be short or long term. Businesses carefully watch advances or declines in overall time spent viewing television (since it is a marker of potential economic momentum in ad revenues), and decide either to buy into the new technology or use their incumbent advantage to block its development, possibly by predatory market practice or by insistence on social or cultural regulation. The rise of video cassette recorder (VCR) use, and the even faster and larger rise of the video game market, have propelled market mergers and acquisition strategies. Given that the Internet generation of services is the fastest yet in its rate of social diffusion, online entertainment market analysis is the premium form of market intelligence in audience research today.

Large multinational companies, with complex interests in all aspects of entertainment, have privatized many online market surveys, many of which are simply beyond the budgets of academic researchers. Some of the best-known North American firms today conducting online entertainment (or media e-commerce) studies are Forrester, Boston Consulting Group and NPD Research, which conduct large syndicated studies for clients like Microsoft, the telephone, digital satellite or cable companies. To use North American marketing jargon, the search is for the 'killer application' – the next great trend in popular online media. How much time will this new media application attract? Will it supplant or be a substitute for old media usage patterns? Will it generate a willing audience conversion from 'free' consumption to 'fee' consumption, to increase profit margins?

The search for transformation of audience use is not an easy one. Relatively scarce leisure time leads to some media substitution, but repeated forecasts of the demise of television, after the advent of the VCR or video games, have been premature. Predicted uses are easy to miscue. Early studies, for example, underestimated the value of the Internet in email or for information sourcing. The 'pot of gold' in new media services online is now projected to be online interactive gaming or interactive video. Surveys count the presence of new media technologies in the home, segment heaviness of new media use, and then ask consumers to identify what they use most often, what kinds of new services they may want and how much they might be willing to pay. The game is to forecast demand. This is a high-risk game, littered with over 30 years of incorrect forecasts. Surveys for new technologies are often looking for markets (with a pro-innovation bias, as we have seen in the early days of videotext) and fraught with problems. People may be unwittingly conservative, or unable to conceptualize what new technologies may mean day to day. To quote one of the veterans of the early Knight Ridder experiments with online publishing in the late 1970s:

> *one of the critical [audience research] lessons to learn is to treat market research from emerging media technologies with caution, because in the 'real' world people do not always want what they say they want or do what they say they will do.*

(Fidler 1997)

To offset this problem, market researchers try to apply Everett Rogers' model of innovators or early adopters, looking to interview only those opinion leaders or lead users who may be out in front of the new media adoption, to aid in their forecast planning (Rogers 1986). Academic surveys on new media use are relatively rare (Kiefl 1995; Livingstone and Bovill 2001). From a policy or social psychology perspective, the fear of substitution (of markets or of social networks, and the attendant alienation) is central to new media research preoccupations.

## HOW RATINGS WORK

The main function of commercial audience surveys, like censuses, is as accounting tools, counting up viewers and listeners in the here and now. But the object is to sell the access to audiences to advertisers. Historically, as the new radio industry turned to advertising as a commercial base, its relative inability to identify its listeners, compared to newspaper subscribers, became a serious impediment to market growth. The struggle to woo reluctant advertisers with a measurement system of equivalent credibility extended over a decade. Audience ratings, then, are the commercial currency for media industries, setting prices for advertising. According to the World Advertising Research Center, trade in TV audiences totalled just over $100 billion worldwide in 2000.

Early commercial studies assumed that the media audience was unproblematically 'there' to be observed and easily measured. Really just head counts, these studies invented the idea of media reach, which can be defined as the potential versus the actual reading, listening or viewing public (that is, defined by activity), or subscription or purchase of a given book, record or satellite TV service (defined by spending). Media reach may be defined in conjunction with a specific medium, a specific publication, an issue of a publication or, even more narrowly, a specific article or picture in a publication. Such categories can be mutually exclusive or overlapping; indeed, overlapping reach is a common characteristic of audiences, which are omnivorous in their media consumption.

The central problem at the heart of commercial media study is how to measure exposure, not access or use. Exposure is ad language for a 'hit' or opportunity to view. Surprisingly, there is still no agreed way to measure exposure, and there are weaknesses in almost every approach.

As we saw in the case of the Everyday Cultures Project (Chapter 11) the easiest way is to ask respondents how many hours a day they watch TV. But people sometimes forget they are doing something else at the time, and fail to report other things they may be doing at the same time. Time spent may not reflect attention paid, so attention measures are necessary. TV exposure may also be conceptualized as programme choice or content preference. Exposure to a programme does not guarantee exposure to ads since, with the advent of the remote control device, people may switch away from the ad. Or they may simultaneously view more than one programme. Different measures of the complex concept of TV exposure have different theoretical implications and therefore different results. Validity of the measures depends on the theoretical perspective of the study (Rubin 1979).

The first method used to track radio listening involved a mail-out survey instrument called a *diary*. Panels of listeners/viewers, selected at random to be representative of the general population, are asked to fill out diaries over 'sweeps' – periods of several weeks in certain seasons (autumn or winter) – for several years, for a small payment, and then mail them in. Stations are outlined in the diary, along with programme titles on a seven-day grid, and radio listeners or TV viewers (called *respondents* to the survey) are asked to record their weekly listening and/or viewing. The efficacy of a diary relies on participants' willingness to train themselves to fill it out as they view or listen, and fill it out correctly. Diaries are useful for the scope of information they can collect over longer time periods.

Diaries are expensive to produce, mail and collect. Despite extensive instructions, they are prone to recording error: failure to remember what one did, to record the channel properly or to comply in the sample week selected. As the complexity of the recording task increases (and as the number of choices grows), the respondent's job becomes much more complex and the risk of recording error grows. The arrival of hundreds of satellite-to-cable TV channels has effectively made diaries obsolete in North America. A recent Canadian experiment comparing diary and meter measurement coincidentally with two independent samples, found diaries overestimate viewership of the mainstream, well-known programmes or station brands, and skew to older respondents, who are more likely to fill them out. Estimates of share per channel could vary as much as 50 per cent, depending on the method (Chahdi and Laurent 1999). But for all their flaws, diaries remain the most cost-effective method to record audience preferences in multiple rural or medium-size metropolitan areas, where other measurement systems are not economically viable.

To overcome some of the problems with diary measurement, the people meter was invented and in place throughout Europe and North America by early 1990 (Kent 1994). In *active people metering*, a set-top microprocessor records the channels we watch or flip through with our remote control device. People push buttons, actively indicating what they are watching. Transmission of the decision can be instantaneous, or organized *overnight*, as is the dominant industry practice. No longer is a half-hour or a quarter-hour measurement all that can be obtained – measurement can be second by second.

Electronic monitoring offers the prospect of catching *flow* – that is, change in audience behaviour over space and time. After the advent of the VCR and remote control device, channel switching escalated. Capturing the flow of channel switching and, in particular, the flow from programme to programme in ever shorter time frames, is a strength of the people meter. For the first time, instantaneous capture of switching and tuning behaviour, virtually in *real time*, is possible when the information is relayed to a central information processor. The people meter has become an important management tool in the media industries, assisting in decisions to keep or cancel existing series, develop new series, optimize scheduling or propel ad sales.

Active people metering is expensive. When provided by commercial entities, meter panels are restricted to major metropolitan markets, where the advertising base can support the trade. So they have limitations in projecting national audiences or effectively representing

## Box 12.1 Key concepts in commercial audience measurement

### Penetration

Percentage of a population with the technology to access a medium. Defines how synonymous the potential audience is with the total population within a given geographical area. In most countries, radio is virtually ubiquitous and penetration is very high. TV has penetrated 99 per cent of North American homes. Penetration figures are important to trace the diffusion of entertainment technology, the trends in consumer spending on entertainment, and the potential competition, displacement or substitution among media behaviours. Penetration figures are usually collected by national statistical agencies.

### Daypart

The number of people watching TV varies during the day. Most watch at night: so-called *prime time*.

### Reach

The spatial dimension of audience studies.

- Boundaries correspond to a hierarchy from local to global.
- First defined by the technology of distribution in various media.
- Percentage of total public in a certain geographic area who have an opportunity to receive a radio, television or other media message.
- May be reported by medium, station, programme or ad over time.

Reach speaks to market size potential. Traditionally, early newspaper, radio and television markets grew up on local market area boundary definitions. As technology over distance improved, reach over distance in national and then international markets was measured. As reach increases, the audience may become synonomous with the total public.

### Reach and frequency analysis

Reach refers to the net size of an audience, while frequency measures the number of times a person was exposed to a particular advertising message or other stimuli during a particular interval. Frequency does not measure actual impact or effect on the viewer, but rather potential for impact or *viewing hits*.

### Rating

Percentage of the total audience with access to the medium who have seen or heard the specific message at a specific time of day. The commercial media divide the week into dayparts: prime time, through the week. Ratings are based on all receivers of a message.

$$Rating = \frac{households\ watching\ a\ programme\ or\ network}{households\ with\ receivers}$$

Rating may also refer to content rating, a label on a television programme that identifies the age-appropriateness of the material for viewing by children.

### Rating point
Where one percentage point is translated to actual thousands (000s) of people reached.

### Share
Percentage of the total audience who have their sets on (i.e. who are actually using a given medium) who have seen or heard a specific message. (Since the base is smaller, the estimate is usually bigger.) Share is based on all users of a medium or message.

$$Share = \frac{households\ watching\ a\ programme}{households\ watching\ TV}$$

### Cost per thousand (CPM)
The cost per thousand (Latin 'mille': thousand) is the basic unit of comparison, the cost of reaching 1000 viewers or listeners with an advertising message (M=1000).

rural or minority tastes. They are prone to error: household individuals may forget to log their individual codes into the remote control device, or forget to turn them off when they walk away. The difficulty in obtaining cooperative members of the public in audience panels suggests to some experts that the statistical differences between fifth- and thirteenth-rated shows could be nothing more than sampling error. Yet advertisers insist on basing the exchange value of a rating on an absolute point. In the US, a difference of 0.5 or less between two programmes can mean millions of dollars in advertising revenues.

The future of electronic audience measurement is *passive meters*, where audience members need do no work. Passive surveillance technology involves some kind of infrared sensor or surveillance transmitter or receiver to distinguish individual viewing, trap location and adapt to capturing simultaneous multi-set use. Such passive metering is dependent upon the diffusion of broadband, high-speed data transmission. Passive meters can measure any number of television sets coincidentally, collect guest information and identify VCR or Internet surfing at the same time. They may even provide a *wrist-watch/watchman*, with the capacity to record viewing out of the home. Metering will furthermore need to capture multimedia use: TV, VCR viewing as well as Internet delivery of media contents.

The technology also enables more precise measurement of ad exposure. The major networks have effectively resisted advertisers' calls to prove the reach of their ads, especially given the rapid diffusion of the process of zapping or zipping. Advertising would be more efficiently bought and sold if direct exposure could be caught. But such measurement would need to encrypt each ad with the equivalent of a universal bar-code, and the very presence of such a code would enable e-hackers to programme VCRs or their remote control devices to avoid ads.

Apparent precision in commercial advertising ratings is an illusion. Commercial audience measurement relies on samples that are prone to under-representing various sectors of the public. They must often be corrected by weighting – that is, inflating the under-represented segment to its known census proportion (or down, if certain sectors are over-represented). Whole populations (college dorms or other public spaces) are left out. Racial minorities are less likely to cooperate on meter panels. And now more than half of the potential sample of TV-metered households refuse. Despite its methodological weaknesses, meter data is pragmatically accepted as a currency value, charting the *technical* market momentum or market fluctuations down or up in audience viewing.

The next challenge is devising accounting systems to measure audience exposure to ads on the Internet. In North America and Europe, new audience ratings agencies (see www.mediametrix.com) are springing up to capture this new market. Like their TV counterparts, such companies design panels to instal 'PC meters' in the home, which record all activity on the PC in real time, 'click by click, page by page, second by second'. The goal is to collect reach data, estimates of unique visitors and other ratings data. Methodological debates include new definitions of 'exposure', such as click-through, page viewed and time spent. But the unexpectedly slow growth of Internet ad markets in North America has delayed methodological advance in Internet audience measurement.

The final challenge is actually employing the Internet to administer online audience surveys, in contrast to telephone or individual house-to-house interviews. Now that Internet access is available to the majority of citizens in North America and some European countries, achieving relatively reliable sampling online is now more feasible. Online surveys share the characteristic of the self-administered mail-out or diary method: they tend towards low response rates. Since there are few sources with exhaustive directories of Internet addresses (like the telephone companies), it is not possible to sample randomly or reliably. There is a self-selected nature to those who choose to participate, and it is not possible to project to the general public, and especially not to those offline. But the speed and ease of administration of online surveys is improving, and a number of countries are experimenting with the creation of sample panels – carefully chosen to be representative of the general public – to conduct surveys on the influence of social issue campaigns and media debates on elections, for example.

Academic interest in empirical secondary data analysis of ratings and the development of new measurement systems has been lacking. The central barrier is lack of access to empirical data, due to financial and structural constraints. Licensing access to continuous audience data is prohibitively expensive, although in some countries university depart-ments have negotiated favourable subscription deals, giving online access to TV meter data. Scholars are thus abdicating a legitimate intellectual and political role in moulding understanding of how broadcasting shapes the context for active media consumers/citizens (Savage 1993: 3).

## THE CRITIQUE OF THE COMMERCIAL RATINGS PARADIGM

While ratings serve important functions in media market exchange, their chief methodo-logical problem from an academic perspective is that they ignore the analytic dichotomy of watching and non-watching. They may systematically overstate viewing. Watching may not imply full attention, or even facing the television! In fact, several observational studies have discovered that we do something else most of the time when watching television. When asked in surveys to estimate time spent watching TV, people sometimes report fewer hours than people meter records measure; so they may subjectively and systemati-cally underestimate time spent viewing, or exclude the time they watch with low attention. Watching and non-watching may be part of the same activity, a seamless web in which we ebb in and out of the message flow.

The second problem is determining what threshold constitutes a *unit* of watching: a second, a minute, as in a people meter, or 15 minutes, as in a diary? The third methodo-logical weakness has been the inability of the ratings systems to coordinate the decentral-ized conditions in the home, more mobility and the use of portable systems such as Gameboy. Finally, most commercially oriented measurement systems are still biased to the more affluent, middle-class majorities that are more attractive to advertisers. They have not yet adapted to the new ethnic diversification of their markets, but there are signs that minorities may be becoming more prevalent in marketing discourses.

In a work published during the so-called people meter crisis in the US, when major networks lost millions in the conversion of measurement systems from a diary-based to a meter system, Ien Ang presented a pivotal critique for cultural studies (Ang 1991). First, she laid bare the self-serving industry justification of ratings as expressions of *cultural democracy*. Ratings are not an expression of *democracy in action*; viewing choices are amongst a pre-limited set of options. Neither are ratings absolute values; they are prone to multiple hidden sources of error.

Ang further argues that ratings are also not a map of the audience. They *map the ways in which the industry defines the audience as commodity*. Commercial audience survey measurement produces a discourse, and the audience glimpsed through the social scientific axioms of this discourse is nothing more than *a collective in which individuals are aggregated*. The parts are the whole. Yet the individuals themselves are not concrete social subjects, nor are they necessarily even aware of what may bond them as an audience. They are a generalized construct that becomes, when quantified, an *abstract* generalization.

Commercial ratings should therefore be seen, not as social science but as technologies of commercial/social control. The surveillance society thesis underpinning Ang's critique

237

raises fears of greater consumer intrusion by the emergence of ever more sophisticated technologies. Mainstream economists (Webster and Phalen) easily oppose the fiction of *complete surveillance*, missing the point that even in Ang's view existing surveillance was necessarily partial. Nonetheless, in the decade since Ang wrote, the emergence of the Internet, sophisticated server systems to track and monitor Internet surfing behaviour and electronic bar-coding in messages, suggest more complete surveillance technologies are both feasible and increasingly commercially deployed. Privacy experts have succeeded in policy spheres in beating back some of the power of corporations in secretly monitoring consumption in this way, but the battle continues (Bennett 1992).

## THE SURVEY IN ACADEMIC AUDIENCE RESEARCH

The Everyday Cultures Project (Chapter 11) represents a case where survey technology was used to map cultural practices across Australia. While not simply 'administrative' in its origins, the goal of the study was to draw conclusions about accessibility and likely areas where public tax support for the arts and cultural policies could maximize participation. Bennett, Emmison and Frow (1999), then, join a long tradition of survey researchers, from the days of Adorno and Lazarsfeld, concerned with new and critical directions to survey research in the study of audiences.

Historical narratives about the use of surveys in audience research oscillate between polar opposites of description and analysis, methodological individualism and social embeddedness, and stand-alone versus triangulated design. Survey technology makes its first appearance in debates over the scale of samples required and the need for accurate estimates in the study of audiences. The focus is around improvements in sampling design, assuring greater precision in descriptive validity for commercial or policy applications in the effects tradition. Many early election studies in the US produced faulty vote projections due to unsophisticated sampling. The shift in the 1960s was to survey design: the study of individual attributes and mapping social change, which may be found in the uses and gratifications (U+G) school. The analytic focus switches to questionnaire development, and specific testing of correlations among demographic and attitudinal variables. There is a self-conscious effort to take the survey tool beyond description, or concerns about statistical precision of estimates, to analysis and hypothesis testing. Finally, the development of longitudinal panel studies of cohorts over time (Rosengren 1994) allows greater attention to patterns of association and models of causality. Various controls for independent variables are introduced. While there is a preoccupation with explanation, it is in this period that we see survey designs as just one part of a triangulated study, often involving in-depth interviews or other qualitative techniques, and a return to the value of surveys as methods of 'deep description'.

The U+G school of audience research has often been identified with the survey approach. It emerged in reaction to the model of direct effects, together with the rise of social cognitive approaches. Widely credited to have led to the now widespread metaphor 'the active audience', the formative thinkers pioneered advances in the operationalization of activity measures. As we will see below, they contribute to the idea of 'productive' consumption, strongly influenced by the tradition of social psychology and growing interest in understanding the social processes of cognition. Unlike the problematic facing the researchers for the Everyday Cultures Project, U+G researchers are more concerned with the underlying transactions explaining how audiences ascribe value to the media they consume. They sacrifice context, so that many of their surveys are more consciously media-centric, as a consequence of their preoccupation with design. They are more individualistic in their focus, often seeking 'most different segments' or 'most similar groups', and tend to be less concerned with structural factors affecting the intergenerational orientation to taste.

## USES AND GRATIFICATION SURVEYS: THREE TRAJECTORIES

We have singled out three trajectories that may be said to characterize U+G. The first trajectory created a typology of gratifications: Why do people use media? The second explored a variety of functions or uses: What do they use them for? The third adapted decision theory in mapping cognitive process: How do people make sense of the media? Indebted to developments in social psychology, U+G studies developed a more complex cognitive and behavioural model in this trajectory than a crude stimulus–response theory allowed.

The starting point is the need/gratification nexus. What needs do the media serve? Needs are not directly observable and may be biological or psychosocial in origin. Early theorists, like Abraham Maslow, explored *basic* survival or physiological needs. Maslow's hierarchy implies a rise from physical needs, such as security or personal safety, to psychological needs, for self-esteem, personal identity and social belongingness, to cognitive needs, such as curiosity (or knowledge, such as the need to know), or expressive needs (the need to play or display cultural markers, or develop a social identity). While there has been some research arguing for a basic 'survival' need for media information (about threats to personal security or the need to monitor the information environment), U+G theorists endeavoured to isolate *media-specific* needs. The focus shifts away from the higher level in Maslow's hierarchy to the need for social functioning, personal escape or parasocial interaction further down the conceptual ladder. In many ways, this debate reflects the epistemological claim that popular culture is more basic than just non-essential luxury or play. Yet much early discussion of needs implied a simple one-way determinism, focusing on innate individual attributes and not their social origins. Needs are not necessarily innate or universal in form (Lull 1995). Our need to belong to an audience or polity, Lull suggests, is gratified in terms of experiences and sentiments that surround family, race, ethnicity, gender, religion, social class or region. In other words, culturally situated social experience reinforces basic biological and psychological needs, while simultaneously giving direction to their sources of gratification. Ambiguities over the origin of human needs suggest that we must think of what the media provide as something not necessarily needed by a person, but used to gratify a yearning.

'Wants' – more ephemeral, less central to well-being – may be the more appropriate level of analysis. Wants are desired but not needed states. Wants set up our understanding of the gratification nexus. In this view, attention should shift to intentional engagement to gratify wants, motivational impulse as it is socially conditioned; a socially embedded, cognitive plan. If a person feels lonely and wants to socialize, but feels shy or inhibited, he or she might turn to the media for vicarious parasocial interaction. This is a parasocial *use* of TV, and the function TV serves is to mimic interpersonal or familial communication. Some critics fairly point out that this chain of reasoning uses rather *tautological* logic, moving from measured satisfaction to imputed need, and forward to a use-value associated with gratification, with no independent way to test these constructs. The alternative approach contrasts *cognitive plans* with feelings: the study of affect (or emotional states) or hedonistic consumption of the media. A review by Gantz of over 20 years of U+G research suggests entertainment makes people feel good, happy, sad, excited, nervous or thrilled. It gets, or keeps, people in the mood they seek (Gantz 1996).

The second trajectory of U+G research identified the complex social ways that TV is used: defining the amount of shared viewing, practices for negotiating type of use, relationship with use or extent of identification with use, and the context of use (in families, among peer groups or alone). During the 1980s, this current of the U+G approach developed its own notion of 'negotiated reading': meaning is decoded by the audience in different ways, with different degrees of audience involvement, depending on the way various cultures construct the role of the 'receiver'. Moving into the area of reception research, a study by Liebes and Katz (1990) carried out a series of surveys to examine how *Dallas* was interpreted by particular groups in different cultures. As we will see in Chapter 13, another typical study of this trajectory is the Comparative European Study of Children and their Media Environment (Livingstone and Bovill 2001). Together with Lull, among others, these researchers led the turn away from the focus on the individual as the basic unit of consumption, and the overly functionalist framework that foregrounds personal psychological needs, to use in the social dynamics of families or other social units (Lull 1980). Viewers routinely engage with television to structure or spend time alone or with others, indulge in talk, seek ambient noise, companionship or entertainment. There may be benefits in social learning, status conferral, role/competence or social dominance. Findings of social psychology, such as people's bias towards seeking confirmatory rather than falsifying evidence, were applied not only to interpretation of events in everyday life, but also to viewers' making sense of television. This bridge has fruitfully extended to cultural studies and the qualitative turn (Livingstone 1998).

An important debate among gratificationists is whether patterns of use (structural or relational) are stable over time. While the composition of underlying audience gratification sets is always changing, the motivations expressed for the choice of media content, and the ways in which this content is interpreted and evaluated, point to the existence of a fairly stable and consistent structure of demand (consonant with a search for cognitive consistency) (McQuail 1998). News, for example, may be most valued, but drama remains most often watched in the majority of cultures. Livingstone has called this the *mean* audience thesis – that is, that audiences are basically conservative, searching for low-cognitive burdens, with tastes sliding to the lowest common denominator (Neuman 1995). Yet the cultural boundedness of these assumptions, especially in mediascapes with a more prevalent public or non-commercial component, suggests gratification may be an outcome of structural determinants. Cultural TV environments like the US, with heavy commercial focus and little public, non-commercial educational production, may support the 'mean audience' thesis; those with more diversified educational and entertainment fare as a consequence of cultural policies may not; we may find instead the 'public intellectual' viewer.

Another central research question among U+G theorists is how to predict habits of taste or repeat viewing. The principle of *cognitive dissonance* suggests people reject media materials and behaviours that undermine existing belief systems (Festinger 1957). Cognitive dissonance is a psychological tenet that guided both the *limited effects* hypothesis in Klapper's era and the *limited uses* theory in McQuail's (McQuail 1998).

One of the most influential of U+G works, which aspires to integrating uses and effects, is the longitudinal Swedish Media Panel Studies, launched in 1975 by Karl Erik Rosengren. Relying on mail surveys, in-depth interviews and a range of other techniques, the studies surveyed 4400 youths and parents in two Swedish cities for 25 years. A longitudinal cross-sectional 'cohort' design was used, allowing researchers to 'control' for time-related, situational and maturational or cohort effects in the data analysis (Rosengren 1994). Financial support of academic funding councils, universities, government education departments and the Swedish Bank enabled a range of over 20 related studies, which suggest that social and family backgrounds are important influencers of future media use. They found that working-class families watched more TV than middle-class households. Families of heavy TV users tended to raise children who are also habitual users. The Swedish Media Panel Studies are notable for their contribution to the study of influence of gender and social background on predicting TV socialization patterns in families and, particularly, patterns of TV habituation, dependency and relationship to supplementing, substituting, stimulating or displacing other leisure activities. The team of researchers developed a spiralling uses and effects chain of interaction between individual characteristics and media use, building on *reciprocal cognitive models*. To quote Rosengren, 'What we see then is a specific pattern of values, attitudes and actions emerging out of a common form of life, patterns which are partly determined by social position (*ways of life*) and partly by individual choice (*lifestyles*)' (Rosengren 1994:147).

The third trajectory of U+G built on marketing and advertising research, to develop extensive insight into consumer cognitive schema and decision-making in the shift from 'mass' consumption. Cognition means the act of coming to know something. Audiences may want to 'keep up' with the news, to learn something from the media, or a whole range of activities on the information/understanding/knowledge continuum in between. For these U+G analysts, the emphasis is on understanding the mental processes that determine how people learn information, form a decision or guide their activity. For the purposes of designing persuasion campaigns, the stages of consumer information processing have been analytically disaggregated and defined to include exposure, attention, comprehension, acceptance, retention and memory. Marketers want to understand how each stage in cognitive/decision-making works. In the flow of the estimated tens of thousands of media stimuli a day, how do consumers decide which message to pay attention to and which not? *Selective exposure*, defined as deliberate behaviour to control perception of a particular stimulus, is the central premise of gratification theories. Selective exposure involves an individual's predisposition to certain choices, the level of attention or involvement in audience consumption, and preference or likelihood of repetitive patterning of taste. How this all works is important in defining the audience activity. *Salience* is the underlying theory behind media attention. The more salient the message, the more likely a person will be to pay attention to the media, and the greater the cognitive, rational or emotional involvement.

To formalize this observation, U+G theorists later developed the *expectancy value* model for predicting media use. This model weighs expected and actual assessment of the benefits or gratifications (whether hedonistic or utilitarian) obtained from media consumption. Expectancy value theorists help us to understand something often dismissed as the 'lowest common denominator of taste' by popular culture theorists. They suggest that where expectations are low and gratifications met, there will be high satisfaction, although low appreciation and attention (Palmgreen et al. 1994). Low-expectancy value explains patterns of *casual, intermittent or low-involvement viewing*, when someone is doing several different things at once, while allegedly watching television.

U+G theorists, then, build models of *active cognitive processing*. Individuals are both *conscious* of their needs and *capable of expressing* them. There is a *logical* relationship between experience and the content chosen, or an *emotional or affective* relationship in this school. Zillman and Bryant suggest that affective arousal and excitement as a result of audiovisual experience can be measured and helps predict future behaviour (Zillman and Bryant 1985). Other, later, scholars also suggest that motives may not be conscious, but reflective of a kind of feeling state: that much audience activity is mood servicing. Reformed U+G analysts (Rubin 1979) suggest that instead of the focus on conscious/affective motives, research should change to *interpretative frameworks* or cognitive schema. Cognitive schema may be understood as the mental maps of meaning by which audiences make sense of their world. Rosengren furthermore identified *problem-solving* as a metaphor for active choice. Critics rebut: 'How *problematic* can lazy leisure be?' Choice may reflect habit or ritual, not conscious decision. The danger on the other side is to be overly individualistic, reducing the social act of viewing to the individual act of cognizing (Livingstone 1998).

## CRITIQUES OF THE USES AND GRATIFICATIONS SCHOOL

The chief theoretical defect with the U+G approach has been the failure to find logical or consistent relations among preference, choice and evaluation, sometimes called utility. It is not clear whether this is due to methodological weakness, or reflection of a reality in which individual media selection is actually circumstantial, inconsistent and weakly motivated. The lack of congruence between attitudes and behaviour is well known. In past studies, interest segmentation explained relatively little variation in viewing behaviour (Frank and Greenberg, quoted in Webster and Phalen 1997). The disparity is between what people say and what they do. What can account for the difference? Choices may be constrained by what is available. Choice may have to be negotiated in company with others. Or there may be a lack of awareness of alternatives. In short, intervening variables may alter the intent to act.

Another problem is with its overly cognitive, rational bias. The roots of gratification theories share many postulates with economic models of rational programme choice (or public choice theory, in political studies). As McQuail has identified, this starts from the premise of the *rational* self-interested consumer who seeks to satisfy a need, exercises rational choice, guided by experience, and expects some utility or gratification. There is little room in this ideal for the emotional, irrational, incremental, habitual or ritual terrain of behaviour.

The U+G approach has also been attacked for overstating the real autonomy of the audience. *Vulgar gratificationism* ignores the everyday social context of media use (Schrøder 1999), and completely separates *need gratification* from the cultural meanings derived. Carried to its logical extreme, if the power of meaning lies in the hands of the consumer, the question of social and economic factors determining individual consumption – the realm of policy and political economy – is invalidated (Matellart and Matellart 1998: 122). McQuail has modified the rational/mechanical model underlying U+G in the third trajectory (above), by emphasizing key linkages between social background and expectations from the media. Indeed, he argues that the *uses and gratifications* approach is not strictly *behavioural*, since its main emphasis is on the social origins of media gratifications and on the wider social functions in facilitating social interaction or reducing stress (McQuail 1998).

The search for a *media imperative*, or affinity for certain media-specific preferences and patterns of interests, habits of use, expectations, and so on, continues to be important in audience studies. It has propelled the rise of psychographic marketing segmentation in advertising and marketing studies, and led the way to new thinking about *value* in the study of media, new space for understanding the role of media practices in the context of lifestyle. Livingstone (1998) argues that there is an opportunity for more specific, qualified accounts of the ways in which audiences are motivated, and convergent or divergent in their appreciation and interpretation of media texts.

While it is fashionable in cultural studies to wholly reject the behaviourist overlay to the diversity of research designs operating loosely under the rubric of uses and gratifications (Lewis 1991; Moores 1993; Schrøder 1999), the tradition does offer some important contributions to how we understand the audience. First, the historical contribution was to emphasize audience *work* or activity, something flattened in earlier effects models. U+G built on Klapper's model of limited effects to study individual media appropriation (for a fuller discussion, see Chapter 15). There are undeniable compatibilities with the rise of marketing science. The focus on hedonism, affect and value, set up the trend away from demographic study to psychographics in the study of persuasion in advertising circles. Indeed, many of the survey techniques, measuring a variety of attitudes, values and reported behaviours, worked within adapted values attitudes lifestyles (VALs) statistical models, using cluster, factor or multivariate statistical analyses to better understand market segmentation. U+G begins to carve out the social space of lifestyles, or what Moores calls *the productivity of consumption theory*, which gained ground in the 1970s.

Where many of the early scholars in this tradition took leave of their earlier counterparts in American administrative research was in the concept of low involvement/low attention viewing. The possibility that people don't care enough about the media to assemble a set of media beliefs and evaluate them was relatively heretical in marketing and TV circles in the commercial media system in the US. By contrast, the idea that there are various values held, with varying levels of intensity, added the idea of use value to the dominant preoccupation with exchange value in audience–media consumption. U+G-style studies are sometimes used in policy circles – for example, to determine competitive positioning or differentiation between media products or brands, or relative perceived value of products in copyright or other hearings. Indeed, it is worth being reminded that some of the early success of the research tradition as it has been practised has been to express, in verbal form, measures that are widely available to measure media use consistently, and establish protocols to measure the dominant associations with certain kinds of media experience (McQuail 1998).

A final area of contribution from U+G study is the idea of an integrated cognitive–affective model. McQuail perhaps expresses it best: the key proposition to be explored is that cultural experience – what happens at the time of attention to the media – can be treated as a generalized process of involvement, arousal, understanding and capture. The essence is to understand the process of freeing the viewer from the dullness of daily life and enabling her to enter into new experiences, which would otherwise be unavailable, as an aid to or substitute for the imagination, enabling joy, anger, sexual excitement, sadness or curiosity. Such work must involve the understanding of taste cultures (Lewis 1991); it aspires to what sociologists call a more *cultural model with a balance between structural determinants and the exercise of agency* (Walsh 1998).

We have seen how a broad-brush survey of cultural tastes in Australia achieves a great deal in comparative generalization in the Bourdieu tradition, but is lacking in understanding in terms of the micro-level specificity of everyday pleasure derived from cultural practice of the sort that may be glimpsed through a U+G prism. The real promise is for cultural studies and U+G models to converge. Lull suggests that although U+G research and cultural studies differ greatly in their theoretical orientations, politics and methodologies, many of their basic conceptions and traditions are not entirely dissimilar. They begin with some of the same assumptions and arrive at several compatible conclusions (Lull 1995). Despite the inadequacy of *activity* as a single general concept, there continue to be valid theoretical and practical reasons for retaining it, but only when it can be clearly defined and empirically tested (McQuail 1998).

# Chapter Thirteen

# The audience survey toolbox: ☐ the questionnaire as lens

How do you *do* an audience survey? This chapter presents a practical toolbox for survey research, built upon the conceptual foundation for quantitative research set out in Chapter 10. We will concentrate on the questionnaire as a lens on the audience, since we have established that surveys are most often 'snapshots' of the audience in time over space. The metaphor of photography is useful when working with surveys, evoking visual expression in 'mapping' audiences in context: apparently documentary in its realism, but equally constructive of its object. What is a defence of audience surveys in light of attacks from cultural studies and critical theorists? We argue that surveys do not necessarily flatten meaning, and that the alternative to deep description in audience studies is breadth of description and power for comparison and generalization. How can researchers guide this method into action?

## DESIGNING SURVEYS AS A SNAPSHOT IN TIME

Surveys ask people questions and accept their answers as data. They look for general patterns rather than exploring in depth why a particular person did a particular thing. Survey design must be appropriate to your research question. Surveys are used if your umbrella question is implicitly representative (how many people would watch? or like?); implicitly comparative (who prefers A to B?); describes a relationship (women use the Internet less often than men); or seeks to influence something (what increases support for regulation of offensive contents on the Internet?) (Sapsford 1999). Don't assume a survey is the best method; have a rationale for its selection. Be sure you understand your survey's purpose: to discover, describe, map or explain. Start by defining a general research question: why it is an important problem, what you mean by the terms you use, and what other factors or subsidiary research questions may be connected. John Cresswell, a noted qualitative sociologist, writing about quantitative research methods (1994), suggests finding focus for your study by asking the following questions (Cresswell 1994: 3):

- Is the topic researchable, given the time, resources and availability of data?

- Do I have a personal interest in the topic to sustain my attention?

- Will the results of the study be of interest and use to others?

- Does the study fill a void, replicate, extend, to develop new ideas in the scholarly literature?

- Is the topic likely to be publishable in a scholarly journal?

## THE SURVEY INSTRUMENT: CHOOSING THE LENS

We can ask survey questions directly or indirectly. *Direct interviewer-administered formats* are face-to-face personal, telephone and computer-assisted telephone interviewing (CATI). Face-to-face interviewing is useful when the ideas explored are complex, or the interviewer presents visual prompts to enhance answer quality. Interpersonal interaction can motivate respondents and improve response rates. However, the technique is slow and expensive, and carries some personal risk to the interviewer who may have to travel in some neighbourhoods they may not choose. Some interviewers may not obtain a high cooperation rate. Some may unconsciously intimidate or get truncated answers. Others may administer the questions in subtly different ways so different answers are obtained. Age, gender and race can introduce subtle cultural bias in the joint construction of meaning. Interviewer-induced variance is thus a large part of survey sample error.

Telephone interviews are used when studies are time-sensitive or opinions need to be mapped repeatedly over time (longitudinal surveys). Collecting voters' responses to an election debate or their views over the course of a campaign are well suited to such designs. Telephone interviewing has the advantages of being relatively inexpensive, fast and amenable to random sampling, but can be undermined by answering machines, competition from telemarketing and the need to 'keep it simple and short'. In a basic telephone survey, the interviewer works with pen and pencil. In computer-assisted telephone interviewing (CATI), the interviewer works from a monitor and software guides administration of the survey. CATI is used for larger sample sizes since it is easier to standardize.

*Indirectly administered formats* include mail or Internet surveys, which ask written questions and rely on the respondent to fill them out. Self-completed questionnaires are often better for sensitive areas where answers may be embarrassing (such as drug consumption in rave culture) or when extensive information is required (diary of daily radio listening habits). They are often used in educational or health research, where personal anonymity encourages disclosure. The defect of self-completed interviews is their low response rate: respondents have little motivation to do the work. Questions are often answered out of order (according to the individual's interest or lack thereof) or not answered at all. In addition, written questionnaires or diaries are less likely to successfully elicit responses to more open-ended questions: the more work a respondent has to do by herself, the lower the response rate.

Your choice of direct or indirect questionnaire radically affects the style of question, the amount of 'briefing' you must give the respondent or interviewer, and the expected response rates. It also influences the degree of control needed over the order and extensiveness of the answers.

# ETHICS IN SECURING COOPERATION WITH DATA SUBJECTS

An effective survey requires special rapport with respondents. Winning agreement to participate involves personal persuasion and establishing trust for the study's objectives and the interviewer. You need to establish your credibility, and declare who you represent. Why did you select them? What is it you want to talk about? How much time will it take? They also have a right to know what you will do with the personal information collected. Since survey research has become deeply contaminated by commercialization – and abuse of personal, confidential information – there is a greater onus on the researcher to legitimate the inquiry.

Response rates on telephone surveys are rapidly declining. Commercial polling and market research are now so widespread that people duck 'junk calls'. Many telephone studies done for marketing purposes routinely obtain less than 10 per cent, and on their own are unreliable. Highly rigorous media industry standards for studies sufficient to set ad rates often call for a response floor of 60 per cent (Canadian Advertising Research Foundation), necessitating up to nine callbacks. In general, academic studies obtaining 50 per cent or more are considered good. Mail surveys routinely have response rates in the 30–40 per cent range. Means of enhancing response rates include offering incentives, callbacks at more convenient times, and regular reminders of the invitation and appointment for participation. Studies on response rates have shown that populist appeals to empowerment (respondents are told 'your opinion counts') are effective.

The test for responsible conduct in survey research is whether the respondent gives 'informed consent', and how we can interpret if it is voluntary and not coerced. In some cases, informed consent may be given after the study, in the form of a veto over disclosure. The introduction to your survey should reveal:

- introduction of interviewer and institution
- how the respondent was selected
- topic and purpose of study
- frame of respondent protection (voluntary cooperation, answers kept confidential)
- likely length of interview.

There is debate over the amount of disclosure of the purposes of a study; some social scientists argue that too much disclosure may bias the results. The British Psychological Society has noted that many psychological processes are modifiable if people know they are being studied (Deacon, Pickering et al. 1999). While deliberately withholding information is acceptable in some circumstances, deliberate deception about the study's intent is not. Special ethical considerations arise when there is risk of harm from disclosure of potentially criminal behaviour, risk of psychological discomfort arising from participation in research about a sensitive topic, or research conducted among minors. Various countries have set legal limits governing a researcher's capacity to guarantee confidentiality. If a researcher is observing drug use at a concert or rave, for example, and obtains personal information about drug consumption from someone later involved in a criminal case, disclosure may be required by law. But it is widely accepted that the ethical standards of academic research work today should encourage a very open standard of disclosure of the study's purpose, unless valid reasons for exception may be demonstrated (see Box 13.1).

## Box 13.1 Concern for respondents

- How will confidentiality/anonymity be assured?
- Who will have access to the results of the study?
- Is the subject matter likely to be painful in any way for the respondent?
- Is there any possibility that an informant will think I have the power to help or harm him or her?
- Is the questionnaire intrusive? If so, by what right do I intrude?
- Is the research consensual? Whose consent is being sought? Are the implications of consent fully understood?
- Is the outcome of the research likely to be harmful to respondents or other interested parties, or make them vulnerable to control?
- Is there a conflict of research interests in this situation, and whose side am I on?
- Does the research reinforce a dominant power relationship or stereotype to the detriment of respondents or other parties?
- How do you plan to destroy the data?

Source: Sapsford (1999: 40); see also Deacon, Pickering et al. (1999: 379)

Ethical issues that deserve consideration include confidentiality, removal of identifiers to ensure anonymity, disclosing information about the purpose and sponsor of the survey, proper interviewer training, and ensuring informed consent. If your topic is especially traumatic, you may consider providing the respondent with access to the study findings or other sorts of post-interview support, through referral to other literature on the topic, counselling or information hotlines (Sumser 2001). Special university peer review of your intended method may be required before you begin your project.

Finally, there are ethical considerations embedded in questionnaire design. Questions may involve sensitive personal disclosure. The most difficult 'talk' is about the socially taboo – areas of sexual, criminal or other 'deviant' behaviour – and here, indirect questions may prove more effective. There are techniques to minimize the perception of threat from disclosure on sensitive or embarrassing questions, by lessening imputation of deviance ('as you know, some religions allow marriage to many spouses'); by lessening psychological immediacy via substitution of reporting on others, by placing them at the end, and by avoiding emotionally loaded or taboo words.

# EPISTEMOLOGICAL BASIS FOR THE SURVEY GAZE

Use of verbal data, qualitative or quantitative, has been an important foundation for audience research. Yet there is much evidence to suggest that verbal data or self-reports may be of dubious reliability, and that we lack a theory of comprehension and communication that can provide a foundation for the way question/answer meaning-making takes place (Cicourel, in Foddy 1993). The general epistemological problems with collecting verbal data are: halo effect, non-attitude, faulty recall. Many of these also affect qualitative research, but what concerns us here is how we manage these problems in quantitative survey design.

## MANAGING THE HALO EFFECT

An interview on culture and the media can be seen as a symbolic battlefield for cultural capital and social status. We know that 'interviewers', especially university researchers, carry social status in interaction with their subjects, which may shape people's desire to cooperate, willingness to please (to get that halo), ability to disclose and type of answer given. Survey questions are inevitably language and cultural context-dependent. Respondents may be self-conscious about their answers (reluctant to disclose what Radway (1984) has called their guilty pleasures), or show marked gender and age variations in willingness to 'play the interview game'. The estimated 25–40 per cent rate of functional illiteracy in advanced western democracies poses serious problems in motivating respondents, and risk of their misunderstanding the question.

What stratagems have quantitative researchers developed to manage the halo effect? The first is *pre-testing language*, asking respondents to think aloud when answering or to 'restate the question in their own words'. Other techniques ask for feedback on question clarity and the perceived relevance of answers offered. The second is to avoid *obvious design flaws* that magnify the halo effect. In the *Canadian Arts Consumer Profile* (1992), the telephone survey began: 'I would like to begin by asking if as a child you recall attending any performance of music, dance or theatre?' Not surprisingly, after this warm and fuzzy start, positive answers to attendance at specific types of performances were suspiciously high. The researchers estimated the likely inflation factor due to the halo effect to be a minimum of 1 in 20, or 5 per cent, but critics suggested this ignored cumulative effects. Attendance at museums in British Columbia (BC) alone could have been overstated by 100 per cent: it was twice what 'turnstile' counts found for the period (Murray 1994: 36). The third method is to *legitimate 'guilty pleasure' disclosure*: making non-conformity more acceptable in the body of the question. To indicate that some people like romance novels, for example, while others do not, begins to legitimate 'low' cultural tastes. Such stratagems in design are also important when probing 'antisocial behaviour', to offset the bias to social acquiescence or 'normalize' dissent. Random probability theory posits that such tendencies may counteract each other in a sample overall. But they never disappear.

Finally, remember that sometimes it is better to *measure things indirectly*. When trying to measure traits of personality that may relate to media use, we seldom ask, 'Do you suffer from low/enjoy high self-esteem', in exploring the views on ads in fashion magazines, for example, since most would deny low self-esteem. Instead, we may ask a variety of indirect questions about the signs of low self-esteem in order to diagnose it (e.g. I feel worthless, I have plenty of good qualities).

## MANAGING FAULTY RECALL

If theories about inadvertent viewing models are correct, then there are cognitive barriers to be overcome in the design of audience surveys: respondents may not recall the specifics of a media interaction, or may answer when they really do not know. Quantitative researchers have devised several ways to overcome recall barriers. They administer visual prompts (magazine covers, say) in a through-the-book technique for magazine readership study. They ask if people have seen a particular ad, then probe for specific recall of contents to do with brands or story elements. In recent reading/viewing questions, the recall period asked for is kept very short (yesterday, the last week, the past month). Questions are often posed in terms of visualizing the daily routine for media consumed while getting up, preparing for work, travelling to work or, conversely, 'epochal' personal and family occasions (birthday, graduation, death of parent, and so on). Or, as Kubey and Csikszentmihalyi did, recall is eliminated by experience sampling or use of direct beeping (see page 173). Multiple snapshots over time of the same cohort of respondents are the best survey designs of all, as the Swedish Media Panel studies found (Chapter 12).

## LOW SALIENCE

The most serious problem is when respondents are not sufficiently interested to recall something, or you are seeming to force them to talk about something they have chosen to ignore. There are two ways to deal with low salience. First, you can allow respondents to skip sections of the questionnaire they don't care about or have no interest in: if they say soaps are their favourite type of programmes, they are not led through painful evaluative questions on news.

The second is to understand cues for salience (so-called agenda-setting impacts) and how to probe for interest from the respondent. Public opinion surveys often ask, for example, 'What is the top media problem facing Canada/Denmark today?' Answers are often related to the frequency of media coverage of issues, as the agenda-setting hypothesis suggests. In an effort to move beyond simple agenda identification, analysts like Gamson (1992) have pushed such questions, by asking supplementary probes: When you think about [*cite issue*], what comes to mind? Would you say [*cite issue*] has affected you personally, or your friends and relatives? Do people you know talk very much about [*cite issue*]? (Gamson 1992: 195).

## MANAGING THE NON-ATTITUDE

Interpreting answers such as 'don't know', 'can't recall', 'undecided', 'no opinion', 'it depends' and 'neutral' is all-important. These represent quite different knowledge states.

In response to a survey about a fictitious public issue, Converse and other analysts of political communication found high levels of respondents (some 40 per cent) expressed an opinion, even when they did not have one, inspired either by a mistake, blindly choosing an answer at random, imputing meaning from the context of the questionnaire, or answering by analogy to other firmly held views (Foddy 1993). Education and involvement have proved the best predictors to non-substantive responses. Those with less formal education are more likely to confess not to know. Those with little interest in an issue are also likely to be predisposed to an easy opt-out. To *manage the non-substantive response*, there are two opposing techniques: asking if people have thought about an issue before posing an attitude question, or asking how strongly they feel about something after they express an opinion, to isolate centrality of views.

Knowledge is obviously important to the history of audience studies. We know that McCombs, the inventor of the idea of agenda setting, hypothesized that its impact is greater for issues on which individuals have no alternative information than from media sources. Variously, we have introduced ideas about the knowledge gap: whether the socially deprived learn less than and thus fall further behind the already informed (Livingstone 1998). This suggests that the media generate different distribution of knowledge and, implicitly, power, as a function of the cognitive differences between viewers. Recent explanations of the knowledge gap refer not only to the cognitive deficit hypothesis to differentiate among social classes, but to motivations and issue salience to account for the gap.

How do we *manage non-attitudes*? The first and best way is to allow the respondent an 'opt-out' clause: using 'don't know' or 'no opinion' as a filter for later questions. A survey about the V-chip, a violence and obscenity blocking device installed in most US-manufactured televisions since 1996, in response to President Clinton's legislation, might ask if people had ever heard of it, or whether they were interested enough in the issue of violence on television to favour one side or the other. A final method is to allow self-styled knowledge characterization. Would you say you are very knowledgeable, reasonably knowledgeable, somewhat knowledgeable or not at all knowledgeable about X? If someone does not know something, or does not feel knowledgeable about it, the researcher has to justify continuing intrusive interrogation.

Early social scientific thinking about cognitive questions was based on a positivist stimulus–response model. Now, a more symbolic interactive or social learning model is accepted at the heart of survey design (see further discussion in Foddy 1993). Sometimes we want to probe whether attitudes can be formed by the introduction of information. One way to do this in a complex area (say, freedom of information or censorship of pornography on the Internet) would be to ask at the outset of the interview for general views, then for reaction to the various arguments of social movements or civil liberties spokespeople influencing public discourse on the issue, then re-test support or opposition for censorship of pornography. Positions may then be pushed in various forms of counterargument or trade-off analysis (see below) which pose scenarios (if, then). The problem, according to Justin Lewis, is 'we have no way of telling if the respondents are comfortable with the way of thinking that has been imposed on them . . . there is insufficient room for respondents to elaborate' (Lewis 1991). Timing or cost constraints often reduce the number of survey probes 'why is that?' which are customary in more informal, unstructured interviews. To correct for this, pilot studies often take the categories yielded from a true open-ended form, analyse the results and base the categories in the final study on the pilot protocol (Schuman and Presser 1981).

## WHAT PEOPLE SAY AND DO

It's universally human to say we want to do something and then not do it, maybe because we can't, we didn't try or something intervened. U+G studies have repeatedly found the relationship between genre preferences and actual programme selection is not direct or strong, due to the menu on offer, mood or social constraints in the viewing decision at the time (McQuail 1998). One may say one wants to read more on something, but for many reasons not be able to, or want to improve the quality of one's reading (perhaps by joining a book club), but soon drop out. Commercial audience research is good at studying this gap and developing prediction models to control for it, for instance, in the area of intent to purchase new information/communication technologies (ICTs); and proprietary market research models exist that track what people say they want to buy and revisit them in six months to see what they actually bought. These longitudinal methods allow us to develop a reasonable discount algorithm. An alternative is to look in the body of your questionnaire for gaps between what people say and do. For example, 40 per cent of British Columbia residents over 18 claimed in a survey they wanted to attend a jazz or blues concert. By probing other areas of behaviour and opinion in the questionnaire, such as preferences for CD audio quality over live performance or for staying home rather than going out (so-called cocooning effect), a discount factor of some 50 per cent was estimated. Prediction is a hazy art. Commercial firms have underestimated phenomena (the rise of audio file swapping on the net, for example) or persistently overestimated demand (for broadband interactive services in North America), all due to the biases of the promotional culture. Introduction of a midpoint on a four-point intent-to-purchase scale (allowing for an undecided choice) helps offset any pro-ICT technology bias in academic study design.

## STRUCTURE AND STANDARDIZATION IN ENCODING MEANING: SETTING THE F-STOP

No less than an in-depth interview, a telephone or face-to-face survey is a conversation that establishes reciprocal trust, turn-taking and interest. The biggest difference is the philosophy of 'structuring' a conversational exchange. Choice of the degree of structure (setting the lens aperture) in questioning turns on the level of social generality you want to employ in analysis, and the scale of measurement. Are you interested in an individual, group or cross-section of a national people? The level of structure or 'standardization' increases with the scale of the interactions. In surveys, there is a continual trade-off between open, reflexive and narrative 'talk' and the need to standardize responses for analysis. Standardized survey questionnaires cost less, in terms of both time and money, than personal in-depth interviews. They easily allow data comparisons across widely varying populations, and deliver better potential for generalization.

Surveys present a continuum of structuring questions, ranging from open to closed. An *open-ended question* seeks an answer the respondent is free to construct. In *Television and the Quality of Life,* Kubey and Csikszentmihalyi asked a simple, exploratory question at the outset: 'What is the one thing in your life you enjoy doing the most?' In the Australian Everyday Cultures study (Chapter 11), a classic question asked respondents, 'Could you indicate in a few words what you think 'good taste' and 'bad taste' entail?' Here you can see that an open-ended questionnaire sets a fairly wide F-stop on the questionnaire lens.

*Closed-ended questions* fix the categories of choice for the respondent. Bourdieu's survey for *Distinction* asked respondents to underline the personal qualities they most appreciated, from a list including 'bon vivant', 'artistic', 'dynamic', and so on. The image has been sharpened through a smaller aperture setting.

Open-ended questions, much more difficult for respondents to answer, are often avoided in questionnaires. The potential text of all the answers may measure in terms of thousands of pages. Respondents have to think harder to choose and frame their answers; analysts have to work harder to sort and name the groups of answers.

Selective use of open-ended questions is helpful to introduce variation in a questionnaire. Open-ends are probably the only way to explore language issues on a broad scale (to see if meanings of key terms are shared, or if new slang or language is emerging), to avoid imposing response categories or specifying too many possible responses.

Open-ended questions are often used to develop the categories for closed questions or indexes. Scales, constructs or indicators take time, trial and error, and science to develop. The story of Greenberg's (1974) effort to develop a viewing motivation scale to assess why children watch TV is typical. To create the scale, he asked British youths to write essays about why they liked to watch TV. Content analysis of the essays yielded eight themes, among them: to pass time, to relax or by habit. Greenberg then created 31 statements to reflect these reasons and administered them to a large survey sample. His subjective taxonomy was checked against a statistical technique to identify if underlying factors or dimensions matched his expectations (see discussion of data reduction below). The Viewing Motivation Scale (Rubin et al. 1994) has been replicated in over a dozen studies as it has been refined.

If respondents are interpreting the question differently, answers cannot be meaningfully compared across populations (Foddy 1993). For this reason, open-ended questions are rarely subjected to statistical analysis in survey research.

The analytic costs of closed-ended questions are well known. They may elicit answers where no opinion or knowledge exists, they may over-simplify or distort issues, they may 'force' or 'coerce' an answer or they may be boring to answer. All these reasons have caused qualitative cultural analysts to oppose excess structure in question design, and challenge the validity of closed questions. Yet the advantages are also well known. In general, pre-setting the answer categories tries to ensure that the questions are asked in as similar a way as possible to as many people as possible, reducing the potential for inter-personal variance in administration. Closed-ended questions are easier to administer, decode and process for large samples. As a telling tale from the field reveals, despite the effort to integrate ethnography and survey work in the European comparative Children and New Media study, most of the report relies on the survey, which was much easier to contrast and compare between the participating countries. Livingstone and Lunt's (1994) work (on TV talk shows) evaluated the use of focus groups versus surveys in explanatory utility. While less useful for understanding the complex relationship between certain texts and context, survey analysis was better at identifying an important intervening variable not pinpointed in focus groups: the importance of age rather than gender or class.

## QUESTIONNAIRE DESIGN IN CLOSE-UP

Questionnaire design must start by anticipating question answers and the contexts under which they are given. Questioning is thus an interactive and elaborative communication process, both art and science. Designing questions involves painting social thought-worlds in words, with trial and error. The keys to self-reflexive sensitivity in question design, common to all forms of questionnaire administration, are:

**A.** respondents must mostly have the same idea of what both a single question and a body of questions are about

**B.** respondents should have the required information sufficient to answer

**C.** the question should be relevant/salient to respondents (so they pay attention and want to answer)

**D.** the researcher should specify as fully as possible the perspective that respondents should adopt when framing answers, to aid in comparability. (Foddy 1993)

The three overarching considerations of questionnaire design are ethical sensitivity, validity (making sure the measure you select is measuring the concept you need to measure) and reliability (when responses are consistent over time).

So how do we begin? The first step in mapping talk is to set up an inventory of the information you need. An example is found with the international team studying Children and New Media in Europe (Box 13.2). You may wish to collect four main types of information: demographic, behavioural, cognitive and affective.

First, you need to know how to describe the basic personal attributes of the people you want to talk to: your 'target population'. This descriptive information is often called *demographic*

## Box 13.2 Inventory of topic areas covered by a comparative European study of children and their media environment

### Access
- Satisfaction with local amenities, freedom within local environment
- Ownership (in bedroom and/or elsewhere in the home) and use of each of 16 media
- Access to computers and Internet in school and home

### Time
- Leisure activities engaged in (19 listed, including 7 non-media-related)
- Typical number of days per week spent on each of 16 media in leisure time
- Length of time spent (hours/minutes) with these media on a typical day
- Times of day television switched on or watched in the home
- Time spent on computers at school
- Bedtime and proportion of leisure time at home spent in bedroom

### Uses and modes of engagement
- Which media child uses personally, which child would miss most, which want to get next birthday
- Which media child chooses when bored/wants to relax/wants excitement/wants not to feel left out/which does child concentrate on
- Which media child finds best for following main interests (names in values/interests)
- For media-related goods (books, magazines, comics, music tapes, computer games, videos, clothes, toys, things you collect), which child buys with own money and which swapped with friends
- For television, how often/when does child flick channels
- What computers at home/in school used for and what is the Internet used for

### Content
- Name of favourite television programmes
- Understanding of who the programme is for (older/younger people), whether child talks to friend about it, whether parents keen for child to watch it
- Type of favourite electronic game

### Social context of use
- Who child spends most free time with
- Who usually watches favourite programme/plays electronic games with

## Box 13.2 continued

- Who asks for advice about computers
- How often does things with parents (eat main meal/watch TV/play or make things/talk about things that matter/talk about things on news)
- Whether child visits friends to use (which media) not available at home

### Parental mediation (for father and mother separately)

- For each of watching television/videos, using/playing on computer, listening to music, making telephone calls, reading books and going out, for which is child told when can/can't do and which media do parents talk to child about

### Attitudes values/interests

- Which of 14 topics interests the child most
- Perceptions of what makes someone the child's age popular
- What will be most/least important when child grown up

### Background and personality

- Who child lives with
- If lived abroad, where they would prefer
- Whether child worries/gets bored/likes being the way they are/finds it hard to make friends

Source: Livingstone and Bovill (2001: 43)

*information*, including gender, age, household size, racial information, employment status, income or occupation, which describes what people are (and a category overlooked in Box 13.2). Factors concerning social background and milieu, as reflected in social class, education, religion, culture and family environment may surface here, and are best modelled on census questions.

The second type of information is also descriptive: it measures *behaviour*, what people say they do, use or buy; their consumption spending on goods and services (such as video games or Internet services). This information is critical in the commercial realm as it affects ad spending. Indeed, the most lucrative consumer segment commands higher prices in ad sales on programmes designed to attract them. The phrasing of behavioural questions needs to be precise. To quote Roger Sapsford (1999):

> *It is no good asking 'Do you have a television set?' when what you want to know is whether the informant actually watches television. Questions must be unambiguous; 'Do you have a television set?' might be answered 'Yes, there is one in the house, it belongs to my Dad', or 'No, but my Dad has*

*one' or even, 'Yes, but our set is rented not owned'. At the same time questions must be as colloquial as possible, to be easily understood and create some feeling for a natural conversation rather than an esoteric checklist (or else the reactivity of the situation may distort the data. 'Do you own or rent or otherwise have a chance of watching a television in your house?' is accurate but cumbersome. 'Do you have access to a television set?' is precise but rather pedantic and formal. Best might be to ask three separate questions: 'Is there a television in your house?' 'Do you watch it at all?' And if the answer is 'No', 'Could you watch it if you wanted to?'*

(Sapsford 1999: 119)

The conceptualization or interpretation of behavioural sets needs to be creative. Kubey and Csikszentmihalyi illustrate the degree of creativity needed in interpreting their taxonomy to organize primary and secondary behavioural data, collected during the course of the day, in another way for their study *Television and the Quality of Life*. They developed observational categories ranging from 'imagining activities', including talking to oneself or meditating, to 'visual and auditory activities', ranging from reading to listening to noises, to oral, physical and work activities.

The third category is *cognitive*, referring to how people think. This is increasingly interpretative rather than descriptive. Thought-worlds are made up of attention paid or knowledge of something (what people think about or what they think they know), perceptions of values (what people believe is morally right or wrong), attitudes (what people would prefer) or beliefs or opinions (how people evaluate certain phenomena). In Bourdieu's study *Distinction,* an extensive set of questions was asked about which film people had seen, and if they were able to name the director and leading actors. Not surprisingly, levels of knowledge expressed were quite low (2 per cent), even among the upper classes. Murdock has likened a survey to 'an interrogation' and Bourdieu himself was uncomfortably aware of how like a school examination was his own survey instrument. Knowledge questions are particularly intimidating to respondents.

Here there must be careful attention paid to nuance: the positive or negative social or ideological connotations of words or ideas; awareness of the barriers of literacy or cultural association with certain ideas; and management of the risk of 'priming' or 'framing' later responses, as the question/answer dialogue continues.

The final category is *affective*, information that is expressive of emotion. These questions ask respondents to describe or, conversely, to project their moods, emotions, feelings or metaphorical associations. Of all categories of questions, these are perhaps the most interpretative and creative. Some use open-ended metaphor or projective techniques, usually in concert with drawing or other non-verbal expression. One way might be to introduce cartoons and ask people to write thought bubbles about the characters. Alternative affective designs introduce a picture and ask people to tell a story about it, looking for the degree with which feelings are projected into the scene (such as telling us what animal a political leader reminds them of). Various scales have been developed (e.g. the semantic differential scale with adjectival opposites) to elicit more colourful and creative associations with moods.

## Box 13.3 Types of questions: camera angles for surveys

Closed-ended questions come in five main types of format. Each is coded or translated into scales in a number of different ways. Then it proceeds down the list (checklists etc.).

### Dichotomous

These are yes/no (two-category) answers to simple, single questions: Did you watch the 11 pm news on TV last night? They are often used as filters, to take those who answered affirmatively through some special questions. Dichotomous questions are easy to code into numbers (1 for yes, 2 for no, with a 9 for no answer).

### Checklists

These questions list a range of items in the body of the question, usually grouped according to type, and then ask which of the following someone owns or uses. Checklists can easily create indexes, they just string yeses and nos. You must specify if a single response to a checklist or multiple response is acceptable. In the latter, answers may total more than 100 per cent. An example of a checklist question in the *Australian Everyday Cultures* survey asked 'Do you have any of the following in your home?', listing eight alternatives:

- Original paintings/drawings
- Signed limited edition prints
- Rock music posters
- Art posters
- Pottery or ceramics
- Sculpture
- Nature posters
- Political posters.

Respondents were invited to check off as many as applied. Checklists act as repeated yesses and nos in coding.

### Ranking

Some questions ask respondents to choose their favourite, second favourite and third favourite TV shows today. The question may not have a prompt, relying on a type of free recall associated with a true open-end, or it may rely on a prompt or aided recall from a list of TV shows read. The most important constraint on asking ranking questions is the difficulty for respondents to sort through their recall and answer. The burden can be reduced by limiting the number of selections allowed. A typical ranking question is: If asked to discuss any of the following issues yourself, which of the following would you be most and least likely to mention? Using the numbers 1 to 7, please rank the following on your willingness to discuss the topics below. Use the number 1 for the topic you are most willing to discuss and 7 for the topic you are least willing to talk about. The topics are . . . education, political affiliation (and so on).

## Rating

Item-by-item rating questions usually ask if people are positively or negatively oriented to something, and by how much. They have most often been called 'Likert scales' to probe extent of agreement or disagreement with an idea. Example: Would you say the quality of the TV series *The Road to Avonlea* is excellent, good, only fair or poor? Often followed by open-ends, e.g. Why is that?

## Trade-offs

Many surveys ask questions about complex issues. Defining the alternative views on an issue is hard. Instead of trying to artificially truncate the perspectives on the issues into a dichotomous answer (some people say, other people say), researchers often try to probe whether views will change as further information about the consequences of a stated view is introduced. The 'trade-off' scenario is an effort to accommodate complexity. An example of a 'trade-off' design may be found in a study on public interest broadcasting in the 1980s under Prime Minister Thatcher's effort to commercialize the BBC.

Would you strongly approve, approve, disapprove or strongly disapprove if the BBC accepted commercial financing as a means of funding its services?
If approve, ask: Would you want BBC television to take advertisements if this meant . . .
. . . less choice of programmes?  Yes  No
. . . more of your favourite type of programme but smaller range of others?  Yes  No
. . . more American programming?   Yes  No
. . . closing down some regional television stations?  Yes  No
. . . less experimenting with new programmes on BBC and ITV? Yes  No
. . . BBC would have a wider choice of types of programmes?  Yes  No
. . . BBC would have better and more expensive programmes? Yes  No

Source: Morrison (1986)

# TECHNIQUES TO MANAGE COMPLEXITY

Many areas of survey research deal with risky social issues that are frequently complex, to do with the ideology of freedom or balance of expression or censorship; national, local or global contents; or interpretative schema for news and other topics. An array of tools exists to manage complexity in question design. The most common in audience research are Q sorts and counter-arguments.

## Q SORTS

As a basis for his provocative exploration of the construction of meaning in the 'field of the politically thinkable' in the relationship between culture and the politics of 'selective democracy', Bourdieu conducted a pilot study that gave respondents 15 cards, each bearing the name of a movement, grouping or party, and asked them to group the cards as they wished. They were not explicitly asked to comment on the categories they applied, or to attach names or descriptions to the groups they established. In a second stage, they were given 24 cards and asked to say which group, movement or party each individual belonged to and then group them (Bourdieu 1984: 591). Part of a larger preoccupation with the modes of opinion production, or consciousness of a political 'line' or reading of political labels or unconscious predisposition, Bourdieu uses these kinds of questions to map a 'provisional diagram of political space':

> *When the respondents were invited to classify a set of movements, groupings or political parties as they saw fit, in general the higher their social position or the greater their educational capital, the more [categories] they produced. The ability to make refined classifications, the readiness to comment on them, and especially, to give names or qualifiers to the categories varies even more strongly by social position, educational capital and also social origin. Such a reading . . . overemphasizes the unequal distribution of political capital . . . technical competence depends on social status . . . One has to also consider the [socially authorized and encouraged] sense of being entitled to be concerned with politics, authorized to talk politics or apply explicitly political principles of classification and analysis instead of replying ad hoc on a basis of ethical principles . . . technical competence is to social competence what the capacity to speak is to the right to speak, simultaneously a condition and an effect.*

(Bourdieu 1984: 409f.)

Q sorts allow respondents to categorize in their own words the ideas you are interested in measuring. These categories or taxonomies may then be used to simplify complexity. In Chapter 17, we discuss the possibility of using Q methodology as a bridge between qualitative and quantitative approaches to audience research.

## COUNTER-ARGUMENTS OR THE VIGNETTE

How can you structure a series or question block to disclose sufficient information to a respondent to allow those with no prior information to form a view? How do you probe those with firm views to consider new information or determine the circumstances under which they may change their view if you are designing a persuasion campaign? To solve the dilemma of 'informed' consent, but at the same time 'balance' the information provided, the counter-argument, factum or vignette has been adopted. Intended to ensure that researcher and respondent have a shared understanding of the topic under investigation, these designs introduce contextual information and repeatedly test for changes in view.

In public opinion research, a counter-argument tries to cover at least two opposing views in a kind of mini-debate, usually citing the authorities endorsing this view, so that both the source and the argument can be evaluated. A factum, used in explorations of legal cases, may set up the facts of the case, the point of law, and invite various 'juror' deliberations. A vignette (derived from the French term for a brief descriptive account, anecdote or character sketch) might set up the aspects of a story, which probes ethical or moral reasoning.

These kinds of questions are perfect for situations where the best answer to a complex topic is 'it depends'. For example, if you want to explore attitudes towards copyright, the online audio file swapping that Napster, Gnutella, or a number of other transient new services provide, would be described, people asked what they think of such a service, and then the various arguments why MP3-enabled music swapping is theft of intellectual property or not would be explored, along with the reasons why. Respondents would then be asked either to rate each of the stakeholder arguments (derived either from the court transcripts of the Napster case in US superior courts, from the media, or official 'promo tional' discourse in company statements, and so on) or a cascade of value trade-offs (Box 13.3) would be presented and initial support for deregulation of such a service tested. Textual criticism is thus a very large part of developing survey design. Or, conversely, earlier models of questions that are theoretically useful in earlier academic studies, might be replicated, with permission from the authors.

Effective use of counter-argument is acutely dependent upon the capacity to distil complex ideas simply and accurately. It is hard to provide a full range of alternative views in a questionnaire, and harder still to frame 'equal' weight to all sides of an issue. Research into the persuasion effects of questionnaires suggests formal balance is less important than providing a cue that counter-arguments are acceptable (Schuman and Presser 1981). Others oppose them on the basis that a counter-argument is not enough to balance a question. The introduction of additional information to guide judgement is dangerously close to the inappropriate error of leading a respondent or 'framing' subsequent answers. It may be said that the respondent is either provided with a strong suggestion of the answer expected or conditioned over time to adopt a certain view. Such question design is among the most interpretative, or qualitative in origin. But mapping discursive ideological terrain is just where audience research gets interesting.

There are no hard-and-fast guidelines that will ensure your questionnaire is a good one. Box 13.4 sets out some common-sense pointers, to bring quantitative questionnaire design into finer focus.

### Box 13.4  Ten guidelines for questionnaire design

1. Ensure your questionnaire reads well: enlist informed consent of respondent, and begin with some fairly easy and interesting questions. Provide an opportunity for comments at the end.
2. Use simple language. Avoid slang or technical terms. Pre-test for levels of comprehension.
3. Be specific. Provide the respondent with a frame of reference (e.g. define what you need). A question like 'What is your income?' has to say who is meant by 'your' (self or family), what is meant by 'income' (salary or all other sources) and what time period.
4. Provide interviewer instructions. Be sure to stipulate if you want one or multiple answers in a checklist.
5. Provide transitions for changes in subject matter, and group like questions together, moving from easy to hard.
6. Make sure the order moves from general to particular, or a logical time or chronological progression. Frame the opinion questions so they are independent of the need for special knowledge initially.
7. Avoid 'and', or double-barrelled questions with any conjunction 'and' in them.
8. Avoid emotionally or ideologically laden terms – watch leading or loading.
9. Provide counter-arguments or factual vignettes. Allow a don't know or opt-out clause. Use Q sorts or trade-off designs for complex ideological issues.
10. Use multiple measures of the key analytic variables and use internal controls to check internal consistency of response.

## MAIN PROBLEMS IN QUESTIONNAIRE DESIGN: THE DARK ROOM

After sampling error, the largest source of error arises from questionnaire design. A typical well-administered survey item can yield up to 50 per cent variance (Roe, cited in Foddy 1993). Most introductory audience research texts are quick to identify the principal threats: order effects, bias, leading or loading, and recency effects.

## ORDER EFFECTS

The order of questions has an enormous influence on survey reliability and validity. We have already seen how the *Canadian Arts Consumer Profile* unwittingly set up a tendency towards inflated reporting of arts attendance by starting with a recollection of childhood. Priming is when a question suggests an answer, which then suggests a second answer in order to achieve logical (or psychological) consistency. An example of priming might be: thinking about acts of random violence in the news recently, would you say you are very concerned, somewhat concerned, not very concerned, or not at all concerned this social problem? And how about violence on television today? Are you very concerned (and so on)? Not only is this question unclear about the form of TV violence (news versus entertainment), it is also set in the context of a recent news story priming fears of random serial-killer violence, which may spill over to judgements of the media.

Pointers on question ordering generally recommend that you go from easy to hard (to establish social rapport), from general to particular (to avoid priming), from the full or wide population to the sub-population, or narrower social group; that you group topics by type and cue the respondent as you go along, moving from low-risk to high-risk questions over the body of the dialogue, to prevent the loss of respondent cooperation.

## BIAS, LEADING AND LOADING

The loaded question leads or clues the respondent to the desired response. An example would be 'Some people say freedom of expression is the most important value on the Internet today. Do you agree or disagree?' The field is obviously ideologically laden to a neo-liberal point of view. An alternative might be 'Some people say we need to protect people from harmful content on the Internet, while others say we have to protect freedom of expression. Which is closer to your view?'

## RECENCY EFFECT

This speaks to the tendency for judgements to be affected by the end or anchor point in a list read. To offset this potential for order of presentation bias within a questionnaire, answer categories may be rotated or read randomly in different order to different respondents. Computer-assisted interviewing scripts can make this a relatively simple tool to administer.

## INTERVIEWERS' INSTRUCTIONS

Major studies have two sets of instructions: those embedded in the questionnaire and those separate, to describe the purpose and design of the study and the reason for certain sections of the questionnaire. Possible objections or clarifications are anticipated, and responses written for all interviewers. The goal is not a mechanical sameness of procedures in administering questions (something unlikely outside a laboratory) but presentation of questions in as similar a way as possible to everyone, so there is reasonable probability that they may be understood by everyone in a similar way (Sapsford 1999). In general, instructions for mail or Internet surveys have to be complete and self-evident to the respondent. Be sure to stipulate when one answer or multiple answers are wanted. If there are questions irrelevant to respondents (they have not seen the ad you are asking about), allow them to skip those questions, and be sure to give them graphic or verbal prompts about where to re-enter the question series. You may add inset boxes for visual cues: if yes, answer Q2; if no, skip to Q3.

Open-ended questions need prompts ('Anything else?') to ensure the respondent completes a thought. Perhaps you want your interviewer to record them in the order mentioned. Finally, perhaps you want to underline how the emphasis is placed on words, or ask interviewers to clarify the meaning of terms unknown to them.

Closed-ended questions in a self-administered survey stipulate 'Please check one' or 'Please check the appropriate category'. Conversely, you may want to record multiple measures ('Please check as many as apply', or 'Please check the appropriate box[es]'). Telephone interviewers administer these instructions aloud.

Finally, it is important to be clear when you want an interviewer to read the list of pre-set answer categories, and when you do not. If you do not read the list, it is a modified open-end, with an 'other specify' open code to catch the odd unanticipated answers. If you do need to read a list, that instruction must appear. In some cases, interviewers are asked to 'rotate' the order of the list read, to offset recency bias.

## SAMPLING IN THE REAL WORLD: COARSE GRAIN

*Probability sampling* methods (outlined in Chapter 10) are labour-intensive, expensive and time-consuming. Confounding most sampling is the idea that often we are studying a population that is unknown: no lists of the sample universe exist. Or, conversely, our target population is such a small minority of the total universe (say, under 10 per cent) that random methods would be an inefficient way to reach them. In this section we look at drawing samples in the real world, without a complete and accurate sample frame available (Sapsford 1999).

The main alternative to probability sampling is *quota sampling*, in which respondents are picked to match the population on the demographic variables that form the basis of the quotas. An example of this approach may be found in the European comparative study on *Children and their Changing Media Environment*, chaired by Sonia Livingstone and Moira Bovill (2001). All 12 countries aimed for representative sampling as far as possible. Quotas were set for age, gender and social class. To do a random sample of children, you would need a list of all students, unavailable in most countries. Another way is to obtain lists of schools (from directories or government listings) and choose several at random; within schools, choose classes at random; finally, within classes, choose children at random to interview. At each stage, it would be necessary to weight the selection according to the number of children taught: otherwise, smaller schools would have a greater chance of selection. Alternatively, one might choose 'representative' strata of school systems (an affluent school, a middle-class suburban school, an inner-city school in a poorer region) and a number of schools within each. One would need to obtain permission to enter the school to conduct the study (and obtain ethical release from the corresponding authorities). As Roger Sapsford (1999: 100) succinctly summarizes, the more you can impose a degree of randomness on the selection of cases, and control the places and times of their collection, the better the representative quality of the sample.

Limited funding in some countries necessitated compromises: age bands were discontinuous and empty in some countries. These imbalances made it inappropriate for the researchers to project their findings to Europe. Where an 'all' or 'total' figure is provided, the researchers chose to present an average of the averages, calculated by giving equal weight to all countries (not proportionate to child population) so they are not simply representative of 'European children' but of the 'participants in the study' (Livingstone and Bovill 2001). We can still use estimates of sampling error on quota samples, as long as randomization occurs across the quota cells.

Many academic studies have to use *non-probability methods*. In preliminary stages, researchers may want to use non-random samples when the research question requires a sampling unit that is not really the population, but the range of ideas or activities characterized. Perhaps the best-known non-probability survey in audience studies is Robert Kubey and Mihaly Csikszentmihalyi's (1990a) naturalistic research on the viewing experience. Kubey and Csikszentmihalyi focused their analysis on 107 US adults, aged 18 to 63, recruited from five companies in the Chicago area. They obtained permission to interrupt the work day, and about a 50 per cent cooperation rate. As they noted, there was no gender balance, and unequal distribution across types of jobs. A number of different non-probability samples were compared, sufficient to cause Kubey and Csikszentmihalyi to argue that the 'data are generally applicable to the research questions posed and the findings characterize, in the main, general trends in viewing' (Kubey and Csikszentmihalyi 1990a: 47).

Other types of non-probability samples are purposive, snowball or convenience samples. *Purposive* is the most frequently used non-probability sample; that is, you may want to study leaders of an Internet subculture on a chatline, identify them by observation over time and then invite them to participate in a survey or experiment. In network or *snowball* referrals, you start with a friend, and ask that person to refer you to someone. You interview that person, and then ask them for another reference. These samples tend to reflect the sociocultural networks of the researcher, representing 'most similar' cultural enclaves. The third non-probability method is the intercept or *convenience* sample, where people may be interviewed at a hip downtown Internet café: patrons tend to be geographically clustered and may share other demographic characteristics. Comparisons to the general population are not reliable: what you have is a sample of people passing a specific point at a specific time – an accident, if you will.

The final and least reliable non-probability sampling method is *self-selection*: those who reply to a bulletin board posting about a study, for example. That some people are more interested and willing to cooperate in your study does not make them at all representative of the universe as a whole.

No confidence limits for non-probability samples may be calculated, and few statistical tests may be applied.

## CODING

Once the survey is completed in the field, you are ready to start the editing. This checks the eligibility of the respondents, whether all relevant questions were administered, and sets up rules for the rejection of partially completed questionnaires (anything less than 60 per cent completed is usually rejected). Editing really just confirms that the instructions to the interviewer or respondent have been followed reliably in filling out the questionnaire.

Coding involves preparing the survey information for transfer to computer data files. We can do this in several ways. With small databases (few questions and under 50 completions) a simple spreadsheet programme like Excel or Access is easily workable. For larger databases, a statistical software package such as SPSS or SAS may be needed.

Codes are the values used to represent different responses. The best time to plan the coding is before the survey is administered: pre-coding the answer categories right on the questionnaire is preferable.

The first job in survey administration is to identify the number of completed interviews or cases in your file. Each interview is a data record, and each has a unique locator number. The file usually starts with some code about the sampling area, date and time of the interview. Sometimes it is important to capture some information about the interviewer who conducted the study, if you have reason to believe you will need to evaluate interviewer variance later.

Once each questionnaire has a unique number, you can begin to enter the data from each variable in your questionnaires. Let's assume you want to create a data set based on 30 closed-ended questions for a questionnaire of about 10 minutes. You have numbered each question from one to 30, but not all questions are single variables. Remember the checklist of arts activities? A list of eight performances, with a dichotomous yes/no against each one. In that case, each type of performance, dance for example, is a variable with values attached, but only one question was asked (see Box 13.3). This would count as eight variables, within an apparently single question.

Most researchers like to give each variable a unique number in series, *in the order in which the questions were originally administered*. It is important that your variable label ('gender', say) also includes the question number. The researcher usually codes single-digit answer codes (0 to 9) against each answer category. For example, the classic Likert agree/disagree scale was used in a battery of statements people have made about economic, social and political issues in the Everyday Cultures Project. For each statement, respondents were asked to circle the number that came closest to how they felt about the issue. The first statement was 'The government has a responsibility to support the disadvantaged'. The variable label was 'responsibility for the disadvantaged'. The researchers made the following coding allocation:

Strongly agree 1

Agree 2

Disagree 3

Strongly disagree 4

No opinion was entered as 9 (which is often reserved for no answer/no opinion).

From time to time (on very large samples), your data file may have to record higher values (instead of 0 to 9 in single digits you may need 00 to 99 in double digits, if you expect up to 100 answer categories) to allow data space for possible answer variations.

With open-ended, narrative answers, experience in qualitative content analysis or discourse analysis in identifying like phrases, metaphors or ideas comes in handy. Each answer category is input in Microsoft Word, or other software, like Nud.ist (for a description of Nud.ist, see Deacon, Pickering et al. 1999). The challenge is to determine which can be grouped together. A name for the attribute or grouped ideas is created and given a number, by hand, beside the open-ended question on the completed questionnaire, and data then entered. Use a sizeable random sub-sample (20 per cent or more) of your completed questionnaires to set up these categories. New ones may be added from the balance of the sample. It is probably better to have more codes initially, so you can later collapse them, than to collapse a category and flatten its meaning prematurely. At the reporting stage, the 'unedited' 'verbatim' answers may be reintroduced to the analysis to make the diverse meaning of a category come to life. This process has much in common with developing categories in 'open coding', associated with the qualitative method called grounded theory. Cresswell (1994) states:

> In open coding, the researcher forms initial categories of information about the phenomenon by segmenting it. Within each category, the investigator searches for several properties or subcategories, and looks for data to dimensionalize, or show the extreme possibilities on a continuum of the property.

(Cresswell 1994: 57)

A few final pointers about coding. Be consistent: if you are using 9 for no opinion, stick with it. Enter all 0s where relevant. Use actual corresponding codes where possible. If you ask age in an open-end, code 23 years as a 23. Finally, try to keep the codes directionally consistent. If 1 means 'strongly agree', then small numbers are oriented to the positive pole. Later coding of 'really like' should not then have a 4. This is called 'standardizing scales' and is important later when you consider data constructs or indices.

## CREATING THE DATABASE

The responses from each questionnaire will be entered into your chosen database or spreadsheet software. Each respondent record will consist of a string of numbers. Let's assume you are using an Excel spreadsheet, with six variables in a string for each of nine respondents. A sample record might look like: '1, 2, 43, 4, 6, 45', where each comma-delimited value represents a respondent attribute or a question response. A representative data file might look like that shown in Table 13.1.

Inevitably, the integrity of your database will be compromised to some degree by typing errors during entry, or logically invalid responses. Typing errors can be eliminated by

Table 13.1   A representative data file

| ID# | Gender | Age | Q1 | Q2 | Q3 |
|-----|--------|-----|-----|-----|-----|
| 1 | 2 | 43 | 4 | 6 | 45 |
| 2 | 1 | 22 | 9 | 3 | 21 |
| 3 | 1 | 18 | 3 | 2 | 68 |
| 4 | 2 | 54 | 1 | 2 | 33 |
| 5 | 1 | 33 | 1 | 4 | 12 |
| 6 | 2 | 37 | 2 | 5 | 15 |
| 7 | 2 | 29 | 3 | 1 | 2 |
| 8 | 1 | 46 | 1 | 6 | 1 |
| 9 | 2 | 22 | 2 | 3 | 24 |

A data map or codebook should also be created.

| | | |
|---|---|---|
| Variable 1: | Respondent ID No. | Values 1..9 |
| Variable 2: | Gender | Values 1..2 |
| | | 1 = Female |
| | | 2 = Male |
| Variable 3: | Age | Values 18..99 |
| | | 98 = Refused to answer |
| | | 99 = No response |
| Variable 4: | Q1 | Values 1..4, 9 |
| | | 1 = Very likely |
| | | 2 = Somewhat likely |
| | | 3 = Not very likely |
| | | 4 = Not at all likely |
| | | 9 = No response given |

having each document input twice by different people, then resolving any differences. This process adds considerable time and expense, and the benefits are generally small, because error effects tend to cancel out due to their randomness.

Logical validation consists of detection and correction. By detection, we should spot an inconsistency such as:

> *Respondent's age:* 19
> *Academic status:* *Attending preschool*

Correction involves checking the original questionnaire to correct an input error or change the offending response to a 'don't know' or 'missing' value.

## CREATING NEW VARIABLES

You may wish to construct three types of new variables: a summary variable, a product of two, or an index or construct. Most of these must be constructed using statistical software packages such as SPSS or SAS.

A *summary variable* allows you to create a logic where answers may be grouped; these are useful for lists of repeated answers. In the example from the BC *Arts Consumers Profile*, it would be possible to create two types of summary variable derived from the reports on attendance to the list of eight activities. The first reports just the number of activities reported from the eight (number cited 1–8). It would then be possible to create an average of the number of activities done to study the tendency to 'omnivore' or 'univore' range of the cultural palette, as Bennett, Emmison and Frow did for their Australian study (1999). Or it might be possible to summarize the responses into 'any' reported on the range of variables 1–8 and 'none', to pick up inactivity.

A *product variable* is constructed as the product between two or more variables, usually to assist in a data control analysis. The most common new variable created is age within sex, with a cross-tab of age and sex answer categories (see the example in Chapter 10). Then each cell is defined by special parameter: female 18–24 is code 1, male 18–24 code 2, etc., in the array.

The final type of new variable is the *index* or data construct. One often used in basic uses and gratifications study in commercial realms is the idea of the Technologically Advanced Family. The Technologically Advanced Family is defined by the number of communication technologies in the household and their time of adoption. It is an additive index, which groups the different technologies (some new to market with low penetration and others in the mass-market stage) reported, and intention to buy, and breaks the groups into advanced, mid and lagging ICT markets. A common political index is constructed around political activism. While the formula for any index may change, it creates a typology based on demographic, behavioural or key attitudinal variables, which is usually frequency-based. Indexes or data constructs are more reliable when they are based on interval or ratio scales for advanced statistical analysis. To create a construct, it is important to look at the direction of the positive or negative poles for the variable. In some cases, you may need to reverse the answer categories after the fact (Sumser 2001).

Each type of new variable can strengthen your analysis. Be sure to include the original source question label in the new variable (e.g. Age Within Sex Q9XQ10) label, and add all new variables at the end of the data file. It is good practice never to expunge the source variables.

## STRATEGY FOR DATA ANALYSIS: FINE-GRAIN FOCUS

Starting out on a data voyage is an act of discovery. You may set out in different ways, but it is important to remember where you started and where you have been. It is less important to discover a specific place (the new world, say) than to see the contours of the continents, major oceans and rivers. This is to say that you are interested in number patterns, and how they relate to one another. One of the fallacious criticisms about quantitative methods is that they are prey to methodological individualism. You are not interested in a specific person's answer, nor a specific variable, but in how they relate to others in your survey. You need some sort of compass. The following plan is based on a methodical mapping of data, which is cumulative, offering a kind of 'constant comparative' method of data analysis (see Cresswell 1998).

The purpose of this section is to outline a strategy for data detection. There are excellent introductions to software packages (see Deacon, Pickering et al. 1999: 336), and fairly good manuals or other information available offline, which will help you process the data. Here we are interested in the data's overall shape and contours, and how to embark on analysing it like a geographer, using the tools of space and search tendencies to group or disperse, as we saw in Chapter 10. Now we need to start several analytic passes over the data: first, the descriptive pass; second, the thematic pass; third, the analytic one that tests hypotheses.

### DESCRIPTIVE DISCOVERY

The first exciting *descriptive* step of discovery is to look at the overall frequency distribution for all answers to your questionnaire. Remember, there are two ways to report answers. The first is the underlying *number of people* choosing that answer category from your sample. The second is what that number represents as a *percentage of the total sample*. If you are using an Excel programme, you will have to embed a formula using your sample size as a base to derive a percentage. In a software package such as SPSS, you start with the 'summarize frequencies' dialogue box.

The frequency distribution reports the following: number, per cent, missing values, valid per cent, cumulative per cent. It is important at this initial stage of data mapping to be sure that you also calculate *means* or *medians* on the questions to do with quantity (time or money spent, and so on) that are meaningful. On the SPSS package there will be something at the bottom of the pull-down menu on frequencies, which is called mean, median or mode, within the 'central tendency' dialogue box.

Once you have a basic count of the demographic characteristics of your sample, you compare it against your universe by using census information. Does your sample show a bias to women, or under-represent senior citizens? At this stage you decide how to operationalize *weighting* to correct for sample biases. Perhaps you choose to weight down or weight up. There are limits to such weighting (counting one young male record for two on a survey of self-esteem would be excessive), and any weighting algorithm can help you determine this.

The next step is to decide how to organize your *cross-tabulations*. Start with the demographic variables key to your initial research question or hypothesis. It is useful to keep the data organized in the way the questionnaire was initially administered. Later you will analyse cross-tabs systematically, but grouped into thematic sections in the way we have seen the U+G questionnaire organized by Livingstone and Bovill (see Box 13.2). In most software packages, the simplest way to access the cross-tab function is on the same pull-down box statistics. Excel spreadsheet users are disadvantaged in cross-tab creation, since each cross-tab will require a separate formula, specifying the selection criteria. The important format decision to be made is how to present the table. Are independent variables on the top, creating columns, or on the side, creating rows? Be sure you know how to read the way a table is percentaged. Pay attention only to the valid per cents on your first read-through. Decide how you want to present 'no opinions'. Do you include them in the calculations of percentages? The rule of thumb is that the larger they are, the more they should be presented as a separate category, that is, kept in the base of percentages.

Let's say we are initially interested in Internet usage again, as we explored in Chapter 10. Look at the difference in each demographic variable. Ask yourself, what is the difference between male and female use of the Internet in our sample? (How many people and what percentage?) Is this difference large or small? The decision rules here on what constitutes large and small are contingent. What that means is that you need to develop a rule of thumb initially to scan the data, but the divider line is not absolute. It is relational: that is, you will be looking at the magnitude of differences on gender across all your answer categories, to see where the biggest ones are and where the smallest fall. In a small sample, look for a difference of at least 20 per cent (or 10 people in a group of 50) to tell you there *may* be something going on. Remember, the decision rule here is operationalized by the confidence limits around your estimates, obtainable from any statistical text or online search.

As we saw in Chapter 10's discussion of a survey on Internet usage, the Chi-square test is a descriptive statistic that can tell us if our random sample is similar to or different from that expected from the population. It is useful to use Chi to help you determine the level of significance to the difference. Chi allows us to ask, 'How does gender use on this variable in our sample differ from that expected from the general population?'

Develop a system of denotation. Perhaps you and your research team will circle the high numbers and box the low. Whatever the system of denotation used when you analyse the variables, record it and keep it consistent, to assist in your later analysis.

Now you seek the overall pattern of gender across all the answers in the data set. What variables in the full data set show the greatest variation on gender? (And the course of your analysis will keep returning to 'why?') Summarize these. Once you have completed the check of gender for all questions, you are ready to start the next demographic variable: age. If you remember from Chapter 10, age had a larger variation in reported Internet usage than even gender, despite similar reported Chi significance levels. Your summary of differences (males +3 per cent, females −3 per cent, around the total on Internet use, under-25s +x etc.) should begin to flag interesting social phenomena. The purpose of this analysis is to determine which, of all demographic variables, show the largest variations.

Many data files have up to five demographic variables on a data set with 30 variables, so you will be looking at 150 potential cross-tabs. It is possible to condense the presentation of the cross-tabulations by use of banner tabulations, which present multiple demographic variables as columns across different questions in series. SPSS does not easily have this capability, but Excel or Access does. After you format the data file by respondent for all questions, you report the data file within the categories you need, re-entering or rotating columns to rows as needed.

You then proceed through key behavioural measures (heaviness of viewing, and so on), and then to attitudinal or cognitive measures systematically, to complete your first mapping pass of the data.

## THEMATIC DISCOVERY

The second analytic pass on the data begins to build the units that will guide your reporting. Remember how you divided your questionnaire into thematic topics? Here the European comparative study on *Children and New Media* will be illustrative. This U+G-inspired study looked at various main areas of the media environment: access, time and use/modes of engagement. The access section begins to look for key patterns of ownership in the home, and importance attached to the various media. The study finds sharply different access across Europe. TV and VCR access are widespread, but bedroom TV cultures are more prevalent in the UK and Denmark (where an astonishing three in five have a TV in the bedroom). Contrary to their expectations, richer, higher-educated families were less likely to have a TV set in their child's room (Livingstone and Bovill 2001: 72) and Internet access from the bedroom is rare. Author Leen d'Haenens finds there is a Nordic edge given to information and communication technologies, and a TV screen bias in the UK. These findings are then compared against the World Economic Forum's (WEF) rankings, to find interesting anomalies. Whereas WEF ranked Switzerland high for overall preparedness for the networked society, if family Internet access is one measure of this preparedness, it is well below Sweden, Finland and Israel (Livingstone and Bovill 2001: 81). The idea in thematic analysis is to compare and contrast your findings against what is known. What is unusual? Where are there surprises, anomalies or discontinuities?

## HYPOTHESIS-TESTING DISCOVERY

Once you have done your thematic summary, you may begin the final pass, which is intended to explore specific hypotheses or hunches about interrelationships in the data. Let's return to the European study of children and their changing media environment. Perhaps you want to return to a thesis expressed by McLuhan that TV supplants reading, or explore whether girls are more likely to read than boys, or boys more likely to adopt interactive media than girls. These are what you call your 'ballot' questions (or the most important questions in your survey), which were designed around these topics. Are the hypotheses supported or refuted by your sample findings? If they are partially supported, under what conditions and why? The European comparative study found that, especially for boys, the increased use of electronic games was associated with the shift from a word-oriented culture to one oriented to image, in a way that McLuhan foresaw in 1964. With this summary of what the data support in your central arguments, you have taken your data mapping and analysis as far as you can, using traditional descriptive statistics and cross-tabs.

---

### Box 13.5  Data detection guide (based on Chapter 10, use of the Internet case)

1. What is the difference between males' and females' use of the Internet?
   (The group of people comparison.)
2. How does gender use in this sample differ from that expected in the general population?
   (The generalization: Chi-square significance.)
3. Among all variables, which show the greatest variation on gender?
   (The context question; the reliability issue.)
4. Of all demographic variables, which show the largest variation?
   (Testing the causal imputation.)
   Repeat cycle for key behavioural and cognitive/attitudinal variables.
5. How do your findings confirm or refute other studies? What is unusual? Where are their surprises, anomalies or discontinuities, and can you explain them?
   (The external validity issue.)
6. Are your hypotheses supported or refuted? If partially so, under what conditions and why?
   (The proof.)

# DATA REDUCTION TECHNIQUES: REGRESSION, CLUSTER AND FACTOR ANALYSIS – FINER FOCUS

Surveys are casualties of their own comparative advantage in breadth or scope of variables examined. As you may begin to see, the larger the survey, the more complex and intensive is the data analysis. It is not unusual for very large academic studies (for example, the Canadian Election Studies run by the Canadian Political Science Association) to take several years in data processing. What is often needed in such large-scale studies are decision tools to reduce the data set: to separate out that data which is significant.

Now it gets complicated: we want to explain how much the dependent variable varies from the independent variable; and more about the strength of the association between the two. The first method is *multiple regression analysis*, which can be found in most statistical packages. How does it work? Assume that you standardize the values in your measurement scales so they are expressed in units of standard deviation. Each score is expressed as a standard deviation from the mean on each of two variables. Some scores will be positive and some negative. The intent here is not to drown in the mathematical formulae (although they are elegant underwater beasts), but to recall that you may use these off the shelf. All you have to do is specify the dependent variable and the list of independent variables you want to test, and the software does the rest.

Regression is used to test models of direct and indirect causal influence. What you are doing is seeing which of the possible determinants is statistically significant, as you 'build up a picture of how each independent variable influences the one after it in the causal chain' (Sapsford 1999: 192). The important benchmark in regression model analysis is the degree of variance it may explain. In discussing the BC *Arts Consumers Profile,* Chapter 10 presented a typical correlation matrix to find, surprisingly, that those who attended pop concerts were also prone to attend jazz, sports and other activities, giving the lie to simple dichotomies between 'high' and 'low', or popular, arts practices. The purpose of the regression was to find which performing arts disciplines had overlaps in types of audience and reported attendance. Unique disciplines, such as country and western concerts or children's plays, showed little or no audience overlap. Ethnic performing arts in Canada showed the strongest association with museums and the model proved reasonably robust in cultural practices, explaining 21 per cent of the variance. A sample table might present just the regression coefficients. In the case of the crossovers, ethnic music obtained a correlation coefficient of .150 and art galleries a coefficient of .310, explaining 21 per cent of the variance (Murray 1994: 84). Other more robust values would be .45 or so, suggesting very strong interrelationships. (For a more extensive discussion of the logic used in interpreting regression analysis, see Sapsford 1999: 192–200.) Regression analysis allows you to tell *which is the most influential independent variable*, to guide further inferences. Regression helps us simplify our explanatory constructs, and allows us to predict the level of magnitude of a dependent variable. To make this tool more effective, you have to make sure that the independent variables are not correlated with each other: collinearity fatally weakens the model.

A second main tool for data grouping or data reduction – *factor analysis* – is very useful in helping winnow concepts. Factor analysis is a method of constructing like types, to identify important dimensions for further analysis. Also it can help determine if the variables are linked – that is, if they are measuring the same underlying phenomenon. Factor analysis is an appropriate method for scale development, since it allows you to mathematically reduce a large number of initial variables to a smaller set of underlying concepts or variables, referred to as factors. The basic aim of factor analysis is to examine a wide range of answers to identify underlying patterns. (For an example of factor analysis in action, see Bennett et al. 1999: 97–101, 292 n. 4.) It may be used to explain the variance in the correlations among a set of variables, where no single dependent variable is specified. Instead, all variables are hypothesized to be dependent upon some unknown independent variable, and the researcher looks at the amount of variance explained by each (see De Vaus 1995).

Adding scores (to create an index of ICTs in the home, for example) is just one way to build a scale. Such scales may be constructed easily if questions use the same number of answer categories and are loaded (high score to low) in similar directions. In order to do this, the questions must also belong to the same underlying concept. A number of specialized statistical tools test for this. Rubin's Viewing Motivation Scale used factor analysis in its development, and his resultant model explained 56 per cent of the variance: a strong proof of its validity.

A final tool is *cluster analysis*, which is useful in the study of lifestyles or subculture. The intent is to group objects or people into some number of mutually exclusive or exhaustive groups, so that those in a group are as similar as possible to one another. In other words, clusters should be very homogeneous internally (within clusters) and heterogeneous externally (between clusters). We won't provide the algorithms here, but what these cluster analyses do is modify arbitrary cluster boundaries until the average distances within clusters are as small as possible, but the distance between the average values across clusters is as large as possible. The best-known clusters are used in psychographic segmentation in lifestyle analysis, resulting in such personality types as 'actualizers', 'strugglers' etc. (McDaniel and Gates 1996: 688).

## REPORT WRITING: HANGING THE PHOTO IN THE GALLERY

How do you go about hanging your survey snapshot in the gallery of public communication? You want to be sure to shed light on it, and hang it in a way that gives the eye a good perspective. Finally, be careful how you frame it. Chapter 10 set out a very sensible map for what a report must do; the object here is to suggest a few language choices that will have profound consequences for your number stories.

More practical language advice will ask you to choose the best terms for your report (respondent, subject, viewer, 'average Dane or Canadian') with sensitivity to the different connotations of objectivism. Data are plural. The tense for data interpretation is present (data have endless life). References to the survey fielding, however, are past tense (the survey is one single snapshot in time). Questions were administered. Don't paraphrase the question: specify it exactly as asked. Disclose open-ended narrative nuance. In addition to these important (creative writing) factors, there are other rules of reportage. Think of data reporters such as Carl Bernstein breaking the Watergate story in the *Washington Post*: develop a 'deep-throat rule', that a data observation or tendency needs to be corroborated by at least three sources before reporting. Seek internal consistency. Bullet-proof your argument by referring to the clear anomalies, and try to explain them. Refer to other studies that support your findings. We conclude by listing some of the potential pitfalls of report writing, most of which have already been identified in this chapter (see Box 13.6, based on Berger: 2000).

## Box 13.6 Ten common reporting pitfalls

1. **Over-generalization:** assuming that what is true of some x is true of all x.
2. **Misreporting the base:** calculating the percentages of your sub-sample administered in a skip pattern on the base of total completions.
3. **Not showing the 'no opinions'.** Failing to explain how you treated missing information.
4. **Quoting a number with no reference to the underlying base** of numbers it represents, or size of sample, or likely confidence limits on the estimates.
5. **'Slamming'** no opinion voters – and disguising it.
6. **Misusing the term average.**
7. **Inferential fallacies:** that if some disliked something, the rest liked it.
8. **Mistaking correlation for causality.** Surveys stop short of 'proving' causality, but they can move beyond causality to present hypotheses about causal relations.
9. **Blurring data reportage with data interpretation** and failing to provide explicit proof of interpretation.
10. **Forgetting to leave a map** of where you went and how you got there for the next explorer.

# Section 6

# Experimental Audience Research

# Chapter Fourteen

# Experimental audience research in practice: conceptualizing effects

We have seen that the statistical tools developed by survey researchers have been extensively applied to map the daily users of media around the world: their attitudes, preferences and engagements with different media. Thanks to the survey methods, communication scholars now have a fairly reliable picture of who says what to whom in our global society. For example, in their book *Consuming Environments*, Budd et al. (1999) note the very high levels of television viewing in the US and Japan. Surveys of audiences regularly indicate that viewing is, in both countries, the third most performed activity after working and sleeping. In addition to this fascination with TV, they also go on to note that Americans and Japanese, relative to other industrial nations, also work longer hours. They speculate about this quantitative relationship as follows: 'television's function in many of our lives derives from its ability to distract us from or compensate us for bad jobs, bad relationships and other unpleasant realities' (Budd et al. 1999: 94). Rephrasing Marx, they seem to suggest that TV is the opiate of the most overworked industrial masses. Powerful polemics, perhaps, but faulty science.

Although survey researchers will be impressed by the generality of the correlation between hours of work and TV viewing in industrialized countries, the conclusion that TV consumption is motivated by escape from hard work would be extremely misleading. For example, there could be a confounding factor in both countries, such as the abundance, quality and diversity of programming, which explains why audiences like to watch a lot of TV. If audiences watch TV because it is better programmed, or if audiences use TV largely because their entertainment options are otherwise limited, or because it is cheap entertainment, then it stands to reason that those with less money and lots of time on their hands would be most likely to turn to television, regardless of how long they work. However, we do not know if this explanation is better, because these variables were not considered. Moreover the reverse causal explanation provides an equally plausible explanation of the correlation: in the most commercialized media systems, those who watch more television also see more commercials, so perhaps they have to work harder in order to acquire the goods promoted on TV.

A significant positive correlation tells us something important about the magnitude and direction of the quantitative relationship between two independently measured variables: lots of TV viewing and long hours of work do characterize lifestyles in some countries, and little TV and a shorter working week in others. But it does not prove the hypothesis that *working long hours causes people to seek passive (television viewing) rather than active leisure*. As critics point out, scientific explanation is valid only when the evidence is consistent with other empirical evidence about the causal relationships under study. Yet careful examination of TV viewership data reveals some pretty important anomalies in the 'opiate of the working masses' hypothesis: the heaviest watchers of TV are, in fact, retired individuals, 55–85, who watch on average 10 hours more per week than the average worker. Moreover, women who work watch less TV than women who stay at home. Also men who are unemployed, or part-time workers, watch more TV than men who are employed full-time.

A correlation represents mathematically the magnitude of an association between two variables: but since Aristotle, causality concerns a more specific contingency relationship between an antecedent (cause) and a consequent (effect) condition. In each of the anomalies above, the argument that the main reason people in the US and Japan watch so much TV is to escape from the drudgery of work, does not apply to many segments of the population. Escapism may explain some individuals' use of TV, but as a generalization, this construct does not provide a very powerful explanation of the complex evidence we have about regular TV viewing in industrialized nations, nor a robust theorization of the complexity of motives for high levels of television watching in Japan and the US. In short, without better-designed research it is impossible to discover if labour escapism plays a significant role in motivating TV viewing in Japan and the US. This is because a quantitative mapping of the degree of association between two variables does not fully constitute what we mean by a scientific test of a causal relationship in societal phenomenon.

Given the importance of television for democracy, American researchers of the postwar era set out to search beyond these correlations between media consumption practices of audiences, to address more pressing issues of determinacy in a mass-mediated culture – the 'with what effect' question – with both trepidation and hope (Lazarsfeld 1955). The problem was clear: however useful, sampling frames and surveys on their own are not sufficient for valid accounts of the social impacts of media. Whether interested in the relationship between cigarette advertising and cancer rates, or media use and violence, anyone interested in effects faces a common research design question: 'How is it possible to go beyond descriptive accounts of the relations between variables?'

## TOWARDS THE EXPERIMENTAL ANALYSIS OF AUDIENCE EFFECTS

The positivist turn was spearheaded in the 1920s by the behaviouralists, who modelled their science on experimental physics. In their laboratories, behavioural psychologists were reinterpreting Aristotle's ideas about logical necessity, looking for a way of scientifically operationalizing determinacy. The defining feature of a causal relationship, they argued, is temporal: the cause must be observed before the effect (x precedes y). The easiest way to study causality, then, is to see if the presence of the antecedent variable x produces the expected state of y, when compared with the state of y in the absence of x. A minimal claim can be made about determinacy, upon the reliable observation that expected changes in the dependent variable y reliably follow independent condition x. In this case, it is said that x is a sufficient condition to change y. The stronger claim of determinacy can only be made when it is observed that the change in the condition y reliably occurs when x has preceded it, but doesn't occur unless x precedes it. In this case, it can be claimed that x is both a sufficient and necessary condition for changes in y. The problem facing audience researchers interested in the 'with what effect' issue, was to imagine and conduct an experiment where it can be confidently determined that *if and only if x then we will find a change in y*. These design challenges and statistical tools used in the quantitative analyses of audience effects research will be elaborated in Chapter 16. We will also set out to track the historical development of the effects tradition, in Chapter 15.

Even though its roots were firmly planted in the positivism debates of psychology and sociology, it was the pragmatic interest of marketing researchers, who first developed new quantitative tools for evaluating advertising campaigns. Subsequently, the desire to guide the management of public opinion with audience research intensified with the onset of the Second World War, leading to the formation of a research group at the US Army's Experimental Section. Among other aspects of war psychology, these social psychologists were charged with finding ways of maintaining both troop and general morale. To do so, they undertook a massive research programme into mass persuasion: throughout the war, this cadre of social psychologists examined how movies and radio could be used as a public propaganda tools to facilitate opinion change. Working on these complex problems, psychological researchers began to develop the quantitative tools necessary for effects analysis. Causality, operationalized in this temporal way, could be studied by a careful statistical assessment of the expectations generated by a clear hypothesis concerning the contingency relations between a stimulus condition (x) and a response condition (y). If the variables were nominal, then contingency tables could be used to compare a sample of observations of the state of variable y in the presence and absence of the determinant variable x. If the dependent condition was measured as an interval or ratio scale, then analysis of variance could be used to statistically compare the sample of observations against the hypothetical model of the null hypothesis (for the terms 'variables' and 'scales', see Chapter 10).

After the war, the pioneers of quantitative media studies, like Lazarsfeld and Merton, became caught up in the broader policy debates raised by the rapidly expanding commercial media systems and the policy questions they posed. Researchers wondered if quantitative sociology might help determine whether these new channels of communication were promoting democracy or 'rendering mass publics conformative to the social and economic status quo' (Merton and Lazarsfeld 1950: 458). Despite the energetic debates concerning the impact of television on cultural taste, beliefs, on election politics and on socialization of a TV generation generally, these authors worried that 'certified knowledge of this kind is impressively slight'. They called for a vigorous empirical effort to determine the impact of media on society generally.

American social scientists embarked on a new programme to improve their research designs and statistical tools, hoping to tease out the contribution of media to public opinion. Quantitative political sociologists like Keys, Katz and Berelson did a series of community studies, which offered a qualified image of the role of media in elections and politics (see, for instance, Katz and Lazarsfeld 1955). Returning to their university labs too, attitude change researchers, like Carl Hovland (1959), challenged the simplistic hypodermic language of propaganda theory. Summing up over 20 years of research, Klapper observed that TV had only a limited and ambiguous potential to influence mass opinion (Klapper 1960): this new medium was both a magical window, helping educate, inform and broaden the public's horizons, as well as a vast wasteland filled with distracting entertainment and mainstream politics, which diminished debate, reading and public knowledge. It all depended on who watched what, for how long, and why and how they watched it. As the empirical evidence continued to accumulate during the 1960s, the propaganda model was eventually replaced by a more nuanced model of media effects among communications scholars (Roberts and Bachen 1981).

The social issue that preoccupied many during the 1960s, was whether children's exposure to images of war, crime and violence on TV was socializing a more aggressive and antisocial generation. Survey after survey confirmed that heavy television viewing was associated with aggressive attitudes and antisocial behaviour. Given increasing empirical evidence concerning both TV violence and youth crime, it was not surprising that psychological researchers began to design experiments to assess the implications of this generation's extensive exposure to TV violence.

## BANDURA'S VIOLENCE STUDIES

Perhaps the most formative of these effects experiments was conducted in the lab by Albert Bandura, who set out to determine whether the modelling of violence increased the aggressiveness of children. It is worth remembering that Bandura was, in fact, using the experimental method of the behaviourists to counter their reward model of learning with the idea of 'imitative' learning (Bandura et al. 1961). In this study, researchers hypothesized that:

> *imitative learning can be clearly demonstrated if a model performs sufficiently novel patterns of responses which are unlikely to occur independently of the observation of the behaviour of a model and if a subject reproduces these behaviours in substantially identical form.*

(Bandura et al. 1961)

They further hypothesized that subjects would imitate the behaviour of a same-sex model to a greater degree than a model of the opposite sex, and that boys would be more prone than girls to imitate aggression exhibited by a model.

The first research challenge was to design the laboratory conditions that would adequately provide a credible test for these hypotheses about imitative aggression. The experiment took place in a nursery school, where subjects observed either an aggressive or subdued model of either the same or different sex in a playroom with a small table and chair and some toys (including a Bobo doll). The participants were divided into eight groups of six subjects each. Half of the subjects were exposed to aggressive behaviour and the other to non-aggressive behaviour. Two adults, a male and a female, served as the role models.

The study included an equal number of boys and girls, who were enrolled in nursery school, of a mean age of 52 months. An effort was made to balance the assigning of the children to experimental conditions based on a prior aggressiveness rating made by the nursery school teacher. In the first step of the procedure to this study, the subjects were brought individually into the playroom area and seated at a table with potato prints and stickers.

In the experimental conditions, after seating the child at a small table, the experimenter demonstrated how the subject could design pictures with potato prints and picture stickers provided. The potato prints included a variety of geometrical forms; the stickers were attractive, multicoloured pictures of animals, flowers, and western figures to be pasted on a pastoral scene. These activities were selected since they had been established, by previous studies in the nursery school, as having high interest value for the children. After having settled the subject in his corner, the experimenter escorted an adult model in, explaining again the materials provided to play with and, after the model was seated, the experimenter left the room for ten minutes.

In the non-aggressive condition, the model assembled the 'tinker toys' in a quiet, subdued manner, totally ignoring the Bobo doll. In contrast, in the aggressive condition, the model began by assembling the tinker toys but after approximately a minute had elapsed, the model turned to the Bobo doll and spent the remainder of the period showing aggression towards it. In addition to punching the Bobo doll, the model enacted a sequence of behaviours (laid the Bobo doll on its side, sat on it, and punched it repeatedly in the nose). The model then raised the Bobo doll, picked up a mallet and struck the doll on the head. Following the mallet attack, the model tossed the doll up in the air and kicked it about the room. This sequence of physically aggressive acts was repeated approximately three times, interspersed with verbally aggressive responses such as 'Sock him in the nose . . .', 'Hit him down . . .', 'Throw him in the air . . .', 'Kick him . . .', 'Pow . . .', and two non-aggressive comments: 'He keeps coming back for more', and 'He sure is a tough fella.' In the control condition, subjects were not exposed to any modelling behaviour.

Subjects were then assessed for the amount of imitative learning in a different experimental room that was set off from the main nursery school building. Before being observed, however, the children were frustrated. The experimenter brought the subject to an anteroom that contained relatively attractive toys: a fire engine, a steam train, a jet fighter plane, a cable car, a colourful spinning-top, and a doll set, complete with wardrobe, doll's pram and cot. The experimenter then explained that the toys were for the subject to play with, but, as soon as the subject became sufficiently involved with the play material (usually in about two minutes), the experimenter remarked that these were her very best toys, that she did not let just anyone play with them, and that she had decided to reserve these toys for the other children. However, the subject could play with any of the toys that were in the next room. The experimenter and the subject then entered the adjoining experimental room.

The experimental room contained a variety of toys, including some that could be used in imitative or non-imitative aggression, and others that tended to elicit predominantly non-aggressive forms of behaviour. The aggressive toys included a three-foot Bobo doll, a mallet and pegboard, two dart guns and a tetherball with a face painted on it, which hung from the ceiling. The non-aggressive toys, on the other hand, included a teaset, crayons and colouring paper, a ball, two dolls, three bears, cars and trucks and plastic farm animals.

The researchers analysed their data with a statistical procedure called Student's T test, which compares the mean number of imitative behaviours for each condition. In the generalization situation, results indicated that subjects exposed to aggressive models reproduced a good deal of aggression resembling that of the models, and that their mean scores differed markedly from those of subjects in the non-aggressive and control groups. Subjects in the aggressive condition also exhibited significantly more partially imitative and non-imitative aggressive behaviour, and were generally less inhibited in their behaviour than subjects in the non-aggressive condition. The authors concluded that, generally, subjects who observed the modelled aggression reproduced considerable physical and verbal aggressive behaviour, resembling that of the models.

In their designs, laboratory researchers needed to identify the various factors that could cause the aggressive behaviours, in order to control for them in one of two ways: either by randomizing the assignment of subjects to groups, or by measuring those factors (gender, aggressiveness, intelligence etc.) that might also explain why some treatment groups were more aggressive. For example, in the Bandura experiments, the children were not only randomly assigned to test conditions, but the experimenters used teacher's ratings of subjects' aggressiveness to test whether the experimental treatment had disproportionately more aggressive children assigned to the experiments.

Through subsequent comparison, the evidence indicated that learning through modelling was differentially influenced by the sex of the model: following contact with the male model, boys showed more aggression than girls, the difference being particularly marked on highly masculine-typed behaviour. Subjects who observed the non-aggressive models, especially the subdued male model, were generally less aggressive than their controls. Boys reproduced more imitative physical aggression than girls, but the groups did not differ in their imitation of verbal aggression. The results of this study provide strong evidence that observation of aggressive models can affect shaping of behaviour through imitation.

In a later study (Bandura et al. 1963a), these researchers set out to determine whether observational learning occurred when the aggressive behaviour was presented in media.

## Box 14.1 Measures of aggressive behaviour

### Imitative behaviour

*Imitation of physical aggression*: this category included acts of striking the Bobo doll with the mallet, sitting on the doll and punching it in the nose, kicking the doll, and tossing it in the air.

*Imitative verbal aggression*: subject repeats the phrases, 'Sock him', 'Hit him down', 'Kick him', 'Throw him in the air' or 'Pow'.

*Imitative non-aggressive verbal responses*: subject repeats, 'He keeps coming back for more,' or 'He sure is a tough fella.'

Since subjects could also direct aggressive behaviours to other toys than the Bobo doll, two other 'partially imitative' aggressive responses were also scored.

- *Mallet aggression*: subject strikes objects other than the Bobo doll aggressively with the mallet.
- *Sits on Bobo doll*: subject lays the Bobo doll on its side and sits on it, but does not aggress toward it.

### Non-imitative behaviour

The following additional non-imitative aggressive responses were also scored by recording how often the subject displayed the following actions.

*Punches Bobo doll*: subject strikes, slaps, or pushes the doll aggressively.

*Non-imitative physical and verbal aggression*: this category included physically aggressive acts directed toward objects other than the Bobo doll and any hostile remarks except for those in the verbal imitation category; e.g. 'Shoot the Bobo', 'Cut him', 'Stupid ball', 'Knock over people', 'Horses fighting, biting'.

*Aggressive gunplay*: subject shoots darts or aims the guns, and fires imaginary shots at objects in the room.

Ratings were also made of the number of behaviour units in which subjects played non-aggressively or sat quietly and did not play with any of the material at all.

Source: based on Bandura et al. (1961)

They hypothesized that modelling effects might be ordered along a 'reality–fiction' stimulus dimension, with real-life models located at the reality end of the continuum, non-human cartoon characters at the fictional end, and films portraying human models occupying an intermediate position. It was then predicted, on the basis of saliency and similarity, that subjects are more likely to be influenced by real-life models. Repeating the procedures and measures from the previous study, with the main difference being that the aggression modelling treatment was either live, projected on a screen in the darkened room, or presented as *Herman the Cat* colour TV cartoon (the female model dressed in a catsuit in a cartoon version of the room). Results again confirmed that imitative learning generalizes to TV models; indeed, the total aggression scores were not only significantly higher for all forms of modelling than the controls ($p > .01$), but the less realistic models produced the greatest aggression on average (Table 14.1). Whereas all types of modelling produced significantly more aggression than the control, the film and cartoon treatments also produced significantly more non-imitative aggression (i.e. generalized to other toys).

Table 14.1   Mean aggression score for each stimulus condition

| Live | Film | Cartoon | Control |
|------|------|---------|---------|
| 83 | 92 | 99 | 54 |

# CRITIQUES OF BANDURA'S EXPERIMENTS

Although the imitative learning hypothesis seems to have been confirmed, Bandura's findings have been called into question by critics who challenge the artificiality of the laboratory experiment, which exposes children to only one violent programme, rather than examining the constant and repeated exposure to and identification with violent stories in conjunction with many other causes of aggressive behaviour (Gauntlett 2001; Freedman 2002). Critics have been most scathing about the construct validity of Bandura's laboratory studies.

*Construct validity* refers to how well the operationalization of the variables in the experimental study actually captures the processes, laws or practices articulated in the causal explanation under investigation. For example, the construct of interpersonal aggressiveness was operationalized as a playful hitting of a Bobo doll. Although this behaviour was observed more frequently after exposure to aggressive models, one wonders if this observation has less to do with interpersonal aggression and more to do with playful acting-out of mock hostility. In laboratory research there is an additional kind of construct validity that we must obviously consider – that is, the degree to which we can generalize from the experimental situation to the world. This kind of validity is sometimes called *ecological validity* and it has led many to wonder if demonstrations of causal processes observed in the lab are similar to those occurring under the natural conditions in which the phenomenon is experienced – whether the contexts observed represent the population of situations occurring in social life.

Ecological validity concerns the degree to which the system of causal relations being observed in the situation matches the system of causal relations in the population as a whole. Since effects research was conducted both in the controllable circumstances of the university lab, in the classroom and in the field (naturalistic experiments), it has galvanized a long debate about ecological validity in experimental research. In Bandura's defence, it can be said that, although this research took place in artificial circumstances, it only set out to demonstrate the possibility of imitative learning in a plausible situation (if not a natural viewing one). But it is clearly not conclusive: the adult models, the differences between their behaviours and that of television characters, and the way these children were primed for aggression with frustration, implies that care is warranted in generalizing these processes to solitary home viewing.

Scholars in cultural studies have been particularly scathing about these early lab studies, claiming they fully exemplify the reductionist tendencies of positivism: they isolate communication processes from the cycles of daily life and regard human subjects as objects to be controlled and observed in the quest for a single causal factor (Buckingham 2000). Contemporary methodological commentators, too, still tend to write off the whole effects tradition because of the shortcomings of these early lab studies, dismissing out of hand their quest to isolate cause–effect relations (Deacon, Pickering et al. 1999).

In spite of questionable assumptions in their quantitative methods, it can be appreciated that these quantitative researchers were confronted by the complexity of studying determinacy in a mediated world: in doing so, they were forced to provide more complex ways of thinking about causality, generalization and comparison in cultural analysis. To condemn these results out of hand as tainted by positivism, misreads this growing awareness of the limitations of the lab among quantitative effects researchers themselves, and overlooks the way these early debates precipitated the development of sophisticated designs and statistical tools.

Indeed, with so much at stake socially and financially, it is not surprising that early laboratory studies served to galvanize a long and lively debate about the effects of TV violence. Recognizing the methodological limitations, there has been a call for more sophisticated research into media violence effects: neither co-relational studies nor 'one-off' lab demonstrations provide ecologically valid accounts of the way young audiences are impacted by the steady flow of violent TV entertainment, news and education. The early theories of social learning effects have been both confirmed and qualified by subsequent research over the years (Comstock and Paik 1991; Anderson and Bushman 2002). In keeping with our 'critical discursive' approach (Chapter 3), we can see, with retrospective wisdom, that those 1960s lab demonstrations helped to extend, contest and complexify our understanding of the impact of watching violent television on children's aggressive behaviour. In the next chapter we will show that, in fact, laboratory aggression experiments were only one relatively minor theme in the broader effects project, where the synergy between laboratory and natural experiments contributed to a multifactoral research approach.

# BEYOND THE LAB: LIFE AS AN EXPERIMENTAL CONDITION

Those who comment on media effects research today need more than a cursory understanding of the finer points of social scientific methodology and evidence evaluation. A dramatic case in point concerns a recent sophisticated study, investigating the effects of watching TV violence, published in *Science* (Johnson et al. 2002). This study is the most recent in a series of longitudinal field studies, or 'natural experiments', into TV's role in the socialization of aggression. A considerable sample consisting of 707 families, with children of a mean age of 5.8, was randomly drawn from two representative communities in northern New York State for this 1975 study. Families were interviewed repeatedly over a 17-year period (1983, 1986, 1992) so that time-based comparisons could be made between the amount of TV viewing throughout childhood and levels of aggression later in life. Researchers were able to test whether levels of TV viewing at different ages (14, 16, 22) precedes aggression and criminal behaviour later in life (ages 16, 22). The advantage of this longitudinal design, then, is that it combines the ecological validity of surveys with the temporal control over the relationship between dependent and independent variables.

In the Canadian news coverage of this study, the CBC newsreader acknowledged that this longitudinal study was unusual in that it was conducted over many years, in an attempt to discover whether children who watch a lot of TV are aggressive when they get older. The results seem to confirm the hypothesis, because, as the reporter explained, it found that of those children who watched less than one hour per day at age 14–16, only 5.7 per cent had engaged in aggressive and antisocial behaviour later in life, whereas of those who watched more than three hours per day, 28.8 per cent had done so. In a subsequent interview, the lead author, Johnson, explained that this result suggests that watching lots of TV may 'desensitize' children to violence. But the reporter then called this conclusion into serious question by stating: 'critics say *that the study made a mistake by linking television viewing directly to aggression*'.

With regard to a direct relationship between media use and aggression, many studies have been criticized for using either observations of play, or teacher and peer judgements of aggressiveness, as the dependent variable. Many suspect that these provide poor indications of real aggression because they can be confounded with subjective perceptions of social power, playfulness, competence and isolation within social networks (Freedman 2002). In this case however, the subjects' aggressive behaviour was measured objectively through documentary evidence, gathered from school records, and criminal evidence, drawn from FBI records. While it is reasonable to assume that such official records underestimate the amount of violence and crime, there is little reason to believe that this 'underestimation' is related to the TV viewing itself.

Because it is costly, longitudinal field research is designed with expediency in mind. Obviously one would want objective measures of viewing behaviour. In this case, the researchers chose to study the patterns of children's viewing by self-reports of total daily consumption. Yet such self-reports are notoriously unreliable estimates of how children use TV. Taking account of this, the researchers asked both the children and their parents to record daily viewing during a sample week. Where these estimates were widely divergent, the researchers averaged the time, hoping to overcome some of those limitations. Such correctives are called for when researchers cannot use the commercial standards of detailed daily diary methods or TV meters.

As the researchers explain, this measure is based on consistent prior evidence that most of children's TV programming contains violence. Yet, such estimates of total viewing are faulty: a more precise measure of children's actual exposure to violent programming clearly would provide a more robust test of the hypothesis. That said, the consequence of this particular design compromise is to underestimate the magnitude of any violence effects, because the statistical comparisons will include many children in the heavy viewing category, who watch a lot of television but little of it violent (for example, heavy-viewing girls who watch sitcoms). In short, the researchers have chosen a very conservative design for testing the effect of prior watching TV and aggressive behaviours.

So what exactly is the 'mistake' implied by the researchers' conclusion that there is a direct causal relationship between heavy television viewing and subsequent aggressiveness? The results show that children who watch more than four hours of TV, also disproportionately grow up in poorer, dysfunctional families and in neighbourhoods where crime and violence are common. How can we say, therefore, that it is TV that causes them to be aggressive? The Canadian news reporter cited a critic, who asserted that, in his opinion, television turns out to be 'relatively minor, in relationship to those other factors', such as violence in the home, the amount of parental supervision, violence in the neighbourhood and at school, which he considered the 'real causes' of children's antisocial behaviour. In short, has the study not confounded the effects of TV viewing with all the other social factors, which better explain why some kids become aggressive later in life?

It must be said that, without knowledge of the details of the research design and the statistical tools used, this longitudinal study might appear to be one more polemic on the effects of TV on kids. Obviously there are many reasons why children become aggressive young adults. Aggressive dispositions, abusive and dysfunctional parenting, and hostile and impoverished communities can contribute to the formation of an aggressive or antisocial personality. Typically, researchers find significant correlations among the many risk factors associated with aggression, including TV viewing. This means that any sample of heavy TV viewers is also more likely to include abused and neglected children from impoverished circumstances. It is equally plausible, then, that, over time, children who experience aggression in their families and communities might also consume more violent media to cope, adjust to or merely confirm their mean worldview. To understand the argument about TV's impact therefore requires some knowledge of the research designs used, and the statistical inference procedures developed for assessing interacting multiple determinate factors. There are two basic statistical tools for analysing multifactoral research designs: the first, called the Analysis of Variance, or Anova, is based on comparisons of expectations of each group's means, under the assumption that there is no difference between the treatments and controls. The second, called Regression Analysis, is based on comparing a predictive hypothetical model of the relative contribution of each causal factor with the actual data for goodness of fit, based on the variation from the model's relationships. In Chapter 15, we will outline the development of these techniques and their contribution to effects research. In Chapter 16, we will go on to outline the basis of the statistical reasoning used in these multi-factor tests of cause-and-effect relations in both laboratory and field studies.

The aforementioned critic implied that these violence researchers took no account of the other factors in the socialization of aggression, confusing the impact of TV with those other causes of antisocial behaviour. However, this standard critique of the violence literature is inappropriate here, for the researchers went to great effort to design research that could both tease out the temporal sequence implied by the TV causality hypothesis, as well as to control for the situational and dispositional factors that can 'confound' interpretations of the multiple interacting causes of aggressive behaviour. This is why these researchers employed standardized scales for measuring poverty and neglect, family abuse severity, as well as levels of community violence, based on standard social work diagnostics administered by professionals. Once these other risks are measured, they are used as statistical 'controls' in an analysis of co-variance, which compares across levels of TV viewing for similar levels of these control factors. After controlling for these co-variates, the researchers were in a position to assess whether television viewing itself has had an impact on aggression over and above each co-variant. The assessment can be summarized in a matrix that shows the analysis of the relationship between an aggressive disposition at age 14 and total TV watching (Table 14.2). The full results can be seen in Table 14.3.

Table 14.2   Television viewing at mean age 14 and aggressive acts reported at mean age 16 or 22 (n = 707)

|  | % Aggressive acts | |
| --- | --- | --- |
|  | Aggressive history | No history of aggression |
| < 1 hr TV | 12% | 3% |
| 3 hrs TV > | 49% | 18% |

Source: extract from Johnson et al. (2002)

Moreover, through a series of separate analyses, it can be seen that the effects of heavy TV watching are gendered: young boys who watch a lot of television are particularly vulnerable to watching violence in media. Not only do they tend to watch TV more, but whereas 45 per cent of the boys who watched television for more than three hours per day at age 14 subsequently committed aggressive acts involving others, only 8.9 per cent who watched television for less than an hour a day were aggressive later in life. For girls, the effect still holds, but at a lower level: 2.3 per cent of TV low-viewing girls, and 12.7 per

Table 14.3    Television viewing at mean age 14 and aggressive acts reported at mean age 16 or 22 (n = 707); full results

| Study group | Television viewing at mean age 14 | | | Adjusted odds ratio (95% CI)[‡] |
| | <1 hour/day % ($n$) | 1 to 3 hours/day % ($n$) | ≥3 hours/day % ($n$) | |
| --- | --- | --- | --- | --- |
| *Assault or physical fights resulting in injury* | | | | |
| Total sample | 5.7 (5 of 88)* | 18.4 (71 of 386) | 25.3 (59 of 233) | 1.57 (1.13–2.16)[†] |
| Males | 8.9 (4 of 45)* | 27.5 (55 of 200) | 41.7 (48 of 115) | 1.95 (1.30–2.94)[†] |
| Females | 2.3 (1 of 43) | 8.6 (16 of 186) | 9.3 (11 of 118) | 1.23 (0.72–2.54) |
| *Robbery, threats to injure someone, or weapon used to commit a crime* | | | | |
| Total sample | 3.4 (3 of 88)* | 9.6 (37 of 386) | 14.6 (34 of 233) | 1.58 (1.01–2.46)[†] |
| Males | 6.7 (3 of 45) | 14.0 (28 of 200) | 20.9 (24 of 115) | 1.46 (0.84–2.53) |
| Females | 0.0 (0 of 43) | 4.8 (9 of 186) | 8.5 (10 of 118) | 2.44 (0.97–6.16) |
| *Any aggressive act against another person* | | | | |
| Total sample | 5.7 (5 of 88)* | 22.5 (87 of 386) | 28.8 (67 of 233) | 1.58 (1.16–2.16)[†] |
| Males | 8.9 (4 of 45)* | 32.5 (65 of 200) | 45.2 (52 of 115) | 1.92 (1.28–2.88)[†] |
| Females | 2.3 (1 of 43) | 11.8 (22 of 186) | 12.7 (15 of 118) | 1.25 (0.70–2.22) |

* Significantly lower level of subsequent aggression in comparison with individuals who spent more time watching television at mean age 14.

[†] Significant association after controlling for the covariates that were significantly associated with television viewing and subsequent aggression. Note: Odds ratios indicate the average increase in the odds for subsequent aggression associated with an increase in the level of television viewing (e.g. from <1 hour to 1 to 3 hours per day of television viewing).

[‡] 95% confidence interval.

Source: Johnson et al. (2002: 295)

cent of TV heavy-viewing girls commit acts of violence later on. In employing a sophisticated design, the researchers are in a position to report that their hypothesis cannot be rejected: 'television viewing at mean age 14 remained significantly associated with any subsequent aggressive act against another person *after controlling for prior and subsequent television viewing*' ( Johnson et al. 2002).

# Chapter Fifteen

## ☐ Experimental audience research: defining the field

### TOWARDS A METHODOLOGY FOR STUDYING EFFECTS

Historians of the social sciences have long acknowledged that the experimental method was practised by early Greek physicians, who, like Galen, tracked the healing of patients who were administered different treatments for an illness or injury. Although their techniques were crude and their comparisons unsystematic by today's standards, these early clinicians made careful measurement the foundation of experimental science. Medieval philosophers (such as Roger Bacon and Galileo) likewise privileged the trial-and-error explorations of these empirics over the abstract deductivism of logicians, helping to make discovery a fundament of valid scientific knowing. During the nineteenth century, these two principles of scientific inquiry were buttressed by the statistical reasoning developed by epidemiologists, who used population maps to diagnose health risks. In the social sciences today, we call any intervention or control a 'treatment', in recognition of these medical origins of the experimentalist methodology.

Population sampling and statistical reasoning spread quickly to the study of 'psychological' experiences as well. Early psychometric judgement scales were developed by Wundt and Galton, who assumed that if subjects could make relative judgements (such as, 'That colour looks more red than green'), then mental events, sentiments and feelings were measurable entities just like heat and mass. To the degree that these experiential scales could be standardized, they could be used for comparisons over time (I feel warmer now), or for the comparisons between different individuals on a common dimension of experience (A reports feeling warmer than B). Psychologists increasingly used psychometric techniques because they offered a more precise quantitative way of measuring variable subjective experiences and 'perceptions', and could be related to observable behaviours. Even Carl Jung experimented with galvanic skin responses as a way of tracing mental associations.

E.L. Thorndike (1874–1949), considered by some to be the father of educational psychology, called for the implementation of a rigorous scientific method, including replication studies for validity, and control groups to evaluate treatments quantitatively. Thorndike's ambition was pragmatic too: he hoped that the scientific study of mental operations, like learning and problem solving, would result in more effective teaching and learning experiences. In an attempt to discover the basic 'laws of learning', Thorndike did much of his pioneering work in an animal lab. His experiments devised maze boxes from which animals had to escape to get food. American behavioural psychologists like J.B. Watson built on this approach, asserting that it was only through objective behavioural tests that a general science of learning could be established. The aim was for behavioural psychology to establish the science of learning on observable psychological measures. The experimental methods should be applicable to animals (who couldn't talk) and humans (even if they could).

# EARLY EVALUATION OF AUDIENCE RESPONSES TO ADVERTISING

The twentieth century took flight upon the optimistic updraft of positivism, floating on the belief that all problems would be solved by experimental science. In 1903, psychologist Dill Scott published his famous work, *The Theory of Advertising*, which asserted specifically that commercial persuasion could be made more efficient if it were founded on scientific psychological principles. Link, a Yale-trained psychologist, who was equally optimistic about the prospect of behavioural psychology, later remarked that, 'The old psychology was a study of how the mind thinks; the new psychology is a study of how the mind acts.' Yet he complained that for all its pretence of science, behavioural psychology had not provided businessmen and advertisers with the requisite tools they needed to understand selling and marketing. He advocated an applied social psychology of marketing, which could systematically use psychometrics in experimental approaches to solve the pragmatic problems facing advertisers, such as improving copy and making advertising more effective.

It is not surprising that, given the importance of persuasion to this industry, early advertising researchers were the pioneers of evaluative media effects experiments. Harlow Gale and Harry Hollingsworth, for example, began to use a standardized psychological measure of psychological impact to assess the 'copy' of ads for persuasiveness. Hollingsworth, in particular, formalized what might be called the evaluative approach to persuasion. He exposed various subjects to different ads and compared their responses on a series of standardized scales, designed to register the basic values the ads communicated, and measure how much subjects liked them. Through these comparisons, he discovered that subjects generally gave higher marks to ads that communicated healthfulness, cleanliness and scientific design. Yet, by contrasting the preferences of women – who favoured efficiency, safety and durability – and men – who were inclined toward modernity, family and animals – he was able to claim a scientific basis for the gender targeting of campaigns ( Johnston 2001: 163).

This idea of a pragmatic psychometric psychology was further elaborated by Daniel Starch (1923), whose *Principles of Advertising* built upon the fledgling measurement techniques of opinion research, because of advertisers' concern with the evaluation of persuasion effectiveness. To supplement the readership surveys being used in the commercial sector at this time, Starch launched a series of extensive evaluation studies in the controlled exposure setting of the 'lab', to evaluate different executions of advertising copy. His research numerically compared self-reported impact statements of subjects to specific message designs. The contribution of Starch was the combined scaling of standardization judgements (including interest, comprehension and retention scales), which together measured the relative 'persuasiveness' of any given ad when benchmarked against many other ad designs, tested on thousands of different subjects. The Starch Index proved to be the first of many such business tools developed in advertising laboratories, based on readers' attention to, retention of and enjoyment of particular executions (distinguished by formal features like colour, size, imagery).

Although these lab studies were rarely related to measures of purchasing behaviour, it would be a mistake to underestimate the enormous practical contribution of the evalua-tive research design, and the paper and pencil test scales that they employed. Unfortunately, the detailed knowledge about specific audiences, their responses to specific ad designs, and their persuasive impact (these studies began using day-after recall to provide a behavioural measure), amassed by advertising research over the last 60 years, is proprietary and not open to public scrutiny. However, the panel approach, which compares the responses of different consumers, has become the standard approach to the pragmatic science of persuasion evaluation that can be found in most marketing texts today.

Humans, however, are political animal as well as consumers, and rhetoric – the scientific study of persuasive communication – also became an important sub-field of political science. Edward Bernays argued that once public opinion could be measured and charted, then persuasive communication could be designed to 'win people's consent'. As he points out: 'Psychologists have isolated a number of compelling appeals, the validity of which has been repeatedly proved in practical application' (quoted in Ewen 1996). Bernays is referring, of course, to the copy testing approach developed for evaluating advertising. He goes on to ask, 'Why not use this experimental model to enhance democratic communi-cation?' Bernays proposed an empirical field of political persuasion research that could map 'what are their present attitudes toward the situation with which the consent engineer is concerned? What ideas are the people ready to absorb?' He imagined practitioners of social communication who were well informed by scientific study of 'appeal to the motives of the public', and could use this research to improve the delivery of knowledge, skills or health information to workers by testing opinions before and after watching a training film, for example. Bernays goes on specifically to identify a number of practical questions about the role of persuasion in a democracy:

> *What group leaders or opinion models effectively influence the thought process of what followers? What is the flow of ideas – from whom to whom? To what extent do authority, factual evidence, precision, reason, tradition and emotion play a part in the acceptance of these ideas?*

(Quoted in Ewen 1996: 378)

The same proactive persuasion research approach was adopted by social psychologists who wanted to evaluate the effectiveness of different media presentations to provide feedback to writers, directors and producers. By the early 1940s, Hollonquist and

Suchman (1944) were reporting how the evaluative tradition developed for copy testing could be effectively applied to radio programmes as well. The problem they addressed was that radio programmes had duration, and that a global response to an evening's listening in a diary told us very little about what the listener actually attended to. So they used a programme evaluation device that enabled listeners to press either a 'like' or 'dislike' button while they listened to different radio programmes. The benefit of this evaluation technology is that the affective response of the subject could be related to specific content or formal aspects of the programme, providing useful insight to programming decision-makers. As we will note shortly, programme evaluation technologies have been much enhanced and developed over the last 50 years, especially in the commercial sector, as the circuits of audience feedback about audience appreciation became the sine qua non of programming commercialized media institutions.

## PUBLIC OPINION AND MILITARY PERSUASION EXPERIMENTS

During the 1920s and 1930s, psychologists like Likert and Thurstone innovated with novel attitude scaling techniques for the psychological mapping of mental life. Preoccupied with the fate of democratic communication in a mass society, these early forays into the psychometrics of ideation used the same principles as survey researchers to develop the experimental science of public opinion based on the scaling of mental life. If individual perceptions could be calibrated on scales from one to 10, then so could attitudes and ideologies. Pioneering political scientists like Lasswell, Lazarsfeld, Key and Berelson began to apply the mathematical techniques of surveying to test the different attitudinal factors shaping election results in the late 1930s and early 1940s. But this emerging opinion science was put to its first experimental test with the outbreak of the Second World War. Given the problem of maintaining morale, the US Army assembled a team of leading social psychologists in what was called the 'Experimental Section' of the Research Branch of their Information and Education Division (Hovland et al. 1949). The scientists of the Experimental Section undertook a series of evaluative investigations of public lectures and films, borrowing the belief and opinion scaling techniques of survey researchers, to compare populations that had seen a propaganda film with those that had not.

This foray into propaganda research began with a basic clinical trial comparing the opinions of a group of 1200 soldiers, half of whom viewed the films (*Battle of Britain, Why We Fight*) with the half who had not. They reasoned that they could establish the impact of the film on opinion by comparing the aggregate levels of knowledge or positive attitudes in the exposure group tested one week later, with a control group drawn from the same population who saw an entertainment film. The test items used were constructed as nominal opinion scales (for example, a true or false answer on a multiple-choice question), so the results were reported as the percentage of all subjects in that group who responded in a particular way. For practical reasons, it was not possible to actually randomly assign the soldiers to either the Treatment Group or Control Group, because this would not be a normal procedure in the Army, so this was not a randomized *between groups design*. Yet in its employment of a 'control group', the Experimental Section conceived of an experimental design that was more rigorous than the evaluative designs of the commercial copy testers and programme evaluators, which only established relative differences in preferences.

The Experimental Section's first study did reveal some *impact of the film on knowledge* (measured by belief items such as 'the Nazis plan to destroy the RAF, then invade England', which was correctly answered by 28 per cent in the control group and 55 per cent in the film group (n=1200). The researchers also noted that the percentage responding 'incorrectly' to another knowledge item dropped from 38 per cent to 20 per cent in the group seeing the film. Although this provided some evidence of *learning effects*, the researchers worried that 'there seemed to be no transfer of the specific material to more general attitudes toward the British' (Hovland et al. 1949: 53). More troubling, some soldiers who saw the film were less knowledgeable *after* viewing than before, and some who didn't see the film actually increased their knowledge without the help of the film.

These first few experiments therefore revealed how truly difficult it was to assess the overall impact of a film. The reason was the wide variation in knowledge and opinions in the target population, who had different ways of interpreting and responding to the film's message. There was evidence that viewing the same film made some soldiers more patriotic and others more despondent. The problem was, that given the variation in the intelligence, prior knowledge and opinions of the soldiers, it was hard to say if the differing effects of the film on individuals cancelled out the group effect on some measures. Moreover, the researchers remained unsure whether the two groups were different in their composition (intelligence, education, attitudes), which meant that other intervening factors might account for the lack of opinion change from the orientation films. Given these methodological uncertainties, the researchers sought a more rigorous way of studying the overall impact of a film, based on measuring the magnitude of change in knowledge or attitudes.

To further control for the possibility that the composition of the groups was different, the researchers then adopted an even more rigorous *before/after design*, reasoning that differences in the composition of the groups would be controlled by comparing the subjects' prior knowledge with their own subsequent knowledge. Thus the statistical comparisons between the control and treatment group would be based on *the change in knowledge or opinion* represented by the difference between the score at T1 (before measure) from T2 (after measure). It was argued that the difference score provided a better way of controlling for group differences than an 'absolute' measure of effectiveness aggregated over groups.

The Experimental Section further adapted the before/after design in their subsequent studies, developing complex factoral designs that explored why media generated limited opinion change from considerable knowledge gain. They particularly wondered if the limited results might be due to differences in intellectual capacity and ideology. In a subsequent series of studies, they compared the magnitude of opinion change effects for different levels of intelligence, using the Army Aptitude Assessment. It was found that a balanced approach worked better for more intelligent soldiers. Their analysis goes to great lengths to explain why the impact of the balanced film varies between better-educated soldiers:

> *The most significant finding, noted earlier, that did emerge from the study was that the [presentation] giving both sides was – as expected – more effective among those initially opposed. It should be realized that the method of utilizing the arguments on both sides of a question is probably very important in determining the relative effects of the communication on either those initially opposed or those initially favoring a particular point of view.*

(Hovland et al. 1949: 270)

They also suspected that intellectual capacity and oppositional attitudes might be important in explaining the long-term 'sleeper' effects of the film exposure (where the magnitude of the effect is greater after three weeks than after one week).

Over the course of the war, these psychologists became familiar with the many research design factors that need to be considered in studying persuasion: audience attention to the film, and specific aspects of a film's content they enjoyed and found believable, the need to get open and honest responses from the soldiers (no officers present), the issues associated with using repeating measures in this second design (how long before the film should the knowledge and opinion test be taken), the role that audience variables (intellectual capacity) have on what is learned, as well as the limitations of statistical analysis of results (effects differ depending on initial attitudes). As a result of their growing research expertise, they asserted the superiority of their experimental designs over the commercial researchers' evaluative designs, which they felt were 'only interested in the box office'. Yet in their pragmatic desire to understand the mechanisms underlying persuasion, they also borrowed from the programme evaluators. They launched a series of experimental assessments of propaganda effects using the programme evaluation (button pressing) techniques developed for measuring radio programmes to explore some of the intervening factors in persuasion, such as interest in and perceptions of the propagandistic elements of the mediated communication. One study compared the effectiveness of a training filmstrip, film and text in teaching orienteering map-reading skills, finding that the visual information was a considerable aid to learning. Another compared dramatic and informational formats for radio shows, and another compared one-sided (propagandizing) versus two-sided (balanced) filmic treatments for their persuasive effectiveness.

Although this body of work was conducted for its practical implications, these psychologists were scientists first and foremost. This work was published after the war, as an academic account of this growing field, less to publicize the findings, which were surely out of date, than to lay the foundation for a method for studying persuasion: 'These experimental studies comprised a large-scale attempt to utilize modern socio-psychological research techniques in the evaluation of educational and indoctrination films' (Hovland et al. 1949: vi). Their overall contribution to effects research was the identification of three basic explanatory factors in the persuasion process that had to be acknowledged and controlled by the experimental design. These were (1) *population variables* (the way different individuals responded to a given film), (2) *film variables* (the way the design and content of a film (authoritative sources, balanced arguments, visualized ideas, entertainment values, etc.) might contribute to interest, learning, persuasion) and (3) *external variables* (factors associated with the social context of viewing, or use such as learning expectations, power, suspiciousness).

## THE SOCIAL PSYCHOLOGY OF NORMATIVITY

Just before the war, experimental social psychologists had been analysing the part played by normative social pressures in the formation of attitudes and behaviour. After the war, keep-up-with-the-Joneses conformism moved to centre stage, in a growing debate about mass-mediated society (Packard 1959). In many cases, the researchers involved in the war propaganda studies (Hovland and Janis among them) returned to their university labs, and the study of mass-mediated social influence. Numerous studies of norms and values, and their relationship to opinion formation and behaviour, were conducted during the 1950s. In most cases, they applied the same experimental approach developed for propaganda, in an attempt to identify the major determinants of credibility, agreement and acceptance of the opinions of others.

Concerned that the spectre of fascism might infect American mass society with similar prejudices, Cooper and Jahoda pointed to the experimental research into the anti-prejudice Mr Biggot cartoon, noting that 'it is difficult in general for a communication to reach people who are not already in favor of the view it presents' (Cooper and Jahoda 1954: 313). They went on to note that subjects confronted with new and challenging progressive information 'may fight it or they may give in to it'. The Mr Biggot cartoon revealed the oft-demonstrated attitudinal responses of either yielding to a persuasive message or resisting it with counter-argument or ridicule. But based on psychoanalytic theories, these researchers proposed a third option, namely that subjects may also evade or equivocate, or neutralize the communication by not 'understanding the message' – that is, by emotionally disengaging or neutralizing its psychological force. To assess these kinds of reactions meant that researchers had to venture beyond their predominantly cognitivist measures of knowledge and opinion, to the deep-seated *attitudes of mind* that underwrote prejudicial judgements and interpretations of propaganda efforts.

Their quest for better measurement techniques were well understood by those researchers trying to measure the relationship between attitude formation and behavioural change. Sheffield's study of latitudes of acceptance and rejection attempted to measure the implied consequences of holding rigid attitudes. Adorno's work on the Authoritarian Personality Project, which conducted thousands of in-depth interviews, was similarly motivated by the need to distinguish those who harboured rationally prejudicial ideas. Although critical of positivism, Adorno was content to use advanced statistical techniques to evaluate these interviews when they helped provide a reliable scale of crypto-fascism known as the F-scale. Several studies showed that this standardized operationalization of prejudicial thought was related to the way individuals differentially responded to persuasive communication.

# EXPERIMENTAL STUDIES OF PERSUASIVE COMMUNICATION

Psychologists believed that designing effective persuasion was complicated by the fact that many factors, such as the intelligence, education and initial opinions, influenced a subject's interest in, comprehension, learning and acceptance of persuasive communication. Building on the finding that some individuals accept while others resist the same message, Janis et al. (1954) began to explore the processes of counter-argument and debunking elicited by persuasive communication attempts. They initially assessed three groups of 55 high-school freshmen for their attitudes to the Russian likelihood of dropping the A bomb. The next week, one group listened to a radio programme that optimistically argued that Russia could not develop the atomic bomb soon, the second listened to the same programme, but it was balanced by an additional segment that argued the exact opposite, while the control group listened to an irrelevant programme. Attitudes were again measured after listening to the programme, and again three months later, after the announcement of the Russian atomic tests were made public.

The results demonstrated the cumulative effects of communication in attitude formation and change: although preparatory optimistic communication had the expected attitudinal effect of convincing the subjects that it would take longer for the Russians to develop the bomb, it also blunted the pessimistic impact of the subsequent test explosion, particularly on subjects' estimates of how long it would take for Russia to develop large numbers of bombs. But the optimistic propaganda made little difference to the emotional impact of the subsequent bomb test announcement, and had only a small effect on the judgements students made of the long-term implications of these developments. In this respect, the one-sided presentation proved less effective than the balanced radio presentation, a result that the researchers view as consonant with the concern with resistance to persuasion as subjects actively debunked the overly optimistic but biased source.

The processing of arguments was further elaborated by William McGuire (1962), whose research explored the various competing cognitive factors contributing to resistance and yielding to persuasion attempts. McGuire set out to discover whether 'priming' resistance, with the ability to critically counter arguments, particularly novel ones, might prevent audiences from accepting strong one-sided arguments. These studies focused on medical opinion and were conducted on students. The changes in attitudes were based on comparisons between two experimental treatments that controlled the different ways of priming counter-argument: by asking students to read articles on medical truisms, or reading

attacks on previously defended and undefended truisms. The tests confirmed the importance of both the one-sided yielding to authoritative information, and the potential of
debunking and critical education in priming resistance to persuasion.

Similarly, Carl Hovland with Walter Weiss (1954) wanted to know whether the 'sleeper
effects' found in previous wartime research were a function of source credibility and
retention. They believed the subjects progressively yielded to the views of a persuasive
communication over time, as their specific suspicions about the motivations of the communicator and counter-argument were forgotten. They designed an experiment to assess
whether the learning and acceptance of communications on four controversial issues,
presented by trustworthy and untrustworthy sources, were similar. The experimenters
presented four newspaper stories, each of which contained a version of opposing
arguments (for example, for and against the selling of antihistamines without prescrip-
tion), to two comparable student groups (a total of 223 subjects), but attributed them to
either a high-credibility (*New England Journal of Medicine*) or a low-credibility (*Life Magazine*)
source. Measures of knowledge and attitudes towards the issues were gathered before,
immediately after, and one month after the presentation.

The results indicated that the credible sources were reliably perceived as more trustworthy, and high-credibility sources were more persuasive than low-credibility sources
immediately after the communication. But the amount of knowledge acquired from
reading the stories was unrelated to perceived credibility. Moreover, one month later, the
persuasiveness of high-credibility sources had diminished and that of the low-credibility
sources had increased (i.e. sleeper effect). This finding was corroborated by evidence that
the names of the low-credibility sources were mostly forgotten, especially by subjects who
were initially at odds with the argument of the story. Studies such as these suggested that
the long-term persuasion effect is related to the evaluation of the source as well as to how
subjects incorporate and forget aspects of the argument.

Hyman and Sheatsley subsequently pointed out that many other factors beyond source
credibility were involved in real communication processes. It is the complexity of persuasion that can explain why so many public health and information campaigns fail. Their
work notes that the laboratory research was identifying many mediating processes
involved in any public communication effort that can explain why audiences do not
always react as expected by message designers. Among the explanations they include
ignorance (and lack of prior knowledge and literacy skills), the poor design of messages
and irrelevance of the issue, the distraction of the audiences' attention, and predisposi-
tional issues such as selective interpretation and psychological resistance, which so often
create variability in the susceptibility to persuasion (Hyman and Sheatsley 1954: 523).

While the persuasion researchers focused on cognitive and belief processes, Irving Janis
and Seymour Feshbach became interested in the affective responses to persuasive communication, because, as they suggested, 'symbols in mass communications can be manipulated in a variety of ways so as to arouse socially acquired motives' ( Janis and Feshbach
1954: 320). They set out to demonstrate this by examining the role that fear and anxiety

play in message processing. They argue that the intervening role of emotion in persuasion is complex: it can be to enhance the salience of the message and promote yielding, to distract viewers' attention, to elicit unpleasant feelings and lead to different kinds of defensive resistance. Their research, therefore, attempted to identify the determining conditions under which the arousal of fear is effective or ineffective in eliciting changes in beliefs, practices and attitudes.

The experiment tested four groups of 50 high-school students who were exposed to one of the three experimental treatments (strong, moderate, mild fear-arousing lecture) or a control presentation, each was tested before and after for their knowledge, attitudes and anxieties about oral hygiene issues. Their level of anxiety was measured as a Likert-style item, indicating the degree (very, somewhat, not at all) of worry about improper care of teeth. But perhaps the most interesting feature of this experimental design was the treatments that controlled for three levels of fear-arousing material, provided a way of testing the 'dose response' relationship between the treatment and the effect. Before and after anxiety scores indicated that the strong fear appeal presentation was most interesting and created more anxiety. Their evaluation of the communication effects indicated that, though regarded as most interesting and authoritative, fear appeals were also unpleasant and were most disliked. The emotional design of this communication did not therefore result in either more or less learning, as tested by the toothbrush knowledge items. Subsequent analysis of oral health beliefs and practices showed that the more factual presentation generated the most conformity with good oral health beliefs and practices.

## TELEVISION, MASS MEDIA AND PERSUASION STUDIES

The postwar debates about conformity and persuasion grew ever more lively with the rapid diffusion of, and growing audience for television. Given their broad interest in Cold War propaganda and the threat of mass conformity, researchers set out to study the complex social influence processes (the source ethos, the structure of argument and appeals to emotion) that made persuasive speech effective for listeners. From these studies of the micro-processes of learning and opinion formation in the psychology labs, there was strong evidence supporting the idea that well-designed messages and advertisements presented by credible sources on TV might achieve a persuasive effect on knowledge, attitudes and behaviour, and that priming the defences of viewers might also make them more resistant to persuasion.

Yet more recent communications scholars often write off the effects laboratory tradition as contributing little to our understanding of media, because these researchers wielded a hypodermic model of communication, which assumed that meaning could be directly injected into the audience guinea pig. To some degree, this critical accusation is understandable. Deeply influenced by the rhetorical tradition, American communications researchers were concerned about the pragmatics of communication (i.e. with ideology and its fate in democracy). Yet this wholesale dismissal of the effects tradition to some degree reveals the cultural critics' fundamental hostility to social sciences – their quantitative methods, approaches and epistemologies. Raymond Williams (1974), though concerned that communications had become dominated by studies of 'mass-media effects', was more charitable to social scientists' methodology, arguing that much of it was indeed 'valuable'. The reason was that in spite of questionable epistemology, at least these quantitative researchers were trying to cultivate a robust conception of determinacy in a mediated world: in doing so, they were confronting the complex issues of causality, generalization and comparison in cultural analysis.

With Williams, we suspect that the blanket condemnation of the effects tradition misreads the dynamism and tentativeness of the social science experimentalism. The *OED* reminds us that experimentalism implies only an 'adherence to empiricist doctrines'. An experiment, it explains, means a trial, 'an attempt', 'a test', or 'tentative procedure' – 'a method, system of things, or course of action adopted in uncertainty whether it will answer the purpose'. To this we might add social scientists' commitment to providing a valid and reliable comparison that provides a valid test of whether the evidence confirms or disconfirms a stated hypothesis – the core issue that underlies the very concept of social science methodology (Stangor 1998). To condemn experimentation for behaviourism's reductionism and positivists' misguided claims of objectivity, clearly misreads the effects tradition's growing familiarity with the uncertainties and limitations of the lab as a venue for audience research. When one carefully reads the early effects studies, it becomes clear that a more accurate term for their approach is the inoculation model, for it is apparent that they did not regard their subjects as *tabulae rasae* or *passive victims*, but rather as active interpreters of the various competing attempts at social influence directed at them through the media. We suspect that the critics' facile dismissal of what was learned from these early studies is unhelpful too, for it fails to accurately contextualize these early studies of reception, or acknowledge the similarity between the processes of persuasion they were exploring and Stuart Hall's much later encoding and decoding model of mediated communication. What remains truly different between these two fields' understanding of social influence was the effects researchers' belief that it was possible to investigate ideology in the controlled circumstances of the lab.

In retrospect, many of their findings must now be taken with a pinch of salt. Given the tendency to over-control the experimental treatment, the study of classroom exposure to faked TV programmes failed to address the many differences between using media in these experimental situations with home viewing. Even in experiments where random assignment to treatment groups helped control for predisposing factors, it seemed inappropriate to declare general laws of persuasion when the sample was unrepresentative of normal populations. Their attachment to the laboratory meant that their studies only demonstrated how a small group of psychology students responded to a specific message in very artificial circumstances.

Often criticized for the banality of their results, the real limitation of this experimentalist programme was that findings were either so specific to the subject pool, or so unique in message design, that psychologists contributed little to what communication practitioners generally already knew about effective communication: that not all audiences fully yield to or assimilate the information in a message; that emotional appeals might sometimes work and sometimes fail; that attention, comprehension and retention were important precursors to, but not entirely predictive of, attitude change; that overly biased information would be debunked; that likeable expert sources could be convincing; and that some people were impervious to ideas because they were bigots.

Yet most communications scholars were aware of the difficulty of generalizing from laboratory findings to audience effects in the mediated world of everyday life. There was increasing disenchantment with the psychologists' laboratory approach, because its exponents seemed so obsessed with isolating a single determinant factor, and in so doing overlooked the artificiality and transparency in their experimental manipulations. Audiences might only see propaganda films and training films once, but to assess the impact of ads, election coverage of politicians, and news on general opinion, one had to investigate the cumulative media exposures that were repeated on a daily basis.

## TELEVISION AND SOCIALIZATION: TOWARD THE FIELD EXPERIMENT

The rapid diffusion of television during the 1950s, and the importance of the news and entertainment it provided, began to broaden the effects research agenda. Himmelweit (1958) conceived of the arrival of TV as a kind of natural experiment, and seized the opportunity to study its longer-term impact on British families, by observing families as they acquired and adapted their lives to television. Because society was structured, Himmelweit did not assume that the effects of television would be uniform across all individuals, families and communities: how could they be, given that some families acquired television and used it regularly whereas others delayed or used it only infrequently? She conducted depth-interviews with over 4000 families, based on a sampling strategy that ensured participants of different ages and classes. This study was not only ambitious in scope, but one of the first examples of a longitudinal audience research design (i.e. one that compared the adjustment of the English family before and after the arrival of television). For children growing up in Britain during the 1950s and 1960s, television was an important factor in the home; but both class and education were also contextual factors that influenced the way families incorporated TV into their lives. The effects of television, therefore, could not be understood independently of these other processes of interacting with the pattern of television use. The researchers used a longitudinal design, tracking these children as they grew up, noting how their media use interacted with broader sociocultural factors, in determining their success at school and their general social development, to document how social class and parental education moderated the impact of TV on children's learning, attitudes and personalities.

The prospects of television culture loomed ever larger in the thinking of American communications scholars during the 1960s and 1970s. By the early 1960s, television sets were found in over 90 per cent of US households, and the average viewing time climbed over the two-hour daily threshold. Wilbur Schramm and his associates' pioneering field experiments helped explain why net effects on group averages could badly misread the complexity of the impacts of television viewing (Schramm et al. 1961). Their work focused on families within a number of communities who were just acquiring TV. Tracking what TV meant in the daily lives of kids, Schramm's work did a lot to complexify discussions of the media's effects on schooling and on children's welfare generally. First, although there were significant differences between TV and non-TV families, there were also clear differences in the children's motivation and capacity to learn from TV. This was because children assimilated TV into their established routines and dispositions. Among his most startling observations, Schramm found that younger children of high IQ watched more TV and did better at school. Conversely, older children of lower IQ watched more TV and did comparatively worse at school. TV's effects were not uniform. For bright young children, TV seemed to be an educational resource; for duller older ones, a mind-numbing distraction.

Schramm and Himmelweit both found that television's effects on children were multifarious and complex. In part, this was because there was no normal child. In their use of TV, children developed regularized media preferences and habits, but these preferences and habits were not uniform across the entire audience. These researchers also found that when TV use was integrated into middle-class families, who emphasized learning, it could contribute to the child's achievements at school; yet, for others, in working-class circumstances, excessive TV use could detract from social and educational attainment. Gender was found to play an important role in explaining the long-term patterns of use and the consequences of media within the home.

Public opinion researchers during this period also studied media effects designing field studies to explore the role of opinion leaders in political and commercial decision-making. Katz and Lazarsfeld pointed out that, unlike lab experiments, field studies are unable to control the dispositional factors that are known to influence the media's impact on opinion change. They highlighted four particular intervening factors that can explain the uncertain effects of mediated communication: (1) the access and interest in getting information, (2) the media channels available (newspaper, radio, TV), (3) the actual content and design of the message, and (4) the intervening individual predispositions such as intelligence and prejudice, which can distort the interpretation of messages (Katz and Lazarsfeld 1955: 22). By controlling for these factors, their community field study of Decatur indicated that for opinions about crime, for consumer products and for political attitudes, social networks and opinion leaders, rather than the news media, had the greatest influence on public opinion. Adding this complexity to persuasion research, the laboratory approach was increasingly subject to concerns about the narrowness and generalizability of the findings (Hovland 1959; Campbell 1963).

The laboratory studies had been moderately successful in demonstrating qualified or limited effects: few studies confirmed the null hypothesis (that mediated communication had no effects whatsoever). Yet on reviewing the contradictory research findings from 300-

plus studies of media effects, Klapper (1960) concludes that it was time to stop worrying about the powerful propaganda effects of mass media. Television, under some circumstances of monopolistic control, might be a powerful technology for propaganda and mind control (as in dictatorships), but it might also be a force for more effective public education, marketing or democratic discussion. Such outcomes would depend on how it was used. American effects research, he suggested, had shown that in a pluralistic and democratic society, television simply legitimated and consolidated the pre-existent attitudes and opinions, 'reinforcing' and consolidating the diverse opinions of pluralistic American society.

However influential, Klapper's review fails to adequately distinguish the differing disciplinary interests of the sociological opinion researchers (Roper, Campbell, Berelson and Lazarsfeld) and the psychological persuasion researchers (Janis, McGuire and Hovland). Surely, to some extent, the debate between experimental and survey research about effects of media might be explained by the assumptions, techniques and evidence gathering unique to these disciplines. By controlling source, content and delivery, laboratory studies often revealed that the form and content of messages were important in opinion change. Field studies, on the other hand, demonstrated that there were no absolute 'hypodermic effects', because selective exposure and audience reception factors always intervene in the mass audience assimilation of those messages. Gradually, *the laboratory* so favoured by psychologists was partially eclipsed and supplemented as a venue for communications research by *the field*, as sociological researchers set out to increase the ecological validity of their studies of mass media effects. In most cases, understanding the social implications of the daily mediation of communication meant going beyond the specific contents to account for how media interacted with other factors in opinion formation, learning and socialization. Reviewing the results of four opinion surveys, Wade and Schramm (1969), for example, examined the role that news coverage played in health, public affairs and science knowledge. These surveys revealed strong relationships between the way individuals used specific media (newspapers and television), and the levels of knowledge and understanding they had. Newspapers, it seemed, were a better source of health and science information than television, for example, as those who read them regularly scored higher on the factual items included in their studies. But correlations in surveys were not proof that media use patterns caused ignorance, for such results could be explained by the different media use patterns of high SES and IQ groups. In controlled exposure tests of what individuals could remember from television news, for example, it was found that although recall of stories was less that 20 per cent of items on a newscast, the level of recall was very similar for newspapers and television.

During the 1960s and 1970s, in light of Klapper's reinforcement hypothesis, the focus on persuasion was slowly being replaced by a more qualified and supple account of the complex processes of mediated social communication (Roberts and Bachen 1981). Among American effects researchers especially, it was argued that through improvements to experimental design and measurement, it was still possible to tease out the specific contribution of media channels to public learning and opinion change. Chaiken and Eagly

(1976), for example, experimentally explored the relative contribution of the complexity of presentation to qualify our understanding of the comprehension and resistance model of learning from media. In an experimental study, they exposed 299 undergraduates to either an easy- or difficult-to-understand persuasive message, which was presented either in the written, audiotaped, or videotaped modality. The communicator's non-verbal expressions of confidence were carefully manipulated within audiotaped and videotaped conditions, but these cues were not found to significantly affect opinions. For difficult messages attitude change and comprehension of persuasive materials were found to be greater when the message was written, compared to a videotaped or audiotaped presentation. With easy messages, persuasion was greatest for a videotaped message, moderate when audiotaped, and least when written; but comprehension of the easy message was equivalent, regardless of modality. The authors suggest a framework that considers the interactions among multiple factors, like the modality of communication in relationship to the information-processing capacities of the subjects, the subject matter of the communication, and the predisposition of students who are habitually primed to 'yield' to information presented in classrooms.

## AGENDA SETTING AND POLITICAL INFLUENCES OF NEWS

Political science researchers had long focused their research into media effects on the cognitive or belief models of persuasion, and particularly on the issue of argumentation and counter-argumentation, which was associated with partisan political broadcasts, especially during elections. Rolling polls and surveys at election time had more or less excluded the role of local newspapers and radio, surmising that they played a minor role in voter decision-making. Broadcast media were thought to increase the level of interest in elections among some voters, but because the media were used selectively, they were considered less important in explaining voter patterns than party affiliation, region, economic status, levels of political involvement, etc. (Campbell et al. 1960).

Based on the prior survey studies of political influence, there was compelling evidence suggesting that very few people actually changed their minds during elections. Media appeared to increase the awareness of election issues, but the 'selective exposure' to confirmatory information seemed to blunt the impact of mediated information (Lazarsfeld et al. 1948). In the Elmira community study, for example, they found that persons reporting extensive use of media during the campaign were less likely to actually change their votes. Although they remain unsure of how television influenced voting, Campbell et al. (1954) note from their election surveys that it is disproportionately watched or rated as an important information source. They predicted quite accurately that opinion research would have to re-examine contemporary persuasion in the light of television's growing importance. But the Michigan Research Center's national surveys seemed to indicate that due to selective exposure, based on ideological dispositions and relatively impartial press coverage, television's biasing influence on election outcomes was reduced (Campbell et al. 1960).

Yet as television played an ever greater role in American elections, and in the foreign policy debates that dominated American politics, particularly during the Vietnam War, researchers attempted to add to the models of voter decision-making, taking into account unexplained variance in voter decision-making. Stokes (1968) suggests that, in the age of television, among the various demonstrated political affiliations of parties and issues, the perception of the leader as a political object was becoming an ever more important aspect of the political decision process. Television seemed to have a unique facility to communicate the authority, credibility and attractiveness of sources, all of which might play an important role in the formation of public opinion, especially at elections.

Both interpersonal communication and source credibility researchers undertook experimental comparisons of different media. Mehrabian, for example, demonstrated in a series of laboratory studies, that source credibility was very much influenced by clues transmitted by body language and facial expression in videotaped presentations (Mehrabian 1972). Similar research on interpersonal judgement suggests that personal presentations by human sources are judged 10 per cent on content, 20 per cent on vocal cues and 70 per cent by visualized information.

Innovative researchers pursued the suggestion by Lang and Lang (1966) that the mass media 'force attention to certain issues', influencing 'what the public should think about, not what they should think' (Lang and Lang 1966: 468). Based on an open-ended interview method, used by Treneman and McQuail to assess the salience of political issues in Britain during 1959, McCombs and Shaw hypothesized that 'the mass media set the agenda for each political campaign, influencing the salience of attitudes toward the political issues' (McCombs and Shaw 1972: 177). Their research combined a content analysis of (political) news stories during the election, with interviews of 100 'undecided' voters, randomly selected from lists of registered voters in the community of Chapel Hill, America. Not only did they notice that over 30 per cent of the campaign news coverage was devoted to the horse race between candidates rather than political issues, but there was also a highly significant commonality between the issues emphasized in the media and the voters' perception of the salience of those issues. They concluded that there was little evidence of party-based selective exposure and a strong indication that the voters' agenda was set by the media agenda as a whole. McCombs and Shaw are careful to explain that correlations between media coverage and issue salience are not proof of causal explanations but, coding the viewers' affective language in their responses, they suggest that psychological factors like salience of affect interact with interest in politics in the use of media. Those with high political interest were more likely to remember getting information on key issues from newspapers. The issue agenda seems to be set across all media; however, public affairs priorities are related to whether voters primarily used newspapers, television or both as sources of information.

Patterson and McLure (1976), in their panel study of political agenda, confirm that there is little evidence that television contributes to the knowledge that respondents have about election issues. In terms of knowledge levels, individuals who followed the campaign on television were no more knowledgeable than those who didn't follow the campaign at all, and much less knowledgeable than those who followed it through newspapers. Using a cross-lagged panel, McLeod, Becker and Byrnes (1974) note that these agenda effects are not uniform for all populations, nor across all operationalizations of 'salience'. Agenda effects from the newspaper for perceived 'issue salience', for example, were greatest among young first-time voters and those who were more committed partisans. Further refinement of the notion of media effects was also undertaken by the 'cultivation' approach, developed by Gerbner and his associates (see Chapter 2).

The agenda-setting cultivation model became the basis of a strategy for using the media in public awareness efforts in the 1980s and 1990s. Communication scholars increasingly acknowledge that media effects should not be separated from the social context of communication, i.e. the networks of human social interaction that exist in communities and households. The role that regular media coverage played in setting the public opinion agenda also had to be considered a factor. A growing cadre of applied communication researchers believed that it was important to take into account the fact that media were biased, that communities were structured, audiences were active, and that citizens' prior knowledge, preferences, choices and attitudes shaped the media's agenda setting.

Based on a strategic public communication model, the Stanford Heart Disease Prevention Programme (Farquhar et al. 1977) used a quasi-experimental field design to evaluate a heart disease reduction programme that launched a massive public information effort in three matched communities, one of which received the two-year media campaign, the second of which received the same campaign, supplemented by personal communication with high-risk individuals (from health professionals), and a third control community. Employing before and after measures on knowledge and levels of dietary, smoking and exercise habits, the study found that after one year, both treatment communities had higher levels of knowledge about the risk factors of heart disease. Moreover, there was significant reduction in saturated fat intake, cigarette smoking and systolic blood pressure in both communities. There was little evidence of additional benefits of the personal communication, with high-risk individuals leading many in the field to believe that public information campaigns were, after all, an effective means for changing lifestyles (Maccoby et al. 1977).

## ADVERTISING EVALUATION RESEARCH

One of the first to grapple with the limited validity and generalizability of laboratory research was the advertising industry. One way of validating its laboratory predictions of brand choice was to cross-validate laboratory and survey results. Reporting over 16 years of copy evaluation, Daniel Starch (1966) wrote *Measuring Advertising Readership and Results*, which summarized over 400,000 interviews, conducted to assess over 45,000 ads taken from the *Saturday Evening Post* and *Life*. With their well-established reliability, the Starch procedure could act as a benchmark against which to calibrate day-after recall scores and even self-reported purchases. Similarly for television commercials, it was possible to use phone surveys to compare 'day-after recall' for pre-tested commercials. Although cross-validation of indexes was costly, it was important to provide the advertiser with a more reliable measure of how much its campaigns were being watched and remembered by the audience.

The Starch Index was, of course, only the first of many evaluation techniques developed by the commercial sector. Because they mistrusted diaries and self-reports of listening and viewing, the commercial audience researchers experimented with tuner monitoring devices, establishing the people meter panels as the gold standard in audience research. Recognizing the limits of post hoc evaluation scales, advertisers experimented with real-time programme evaluation devices, which can plot changes in audience responses over time (recording tuning information), and pioneered real-time programme evaluation systems, by providing buttons and dials for audiences to indicate their appreciation. An interest in measuring the size of the audience, and their preferences and interests through scaling interest, enjoyment and retention, was operationalized by the radio broadcasters and the film studios. Many novel tools and techniques for measuring learning and attitude change flowed from the commercial sector's interest in audience responses to programming and ads. For example, the magazine sector developed eye-tracking devices, which allow the experimenter to observe exactly where a person 'looks' in a photographic image, to supplement evaluative and recall indexes. These laboratory findings could then be used to predict field studies of day-after recall.

The social–psychological model of belief-induced attitude change, developed by the persuasion researchers was enthusiastically applied in the field of marketing psychology to target campaigns on brand attitudes (McGuire 1962). While acknowledging the benefits of semantic differentials and other kinds of measures to isolate the dimensions of beliefs about products (power, effectivity, evaluation), Krugman still rejects the idea that a complete change in 'attitudes' should be expected 'prior to changes in behaviour'. Krugman (1965) notes that the limited effects model of Klapper and others 'was based upon analysis of largely noncommercial cases and data' (Krugman 1965: 349). He argues that the accepted theory is that 'advertising's use of the television medium has limited impact' because audiences rarely felt converted, and TV advertising appeared to be trivial and silly. He goes on to note that 'what is lacking in the required evaluation of TV advertising is any significant body of research specifically relating to advertising attitudes and these in turn to purchasing behaviour or sales' (1965: 350). He then points out, however, that the 'economic impact of TV advertising is substantial and documented. Its messages have been learned by the public . . . yet the lack of specific case histories keeps researchers from concluding that the commercial use of the medium is a success' (1965: 351).

Discussing the evidence gathered around advertising exposure and remembrance, Krugman points out the need for a unique theory of learning of 'lesser ego-involvement' material, in which repetition outweighs attitudinal predisposition as a factor in persuasion. He calls this second kind of perceptual learning, 'persuasion without awareness', distinguishing between the commercial and academic 'results' of impact studies as indicating two 'entirely different ways of experiencing and being influenced by mass media'. Krugman's studies concern the relationship between psychological involvement in the subject matter of the ad as a factor in the persuasive impact of televized advertising messages. The distinction between low- and high-involvement persuasion, processes concerns the number of 'bridging experiences', or connections, between a viewer's own life and the message content. In low-involvement persuasion, researchers must look for gradual shifts in perceptual structure, while for high involvement they must look for the more classic 'conscious opinion and attitude change' (i.e. in the cognitive–affective structure of conscious agreement and resistance). 'Does this suggest that if television bombards us with enough trivia about a product we may be persuaded to believe it? On the contrary it suggests that persuasion as such, ie overcoming a resistant attitude, is not involved at all' (Krugman 1965: 353).

In his attempt to test out this theory of two kinds of learning, Krugman (1972) used electro-physiological measurement systems, developed for brainwave analysis, to chart real-time fluctuations in mental activation while watching television footage, for low and high involvement. His results indicated that a persuasion without the awareness model might help to explain the processes. Further experiments confirm that a 'dual processing' model may offer a fuller account of persuasion than the belief-induced attitude change model favoured by the opinion researchers and cognitive social psychologists (Petty and Cacioppo 1985).

Acknowledging the many mediating factors in persuasion, advertising researchers were quick to realize that laboratory studies of the relative attractiveness of an ad provided only one vague indicator of purchase decisions. For practical reasons, advertising evaluators set out an account for exposure and retention in their estimates of the effectiveness of ads. Michael Ray (1973) provided a summary in the form of a general model for advertising's influence that could evaluate the different routes to the formation of brand preferences and increased likelihood of brand purchase. Ray's multi-factor model was further developed by Batra and Ray (1986), through a series of reception studies that isolated the importance of the perception of the ad itself as part of the persuasive impact. A major pre-occupation in their work became the modelling of the complexities of purchase decision-making. More precise models of the cognitive and affective processes involved in learning from television advertising were enabled by refinements in attitude measurement techniques. Similarly, Mitchell (1983) reports a series of studies that demonstrate the importance of adding measures of the visual and emotional dimensions of meaning in accounting for how subjects process and remember the information in ads. Reporting a series of experiments where visual and verbal content are carefully manipulated, Mitchell suggests that there are two information processes involved: a perceptual stage, in which attention to the stimulus is not entirely conscious, and the actual interpretative processing of the visual and verbal information content. Both the visual and verbal components con-tribute to the brand attitude, measured two weeks after a series of exposures jointly through the formation of an attitude to the ad (enjoyment, interest, persuasiveness) and by eliciting product thoughts and brand beliefs.

The ability to measure the affective dimension of style and brand attitude has preoccupied more recent forms of advertising evaluation. Burke and Edell (1989) emphasize the progress being made in the ability to account for the 'affective dimension' of advertising's impact on brand attitudes and purchase decisions, and identify the links to advertising effectiveness. Their model suggests that the measurement of 'feelings' is a way of tracing the different judgemental processes that ultimately determine the ad's impact after exposure and comprehension. These include the judgements of an ad's characteristics, the evaluation of the brand's attributes as communicated through the ad, the attitude formed about the ad, and finally, their contribution to attitude to the brand.

Burke and Edell recruited 191 paid subjects from the general population for a television programming study, and embedded a degree of exposure (5 exposure versus 10 exposure) to six 30-second television test ads (and four rotating filler ads) for products that were not yet available in the area (potato chips, a band, fruit juice, salad dressing, outboard motor, photo service). Subjects were scored for overall response to the ads, with a 56-feelings rating checklist and a 25-scale semantic differential for the ads' characteristics. Brand attitudes were measured on four attribute dimensions of evaluation and likelihood to buy. After factor-analysing the feeling scores, three kinds of feelings were noted: upbeat feelings, warm feelings and negative feelings. The affective semantic differential judgement scales for attitude to the ads revealed the following three dimensions: evaluation, activity, gentleness. Through a complex series of predictive models, they argue that ads that make viewers 'feel' upbeat, warm and negative not only have a significant effect on the judgement of the ad, but also on their attitudes to the brand as well, but in different ways: because different feelings co-occur but can have countervailing effects, each dimension of feelings must be measured and entered into the predictive model separately. For example, the elicitation of negative feelings may work through the evaluative judgement (phoney, informative, annoying, fearful) made of the ad and therefore transfer to the brand, even without a positive evaluation of the ad.

Marketing evaluation research techniques were applied to television programming as well. Programmers, like advertisers, conduct many proprietary experiments in audience responses to build the programme audience. Evaluative research, conducted on test panels of targeted viewers, are used extensively in the programme decision-making of television networks: (1) as a diagnostic tool to assess how a programme has performed, (2) as a prediction tool to anticipate how a programme will perform for a particular time slot or target audience, and (3) as a promotion-planning strategy to strategically boost the ratings for a show by knowing its strongest features. Menneer (1987) reports a series of panel studies of BBC pilots, and the relationship between the early audience appreciation index (AI) and longer-term growth in audience size. The figures for the appreciation index for the social-realist soap opera *EastEnders* show how the improvements of the AI technologies helped the BBC to improve one of its most successful soap operas.

Political evaluators have also invested heavily in new 'real-time' TV ad evaluation systems, such as the PEAC system, which was originally developed for educational research, but found its greatest use in political campaigning. The constant monitoring allowed researchers to track undecided voters as they responded to the debate between Reagan and Mondale during the 1984 US election. Other researchers have used GSR (galvanic skin response) and HR (heart rate) as indicators of fluctuations in emotional responses while watching (liking the ad), which might be equally important in predicting whether the ad is effective in terms of retention and formation of positive brand attitudes or 'selling' political personalities during elections (Kline 1997).

## EXPERIMENTAL APPROACHES TO MEDIATED LEARNING

There was similar enthusiasm in education circles with regard to the potential of using mass media to educate. Some early critics of TV fretted that the onslaught of visual information might affect brain development, alter attention mechanisms or overwhelm the information-processing capacities of children, by eliciting trance-like, uncritical mental states. But TV, the advocates countered, could also be an effective communicator of knowledge because of its novelty, its interesting characters, and the power of visualization, which, when combined, afforded this medium a unique potential to make information more enjoyable for learning. As a lively audiovisual medium, television was accessible and engaging in ways that books were not. Sound and image could enhance rather than diminish learning.

Oddly enough, media theorist Marshall McLuhan was among the first to test the educational possibilities of television, by experimentally comparing his students' learning from watching a film, hearing a lecture or from reading. One group received information via radio, one from TV, one by lecture, and one read it themselves (McLuhan 1964: 271). Each group was then administered a quiz. McLuhan notes, 'It was quite a surprise to the experimenters when the students performed better with TV-channeled information and with radio than they did with lecture and print – and the TV group stood well above the radio group' (McLuhan 1964: 271). McLuhan believed his results would stand classic teaching methods on their head, by drawing attention to the way in which TV dramatized 'auditory and visual features' in ways reading and lecturing did not. Television was a cool medium, requiring intense total involvement, because information was presented to both eye and ear. Print and reading, on the other hand, invoked a more linear rational decoding, rather than the synaesthetic sensorium of a TV image. (McLuhan 1964: 269).

Believing that programming content was cognitively processed as 'information', educationalists have continued to test how much children comprehended and learned from TV. They mostly used the evaluation design: expose children to TV programmes and test them afterwards with quizzes. Research on educational television's impact on learning has indicated that television didn't pacify and mesmerize kids. Children were savvy viewers of TV in the classroom, because they gained skill at using it at home for leisure; quickly picking up the conventions (grammar) of TV and developing sophisticated ways of interpreting the stories – motives of characters, contexts of behaviour, and conventions of narrative exposition (Salomon 1983). They actively engaged with TV programmes in order to make sense of their world. Children are active and capable learners, and depending on their developmental and cognitive abilities and their family backgrounds, could benefit from educational media (Anderson and Collins 1988). TV in schools, it was argued, could therefore be an effective communicator to the young, especially because of its novelty, its interesting characters and visualization, which, when combined skilfully, granted TV the unique potential to make learning more enjoyable (Palmer 1988). When used creatively in the classroom, it could make children enthusiastic about learning while still communicating abstract concepts more effectively than books (Calvert 1999).

Yet the early field research also fostered an appreciation of the complexity of mediated public education efforts. As with advertising, educational audience researchers were therefore inclined to acknowledge TV's ambiguous potential when studied in the context of daily life: this medium was both a magical window, helping educate, inform and broaden the public's horizons, and a vast wasteland filled with distracting entertainment and mainstream politics, which diminished debate, reading and public knowledge. It all depended on who watched what for how long, and why and how they watched it.

The test of potential for educational TV was *Sesame Street*. The CTW (Children's Television Workshop) launched *Sesame Street* to level the educational playing field for underprivileged preschoolers. Although television was an effective teacher in the classroom, it was much harder to provide similar results in the home. Following the commercial model, the CTW did a lot of formative research in its learning laboratories, to fine-tune its formats and content. But its subsequent field evaluations revealed classically ambiguous prospects concerning the use of TV for the benefit of the underprivileged. The educational benefits of regular watching of *Sesame Street* seemed to depend on the quality of parental support and encouragement, which was less frequent in precisely those homes that programme targeted (Lesser 1974). In short, although television was capable of contributing to children's education, it was going to require sizeable public resources to achieve this modernist vision.

Aware of these competing claims about the role of TV in children's learning, Tannis McBeth Williams used the idea of *natural experiments* to design one of the landmark studies of these profound changes taking place in communities, schools and families with the introduction of television (cf. the Himmelweit study mentioned above). The researchers recognized that by 1973, there was a closing window of opportunity for studying the impact of TV on family life – because everybody now had a TV set. But in the Canadian province of British Columbia, a fortuitous set of circumstances enabled the study team to undertake a powerful natural experiment. Due to the mountainous topography, some mid-sized communities in this province had been buffered from the onslaught of television. One of the communities, which the researchers called Notel, had been without television reception at all. A similarly sized and situated town, Unitel, only had the national broadcast signal (CBC) creep into its valley. Both of these communities were poised to receive new transmission towers that would bring both the private Canadian network (CTV) and three American networks into their communities; these were already available in the neighbouring community, Multitel. Recognizing the passing of this historic moment, a team of researchers rushed into the three communities to survey family members and gather other relevant data from the communities before television arrived. Two years later, they returned to each of the communities for a second data-gathering session, and the results of this study were published in 1986 (Williams 1986).

Williams' rather comprehensive account documents the longitudinal effects of television on school performance (especially reading), on aggressive behaviour, and on the participation in and use of community leisure resources. There was strong evidence of both direct and indirect effects. Direct effects were indicated by the fact that those children who watched more violent television programmes also exhibited more aggressive behaviour in the playground two years after the introduction of TV. The increased aggressive behaviour among Notel boys (but not Multitel), two years after the introduction of television, when measured by observing physical and verbal aggression during free play, and corroborated by peer and teacher judgements, implies that this is a causal relationship (Joy et al. 1986). But this finding is confounded by the ageing process of the children, who also got more aggressive as they got older.

Williams' project is unique because it also set out to explore indirect or 'displacement effects' in context. Such effects do not relate to what the child does while watching TV, so much as what they do not do while they are watching – the activities the child foregoes to spend time with media. Indirect effects, for example, provide a ready explanation of why television 'slows down the acquisition of reading skills'. The trend is weak, but persists when controlled statistically for IQ. Williams explains that 'at least for some children, time spent with television probably displaces reading practice'. The amount of reading involves a trade-off between one media over another – or a 'substitution' based on their functional similarity. But the amount of displacement is not uniform, rather depending on personal and environmental circumstances. With this in mind, the researchers note that 'brighter students probably move on to reading for pleasure more quickly and families of higher SES (socio-economic status) are more likely to emphasize print as a medium for learning' (Williams 1986: 71). The implications of this finding are that television is more important in the early school years, when time spent with television has greater potential to influence school achievement, especially for less intelligent and less motivated children, who require additional reading practice and parental encouragement for this activity.

Educational researchers since have come to believe that television in the home could both contribute to the welfare of children, by promoting learning, and sidetrack children's developmental projects, by distracting them from school-work and reading. All of these interacting contextual factors must be accounted for in any account of media effects. Huston and Wright's longitudinal Topeka Study, conducted between 1981 and 1983, followed two 'cohorts' (consisting of several hundred children aged three to five and five to seven) through a two-year period, in order to see what actually happened in the home. They tracked each child's television use using one-week diaries, gathered every six months, as well as undertaking interviews and monitoring parental viewing. The major purposes of this longitudinal field study were to identify patterns of 'developmental continuity and change in children's early television viewing', and to discover how those patterns are 'related to family environmental influences and to children's cognitive skills and social behaviour' (Huston and Wright 1996: 38). Their study took account of (1) the diversity of content and the variations in children's patterns of media use, (2) the developmental sequences underwriting children's media use as a cognitive activity, and (3) family patterns of regulation and media use in the socialization of young children.

A similar field experiment was conducted beginning in 1990. The team tracked two cohorts of 240 slightly younger children (two and four years of age) for a four-year period. In addition to diaries, this study employed daily-use telephone surveys, interviews with parents and children concerning media use, as well as gathering measures of vocabulary, school-related success, knowledge about emotions and teachers' expectations of success. Children's programme preferences are established very early in life, are gendered, and continue as their thinking and understanding grow more complex. Yet, particularly, for younger children, a large amount of viewing is of programming often chosen by adult members of the family. When they go to school, the total amount of time that children watch decreases – but so does their interest in educational programming. Cable in the home also impacted programme choice by increasing the range of cartoons available and diminishing viewing of educational productions. The researchers' audit of home viewing revealed that whereas younger children develop an early passion for cartoons, they also develop an appetite for drama with more complex plots, sports, sitcoms and crime shows, so that by 10–12 years, the dark and cynical *Simpsons* and romance-themed comedies like *Seinfeld* become perennial favourites.

These researchers also showed that, while children are young, watching *Sesame Street* can support the acquisition of reading skills in families where there is parental encouragement across social strata, but not in families that don't encourage their children to learn from TV. Family support for educational viewing early on improved the child's reading and vocabulary at age seven. The slower acquisition of literacy is also contingent on whether parents read with children and provide them with books. In families where children were left to watch cartoons, and offered no other support, children showed the effects of TV with reduced vocabulary and reading scores: 'These demographic variables appear to affect the child through the parent and the kind of environment the parent supplies for the child' (Huston and Wright 1996: 46). Huston and Wright go on to note that 'parents' own viewing habits and preferences are a powerful source of modelling' and that 'those families that provide more guidance and regulation have children who watch and benefit from educational programmes'. These researchers suggest the family must be understood as the 'core socializing force' mediating television's effects on children.

In recent reconsideration of the long-term effects of early exposure to educational television broadcasting, Daniel Anderson et al. (2001) found 'a much stronger support for content-based hypotheses'. The researchers found that:

*viewing educational programmes as preschoolers was associated with higher grades, reading more books, placing more value on achievement, greater creativity and less aggression. These associations were more consistent for boys than for girls. By contrast, the girls who were more frequent preschool viewers of violent programmes had lower grades than those who were infrequent viewers.*

(Anderson et al. 2001: vii)

## TELEVISION AND THE SOCIALIZATION OF AGGRESSIVE AND ANTISOCIAL BEHAVIOUR

If television was such a powerful tool of learning, what were children learning from watching those high-action police dramas that seemed to be their preferred entertainment at home? In the US, the Surgeon General's first report on media violence, issued in 1972, added a scientific clang to the alarm bells that were already ringing about rising rates of violent crime as the baby-boom generation entered its oedipal rebellion phase (Comstock et al. 1972). Content analysis had revealed that North American children's media were consistently filled with programming that emphasized, and sometimes celebrated, the use of force, revenge and antisocial behaviour. Viewing surveys repeatedly found that children, but especially young males, preferred the most violent cartoon and action adventure programmes, inadvertently exposing themselves to thousands of symbolic slayings and fights each year (Wilson et al. 1998). Yet the industry maintained that violence on television was just entertainment: a good story enjoyed by children, but one that didn't harm them. So it fell upon experimental audience researchers to explain how the representation of violence in media contributed to violence in society.

The researchers approached this issue in a number of ways: by comparing rising crime statistics in America with other countries (with less violent media), by studying the correlations between TV watching and aggressive behaviour, and notably in the laboratory, where an experimental approach set out to measure changes in the behaviour of children exposed to violent shows or films. Since the problem seemed especially acute for the very young, many of the experiments used cartoons such as those featuring the Road Runner as a stimulus. By carefully viewing children's behaviour after watching, they hoped to demonstrate whether watching 'symbolic violence' increased the likelihood of aggressive attitudes and behaviour or, as other psychologists maintained, whether the imaginary participation in violent fantasy might reduce aggressiveness through a cathartic psychological release of pent-up emotions and frustrations.

Early laboratory experiments hypothesized that since aggression was 'provoked behaviour', it was necessary to create feelings of anger and hostility as the pre-conditions for subsequent violent behaviour. Aggression was largely understood as a complexly motivated behaviour: an emotional response to a 'threat' to the organism, which caused feelings of anger, frustration and hostility. To the degree that watching violence generated arousal, television could stimulate or 'dis-inhibit' latent aggressive behaviours. Zillman (1978) articulates three aspects of the aggression drive that could be impacted by viewing violent content: the dispositional component, which is the propensity to 'act' aggressively; the excitory component, which is a function of the physiological arousal state, induced by the perception of provocation or threat; and the experiential component, which is the cognitive or attitudinal processes through which the individual recognizes and interprets his or her own arousal, the situation and the appropriate response to the provocation. Zillman's research suggested that it was important to map the 'excitation transfer' on these three components. A number of behavioural measures of aggression were developed, including fighting, attitudes, self-reports of feelings of hostility/anger, physiological states of arousal, and the disruptive social interactions and play behaviours of children (for example, Bandura's notorious measure of children's hitting of a Bobo doll; see Chapter 14), or administering punishment to a recalcitrant or hostile confederate through pressing a shock button. But in the laboratory, one had to assume that a single exposure was sufficient and that the emotional effect would last long enough after the exposure to be measurable.

It is with regard to the cognitive component of aggressive behaviour that psychological researchers also argued that watching violence might 'cue' subsequent aggressive thoughts and behaviours, making individuals more angry and vengeful in subsequent situations (Berkowitz 1964). Frustration and provocation created conditions that also elicited aggressive cognitions: media enactments supplied the cues that facilitated the formation of mental representations of behavioural responses to situations. Aggressive behaviour is therefore better understood as a 'learned behaviour' in which the construction, consolidation and priming of aggressive thought networks increased the likelihood of aggressive responses. Learning aggression was a matter of strengthening associations between certain kinds of situation and certain kinds of response. What mattered was what the child learned while watching, not how watching made them feel.

Widely influential in this way of thinking about television was Albert Bandura's social learning theory, in which he argued that children modelled their own behaviour on that of fictional characters they encounter in the media – an effect that was enhanced by the processes of identification (Bandura 1973). Modelling had to be understood as a complex social learning process. Since multiple factors influence the outcome, not all children will respond identically to the same programme. Identification accentuates the processes of learning, to the degree that if children like aggressive characters and want to be like those characters, then the learning of aggression would be facilitated. To understand the long-term effects of TV, researchers needed to examine more closely who children identified with, and what kinds of role models they incorporated into their own self-systems.

The limitations in the application of laboratory research results to the study of consequences of mass-mediated aggression are obvious: it assumed that watching one video or playing a game would produce an emotional effect, instilling and justifying feelings of hostility and anger that would then be directed against both the animate and inanimate objects. Yet even among younger children, there were only marginal main effects, and mostly on rambunctious play behaviours or verbal expressions. The point is that fighting, punching and kicking is a rare behaviour in both primary schools and labs. Moreover, exposing children (who normally watch three hours every day) to one ten-minute episode of *Road Runner* in a lab setting might hardly be expected to put children in a rage. It was not clear that watching fictional, and especially cartoon, violence always produced feelings of hostility (instead of general 'activation' or pleasure). Nor was it always true that control subjects would not feel angry or frustrated for other reasons, such as disposition, gender or mood state.

Arguing that these social learning mechanisms needed to be demonstrated outside of the laboratory, Stein et al. (1972) provided one of the more definitive evaluations of programmatic content effects. First, they argued that effects needed to be studied in a natural setting. They chose the nursery school as a more appropriate context to observe children than the lab. Second, they argued that a single exposure is not an adequate treatment: their approach was to provide children with a steady 'diet' of specific programmes that were either violent, pro-social or neutral. Third, they suggested that a more complex multidimensional measurement approach, which could statistically control for various competing explanations of the aggression or cooperative behaviour they observed, would provide a more comprehensive test of the effects of exposure. Under these circumstances, and controlling for factors such as prior aggression and intellectual capacity, this research did indicate that media content was a factor in children's social learning. But the effects are far from overwhelmingly large. These early forays into understanding media's effects on aggression provided far from definitive proof that watching television was a major factor in cultivating aggressive feelings, attitudes and behaviours in children. (For the controversy, see Anderson and Bushman 2001; Freedman 2002.)

Most effects researchers now acknowledge that from the scientific point of view, the evidence from laboratory studies of violence is inconclusive. Nor is it clear to what extent the causality is unidirectional. Goldstein notes: 'The reasoning underlying this research is that exposure to violence activates aggressive associations and images. These in turn heighten the preference for further exposure to violence' (Goldstein 1998: 59). Indeed, the process of becoming aggressive and antisocial is complex. Researchers acknowledge that aggression is not due to TV alone: 'the existing research suggests that childhood aggression is often a product of a number of interacting factors' (Huesmann et al. 1997: 183). Over the child's life course, aggressive and antisocial behaviour is also correlated with lack of self-concept, poverty and broken families, which are also predictors of antisocial behaviour, crime and aggression. In one hallmark longitudinal project, Huesmann and Eron (1986) reported on 600 youths studied over 22 years. This study found that criminal acts at age 30 correlated with both the total amount of time of television viewing at age eight and a preference amongst boys for violent television. It was the interaction of 'extensive exposure to violence coupled with identification with aggressive characters [that] was a particularly potent predictor of subsequent aggression for many children,' they argued (Huesmann and Eron 1986: 185).

These longitudinal studies convinced researchers to pay closer attention to the relationship between television viewing and other factors associated with aggressiveness. Eron cites similar evidence from longitudinal studies of the development of aggressive disposition to explain the effects of television on some boys: 'Consistency supports the contention that aggression is a personality trait that characterizes the individual over time and across many situations' (Eron 1997). The effects of violence would therefore be expected only among heavy users of violent media – where long-term effects would be strongest – namely young males. As Eron notes, 'an environment full of deprivations, frustrations and provocations is one in which aggression is frequently stimulated'. For many boys, watching violent TV or video games is simply a typically male pleasure. Yet within highly stressed families, media can interfere with the formation of 'the children's self-regulating and internal standards for behaviour'. As Eron goes on to explain, a 'child with weak or non-existent internalized prohibitions against aggression or one who believes it is normative to behave in this way, is much more likely to use aggressive scripts' (Eron 1997: 144).

There is a growing group of quantitative researchers who focus on the variables within the family context that impact on children's violent media use in the home and therefore contribute to the socialization of aggression (van den Bergh and van den Bulck 2000). In their field experiments, some researchers have observed that for very young children, family discipline style, as well as encouragement of the imagination, can be important influences mediating the effects of TV violence on judged aggressiveness and activity levels of children (Singer et al. 1984). Desmond et al. suggest that 'although all children are exposed to aggressive behaviour in the home or through media, families differ in self-restraint, comments about aggression, or in discussions of alternative behaviours' (Desmond et al. 1990). Several researchers have demonstrated how coaching parental mediation influences viewing preferences, identification, and assimilation of violent and fearful media content (Rose et al. 1998). Others have noted that restrictions, monitoring, co-viewing and verbal intervention on the development of media consumption habits can play a role in moderating the socialization of aggression (Korzenny 1977; van der Voort 1997; Valkenburg et al. 1998).

Applying Bandura's social learning models, Robinson et al. (2001) reason that reducing children's media exposure could lessen their identification with aggressive heroes and reduce their enactments of domination scripts in their playground interactions. In the case of obesity, three media-related mechanisms have been found in the literature. First, that children substitute watching TV for more active play; second, that in watching more TV, children will be exposed to more snack and fast-food advertisements; third, that children develop a particular habit of eating while they watch. Robinson et al. developed a schools-based programme for reducing that risk through media education. At the test school, researchers found children in the media risk-reduction intervention had reduced their TV viewing by about one-third. They also found that, after six months, the weight gain in the treatment schools was significantly lower. Moreover, based on ratings of playground aggression, frequencies of bullying and rough-and-tumble play were about 25 per cent lower in the treatment school than those at the control school.

# CODA

From the beginning of the twentieth century, when advertisers first set out to evaluate the persuasive impact of their copy, researchers addressed the most pressing practical questions of the modern period. In presenting this overview of the experimentalist tradition, we have focused on four of these: (1) What makes propaganda persuasive? (2) Do media threaten or enhance democratic decision-making? (3) Can media enhance learning and public education? (4) Does watching violent programming contribute to aggressive children? Of course, many other issues were investigated experimentally, which we have not discussed here. Yet we hope it is clear why the statistical comparison of evidence gathered under carefully controlled situations emerged as the favoured method of those designing and managing public communication efforts.

Effects research has often been ridiculed by humanist critics for its pragmatism, its mindless adherence to positivism, and its failure to appreciate the complexity of communication. Laboratory researchers, the critics chided, could never discover anything of importance, relying as they did on the responses of convenience student samples, to simplified communications situations and unrealistic stimulus materials. To some extent, these allegations were true of the early practitioners. The experimental approach was deployed less often to discover new theories than to construct a valid test of the role that particular variables and communication techniques played. Although no unifying laws of persuasion were discovered, it still seems fair to say that this research was of some interest, for it did illustrate the many factors influencing use of media, learning and persuasion effectiveness – from source credibility to visualization.

It also seems fair to say that, in their quest for valid tests of causal processes, the effects researchers also confronted the deficiencies of their own methodology. The early craft of experimental design was based on comparison of evidence gathered from controlled samples of subjects in carefully controlled situations. But a science develops from the criticisms of other scientists. The last 50 years of experimental audience research has made a threefold contribution to our understanding of mediated communication processes. First, as we have already argued, the evidence of limited effects from these laboratory studies was important in challenging the prevailing theory of a passive mass audience: it replaced the so-called hypodermic needle model with a medium theory that recognized the many different factors involved in mediated social influence processes.

Second, the experimentalist researchers were forced to develop better ways of observing and measuring small effects on audiences. They did so, both by refining their understanding of the mental processes involved (attention, comprehension, resistance to persuasion, judgement and evaluation, attitude change, choice and intentionality, etc.), and by improving the sensitivity and reliability of their survey techniques for measuring perceptions, cognitions, attitudes and affective responses of audiences, including new technologies like eye-tracking, semantic differential and physiological programme evaluation.

Third, effects researchers came to acknowledge the lack of ecological validity of even the best designed laboratory studies, so they took the *logic of controlled comparison* into the field. Confronting the complexity of studying the impact of media on diverse populations *in situ*, effects researchers have innovated in field research and pioneered multivariate statistical tools, including sampling strategies (panels, split halves), and inferential statistics (Anova, Regression Modelling), in the course of developing field research designs such as natural experiments, community clinical trials and longitudinal surveys.

No single investigation is ever definitive, in proving or disproving a theory. A science rests on knowledge that is constantly debated and based on a cumulative sifting of evidence. An important aspect of the debates about media effects is the growing sophistication of research design. Anyone interested in studying the impact of media therefore needs to account for both the complexly interacting situational factors shaping the use and impact of media on audiences, as well as the methodological issues encountered in studying them.

# Chapter Sixteen

## The experimental audience research toolbox: the controlled experiment

### EXPERIMENTALISM AND ITS LIMITATIONS

Cultural theorists like Ien Ang have often dismissed the media effects research tradition out of hand, for its incipient positivism. It has become increasingly common for cultural studies scholars to berate effects researchers for their missionary scientism, which applies tests of statistical significance 'as instruments of torture on the data until it confesses something which could justify publication in a scientific journal' (Cumberbatch 2001). These critics often claim the moral superiority of humanist contextualism to the ruthless objectivism of science, because science regards human subjects as objects to be controlled in the scientific quest for causal generalities isolating the communication processes from the cycles of daily life (Barker and Petley 1997). Such critics condemn all psychological studies of media effects with the same brush strokes as if this social-science tradition exemplified the worst reductionist tendencies of behaviourism.

Having just reviewed the effects literature, we can agree that some behavioural psychologists did set out to study persuasive communication in the controllable circumstances of university laboratories or classrooms, where subjects were readily available and pliable participants in their forays into the 'laws of human nature'. These behaviouralist pioneers rarely reflected on how the laboratory limited their ability to generalize from their experimental situations to the world writ large. For this reason, their behaviourism became the justifiable target of those social critics of quantitative audience research. We think it is fair to say that many of those lab studies contributed little to the science of audiences, because the situations they observed bore so little relation to more complex conditions in which daily social communication is transacted and experienced. In short, these researchers failed to adequately operationalize the complex social processes, or cultural practices, implied in their causal explanations. Yet we think that the experimental methods developed by 'effects researchers', are too narrowly equated with the pragmatism that motivated these audience researchers, and fail to acknowledge the many other methodological innovations, undertaken by effects researchers, like Himmelweit, Schramm, Williams, Huesmann and Huston, who, recognizing the limitations of the lab, pioneered field experiments to test out their theories of the media's impact on social life.

It is clear that effects researchers are now rarely naïve positivists. As we saw in the last chapter, experimental forays into media effects did precipitate an ongoing and increasingly sophisticated debate about quantitative design strategies for managing error. Every trained social scientist knows that one study can never 'prove' a causal theory. Rather, over time and through critical evaluation, the weight of evidence that accumulates favours some tentative explanations over others.

Perhaps the most important methodological critique emerging within the effects tradition, concerns ecological validity in experimental research design. Indeed, ecological validity is now a widely accepted criterion with which to evaluate all communications research. Audience effects researchers must be especially mindful of the many contextual factors that impinge upon the dialogue between researchers and subjects. But this issue of intrusiveness must be applied to all empirical inquiry, including reception and ethnographic accounts of the audience. As the discursive model of the research process outlined in Chapter 1 points out, the insertion of an observer into a household or workplace is never neutral: in undertaking observations, we are always 'constructing' a unique definition of that situation as a place of scientific investigation, and a new definition of the human subjects who inhabit it, as being observed, studied and interrogated in the name of scientific inquiry.

Causal relationships prove hard to define, hard to isolate, hard to measure and harder still to demonstrate convincingly in the field or lab. Most contemporary effects researchers are therefore keenly aware of the many potential sources of uncertainty that plague the social sciences generally, and experiments in particular (Devereux 1967). The following discussion is intended to outline the basic rationales of inferential statistics used in controlling error. We have included this because we believe that knowledge of statistical inferences provides a useful tool for improving validity by accounting for error. This emphasis on statistical inferences does not imply that we are downplaying other aspects of research design and conduct. It is merely intended to point out that from the moment we begin to formulate our hypotheses and operationalize our variables, we need to understand the logic of comparison that helps us evaluate our findings.

The following toolbox discusses three highly practical ideas underlying experimental research design. The first concerns the operationalization of causal relations as testable hypotheses; the second outlines some parameters of experimental design that help frame the methodological decisions made in experimental studies; the third introduces the basic inference tools, now mostly computerized, that are used in evaluating the magnitude of the effect both in the lab and in the field. This discussion is not, however, meant to be exhaustive; rather it is intended for those who want to understand the issues underlying contemporary experimental research approaches, and have the basic language of statistical inference used in designing and conducting a study of media effects. It should be equally useful for students who only wish to read and evaluate the work of others. As we have seen in the long-standing debates about media violence, knowledge of quantitative statistical reasoning is particularly important for advocates who wish to participate in controversial public debates about media risks, including obesity, literacy, health and media addictions, where the validity of evidence is carefully scrutinized and often contested by industry.

# TOWARDS AN EXPERIMENTAL METHOD

## OPERATIONALIZING THE CAUSE–EFFECT RELATIONSHIP

The desire to understand why things change is at the root of an inquiry into determinacy relations. Perhaps the most practical idea in the effects researcher's kitbag, then, is an operational definition of causality. We have argued that the analysis of determinacy must not only establish the degree of association between two independently measured variables, but also meet three additional conditions of a cause–effect relationship between those variables: (1) the independent variable must precede the dependent variable in time; (2) there should be no intervening variables or spurious linkages; and (3) there must be a clear explanatory rationale of the direction of influence (see Gray and Guppy 1999).

To distinguish between 'associations' and 'determinacy', researchers have formalized both the temporal and directional assumptions of these causal conditions. Adapted from physics, causality can be defined as a temporal relationship between two independently observed variables, such that the presence (or onset) of the antecedent cause (X) produces a change in the state of the effect ($\Delta Y$). The convention is that the antecedent condition is called the *independent* variable, in order to signify the direction of its influence on the *dependent* variable. The minimum requirement is that a cause must be observed *prior* to the expected change in the dependent variable. We can represent these temporal and directional conditions generally as a model of the causal process, in a statement that says:

$$\text{if } X > \Delta Y$$

The use of the arrow in no way implies that the change in Y is entirely a result of X, but rather that in studying causality we are only interested in the part of that change that can be attributed to X.

## TESTING THE HYPOTHESES

The idea of experimental proof also requires a procedure for deciding between competing explanations of our results. Our general model of the causal relationship is operationalized in time as a process of change, which helps us formulate the hypotheses as probabilistic expectations of repeated observations of the dependent and independent variables. To test for a causal relationship, we must both establish that a predicted change in the dependent variable follows the independent one, and determine whether such changes can confidently be attributed to the independent variable.

A scientific argument cannot provide absolute proof of a determinate relationship, but only eliminate explanations. Proof is constituted *through process of evaluating competing causal explanations* stated in the form of hypotheses. Our hypotheses are formulated as two predictions that *compare* our expectations if the causal relationship holds, with our expectations if it does not. All that we assume in calculating these expectations is that X must be observed independently, and prior to ΔY. The convention is to expect *the null hypothesis* – that is, to confirm the prediction that no causal relationship exists between the dependent and independent variables. More formally, the null hypothesis states that *the probability of changes* in the dependent variable when X is present will be no different than the probability of changes occurring without it. The alternate hypothesis predicts that the probability of changes in the dependent variable (ΔY) are greater when the independent variable has been observed. Causal hypotheses are compared as follows.

H0: prob of ΔY given X = prob of ΔY given no X
H1: prob of ΔY given X = prob of ΔY given no X

The statistical test for determinacy compares these two conditions: the expectation when X the independent variable was present, and when it was not. The grid in Table 16.1 represents these two expected outcomes in tabular form, and the inferences we might draw.

Table 16.1    Expectations for independent observations of X and Y in sequence

| Independent variable | Dependent variable | |
| --- | --- | --- |
| | ΔY | No ΔY |
| X | H1: causal relation *sufficient condition* | H0: no causal relation *random variation* |
| No X | H0: no causal relation *random variation* | H1: no causal relation *necessary condition* |

Causality can be tested by statistical evaluation of the probabilities predicted by the null hypothesis: if the differences are small, then it must be said that there is no evidence that X is a *sufficient condition* **to change** the state of Y; but if there is a large difference between the two probabilities, then we cannot be certain that there is no effect. This statistical logic of comparison is the basic principle of quantitative experimental design.

## DESIGNING EXPERIMENTS

Experimental inquiry starts by asking: if X causes a change in Y, how can I observe that relationship in such a way to confidently say whether X *significantly contributes* to that change. Experimental design refers, then, to a process of decision-making through which the researcher attempts to optimize the validity of the study. Design decision-making considers the sampling strategy, its size and frame, the measurement techniques and instruments used, the situation in which observations are made, and the treatments or comparisons for testing the hypotheses. The objectives of design are twofold: first, the experimenter wants to contribute to scientific debate by optimizing the study's explanatory power; second, the researcher wants to be confident that the conclusions he or she draws are justified by the observations made of the causal relationship. Since the word 'contribute' does not assume that X is the only reason that Y changes, design subsumes some speculative reasoning in which the researchers also clarify how they will *control* for spurious or confounding factors that could lead to erroneous conclusions.

In the previous chapter, we discussed the many different examples of effects research. We can identify three typical approaches to experimental method, based on the trade-off between the ecological validity of the study and the potential to control or account for competing explanations: (1) the natural experiment, (2) the field or clinical trial, and (3) the laboratory experiment. At one end of this spectrum is the *natural experiment*, in which the researcher optimizes ecological validity by observing the causal relationships natura-listically, or *in situ* – that is, observing the process when and where it occurs, without intervention. Naturalistic experiments, however, do require controls in the form of a time- and place-based sampling frame, in order to ensure an unbiased estimate of the occurrence of a causal relationship. This approach is perhaps best exemplified in the work of Robert Kubey and Mihaly Csikszentmihalyi (1990b). The advantage of a natural experiment is its ecological validity – that is, our confidence that the evidence we have gathered occurs with the same frequency, and in same context of the patterned flow of everyday life.

In the *field trial*, the determinacy relationship is also observed *in situ*, and usually for a con-siderable time, but the researcher controls the sample in such a way as to ensure that groups differ in relation to the independent variable. In clinical trials, the treatment is administered by the experimenter, but in most field studies, the competing explanations are controlled by identifying groups of subjects in which the independent variable is known to differ naturally. Perhaps the best example of this field experiment approach was the Williams et al.'s (1986) study in which the researchers compared three similar com-munities over two years, before and after multiple television channels were introduced. The disadvantage of this approach, however, is the enormous costs and resources necessary to do longitudinal field studies. In many cases, the sample size is huge so that we can account for the diversity of circumstances surrounding audience behaviours, and make up for the high subject drop-out rates.

In a *laboratory experiment*, the researcher chooses to increase explanatory power by control-ling both the sample and the situation, to ensure that the comparisons provide a valid test of the hypotheses. In a *controlled experiment*, the assumptions about the causal processes are built into the treatment. A treatment refers to attempts by the researcher to manipulate the subjects' experience of the independent variable, and related aspects of the situation in which the subject experiences it. Assuming random assignment to experimental condi-tions, the researcher can distinguish the changes in the dependent variable that are due to the treatment, from changes due to other situational factors. In clinical trials, the compar-ison is between two or more *treatment groups*, which are carefully controlled with respect to the presence or degree of the independent variable. The word treatment is a carry-over from the health sciences, where the administration of some cure to one group and a placebo to another, defines the control. The groups that receive any kind of treatment constitute the *experimental groups*, while the subjects that do not (which provide the baseline for comparison) are called the *control group*. We have already discussed the Bandura study as an exemplar of this experimental approach (Chapter 14). The advantage, as we saw, was the precision with which the researcher could study the imitation hypothesis. The disadvantage mainly concerned the limited ability to generalize the findings to other circumstances.

There are two ways of framing the sampling controls in a lab experiment, depending on the assignment of subjects to conditions. Referred to as the *clinical trial (between-subjects) design*, many laboratory experiments compare a group of subjects randomly assigned to the treatment condition where it is known whether the independent variable occurs, with similar subjects in a control group. But an alternative is a *factorial (within-subjects) design*, where the experimenter compares the same subjects under different treatment conditions, comparing across situations in which the subjects experience the treatment with a condition when they do not. For example, if we want to compare the play behaviour of a sample of boys aged four to six years, before and after watching two different cartoons – one that has character toys associated with it and the other that doesn't – we can structure our experiment in two ways. We can compare the play of two groups of matched subjects who watch either cartoon 1 or cartoon 2. In this case, the comparison is between the groups. Or we can watch the same boys playing after watching both cartoons (randomly altering the order), comparing each individual's behaviour under the two conditions. In either case, if the sampling is randomized and the circumstances of exposure are the same in most respects, then any significant difference in the boy's play behaviour can be attributed to either chance or the difference in the cartoons.

## OPERATIONALIZING CHANGE

Directionality and temporality are the key aspects of experimental design. Since our goal is to observe a specified *process of change* in the dependent variable (signified as $\Delta Y$), the basis of all comparisons for testing our hypothesis is that the dependent variable is a material process, taking place in time and having duration, so we must observe it at two moments – an idea we can express mathematically as dependent variable $\Delta Y = Yt2 - Yt1$. All tests of change are designed as a time-based series of observations, which use a specified sampling strategy that anticipates the duration of the causal process and specifies who is to be observed, when and for how long. In before and after studies, the control is designed to ensure that the treatment is administered to the experimental group at a known time between sampling moments T1 and T2.

Audience researchers must be particularly mindful to clarify the temporal considerations in their causal hypothesis: for example, Carl Hovland's discovery of the 'sleeper effect' revealed how comprehension scores sampled immediately after reception of a communication must be distinguished from the long-term persuasion, because active cognitive processing and opinion formation take place over a considerable period (Chapter 15). Similarly, Stein and Friedrich specified in their treatment a 'media diet', sustained over a ten-day period, because they did not expect an effect of measurable magnitude after a single exposure to violent cartoons. These examples remind us that all experimental designs must clarify the duration of the determinacy relationship to ensure construct validity and to formulate an appropriate sampling frame.

## TESTING THE HYPOTHESIS: CONTINGENCY ANALYSIS WITH NOMINAL VARIABLES

To apply these considerations in experimental design, let us imagine that we want to study the relationship between children's watching of violent TV programmes and aggression. (Before you read on, you may want to go back to Chapter 10 to refresh your understanding of the statistical terminology used in the following hypothetical experimental studies.) Our ambition is to determine whether watching violent television (independent variable = content of the TV programme) increases the likelihood of aggressive behaviour (dependent variable = subsequent aggressive behaviour). We must therefore operationalize both 'watching violent TV' and 'aggressive behaviour'. Clearly this is no easy task, but for now let us say that each observation of the independent variable can be reliably coded for the presence or absence of violent TV programming (Violent TV programme = 1 or non-violent programme = 2) in the one-minute period prior to the observation of the child's behaviour. We will operationalize the dependent variable ($\Delta Y$) with a simple nominal measure made during the two-minute period following the coding of content. To do so, assume we can code aggressive behaviour (1 = no aggression, 2 = behaved aggressively) based on the observation of all acts of verbal and physical threats, hitting, throwing at or tripping. The hypotheses below state the alternatives we must investigate.

> H0: Children do not act aggressively after watching violence on TV.
> H1: Watching violent TV causes children to become aggressive.

Let us start our discussion by imagining a naturalistic experiment in which we observe 2000 children in homes after school (4–6 pm). Our sampling strategy specifies a random observation of 2000 households, between 4 and 6 pm, for one minute, noting if the child is watching television, and whether what they are watching contains violence. We will then code each child's actions during the next two minutes, noting if the child's behaviour includes any aggressive acts. Table 16.2 provides some hypothetical data.

We find that descriptive statistics can tell us a lot. Examining the data above we find that, of the 2000 observations, only in 50 per cent were children actually watching TV after school, because in many of the observations we made, the children were either playing or socializing. Clearly, we made a lot of observations that were not pertinent to our causal hypothesis, but this effort is not entirely wasted, for we have a baseline indication that

Table 16.2   Hypothetical TV violence study: observation data

| Independent variable | Aggression observed | No aggression | Totals |
|---|---|---|---|
| Not exposed to violent TV | 85 | 1704 | 1879 |
| Watching non-violent TV | 14 | 865 | 879 |
| Other activity | 69 | 839 | 1000 |
| Exposed to violent TV | 21 | 100 | 121 |
| Total households | 106 | 1804 | 2000 |

even without media exposure some children (6.9 per cent) will act aggressively. It was also clear that children are aggressive even after watching non-violent TV programmes (1.4 per cent), although aggression was observed after violent TV in 17 per cent of the observations. We can conclude that the occurrence of aggressive behaviour in the after-school period is rather infrequent (only .053 of our observations), which justifies our decision to undertake a sizeable sample.

We might, at first, be tempted to compare the observations of children exposed to violent TV programmes (21/121 = 17.4 per cent) with those that weren't (85/1879 = 4.5 per cent), but thinking carefully about the null hypothesis, we will recognize that this comparison confounds the aggression that occurs in after-school play sessions (other activity category) with that after watching non-violent TV. A more precise test of the hypothesis would derive from comparing the probability of aggressive incidents after watching TV violence with that after watching non-violent TV. Our inferential statistical analysis will therefore only include the 1000 observations in our sample, in which children were actually watching TV.

Since both of these variables are nominal, we interpret the contingency table in a manner similar to the Chi-square test (and under similar assumptions about observed and expected values), to see whether aggressive play occurred more frequently in periods after watching TV violence than would be expected by chance.

How, though, can we determine whether the frequency of aggression after viewing violent TV is significantly greater than it is without it? Assuming there is no effect of violent TV, we expect the same proportion of children to act aggressively after watching violent TV as after watching non-violent TV. Using the marginal totals, we calculate that of the 121 children who saw violent TV, the expected frequency of children acting aggressively is ($Fe = 35 \times 121/1000 = 4$), and (121 − 4 =) 119 who would not. Since our actual data found that 21 children acted aggressively and 100 didn't, we surmise that there is a directional tendency for viewers of violence to be more aggressive. The chart in Table 16.3 uses the formula (fe = row marginal × column marginal/n) to calculate the observed and expected values for the contingency table.

Table 16.3  Calculation of the expected values for the contingency table from the hypothetical observed data

| Observed values | Aggression | No aggression | |
|---|---|---|---|
| Non-violent TV | 14 | 865 | 879 |
| Violent TV | 21 | 100 | 121 |
| | 35 | 965 | 1000 |
| Expected values | Aggression | No aggression | Row marginals |
| Non-violent TV | $35 \times 879/1000 = 31$ | $965 \times 879/1000 = 848$ | 879 |
| Violent TV | $35 \times 121/1000 = 4$ | $965 \times 121/1000 = 117$ | 121 |
| Column marginals | 35 | 965 | 1000 |

Before rejecting the null hypothesis, however, we must evaluate the contingency table with the Chi-square statistic, using the following formula:

$$\text{Chi-square} = \text{sum } (fo - fe)^2/fe$$
$$= (14 - 31)^2/31 + (21 - 4)^2/4 + (865 - 848)^2/848 + (100 - 117)^2/117$$
$$= 9.32 + 72.25 + .34 + 2.47$$
$$= 84.38 \text{ with } (2 - 1)(2 - 1) \text{ degrees of freedom}$$

We can use the Chi-square statistic to test for independence between these nominal variables, because it provides a calibration of the expected magnitudes of the sum of the differences between the observed and expected frequencies given the number of distinctions in our variables, or degrees of freedom. Looking up the Chi-square statistic at the .01 confidence limit $(X = 6.635)$, we reject our null hypothesis based on this data.

## TESTING CAUSAL HYPOTHESES ABOUT SCALAR VARIABLES

The nominal measures we have used, however, provide a rather imprecise test of our hypothesis, because we have only observed whether the child enacts at least one aggressive behaviour in the time period. It may be reliable and easy to use, but its explanatory power is limited because it fails to represent either the intensity or the frequency of aggressive acts. It also conflates a number of different types of aggressive response – both playful and hurtful – into a single construct. So imagine instead that we operationalized our dependent variable as an ordinal scale, by coding the child's behaviour as follows: 0 (no aggression), 1 (mild verbal aggression), 2 (lively imaginary aggression), 3 (pushing and confrontation) and 4 (hitting with intent to hurt or injure). We now have a measure of the 'intensity' of aggression. Since the scale is ordinal, each category has a specific meaning, but with an implied increase of intensity as the number increases. Descriptive statistics are always a good starting point for understanding any data set. Examining the frequency for our ordinal measure for the same sample of 1000 children who were

Table 16.4    Descriptive statistics for dependent scalar operationalization of aggressive behaviour

|  |  | | Behaviour observed | | |
|  |  | Frequency | Per cent | Valid per cent | Cumulative per cent |
| --- | --- | --- | --- | --- | --- |
| Valid | no aggression noted | 965 | 96.5 | 96.5 | 96.5 |
|  | mild verbal aggression | 11 | 1.1 | 1.1 | 97.6 |
|  | lively playful aggression | 20 | 2.0 | 2.0 | 99.6 |
|  | pushing and shoving | 2 | .2 | .2 | 99.8 |
|  | hitting to hurt | 2 | .2 | .2 | 100.0 |
|  | Total | 1000 | 100.0 | 100.0 |  |

watching TV, we might expect the descriptive statistics from our SPSS analysis to look like Table 16.4.

Displaying the frequencies as percentages confirms once again that the predominant behaviour is 'no aggression' (96.5 per cent) while watching TV in the after-school period. We know that in this sub-sample of 1000 children, only 3.5 per cent will exhibit aggressive tendencies while watching TV. We note as well that aggression is not only relatively rare but of low intensity, consisting predominantly of verbal and playful aggressiveness (3.1 per cent). Real pushing and fighting is not a common behaviour during television viewing (.4 per cent).

If we have chosen to measure our dependent variable in this way, how can we evaluate whether the intensity of aggressive acts is significantly greater after watching violent TV, than after watching non-violent TV? One approach would be to compare the average aggressiveness scores of those that saw violence with those that watched non-violent TV. Rephrasing our null hypothesis we might predict the following.

> H0: There will be no difference between the average aggressiveness ratings of children watching violent programming compared with those watching non-violent programming.
> H1: the aggressiveness of those who watched violent programming is on average higher than for those who watched non-violent programming.

Applying our ordinal scale to the same 1000 observations of the TV-watchers above, we can calculate the average aggression rating of .14 for the whole sample. For the 879 children who watched non-violent programmes, the mean aggression rating was .1, whereas for those who saw violence, the mean was .23, or about twice that of those who saw non-violent programmes. But is this significantly larger? Table 16.5 displays the means and standard deviations to be tested under the null hypothesis.

Table 16.5   SPSS output shows means and standard deviations for calculation of student t statistic

Report

Behaviour observed

| TV content | Mean | N | STD deviation |
|---|---|---|---|
| non-violent TV | 2.84E-02 | 879 | .25 |
| violent TV | .33 | 121 | .78 |
| Total | 6.50E-02 | 1000 | .37 |

Group statistics

Behaviour observed

| TV content | N | Mean | Std deviation | STD error mean |
|---|---|---|---|---|
| non-violent TV | 879 | 2.84E-02 | .25 | 8.39E-03 |
| violent TV | 121 | .33 | .78 | 7.08E-02 |

The statistical test used for comparing the magnitude of the difference between two means is called the *student t*. What this statistic does conceptually is compare the variance expected for two samples with different means, with that expected for a single random sample with a known mean. Remember, the total sample mean is not an absolute number, but an estimate of the magnitude of error based on the distribution of aggression scores in the sample. As discussed in Chapter 10, if randomly sampled, we can generally assume that these aggression scores will be normally distributed around the mean of that sample, and the mean will provide an unbiased estimate of the population mean.

We note that the mean and variance are small numbers, in large part because there are so many observations rated 0=no violence observed. In fact, our ordinal scale does not provide a normal distribution, but rather one that is heavily skewed towards the zero. We will ignore this issue for the time being by assuming that calculation of the standard deviation will incorporate a standardized comparison of the frequency of aggressive and non-aggressive behaviour.

The standard deviation is the key statistic used in the calculation of this statistic because it provides a standardized measure of the dispersal of these scores around that mean. The logic of the student t test can be understood in this way. If there is no difference in group means attributable to what they watch, then the standard deviation for the whole sample provides a suitable estimate of the variability for the whole population. Figure 16.1 shows the two distribution curves for these estimates: one calculating the standard deviation, based on the assumption of no effect, comparing that with the actual difference of known size.

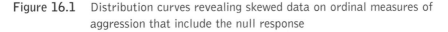

**Figure 16.1**   Distribution curves revealing skewed data on ordinal measures of aggression that include the null response

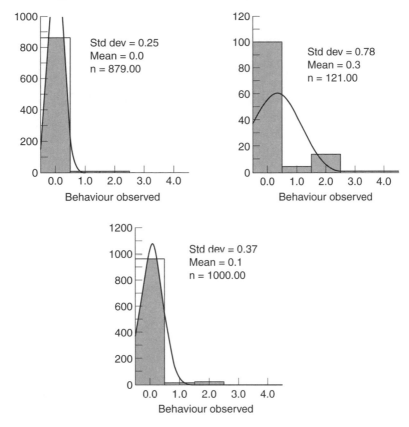

The procedure for testing these three distributions is to compare the standard deviation around the mean for the whole sample, with that for the non-violent TV and violent TV groups separately. The formula for calculating the student t statistic is as follows.

$$T = X_1 - X_2/Sp \text{ square root } (1/n_1 + 1/n_2) \text{ with degrees of freedom } n_1 + n_2 - 2$$

Where $X_1$ and $X_2$ are the means of Group 1 and 2 respectively, and $n_1$ and $n_2$ represent their sample size.

Substituting in this equation for Sp (total standard deviation) =

$$(n_1 - 1) n_2 + (n_2 - 1)S^2_2/n_1 + n_2 - 2$$

The student t statistic is used to compare the likelihood of a difference between group means $X_1$ and $X_2$ with standard deviations $S_1$ and $S_2$, with that pooled Sp calculated for the sample as a whole. In this way, the student t statistic helps us decide if the standard deviations calculated around these two separate means are significantly smaller than that for the sample as a whole.

Table 16.6   SPSS output for student t test differences between means

Independent samples test

| | Levene's test for equality of variables | | t-test for equality of means | | | | | 95% confidence interval of the difference | |
|---|---|---|---|---|---|---|---|---|---|
| | F | Sig. | t | df | Sig. (2-tailed) | Mean difference | Std error difference | Lower | Upper |
| Behaviour observed | | | | | | | | | |
| Equal variances | 289.514 | .000 | −8.733 | 998 | .000 | −.30 | 3.46E-02 | −.37 | −.23 |
| Equal variances assumed | | | −4.238 | 123.389 | .000 | −.30 | 7.13E-02 | −.44 | −.16 |

Again, we note that our group means differ significantly. In fact, the likelihood of differences between means of this size is $p. > .001$, which means we accept that in rejecting the null hypothesis we would be wrong 1 out of 1000 times.

# REGRESSION MODELLING

Still more explanatory power can be achieved in the design if both the dependent and independent variables are scalar. For example, in the above example, if we had also measured the intensity of the violence that the children watched on TV, using a numeric scale from $0 =$ no violence to $5 =$ lots of violence, we could develop a predictive model of the relationship between seeing more violence on TV and the intensity of aggressive behaviour following exposure.

The assumption of directionality in our definition of causality implies that as the intensity of the independent variable increases, we expect that changes in the dependent variable become both more likely and larger in magnitude. We also expect that the intensity of the dependent variable decreases if the cause diminishes. We are therefore able to formulate a more precise mathematical model based on this hypothetical linear relationship between independent and dependent variables. Assuming again the normal variation in both the dependent and independent variables, our mathematical model can be represented as a hypothetical straight line of a constant slope. Much like the correlation, if there is no relationship between the normalized dependent and independent variables, the slope of the line expected is 0. But in this hypothetical case, the modelling of a relationship meets both criteria for causality, because we have ensured that the independent variable occurs prior

Table 16.7   SPSS output describing observations of intensity of the violence in hypothetical TV content

TV content

| | | Frequency | Per cent | Valid per cent | Cumulative per cent |
|---|---|---|---|---|---|
| Valid | no violence | 879 | 87.9 | 87.9 | 87.9 |
| | very mild violence | 21 | 2.1 | 2.1 | 90.0 |
| | cartoon fighting | 88 | 8.8 | 8.8 | 98.8 |
| | war cartoons | 6 | .6 | .6 | 99.4 |
| | realistic fighting | 3 | .3 | .3 | 99.7 |
| | brutal killing | 3 | .3 | .3 | 100.0 |
| | Total | 1000 | 100.0 | 100.0 | |

to and predicts the direction of the specified changes in the dependent variable. Our statistical test for confirming the null hypothesis must determine whether the best-fitting line for our data has a slope $= 0$. If there is a relationship, then the slope would be significantly greater than 0. The regression statistics calculate the dispersal of the actual data points around a linear model that best fits the data set. The 'goodness of fit' of the regression line's predictive model is indicated by the value of r squared, which also provides an estimate of the total amount of the variance in the dependent variable, which can be explained by the independent one. The closer that r squared is to 1, the more of the variation in our data set our model has explained and the better the goodness of fit.

# IMPROVING EXPLANATORY POWER THROUGH DESIGN

## FROM NATURALISTIC TO CONTROLLED EXPERIMENTS

So far we have represented the causal process with the simple model if $X > \Delta Y$. This model assumes it is possible to examine ongoing causal processes in isolation from other factors that influence the dependent variable. The problem with this assumption, as we have seen, is that media use, in most day-to-day situations, entails many countervailing factors that, interacting together, may influence the change in the dependent variable. Most effects researchers know that many different factors contribute to the social communication of aggression – like the presence of toy weapons, which might also influence the social acting out of aggressiveness. We must assume too, that the causal process can interact with situational factors – like presence of peers or parents, or whether the TV is in the child's room – in the socialization of aggression. So unless we know how to account for these situational variables in our analysis, they will continue to confound us and blunt claims of significant effects (Garbarino 2001), which is why experimental researchers developed research designs that enabled them to account for these alternative explanations of their evidence, by 'controlling' some of the expected sources of error: first, through better sampling; second, by controlling the treatment situation to isolate the independent variables' contribution; third, by complexifying statistical tools for multi-factorial experiments.

## SAMPLING STRATEGY AS CONTROL

The basic control in experimental research is a random sample, for it is the assumption of random distribution that enables us to estimate the magnitude of error based on the distribution found in the sample. Yet natural experiments, especially longitudinal ones, are costly and arduous affairs, plagued by high drop-out rates, while subject to the same accusation that the intrusion of researchers (or cameras) makes even the most unobtrusive field experiments transparent to the subjects. For instance, although our study gathered random observations of 2000 different children, because a large number were just playing and socializing, only 1000 subjects were included in the comparison used to test our hypothesis about violence on TV and aggression. Moreover, as frequent as violent content is on TV, because of its temporal distribution within programmes, we observed only 121 acts of aggression in a random sample of programmes watched. The difficulty of a time-based naturalistic sampling of after-school behaviour is that we have gathered a lot of data that ends up being excluded from our statistical tests of the experimental group. Obviously, we might have preferred to have greater numbers of observations to test our effects hypothesis. This means we have to gather even larger samples.

In fact, we have observed many more instances of children *not becoming more aggressive* after watching TV violence (100) than we did of children acting aggressively (21). Moreover, the naturalistic sampling frame we used observed each child only once. This means that we don't have any way of knowing whether the 35 subjects who were aggressive were behaving 'normally' (for that subject) during this observation. And, because children infrequently act aggressively at home, we ended up with only 35 individuals in our statistical evaluation of the aggression effect. We are still left wondering whether our sample of 35 aggressive acts was based on a small group of children who are habitually aggressive, and also who disproportionately like to watch violent TV.

More importantly, perhaps, because we had not considered the context of children's after-school experiences, our ability to comment on the circumstances in which those 35 children acted aggressively was limited. Because our statistical tools are rooted in calculating the probability of error terms, we first need to consider how a *sampling strategy* can strengthen our assessment of competing explanations of the effect. Unfortunately we also had to exclude 1000 observations where the TV was off, which might have provided a baseline against which we could have compared viewing both non-violent and violent TV. So we cannot say whether after watching TV, children act or play more aggressively than they do without the TV on, or whether the presence of another child makes the watching of violence on television and acting aggressively more likely than when watching non-violent television.

To get around these limitations of our sample, let's imagine another study in which we adopt a *quota-based field study sample*. This new approach is intended to improve confidence in our test comparisons by increasing the number of observations in each condition, and enabling us to compare each subject's response across all three situations. Sometimes referred to as a factorial or 'repeated measures' design, our purposive sampling frame sets out to randomly observe 200 different children after school, three times each with the TV off, three times after watching a violent TV programme and three times after a non-violent incident.

Table 16.8  Chart showing quota sampling design and hypothetical mean aggression scores

| Sample of children n = 200 | No. of observations for each child | Observations for condition | Mean aggression rating observed | Standard deviation |
|---|---|---|---|---|
| Not watching TV | 3 | 600 | .13 | .35 |
| Watching non-violent TV | 3 | 600 | .02 | .22 |
| Watching violent TV | 3 | 600 | .33 | .41 |
| Total | 9 | 1800 | .18 | .32 |

Looking at the imaginary data above, we can note that the mean aggression score is greatest after watching TV violence (.33) and lowest while watching non-violent TV (.02). A moderate aggression score (.13) is observed in the non-TV condition, probably due to the fact that many children with the TV off engage in after-school horseplay (about 8 per cent, as noted earlier). We have used the t statistic to evaluate the size of differences between the means in two groups, usually a control group and an experimental one. To compare the means of these three conditions we will use the companion Anova (Analysis of Variance) procedure, which can help us test the magnitude of differences between the three or more group means. Although small, it is important to note that these differences are based not on comparing groups, but on *how the same subject acts in these three different conditions*: when they are not watching TV at all, after they have watched non-violent TV, and while they are watching violent TV. Because the comparison is between conditions, we don't calculate the between-groups sum of squares, but the between-subjects equivalent. Although the mathematics are beyond the scope of this toolbox, the Fisher Exact, or F, statistic is basically the same as for a comparison between experimental groups, except in this case we compare the mean standard deviations for the between-subjects scores with mean standard deviation for the within-subjects scores. The Anova procedure would partition the error estimates into *within-subjects* and *between-subjects* variations, and calculate the ratio between them for known degrees of freedom (df = # of groups −1 = 2). The key measure of significant differences is the

$$F = \text{Mean } S_{between}/\text{Mean } S_{within}$$

The F value increases as the magnitude of the variation between groups becomes greater than that within those groups, so values of F greater than that calculated at the .001 level for two degrees of freedom disconfirm the null hypothesis.

In reducing the sample to 200 children, we have to some degree sacrificed the *representativeness* of the sample in relation to the population. On the other hand, our confidence that our statistical comparisons are valid has been improved by our sampling strategy (600 observations in each of the three conditions) and because those differences have controlled for the variability of the individual subject's propensity to aggressiveness. No research design is perfect, so good research design depends on making thoughtful trade-offs.

## EXPERIMENTAL CONTROLS

Another way we can account for confounding factors is by controlling the situation in such a way that we can confidently distinguish between our experimental groups. Experimental controls can be achieved by specifying comparisons where the independent variables are *isolated*, so that there are no other factors contributing to the differences between our comparison groups. In our naturalistic hypothetical study, for example, we had no way of accounting for the presence of peers, which could influence the degree of a subject's aggressive response to a violent TV show. So now we might attempt to design an experiment that controls for the presence of peers. Imagine a matched sample of 200 boys randomly assigned in dyadic pairs to two groups: one group watches a violent episode of *Power Rangers* and another *Sesame Street*, in an after-school programme. After the programme, the TV is turned off and some toys are brought into the room so that the potentially confounding factors of aggressive toys and peer presence are eliminated. The experimenter observers what toys children play with and how they play with them.

Table 16.9   Hypothetical result from controlled exposure study

|  | Aggression rating | Standard deviation | Total |
|---|---|---|---|
| Group 1: watched *Power Rangers* | 3.0 | .33 | 200 |
| Group 2: watched *Sesame Street* | 1.2 | .09 | 200 |

Assuming random assignments, these controlled treatment conditions not only eliminate measurement error in the independent variables, but increase our confidence that differences in aggression scores between the group means must be because one group has seen a violent programme and the other has not. Controlled in this way, the student t statistic provides a fairly robust test for the null hypothesis about media violence and playful aggression.

The problem, of course, occurs when we generalize from the specifics of the experiment (cartoon violence, dyadic boy groups, artificial situation) to children's everyday behaviour. Three assumptions feature prominently in the critiques of laboratory research of this type. First, with regard to the samples and sampling strategies, experimentalists have used random assignment as the basis for ensuring the equivalence of the groups; but their studies are often already skewed by convenience samples (i.e. undergraduates) or by selection processes that could alter the results in other ways because of interaction effects (for example, comparisons across age for learning from TV, or violence research that doesn't control for gender as an important issue of sampling). Mindful of these assumptions, most experimental researchers report tests of whether their group assignments are normally distributed with regard to criteria variables, at least those that might reasonably be related to the causal relationship – for example, gender, age, class, education, etc.

With regard to experimental treatments and controlled situations, there is also good reason to examine carefully whether the controls seem plausible to the subjects and provide the basis for a useful comparison. In their reliance on laboratory controls, social psychologists have been rightly criticized for being transparently manipulative, simply to economize or simplify the study of audience practices. Researchers schooled in psychological methods can easily overlook the fact that to everyone but a psychology student, a laboratory is a non-natural situation in which the expectations and behaviours of subjects are set by environmental conditions and artificial definitions of the experimental situation. One might wonder whether the treatment is actually sufficiently different from the control situation. For example, in a disguised advertising effectiveness study, where test ads are inserted into programme material, we might want to check whether the subjects were actually watching the TV during the exposure.

Every controlled experiment makes a number of important assumptions that can and should be checked statistically. This means measuring possible confounding factors and then accounting for them in the data analysis. The first assumption to check is the randomized assignment. Data can be examined to check if the groups are comparable in key ways (especially, for example, their preferences for aggressive TV shows and perhaps their disposition towards aggressiveness). The second is that the treatment is the only difference between the two groups. For example, did different researchers (male and female) make the observations? The third is that both groups respond to the intervention in the same way. Did the children watch equally intently? The fourth is that there are no other (unobserved) factors in the environment or in the treatment process that might also influence the causal relationship. For example, did all the dyads know each other equally well? Each of these potentially confounding situational factors can be controlled in field studies *by measuring them as control variables.*

## COMPLEXIFYING STATISTICAL MODELS IN EXPERIMENTAL RESEARCH

We have argued that it is important to complexify our representation of causal relations to account for multiple and interacting factors in communication transactions. We can represent this multidimensional idea of determinate systems by a general formula where we seek to determine if $X > \Delta Y$ in situations where n other factors may also influence the dependent variable (i.e. also $A > \Delta Y$; $B > \Delta Y \ldots N > \Delta Y$). Although they are well beyond the scope of this toolbox, researchers can avail themselves of powerful new statistical tools for studying such systems of determinate relations where there are many factors influencing the dependent variable. For example, having controlled for the presence of peers in the previous study, we might then develop a more complex factorial experimental design that compares children's aggressiveness after exposure to violent and non-violent TV, when they are alone or with peers. Since it would be difficult to employ a repeated-measures design in this case, we will assume random assignment of matched individuals to each condition.

Table 16.10    Hypothetical result from a two-factor design studying toy play after watching violent television alone or in pairs

|  | Peer | Solitary | n= |
|---|---|---|---|
| *Sesame Street* | 1.2 | 1.1 | 100 |
| *Power Rangers* | 1.3 | 2.1 | 100 |
|  | 100 | 100 | 200 |

The inferential statistics we require for such a multi-factorial experiment are really just a more complex analysis of variance, called a Multiple Analysis of Variance (Manova), which examines the relationship between two or more factors (violent content; presence of peers) each of which might contribute independently to aggression, and which might also interact with each other. A similar logic of partitioning variation applies to the analysis of co-variance, which accounts for the standard deviations around the mean for each factor considered independently, and then again after the contribution of control factors have been accounted for. The hypothetical result above, for example, would hint at an interaction effect since children with peers play more aggressively only after watching violent TV, compared with when they are playing alone.

The legacy of 70 years of audience research has revealed the many kinds of error that exist due to sampling, context and interaction effects in experiments. Thinking situationally about treatments is an important part of contemporary experimental research design. Although these multidimensional inferential statistics are beyond the scope of this book, suffice it to say that most researchers today are using either multiple regression modelling, analysis of co-variance and multi-factorial designs to investigate the complex multi-determinate relations required by effects research. This means effects researchers must acquaint themselves with some rather complex statistical procedures. Students who want to undertake experimental research should consult more advanced texts on multivariate research design, especially if they are interested in field research (Skinner et al. 1989; Afifi and Clark 1996).

Another important advance in statistical procedures is the use of co-variance analysis to study interacting causes by mathematically partialling the independent contribution of each variable in a multivariate regression model. For example, perhaps we suspect that acting aggressively is contingent upon the child's identification with the protagonist in the programme. So we might modify our field experiment so that we measure both the degree of aggression in the programming (X1) and, through a questionnaire, rate the subjects' identification with different programme characters (X2). We can now calculate the variance explained by a model that includes only the single independent variable (X1 > ΔY), with one that includes both independent variables (X1 and X2 > ΔY). If these independent variables both independently contribute to aggression, then the model accounting for both variables will fit the data better than the model for just one. The predictive models can be compared and the partial contribution of various factors estimated, which is why, when designing field research, we often look for ways to control these alternative explanations by measuring the potentially confounding factors. The Johnson et al. (2002) study, discussed in Chapter 14, for example, employed such a co-variance analysis to examine whether heavy viewing of TV violence contributed to aggressiveness later in life, after accounting for other factors such as family and neighbourhood. It is worth noting that many effects researchers are gravitating towards the multiple regression risk models used in epidemiology, which has established a number of new criteria for evaluating causal evidence: (1) strength of association, (2) directionality, (3) specificity, (4) temporality, (5) determinacy gradient, (6) plausibility of causal explanation, (7) coherence with other evidence, (8) weight of experimental evidence, and (9) analogy (Bradford-Hill 1965, 1966).

## MEASUREMENT FACTORS IN EXPERIMENTAL DESIGN

We have argued that the twin tools of experimental research are good measurement and well-designed tests of evidence. The old adage about asking a silly question is meaningful to the effects researcher, because it doesn't matter how well designed the inquiry process if the variables are badly operationalized. Nominal variables are based on a mutually exclusive classification system, so the researcher can only make predictions about the frequency of the dependent variables' occurrence. Scalar variables are based on measurable differences in the intensity on a numeric scale, which enables us to employ more precise predictive models of the changes. So it is worth considering carefully the way we will be measuring our dependent and independent variables before we design the research. Moreover we must understand the different assumptions being made by the statistics we use to describe and assess our results.

There are four possible combinations of levels of measurement that we encounter in experimental research. It is important, therefore, to realize that the statistical procedures used for each of these designs will depend on the levels of measurement we have chosen. In this book, because we are not teaching statistics *per se*, we will not explain the rationale for these different statistical procedures, but rather provide some examples that can guide

Table 16.11    Rules of thumb for considering statistical procedures for different levels of measurement

| Type of design | Dependent variable | Independent variable | Statistic |
|---|---|---|---|
| Contingency | Nominal | Nominal | Chi-square |
| Compare groups; factorial | Nominal | Scalar | Student t; Anova |
| Compare treatments | Ordinal | Nominal | Non-parametric |
| Clinical trial; factorial | Ratio | Scalar | Regression; Manova |

the beginning researcher in his or her use of statistical packages. Table 16.11 shows some rules of thumb to use when thinking about appropriate statistics for different levels of measurement.

## THE LIMITS OF UNCERTAINTY

Experimental design employs the strategy of control as the key tool of validity. A control, we have suggested, does not refer only to a manipulation of the subject, but rather to the various ways that a researcher can account for all the sources of error in the inquiry process. It is through thoughtfully designed controls that the experimental researcher strives to eliminate competing hypotheses and alternate explanations of determinacy relations. Competing explanations are evaluated through comparisons of the evidence. The strategy of experimental control is ultimately based on the desire to make different subjects' experiences of media comparable. By pre-selecting the media content and ensuring all subjects see it, we can reduce the uncertainty associated with diverse viewing patterns. By ensuring the exposure is of constant duration and viewed in similar context, we become more confident that it is the subject's relationship to the content that matters; and if we have undertaken a representative sampling strategy that includes different kinds of subject, we may even be willing to generalize our findings to the population at large. In short, by carefully framing and orchestrating the experimental conditions of evidence gathering, experimental researchers strive to achieve greater explanatory power with less work through good research design.

Yet it is sometimes argued that the strategy of control used by experimental researchers is better suited to testing rather than exploring causal relations. It must be acknowledged that experimentalism in social sciences sometimes manifests itself as a paranoia about error, which can lead to an over-controlling attitude and rigid criteria for validity or proof of harm. The radical scepticism of behaviourists, especially, led to overly conservative trade-offs in research design (Devereux 1967). Yet some effects researchers have come to believe that the diagnostic application of statistics (factor analysis, model building, cluster analysis) holds great promise for a more diagnostic media effects project. Imbued again with a spirit of scientific discovery, media effects research can benefit enormously from multi-factorial statistical tools, which now enable communications researchers to conduct complex experimental field studies. Exploring complex data sets gathered in the field uses statistics to detect patterns, and thus develop hunches derived from evidence into testable postulates. Unfortunately there is no space here to justify the diagnostic use of statistics, but merely to assert our hope that the spirit of discovery can once again become an accepted part of media effects science.

# The Dual Challenge of 'Convergence' in Audience Research

# Introduction: the dual ☐ challenge

A research field can never just rest on the laurels of its past achievements. There are always fresh empirical phenomena emerging in the social landscape that need to be understood through investigation and theorization. Similarly, since no method is perfect, there are always methodological shortcomings that require researchers to try both to improve their existing tools and to develop new ones. The emergence of new technologies may in itself enlarge the audience researcher's analytical toolbox. In this section, we address some of the most prominent challenges facing audience research in the years ahead. Most of them have already been touched upon throughout the book, but here we wish to take the opportunity to deal with some of them more extensively, looking at ways in which our field of research is being innovated, in response to both new communicative phenomena emerging in contemporary society, and the methodological ambitions of audience researchers, always wishing to secure greater explanatory power for their findings.

The scope of this book does not permit us to go into detail on everything that might be said to be in some sense relevant to the study of audiences. Therefore we are not going into the challenges posed by processes of *globalization*, even though it is perhaps in the field of media and communication – often described as the emergence of a communicative 'global village' – that the legitimacy of the concept of globalization has been less contested than it has in other areas, such as economics. Suffice it to say that the globalization of communication calls for a wave of comparative audience research across cultures, as the local uptake of (usually American) standardized media fare may lead to very different cultural experiences and effects around the world. Among the prominent academic analyses already made of such processes, we recommend that you look at the comparative *Dallas* reception study by Liebes and Katz (1990), the comparative study of news audiences in seven countries across the globe directed by Jensen (1998), the triangulating comparative study of European children's use of old and new media directed by Livingstone (Livingstone and Bovill 2001), and the recent worldwide study of the Disney phenomenon (Wasko 2001).

Another challenge for audience research that we cannot address systematically here is the dramatic growth in commercially *applied research* over the last couple of decades. The phenomenon itself is by no means new – we need only remind ourselves of the use of audience measurement in the fields of advertising, publishing and broadcasting through the twentieth century (see especially Chapter 12). What is relatively new is for communication studies as a discipline to move to the epicentre of contemporary society, as a strategic tool for management efficiency and as a vital part of so-called expert systems (Giddens 1991; Beck et al. 1994), which use knowledge about communication to provide both the glue of internal cohesion for private and public organizations, and the lubricant of smooth and efficient relations between the various internal and external stakeholders of modern organizations and communities.

Audience research and user research are becoming unquestionable parts of this process which, following Fairclough (1993), we may term the 'technologization' of communication. Behind this term we find media institutions that are supplementing the quantitative base of their research with a wide array of qualitative methods, in their quest to understand and control audiences. We also find a mushrooming field of communication analysts and consultancies (often associated with the notion of 'public relations') boasting their intimate reliance on the cutting edge of the communication research frontier, offering their services to businesses and public organizations.

While stressing the control aspect of the technologization of communication research, we do not wish to imply that these strategic measures do not sometimes also work for the benefit of the audiences and users involved. Since the declared goal of these endeavours is often to promote relations of reciprocity and dialogue, while also improving organizational efficiency, the process remains poised uneasily between containment and empowerment (Grunig and Hunt 1984).

We now turn to a more thorough discussion of the challenges presented by the notion of methodological pluralism itself and by the increasing role of interactivity in contemporary mediated communication.

# Chapter Seventeen

# Convergence of methodologies: □ rethinking methodological pluralism

The methodological challenges perceived by quantitative and qualitative audience researchers alike all have to do with our being spurred on by a profound commitment to work towards greater relevance and explanatory power for our analyses of the audiences and users of mediated communication.

As a fundamental condition of empirical research, we have to live with the duality of, on the one hand, contributing to the advance of human knowledge about communicative processes, and on the other hand, the inherent temporariness of our theories and findings. We nevertheless strive constantly – in accordance with the epistemological objectives of discursive realism (Chapter 3) – to perfect our work in the service of greater 'truthlikeness'. Therefore, we are always trying to improve the scientific credibility of our work, by reflecting on how to innovate the ways we conceptualize and implement, from within our different disciplinary or more or less interdisciplinary camps, the scientific criteria of reliability, validity and generalization.

The conventional way to understand how the quantitative and qualitative approaches live up to these criteria, as we also dealt with them in Chapter 2, is encapsulated in the following quotation from a standard textbook: 'Quantitative observations provide a high level of measurement precision and statistical power, while qualitative observations provide greater depth of information about how people perceive events in the context of the actual situations in which they occur' (Frey et al. 1991: 99).

Translated into research criteria, the two approaches thus have their strong and weak sides. Qualitative research has greater ecological validity, because informants can put items on the agenda, researchers can probe, the data are strongly contextualized, etc. Quantitative research, conversely, has greater reliability, because its more formalized procedures of data collection and analysis increase the likelihood of obtaining consistent data and consistent codings; and its findings have greater generalizability, because of the larger samples and the sometimes random techniques used to recruit them.

Two European researchers, Friessen and Punie (1998), summarize the complementary strengths and weaknesses by saying that in quantitative methods we have a tool that can tell us a little about a lot of people, while qualitative methods enable us to say a lot about a few people. They go on to make a plea for the research strategy often referred to as *triangulation,* in which multiple (quantitative and qualitative) methods are used on the same object of study, in order to compensate for each other's weaknesses and together provide 'a better insight into the phenomenon we are studying' (Friessen and Punie 1998: 73). To continue along their proverbial line of reasoning, we might say that by adopting a triangulating approach we shall be able to say a lot, or at least more, about a lot of people.

We shall return below to the notion of triangulation and discuss Friessen and Punie's study as an excellent example of triangulation, but before doing so we shall dwell a little on initiatives that have been taken *within* the qualitative and quantitative camps, by researchers committed to improving their conventional methodological procedures, even if this means sacrificing some of their sacred cows, learning from credibility-enhancing practices imported from the other camp. Using reception research and survey research as examples of the spirit of cross-fertilization found in many quarters nowadays, we shall therefore take a look at qualitative researchers who wish to present findings that say a lot, and *with greater reliability*, about *more* people than has been normal in reception research, and at quantitative researchers who wish to say *more*, and *with greater validity*, about a lot of people than the typical uses and gratifications (U+G) study has been able to do. Finally, we shall consider ways of not just juxtaposing different methods sequentially, as in triangulation, but fully integrating them into one empirical design, as is possible in the often overlooked approach known as Q-methodology.

## INCREASING VALIDITY: SELF-CRITIQUES IN SURVEY RESEARCH

One of the most relentless methodological self-castigators within the U+G tradition has been Keith Roe, whose work has been associated especially with children's and adolescents' uses of the media (Roe and Muijs 1995). He is critical of questionnaire reliability, because it has been found that 'even after proper piloting, systematic major misunderstanding of questions occurs without interviewers being aware of it' (Keith Roe 1996: 91). He also believes that U+G researchers 'have been too concerned with the (very important) task of assessing reliability, at the expense of the still more important issue of validity' (1996: 90). He further points to the widespread occurrence of measurement error in survey research:

> *A typical survey item, even when well administered to a proper population sample, can yield up to 50 per cent non-valid variance. . . . We all know of this and, as with all deeply disturbing thoughts, we usually do our best to forget it whenever we can. We dismiss the qualitative critiques as 'unscientific' and if someone breaks ranks from within, the usual response is to offer platitudes, dismiss the heretic as a methodological purist (if not troublemaker), and promptly go back to business as usual. This strategy . . . has prevented any real methodological development, and has given extra ammunition to critics.*

(Keith Roe 1996: 87)

This critique does not come from someone who is busily deserting camp and on his way towards wholehearted adoption of a qualitative approach, which in many ways he finds just as deficient. Roe instead urges qualitative and quantitative researchers to cross-fertilize their work, because 'in many respects, they are doing an equally poor job' (Roe 1996: 90).

Walter Gantz, another established figure in the field, arrived at similar conclusions after having critically reviewed the merits of U+G research over a couple of decades (Gantz 1996). Gantz concludes that while the achievements of the U+G tradition are indubitable, the studies conducted within this tradition often have a very low explanatory value. In fact, his verdict is close to agreeing with that of the outside observer Justin Lewis, who observes that 'quantitative surveys have creaked and cranked their way to unconvincing conclusions' (Lewis 1997: 88). Stopping short of such a devastating conclusion, Gantz points to the need for doing something about 'the bias in research methods employed up until now':

> *The research agenda is likely to require alternative, if not innovative, methods of data collection. Interviews will need to be a mix of open- and closed-ended questions. Probes will be critical; interviewers will need to ask respondents what they mean when they say, for example, that they turn to television to be entertained or they watch out of habit . . . gratifications scholars will need to be creative and, as needed, supplement survey research . . . with depth interviews, where respondents are given ample opportunity to reflect and describe the nature of their relationship with media content.*

(Gantz 1996: 26–7)

This sounds very much like a plea not merely for qualitative pilot studies to precede the 'real' quantitative research, but for the adoption of a systematic strategy of quantitative/qualitative triangulation, with the purpose of drawing more authentic lifeworld data into one's analysis of media perceptions and experiences.

A different kind of qualitative critique of the data collection of survey research has been put forward by linguistic researchers who approach the standardized survey interview from the perspective of conversation analysis (see, for instance, Suchman and Jordan 1990; Houtkoop-Steenstra 2000). Here the ambition is to explore what can be done in order to improve the credibility of questionnaire research as questionnaire research.

These researchers carry out what we might call 'reception studies' of the standardized questionnaire as it is conventionally used in the situational interaction between interviewer and respondent. They ask how respondents make sense of the combined pre-scripted and locally produced dialogue of the research encounter. The main issue is whether the respondents' understanding and handling of the conventions of the questionnaire-based speech event are sufficient to make their 'performance' as research subjects reliable and valid. These studies thus go beyond the mere testing of questionnaire wordings, as they analyse the turn-taking in the standardized interview as an interactive practice that is jointly accomplished by interviewer and respondent.

Stressing that the interviewer is more than a mere mediator of the pre-scripted question-naire text, Stax (2000) explored how well respondents in a telephone interview were able to discriminate between and orient to the pre-scripted utterances read from the question-naire and the spontaneous turn-taking caused by respondents' need for clarification of the meaning of certain questions. Finding that many respondents were not able to do this, she expresses concern over the implications for data reliability and validity of such imperfect discrimination.

For instance, she finds that when faced with questions using a four-point rating scale, many respondents fail to use format-fitted answer categories like 'Agree' and 'Partly disagree', and instead fall back on more colloquial replies like 'That's fairly obvious'. Even when a format-fitted answer is secured immediately afterwards, by the interviewer re-invoking the scalar design, some respondents – complying somewhat grudgingly that 'I guess I sort of agree then' – might well believe that both their format-fitted responses to probes *and* other qualifying remarks will be recorded. Thus the recorded answers might not reflect the respondents' positions. Stax therefore recommends that interviewers should explicitly request, and if necessary insist, that respondents follow the 'rules of the game' of standardized interviews and not resort to everyday replies.

The critiques, from within and without, of quantitative approaches, thus show that remedies to the various problems of the questionnaire approach may take quite different forms, depending on the objectives of a particular survey project.

## INCREASING RELIABILITY AND GENERALIZABILITY: SELF-CRITIQUES IN RECEPTION RESEARCH

Always strong on validity, the qualitative path pursued by reception research has been beset by other problems, as most reception studies have analysed the media experiences of only a handful, or two, of informants, and usually presented insufficient evidence of the credibility of the interpretative process. Even if researchers working within the tradition would not subscribe to the devastating critiques coming from 'enemies' in the opposite camp, many have taken note of the methodological weaknesses pointed out by critics. Rosengren, for instance, points out that reception analysis is 'based on anecdotal data and defined as unformalized, exegetic studies of the meaning of individual experience . . . these studies, as a rule, neglect otherwise generally accepted tests of reliability, validity, and rep-resentativeness' (Rosengren 1993: 13).

One of the first and most persistent reception researchers to address credibility criteria has been Birgitta Höijer. From early on, drawing on her social science background in empirical fieldwork, she has admonished reception colleagues, coming from the introspec-tive text-analytical practices of the humanities, that qualitative empirical work requires systematic methodological reflection and planning, so that one doesn't fall for the 'typical example' in the interview transcript: 'From one or two concrete, vivid instances we assume there are dozens more lurking in the bushes – but we don't verify whether or how many there are, and there are usually fewer than we think' (Höijer 1990: 19). A similar critique is put forward by Bergman (1998), who is particularly concerned with the interpretative coding of the transcript, usually characterized dismissively with two-word labels like 'thematic analysis', 'discourse analysis' or following the principles of 'grounded theory'. She accuses reception researchers of having a magician's attitude to the reader, because the way they show their results corresponds to pulling a rabbit out of a hat – nobody is initiated into the actual analytical procedures used.

As we have argued above in connection with media ethnography and reception research, the first reliability-enhancing requirement is simply that the analyst must systematically and carefully describe all steps in the analytical process, including the researcher's pre-understandings of the issues, and specify exactly what was done and how. Second, all analytical points must be supported by extensive illustrative quotations from interview transcripts. Liebes (1984) showed the way (never taken up by later researchers) by publishing a two-column analysis of one full *Dallas* interview, with the transcript in one column and the analytical observations in the other. The implication is that this 'reading over her shoulder' during the analysis of a specimen interview enlightens other scholars about the analytical procedure followed in the other interviews as well: how she relates empirical observation to emerging themes and underlying theories.

Another reliability-increasing measure would be, time and funding permitting, to subject one's analysis to peer audit. This procedure, which was followed by Mick and Buhl's (1992) advertising reception study, gives congenial colleagues or paid scholars access to the data sets and the draft report for re-analysis of the data-material, so as to discover analytical points not sufficiently empirically grounded, or interesting phenomena not discovered in the data, as well as considering the justification for the theoretical claims made on the basis of the analysis. Any analytical discrepancies discovered through such a process can then be negotiated and clarified, and the truthlikeness of the findings thereby increased. A similar procedure using computer-aided coding by two independent coders was also followed by Drotner (2001).

The lack of interest in the systematic pursuit of reliability in qualitative audience research has had the character of an almost unconscious sin of omission. Reliability was ignored, either because it was too time-consuming in the research process or too voluminous in the research report, and often not believed to be of great consequence for the ultimate insight produced. In contrast, the frequent absence of generalization in qualitative research has been the result of sustained theoretical and political reflections among qualitative researchers.

The theoretical position against generalization goes back to the days when the differentiation between reception and ethnographic perspectives had not yet been clearly theorized (Drotner 1994), but it has lived on within the radical constructionist camp until the present day, based on the belief of some that generalization is undesirable if not impossible. This is because, when we engage audiences empirically, we are entering the difficult territory of 'the endlessly shifting, ever-evolving kaleidoscope of daily life' (Radway 1988: 366).

This multidimensionally complex everyday world can only be adequately studied through 'the principle of methodological situationalism' (Ang 1991: 162).

Following this position, we should therefore not delude ourselves that we can ever hope to make generalizations about the whole quilt of the audience, but only do a kind of gentle comparison of a few patches, because 'generalizations are necessarily violations to the concrete specificity of all unique micro-situations'. In other words, we should not attempt to say something general about 'the whole world of actual audiences, because the very fluid nature of that world resists full representation' (Ang 1991: 164). Moreover, to generalize about audiences, especially in the form of audience ratings, is politically undesirable because it may serve the purpose of containing and controlling the audience in the interest of commercial communicators.

Against this position, other researchers argue that however theoretically defensible the situationalist perspective may be, no methodology is inherently biased in terms of promoting some forms of power rather than others (Jensen 1995: 125). Moreover, it has been argued that as a socially committed audience researcher, one even has an obligation to generalize about audience practices, because it is only by delivering structured pictures of audience behaviours, tastes and evaluations that one can hope to intervene in public debates with policy-makers and the public at large about media political issues (Schrøder 1994).

According to this view, qualitative audience researchers should always view their object through a 'lens' that is alert to the discovery of tendencies, categories and types, even with very small numbers of informants. In a theory-generating study of TV households, Jensen et al. (1994) thus suggested that their nine households could meaningfully be seen as giving rise to three ideal types of viewer, which they labelled Moralists, Pragmaticists and Hedonists (see Chapter 3). This typology was later operationalized for a representative survey by a commercial broadcaster interested in understanding and controlling the audience better as part of its TV schedule planning. It was also used, however, as an intervention into educational debates about audience tastes, where it may have contributed to undermining the stereotypical images of popular viewers held by elite-based educators.

In the same way, Jhally and Lewis's reception study in the US of the black situation comedy *The Cosby Show*, was helpful for illuminating television's role in maintaining and challenging ethnic stereotypes, precisely because it generalized about the differences of reception along lines of ethnicity, gender and social class (Lewis 1991). In another study, of news reception, Lewis deviated from the tacit agreement among reception researchers to never offer the actual number of informants sharing the reading of a programme or programme detail. On the perception of a news item about a male politician's speech, for instance, he reported unusually that 'of the fifty respondents, forty-one incorporated references to the speech into their readings, thirty-eight incorporated references to his reception, and only twelve incorporated references to the story's history' (Lewis 1991).

Maybe this numerical honesty was a result of Lewis having no less than 50 informants, rendering numerical indicators more meaningful. In the early days of reception research, in studies involving 12 or perhaps 16 informants, researchers refrained from offering observation like 'five out of the eight women interviewed thought that . . .'; they usually preferred pseudo-quantitative specifications such as '*most* female viewers' or 'this type of reading was *often* found in the data' (Schrøder 1989: 15), presumably as a result of a combined urge to generalize and also to gloss over the very modest number of informants. Lewis (1997) suggests that the reason may be found in 'the lingering suspicion of numerical data' that had 'degenerated into a habit' (Lewis 1997: 84), but goes on to argue for the importance of numbers in qualitative research: 'it is important for us to know, roughly, the number of people who construct one reading rather than another' (Lewis 1997: 87).

Interestingly, the moment a qualitative study ends up with a typology, assigning the different informants to the different types (as is the case with the reception study discussed at length in Chapter 7), quantification becomes a simple task: you can easily count how many belong to each type. However, the quantified 'map' that is constructed on the basis of the qualitative typology can never represent the whole picture of the qualitative analysis. A lot of observational and verbal detail is lost *in* the quantified map and must be supplied *along with* the map, in the form of a traditional qualitative report with analytical interpretations and quotations from transcripts, if the study is to preserve the situational and contextual complexities that informant readings are made of. The quantitative typology remains a heuristic device for summarizing complexity.

Pursuing the logic of generalization towards its quantitative limit, one could ask whether qualitative audience research could – and should – aspire to emulating survey research in terms of representativeness. First, it probably couldn't, as the amount of data collected from a nationally representative sample would be so large as to defy analysis in conventional qualitative terms. Second, we believe that it shouldn't, because the objective of qualitative research – to explore the diversity and range of a communicative phenomenon – does not make it necessary, which is why the usual recommendation about sample size in a qualitative study is to stop interviewing when no new data seem to be emerging.

In most cases of practical reception research the sample size will be decided by tough cost–benefit considerations, like how many informants does our funding (or time constraints) enable us to involve? Commercial broadcasters normally find that two or four focus groups, with the relevant viewer segments, are sufficient to form the basis for editorial decisions.

This said, reception researchers may sometimes have an urge to move beyond diversity towards typicality, desiring to produce findings that are far from representative in the statistical sense, but that may nevertheless command a wider explanatory reach than the typical small-scale study. Recent experience within the field shows that researchers may reach interesting results by interviewing relatively large numbers of informants, who may be recruited so as to be typical of a specific population segment, as when Stald (1999) interviewed 103 children from three different age groups about their use of computers, in a variety of settings and with a variety of methods. All other things being equal, the credibility of a reception study will increase with the number of informants engaged. Jhally and Lewis's *Cosby Show* study, with its 50 interviewed groups, distributed along ethnic, gender and class lines, thus commands greater explanatory power as regards the American viewing experience of this programme than if they had engaged 10 such groups.

## INCREASING EXPLANATORY POWER THROUGH TRIANGULATION

If quantitative and qualitative methods have reciprocal strengths and weaknesses, what is more logical than to design one's research project so as to draw on both? This is basically the rationale underlying the recommendation to use methodological triangulation in audience research as in other kinds of social research.

Going back to Denzin (1970), triangulation is sometimes quite broadly defined as 'a comparative assessment of more than one form of evidence about an object of inquiry' (Lindlof 1995: 239), so as to include in a project *multiple sources* of data (Lindlof gives the example of using differently positioned informants), *multiple investigators* or *multiple methods*. The first two appear to us to be basically a question of how to improve reliability, whereas the third type is more in agreement with the method-oriented way we have used the concept in the rest of this book, and with the most widespread use of the term in the field of communication research.

Triangulation can thus be implemented both *within* one of the major approaches, as when a qualitative study uses two or three different qualitative methods (interview, diary, observation), and *between* the major approaches, as when a study collects both quantitative and qualitative data sets: 'Both types of observation can be used together profitably to achieve triangulation, which enhances both the precision of the data gathered (with quantitative observation) and the contextual influences on those data (with qualitative observations)' (Frey et al. 1991: 99).

Triangulation proper, in which *primary* data sets are being collected using both qualitative and quantitative methods, should be distinguished from research designs that use one method as an *auxiliary* strategy for gathering information to be fed into the research material of the other. The auxiliary mode of method combination (which Jensen (2002c: 272) calls 'facilitation', because one method is used to facilitate the endeavour of the other) has been dealt with numerous times in this book, in connection with the discussion of the four approaches, as when the wording of a survey questionnaire about gratifications from TV is based on a few qualitative interviews with individuals from the target group, or when the relevance of a qualitative study of horror movies is secured by first doing a small-scale survey of the target group's tastes in this area.

Triangulation can be defined as the sequential execution of two or more primary studies of the same communicative phenomenon using different methods. It is based on a logic where the respective strong aspects of the quantitative (reliability and generalization) and qualitative (validity) approaches supposedly join forces and, supposedly cancelling out their respective weak aspects, produce findings that, on aggregate, have greater truth-likeness and explanatory power than either method would have been able to produce if applied on its own.

Friessen and Punie's (1998) study of ICTs (phone-related media, TV-related media and computer-related media) in Holland and Belgium, may serve as an example of the insights that a triangulating research design can offer. The purpose of the triangulating project was to investigate the ownership, use and acceptance of ICTs, and the meanings family members attached to ICTs in the context of their everyday life. The study was particularly interested in so-called 'busy households', because such households were assumed to practise a high degree of 'task combination' and therefore to be interested in the time-saving opportunities offered by ICTs. The project was thus interested in the relationship between time pressure and time problems on the one hand, and ownership, use and acceptance of ICTs on the other (Friessen and Punie 1998: 77).

The qualitative study was conducted in Amsterdam with seven households, who were defined as 'busy' on the basis of their being double-income families with young children. The qualitative fieldwork itself was conducted in a triangulating mode, as the principal method of the semi-structured interview in the home was supplemented with observation during the interview and mental mappings of the house. During the interview, both partners were asked about such aspects of everyday life as their professional careers, internal organization of housework, important social networks, the time structure of an ordinary day, use of ICTs and buying motives for the last two ITCs. The interview transcripts were analysed bottom-up, using a combination of grounded theory and discursive-repertoires analysis, the emphasis being not on what people actually do with ICTs, but on 'the way they talk about ICTs, and the recurrent metaphors, images and expressions they use to describe their own behaviour' (Friessen and Punie 1998: 76).

The quantitative survey was conducted in Brussels, asking members of 356 representative households, through face-to-face-administered questionnaires, about their ownership and use of ICTs, as well as about their organization of time in daily life, mainly through closed-ended questions. On the basis of six questions about time use, especially the availability of 'leisure time', the respondents were divided through cluster analysis into four groups, distinguished according to a linear decrease in available leisure time. The most 'busy' type of family (Cluster 4) was thus defined as those who have fewer than three hours a day to spend on what they perceive as 'leisure activities'. They deviate considerably from the busy households of the Dutch study by only half of them having a double income, and only four out of five having children. The 'busyness' of the Dutch households is thus based on an assumption that double-income families with children are busy, while the Belgian notion of busyness is based on the respondents' subjective evaluation of available leisure time. When comparing the findings of the two studies, therefore, it should be borne in mind that the social groupings investigated do not have identical life conditions.

In true positivist fashion, the Belgian study deductively formed two hypotheses for empirical verification about the relation of busy households to ICTs:

- busy households own more ICTs compared with less busy households

- busy households report to have more communication problems compared with less busy households (that's why they need more ICTs to overcome them!).

In the Dutch study, the researchers were curious 'whether ICTs were actually perceived and used as solutions for time and coordination problems' (Friessen and Punie 1998: 83). It was found that most households did in fact have a considerable number of ICTs in the home, but there did not seem to be an explicit connection between the acquisition of a mobile phone and a desire to overcome time and coordination problems – in most cases, the reason for acquiring one had to do with demands from the workplace. However, once they had the phone, it was felt to come in handy for solving family coordination problems.

The most striking aspect of the Dutch informants' discourses about ICTs was that the meanings expressed were characterized by ambiguities and paradoxes. ICTs can be both a burden and a boon: with many technologies there was an unresolved tension between their time-saving and time-consuming properties, and their ability to sometimes increase, but at other times reduce, flexibility in daily life. For instance, telework is enabled by inter-active technologies and may sometimes provide flexibility, but at other times may lead to an intrusion on one's privacy.

In order to test its hypotheses, the Belgian study crossed, on the one hand, data on ICT ownership and perceived communication problems with family and friends, and on the other the four groups distinguished by their being gradually less time-constrained in daily life. Leaving details aside for present purposes, both hypotheses were confirmed. Busy families do 'have quite a sophisticated ICT-culture at home' (Friessen and Punie 1998: 87), although the statistical linearity between the figures for the four clusters was not perfect, and they do report having more problems reaching the people who belong to their primary social networks. Friessen and Punie emphasize, however, that the difficulty is a relative one: none of the four groupings reports serious problems in this respect.

Reflecting on the benefits of their triangulated design, they conclude that the qualitative and quantitative modes of analysis 'are indeed complementing each other very well' (Friessen and Punie 1998: 89). The sophisticated ICT infrastructure found in the busy households by the small-scale Dutch study was confirmed by the representative Belgian study, and the slight non-linearity of the Belgian ownership statistics can be explained by the ambiguities of meaning surrounding the informants' ICT talk in the Dutch study. Moreover, the authors observe that the different types of finding will be 'useful to develop the research tools for the next stage in the different projects' they are working on.

The Dutch/Belgian study is thus an illuminating example of what a triangulating design has to offer in terms of both explanatory and tool-development benefits. This is in accordance with the view on triangulation that one finds in many textbooks:

*Both types of observations can be used together profitably to achieve trian-
gulation, which enhances both the precision of the data gathered (with quantitative observations) and the contextual influences on those data (with
qualitative observations). Using both types of observation also provides a
way of assessing the accuracy of the findings from one operational procedure
by comparing it with a different operational procedure. If the findings
support each other, both procedures are corroborated. If the findings are
different, however, this does not necessarily mean that the data are questionable. The difference could be a result of the types of data that are acquired
through quantitative and qualitative observations.*

(Frey et al. 1991: 99)

In the case of Friessen and Punie, we clearly have a case of one approach corroborating
the other. So far, so good. But what about the reverse situation – if the two types of
analysis end up with contradictory evidence about a phenomenon? According to the
having-your-cake-and-eating-it logic of Frey et al., there is nothing to worry about in this
case because, after all, we do know that quantitative and qualitative observations produce
very different data!

We believe that the best way to conceptualize the benefits of triangulation is probably
not to make too strong claims for our triangulated findings either way. In other places
in this book we have used the heuristic metaphor that a research method can be likened
to a 'lens', whose grinding produces a particular perception of the object looked at. It
follows from the lens metaphor that we should *expect* different methods to produce
different results, and therefore not be reassured by the 'sameness' of our findings. For
one thing, in qualitative designs, we are looking at the empirical phenomenon through
the complexifying lens of informants' lifeworld-based discourses, whereas in quantitative
designs we are looking through the homogenizing lens of the researcher's categories of
investigation as they appear in the questionnaire. Therefore, when we get different
findings from different methods, the challenge is to understand why.

In other words, when observing the same communicative phenomenon with different
methods, we should always put our energy into interpreting what the probable relationship
between the findings may mean. Since, in triangulation, we are exploring more or less the
same communicative phenomenon, we should expect some kind of complementarity to our
findings, but never a simple underlying arithmetic for combining them. This is also because
the notion of 'same object' should always be taken with a pinch of salt. In the case of
Friessen and Punie, the phenomenon investigated in both countries is people's use of ICTs
in daily life, but when the 'busy' people used as respondents are defined in one study in sociodemographic terms (double income, with children), and in the other in terms of perceived
amount of leisure time, we are already moving away considerably from the idea of sameness.

Another reason why triangulation is not a methodological panacea, is that the triangulated
methods bring their inherent strengths and weaknesses with them into the joint design. A

superficial questionnaire-based survey of TV gratifications does not all of a sudden acquire greater validity by being juxtaposed with a small-scale audience ethnography of domestic viewing behaviour. Nor does the latter become more representative through such a juxtaposition. Along these lines, Jensen (2002c) suggests that we should pursue the option of 'complementarity' as a different, and perhaps more challenging, kind of methodological combination, in which 'different methodologies may be best suited to examine different aspects of a research question, and not necessarily in the same concrete empirical domain' (Jensen 2002c: 272). An example of the pursuit of methodological complementarity would be a study that aimed to explore the phenomenon of *national identity* in a given country through separate studies of, say, relevant domestic TV fiction through semiotic analysis; national attachment and national pride, perhaps expanding into national tastes and attitudes, through questionnaire-based surveys; and perceptions of the national soccer team's participation in the world championships (the team's qualities as contrasted with opponent national teams, the specific games, the organization of daily time schedules for making viewing possible, etc.) through depth-interviews. However illuminating such a study may be for our understanding of national identity, the findings from each of its parts should never be seen as more than the pieces of a sociocultural jigsaw puzzle, whose full picture will eternally elude us.

As we have demonstrated, triangulation in whichever form is a promising example of methodological pluralism. To adopt it can be a significant symbolic act of methodological unorthodoxy. And it is a methodological strategy that can easily be carried out also on the smaller scale normally required by student projects, in connection with an audience methodology class.

But it is also a strategy that really requires no one to change fundamentally, since each method enters the joint design fully intact, with its inherent strengths and weaknesses, and is sometimes implemented in a division of labour that leaves the qualitative part to a researcher with origins in the humanities, and the quantitative part to someone familiar with social science statistics. In the following section, we shall take a look at a methodology that attempts to take methodological pluralism beyond juxtaposition and develop a research design where the quantitative and qualitative aspects are integrated into one methodological operation.

## INCREASING EXPLANATORY POWER THROUGH METHODOLOGICAL SYNTHESIS

We dealt briefly with the method of Q-sorts in Chapter 10, where it was seen basically as one tool in the quantitative arsenal of audience research. It has often been practised as such, especially in social psychology, but it has always also held the potential of incorporating a qualitative dimension, as when some researchers have asked respondents to accompany the card-sorting task with think-aloud reflections, or have returned to respondents in order to have them comment on their reasons for placing the attitude-revealing cards the way they did on the Q-grid.

On the whole, however, Q-methodology has lived most of its life at the margins of social science research, perhaps as a consequence of the difficulty of positioning it squarely within either of the major camps. It has been little used in communication and audience research. We therefore devote a few pages to a presentation of the method here, in order to hopefully whet the reader's appetite for more, which can then be found in introductory texts such as Rogers (1995) or Brown (1993) (see also (http://www.rz.unibw-muenchen.de/~p41bsmk/qmethod/). If nothing else, our discussion of Q-methodology may heighten your ability to reflect critically on the pros and cons of different methods, and ponder what lies at the heart of the qualitative and quantitative approaches.

Q-methodology is a method for mapping people's subjective universes of meaning in a particular field of experience, such as their perceptions of the portrayal of gender in advertising, their experience of the internal structures of communication in an organization, or their sense of national identity in a globalized world. In our presentation of the method, we shall draw on a research project about national and supranational identity (Schrøder and Hansen 2002). The purpose was to explore how people in a small European country like Denmark experience their identity as national citizens, at a time when the country's membership of the European Community may be pulling people towards some sense of attachment to the supranational entity as well. The informants are members of the national media audience, whose identities have been substantially shaped by years of media portrayals of nation and supranational affairs.

The first stage of a Q-project consists in capturing, in a finite number of statements or claims, the essential features of the discursive terrain in question. Depending on the issue in focus, this may be done through a number of depth-interviews about the field, designed to elicit a wide range of perceptions about it, or through a thorough analysis of the public debate about the issue in the media. Each major discernible position in the discursive terrain should be represented through an equal number of statements that express the many-faceted character of the position, so that the set of statements form a miniature representation of the discursive terrain being investigated (Box 17.1). In the study of national identity, 12 statements were chosen to represent the variety of sentiments making up each of three prominent positions on the issue, defined by the researchers' hunches: 'Nationalists' (nation as a core value); 'national pluralists' (some openness towards a union of nations); 'supranationalists' (belief in the vision of a united Europe). Instead of statements, Popovich et al. (2000), in their study of high-school girls' perceptions of advertising stereotypes, used different types of advertisement that portrayed women differently.

In the second stage, the statement-claims are used in random order as the interview guide for individual, structured, qualitative interviews about the issue. Each statement, printed on a small, numbered card, is read aloud by the interviewer and handed to the participant. It thus serves as the input of a dialogical speech event, in which participants think aloud as they negotiate their stance, with the interviewer facilitating the process by probing in order to clarify the participant's position on each statement in turn. The main difference so far, in relation to the typical semi-structured qualitative interview, is that the turn-taking

## Box 17.1 Q-study of national identity: examples of statements mapping the discursive terrain

1. Our identity as Danes will become more and more blurred if Europeanness is promoted. (N)
2. I want a European Union with countries that are as politically and culturally different as they are different geographically. (PL)
3. I think of myself first as a European, then as a Dane. (SN)
4. If someone said something negative about being Danish, I would feel that something negative had been said about me personally. (N)
5. One day it will become necessary for Denmark to join the Euro (the common European currency). (PL)
6. Integration between the EU countries ought to move faster. (SN)

Total number of statements used for study:
N = Nationalist statements (12)
PL = Pluralist statements (12)
SN = Supranationalist statements (12)

between interviewer and participant is structured by the obligatory progression through the randomly packed cards. Another difference is the relatively high number of informants (30) who took part in the study. The interviews are audiotaped and transcribed.

In the third stage, the participant is asked to place the cards one at a time, as a kind of puzzle game, onto a scalar grid representing a continuum with (in this study) nine positions from 'Most agree' to 'Most disagree'. In practice, this occurs immediately after each card has been responded to verbally, and thus overlaps with stage two. As the grid is gradually filled with the 36 cards, the participant is free to reposition individual cards, so that ultimately the grid comes to express the participant's meaning universe on the issue (for an example, see Figure 17.1). In the study of gender roles in print advertising mentioned above, the appropriate stimulus material would be the actual ads rather than verbal statements.

In relation to a survey questionnaire, this is where the crucial difference lies. All the 36 statements of the Q-study could equally well have been used in a classic survey, but in that case, each answer would in principle be unrelated to all other answers. The effect of placing all 36 statements on the grid is that each response becomes related to the 35 other responses, so that a *relational map* of the participant's meaning universe is produced.

As the fourth stage, the relational maps of the 30 informants are subjected to computerized factor analysis (Chapter 13), correlating the similarities and differences among the participants' meaning universes, and discovering the patternings of meaning expressed by the participants through the card sorting. The end product is a number of 'factors' that

Figure 17.1    Q-study of national identity: example of participant's card sorting of the
36 statement claims

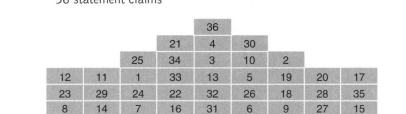

Informant #1, Copenhagen, Female, Bus driver, 42 years of age

each comprises a grouping of participants whose card sortings are similar, compared with the sortings of other participants. The national identity study found four statistically significant factors, each characterized by aggregate card placements that distinguish them from the other factors.

Experienced practitioners of Q-methodology often claim that the method is relatively statistics-free and user-friendly:

> *The focus is on quality rather than quantity, and yet some of the most powerful statistical mechanics are in the background, but sufficiently so as to go relatively unnoticed by those users of Q who are disinterested in its mathematical substructure.*

(Brown 1993: 94)

However, it must be stressed that researchers without some knowledge of statistics will have a hard time using the downloadable software (see http://www.rz.unibw-muenchen.de/~p41bsmk/qmethod/), especially when it comes to undertaking the factor rotations necessary in order to highlight the salient differences between the groupings produced by the first round of the factor analysis.

In the fifth stage, the position of the participants making up each factor is interpreted on the basis of the factor scores, arranged as a Top 36 from 'Most agree' to 'Most disagree' (see Box 17.2). In the national identity study, after extensive interpretative work on the factor scores, the four factors could be characterized as Wholehearted Europeans, Pragmatic Europeans, Euro-sceptical Danes and Danish Danes, comprising 13, 11, 7 and 3 participants respectively.

A purely qualitative analysis might also have come up with such a typology of different national identities. The advantage of obtaining the types through computerized factor analysis is simply that the computer is able to handle the enormous amount of data similarities and differences much more reliably than the brain of the human scholar. The

## Box 17.2  Q-study of national identity: the factor profile of Factor One – 'Wholehearted Europeans' (based on ranked statements, excerpts)

Statement no.                                                                    Z-scores

Top six

31.  It is possible to be a citizen of a united Europe without
     all Europeans having to be the same.                                         2.058
6.   One country cannot control its future on its own.                            1.752
32.  On the whole Denmark has benefited from its EU
     membership.                                                                  1.352
33.  In the future Danes must be able to command both Danish
     and English in order to be able to cope in Europe.                           1.308
34.  If the EU works according to the principle of subsidiarity,
     it is possible to both support a united Europe and to
     preserve Danishness at the same time.                                        1.302
36.  There will be better room for national minorities in a
     united Europe, because a united Europe is more capable
     of handling such differences.                                               1.046

Bottom six

26.  I believe that integration between the EU countries has
     gone as far as it possibly can.                                            −1.295
3.   The globe's population can be naturally divided into
     nations.                                                                   −1.349
15.  Danish culture is worth preserving because it has
     existed for more than a thousand years.                                    −1.375
5.   I feel that aliens in Denmark dilute our national
     identity.                                                                  −1.484
9.   It would be difficult for my parents if I didn't marry a
     Dane.                                                                       −1.610
7.   Your sense of belonging to your country comes before
     anything else.                                                             −1.797

Source: The top statement for each Factor (Grouping) is the one this
grouping most agreed with, the bottom statement the one they least agreed
with. The complete data for the four factors can be seen in the pdf version
of the article by Schrøder and Hansen (2002).

validity cost, conversely, lies in the data reduction required in order to distil the complex discursive negotiation of each statement-claim down to one square on the Q-grid. Pulling in the opposite direction, however, is the fact that this reduction is carried out subjectively by the participants themselves, not by the interpreting researcher. It is not without justification, therefore, that Q-methodology is also called 'the scientific study of subjectivity'.

The factor analysis also tells the researcher which participants in each factor grouping are particularly typical. The researcher can, therefore, in the sixth stage, go back to the interview transcripts of such typical specimens, in order to put some discursive meat on the analytical skeleton supplied by the factor analysis, regaining some of the qualitative thick description that was lost during the statistical operations. The end result of the analysis – its substantial findings – is therefore both a generalized and detail-rich profile of the prominent positions in the discursive terrain of national identity, or whatever the area of experience singled out for Q-methodological analysis (see also Lindlof and Shatzer 1989).

As we have presented the procedures and mechanics of Q-methodology, we have tried to keep track of its dual orientation towards both qualitative and quantitative modes of analysis. Like triangulation, Q-methodology is not a miracle solution to the shortcomings of traditional methodologies. We have merely tried to argue that when it comes to the investigation of subjective experiences of media offerings and communicative practices, Q-methodology offers an approach that, in some respects, combines the best of both worlds.

# Chapter Eighteen

## ☐ Convergence of media: towards a new sense of 'audience'

We opened this book with a portrait of the audience of the reality show *Big Brother*, in order to emphasize how contemporary media audiences are moving away from an identity sometimes epitomized as the 'couch potato', towards a role more aptly characterized as a 'communicative juggler'; away from being relatively inactive *recipients*, towards being increasingly active, even interactive, *users* of mediated communication (for details, see Chapter 1).

Throughout the book, as we have developed our agenda of methodological pluralism for audience research, alongside our focus on 'classic' media audiences, we have incorporated examples of interactive audience practices into our discussions. Now is the time to more systematically face the methodological challenges of how to explore increasingly interactive audiences.

## CONCEPTUALIZING INTERACTIVITY

A good way to unravel the sometimes ambiguous notion of *interactivity* is to consider it through the conceptual framework first offered by Bordewijk and van Kaam (1986) and since elaborated by other scholars. Here we follow the model put forward by Jens F. Jensen, which starts out by focusing on television as an increasingly interactive medium, but which follows the path invited by technological convergence towards a general theorization of interactivity (Jensen 2001).

Jensen's conceptual map of interactivity is based on the different kinds of social power relations that can be distinguished between information providers and users, independently of the technical design, forms of presentation and specific content of the media in question. The variables that constitute the two-by-two model of four idealized interactive patterns have to do with the *production and control* of the information traffic between *providers and users*, as shown in Table 18.1. On the one hand, an information product may be seen from the perspective of its production by either a centralized institutional information provider or by an individual consumer-user. On the other hand, it may be considered from the perspective of whether the distribution (what and when to access the information) is controlled by a central provider or a consumer–user.

*Transmission* is the characteristic communication mode of the broadcast mass media, where 'consumers in principle receive exactly the same information and often receive the information synchronously' (Jensen 2001: 364), when they switch on to the predetermined

Table 18.1    Matrix of four idealized types of media-related interactivity

|  | Information produced by a central provider | Information produced by the consumer |
|---|---|---|
| Distribution controlled by a central provider | Transmission e.g. broadcast television, radio, films | Registration e.g. opinion polling, video surveillance, web log |
| Distribution controlled by the consumer | Consultation e.g. newspapers, CD-ROMs, WWW, libraries | Conversation e.g. telephone, mail, email, chat rooms |

Source: based on Jensen (2001)

flow of news and entertainment. In this mode, the consumer has minimal power over the cultural meanings received, and the interactivity (if indeed we wish to use this term at all) is limited to the act of turning the apparatus on or off. Before the age of broadcasting, we may see the role of the Church as one that represents many of the features of the transmitting mode.

With *Consultation*, the archetypal example of which is the library, the information is produced and owned by a central provider, but it is the individual user who decides what to access and when. Thus we may speak of a kind of power-sharing with respect to the cultural meanings involved, since the content is controlled by the media organization, but a high degree of selective interactivity is required of the user. Consultative media thus offer great freedom and flexibility, 'making more individual and selective uses possible' (Jensen 2001: 366).

With *Conversation*, where the telephone conversation may serve as the most obvious mediated form, 'the information flow runs in both directions, between two individual consumers, and there is an equal exchange of information' (Jensen 2001: 364). Obviously there is also a central provider involved in the interaction, but unlike in the other modes, only as a technical facilitator that does not intervene in the exchange of information itself. Many will see this mode as the genuine interactive form of communication, because the interaction is not merely between humans and media (as with consultation), but between humans with a high degree of mutuality.

*Registration* is the reverse of consultation, as the information is provided by an individual user, but processed and stored by a central organization, with the aim of monitoring and controlling the future behaviour of the user. In other words, the user makes information about him/herself available to the collecting organization, as when opinion polls from voters are used for political campaigns, or bar-code information about shoppers is used to tailor marketing initiatives to consumer segments or even individual consumers. The logging, through so-called 'cookies', of individual traffic on the World Wide Web is a case in point:

> *Communication on the net leaves tracks to an extent unmatched by that in any other context – the content is easily observable, recorded, and copied. Participant demography and behaviours of consumption, choice, attention, reaction, learning, and so forth, are widely captured and logged.*

(Jones 1999a: 6)

The multiple potential audience activities of the *Big Brother* audience, outlined in Chapter 1, include examples of both transmission, consultation, conversation and registration. We suggest you go back to our account of these activities and try to match them with the four idealized types just described, remembering that some of the audience activities may belong to more than one type.

As the examples (Table 18.1) of the four types of interactivity indicate, none of them are entirely new to our civilization, brought about by new communication technologies. They have all existed in some form for a century or more. What *is* new about the interactive modes in the current age is their potentially simultaneous *convergence* on one or two common technological platforms, that of the computer/TV. The precise technological nature of these platforms is developing as we write, as broadcasting and print media are finding their way into the digitized universe of the computer/telephone, and the TV set is incorporating a multitude of interactive services, including some kinds of web access formerly associated only with the personal computer. The mobile phone may be turning into a hand-held TV/computer, as a video camera facility offers users virtual eye contact.

Another innovative tendency is the *intensification* of the non-transmitting modes of interactivity, whereby an increasing amount of time is spent with media technologies that enable consultative and conversational practices and, by implication, also registering practices. Television itself, operating under global multichannel conditions, with the possibility of recording and supplemented with teletextual services, is becoming less and less a transmitting media:

> *All of a sudden TV becomes a random access medium, more like a book or newspaper, browsable and changeable, no longer dependent on time or day, or the time required for delivery . . . Once we begin to build it in its most general form, bit radiation, TV becomes a totally different medium.*

(Negroponte 1995: 49–50).

While it is risky to make predictions, especially about the future, it is unlikely that audiences will disperse completely into individualized viewing habits. We believe that to a large extent, TV audiences will continue to receive broadcast messages simultaneously, for instance, in order to share the simultaneity of experiencing events that are important to an interpretative community (like a nation), both in the factual and fictional realms. But they will be more consultative about the way they select the object of exposure, and they will engage more in various forms of individual-to-individual or community-building conversations about what they have watched, and they will be more closely monitored by centralized information providers and collectors as they do so.

It follows from these (non-original) predictions about rapid media convergence and increased audience interactivity, that the matrix model (Table 18.1), with its neat divisions and categories, is becoming more and more of an analytical abstraction, and less of an illustration of audience practices in the real world. With the technological and functional convergence of information services:

> *the matrix seems to deny itself to a certain extent. The very construction of the matrix and its application to current media phenomena demonstrates that the characteristic patterns and the sharp distinctions disintegrate in favour of more complex and hybrid information patterns and media forms.*

(Jensen 2001: 388)

Still, the idealized model may help us grasp more precisely which dimensions are involved in existing and emerging forms of mediated interactivity.

## METHODOLOGICAL IMPLICATIONS OF CONVERGENCE AND INTERACTIVITY

As the *Big Brother* example shows, to be an audience member in the contemporary media culture implicates communicating individuals in multiple activities. This requires audience researchers to use multiple methods in order to describe and explain the mediated social and cultural processes that shape our future, and to do so in a holistic perspective that may focus on audience practices, but not without relating them to agents who operate at other points in the communicative circuit, and to social and cultural processes in the wider society (see Chapter 3). The ultimate aim is to enable us to draw differently scaled maps of how individuals and groups orient to, make sense of, and appropriate the converging, interactive media coming into their everyday lives.

For instance, we need to explore, on the macro level, the navigational resources and strategies that users employ for orientation, access and selection of material in the multimedia information-saturated universe. We also need to explore, at the micro-level, how users navigate in and make sense of the media technologies and their contents, how indeed they are sometimes – when zapping, web browsing or playing computer games – actively and uniquely co-producing the audiovisual object they are experiencing, as members of social and cultural communities, whether real or virtual, pre-existing or constituted by the communicative activity.

In order to do this, we can draw on the established methods of audience research, as presented and discussed in this book, both in isolation and in combination, as discussed earlier under the heading of 'triangulation' (Chapter 17). Jones (1999a), while agreeing with this view, worries that:

*when it comes to Internet research, our methods are not . . . scalable. Can our methods efficiently build on one another, or is it the case that as we apply multiple methods we are unable to achieve the sum promised by their multiple application?*

(Jones 1999a: 25)

As stated above, we believe that the problem of 'scalability', or complementarity, of methods is one that is epistemologically inherent to triangulation. The best we can hope to achieve through triangulation is a more faceted illumination than would be possible using any one method. While triangulation is thus basically the same thing, with the same strengths and weaknesses, irrespective of whether the audience is more or less interactive, we believe that the concrete nature of the more interactive technologies requires tailor-made triangulating research designs for some purposes. Finding our inspiration in the recent adaptations to communication research of engineering's 'usability testing', we shall present one example of such a research design below.

First, however, we wish to point out briefly how the established methods may be used for exploration of the audience–users of interactive media. In doing this, we retain a core (but not exclusive) focus on 'audiences' as individuals who make sense of a communicative phenomenon produced by an institutional provider: as when a citizen checks the latest update from a net-based news provider, or parents consult the advice offered by a NetDoctor website; as when web chatters gather around and discuss a media product such as a reality programme, a rock band or a controversial novel; or as when computer game addicts pursue their playful passion online, in virtual space on the Internet.

While audiences in the classic sense of the term thus remain central to our work, we have to recognize that as audiences are increasingly turning into 'users', it is becoming impossible to draw the line between mass-mediated and interpersonal communication:

*It is still not clear, and it may be unclear for a long time to come, at which level of communication (mass, interpersonal, group, organizational, etc.) the Internet operates: whether it operates on multiple levels (it seems likely that it does) and, if so, whether it can operate on multiple levels simultaneously (this, too, seems likely) and, if it can, with what consequences for our under-standing of the people engaged in Internetworked communication?*

(Jones 1999a: 9)

The once purely interpersonal medium of the telephone may serve as an example. Today, even an old-fashioned telephone gives its user access to a host of 'interactive' services, provided by institutional actors, while the mobile phone has converged with the rest of the digital universe in giving access to various 'levels' and 'media' of communication. As we write, the new generation of consumer mobile phones will enable users to access TV channels on their display. Similarly, the participants in a web chat group about soap operas are simultaneously engaging in interpersonal communication with other participants and, jointly with other participants, producing a public record of their interaction that is open to the spectatorship of an unlimited audience.

The study of the dispersed 'audience' of centrally provided information is therefore converging with neighbouring fields in the general area of communication research, such as interpersonal and group communication, as the 'user–communicator' becomes the point of departure of any study of mediated communication, on different technological platforms, in different semiotic modes, as the realization of different individual or group-anchored social practices. In the example of triangulation discussed above, Friessen and Punie (1998) thus investigated not 'audiences', but the users (defined as individuals in families) of information technologies *as technologies*, used as a response to needs in, and with an influence on, everyday life, irrespective of the cultural content provided through the technological channels.

In a quick run-through of the different methods for exploring interactive media, then, we may use them all in old-fashioned style: we may do mail or telephone *surveys* of people's access to and ownership of new information technologies, the time spent using them, and the attitudes users have towards them; and we may do *observation* studies of teenagers in a cybercafé, as they spend time on a game platform or on a chat site; and we may conduct reception *interviews* with people who use the Internet as a news provider.

But we may also take our research methods themselves onto the net, after carefully considering what is to be gained and lost by choosing this technology and medium for our inquiries. As regards the administration of *survey* questionnaires through the net, Witmer et al. (1999) warn that although this approach may serve to reduce costs, the problems in securing an adequate response rate appear to be somewhat greater than with snail-mail surveys. Therefore, due to the ease for the user of deleting the questionnaire just by the touch of a key, they suggest that 'on-line survey research requires incentives for participation, introductory messages separate from the instruments, and safeguards against alteration of the questionnaires' (Witmer et al. 1999: 157). Also, net-based surveys have to deal with problems in reaching representative samples.

For the media ethnographer, the Internet offers a unique opportunity to overcome the so-called Observer's Paradox (discussed in Chapter 1), according to which we cannot observe in a sustained manner how people behave when they are not being observed, without observing them, and with the consequence of potentially altering their behaviour. On a web chat site (such as the one connected with the *Big Brother* programme), we *can* observe people as they are interacting naturally about a TV programme or cultural phenomenon in a setting of their own choosing, without any awareness of being observed by a researcher. Baym (2000), who conducted a pioneering virtual ethnography of a Usenet newsgroup about soap operas, finds that her approach has added an entirely new dimension to audience research, because of the inherent limitations of the focus group approach: '[The] methodological reliance on the focus group rather than on the observation of spontaneous and naturally occurring fan talk has obscured how this talk is used to negotiate relationships among viewers as well as between viewers and shows' (Baym 2000: 13).

Virtual ethnographies of audience interaction in a newsgroup or chat forum thus provides an opportunity to observe, in the condensed form of a self-constituting interpretative community, soap viewers' everyday talk about a shared fan object. Baym's study enables her to map:

> *how participants dynamically appropriate a wide range of resources drawn from the structure of Usenet and the soap opera text and combine them with other resources in unpredictable yet patterned ways, ultimately constructing a social space that feels like a community.*

(Baym 2000: 24)

Although one should be clear about the ethical implications of 'spying' on chatters, web interaction does offer the audience researcher a unique chance to understand authentic interpersonal communication, as it is constituted under the specific conditions ruling in the cyberworld.

One issue that has been occupying theorists is whether such Internet groups can legitimately be called 'communities'. Following the discursive foundation of this book, we agree with Fernback (1999) that the essential property of any kind of community is not its locatability in physical space, but its symbolic (i.e. discursive) existence as a meaning complex in the minds of users who feel a sense of belonging to the cyber-community. Cyber-communities are characterized by all the fundamental aspects that constitute social groups: common value systems, norms, rules and the sense of identity, commitment, etc.: 'So, if . . . communication is the core of community, then a community is real whether it exists within the same physical locality or half a world away via the telephone wires' (Fernback 1999: 213).

The immediate methodological implication of doing web ethnography requires that the researcher should be familiar with discourse analysis and ethnomethodologically inspired conversation-analytical tools, because the data materializes as written turn-taking patterns on the screen. An inherent limitation of relying on the web ethnographic approach alone, is that the web dialogues in isolation are unlikely to provide data about all the dimensions of the audience experience that the researcher is interested in exploring. For further methodological directions about virtual ethnography, see Hine (2000).

The possibility of conducting interviews on the net is emerging as an enticing methodological challenge for reception researchers. With net-based chat groups, this option only requires that an observing ethnographer makes the transition from pure observer to participant in the virtual group's exchanges of opinion. Baym made this transition and declared her research intent to the newsgroup, winning the consent of the other participants. Apart from twice sending them an open-ended questionnaire, she never reminded the group of her analytical monitoring during subsequent interactions.

The community character of some cyber-groups does not mean that all virtual gatherings are communities; nor does it mean that researchers can deal with virtual communities the same way they would deal with real communities, because 'virtual interaction transforms the way people relate to each other' (Fernback 1999: 203). This is no less true of the particular form of virtual interaction that goes on in net-based focus groups.

Among the advantages of conducting focus groups on the net – apart from the cost-saving aspects and the possibility of bringing together geographically separated participants – are, for instance, the anonymity of net groups, which may have a liberating effect on the kind of person who would be taciturn in a face-to-face focus group. Conversely, due to its reliance on written competencies, net-based focus groups can be heavily biased against those with little education, not to mention the functionally illiterate, leading to severely flawed data.

Among the other issues that have to be taken into account by online focus-group researchers, are whether the subject matter lends itself particularly to discussion in a cyberspace forum (as in the case of a study of users' website experiences), and how Internet access and literacy in the population studied may affect representativeness. For further guidelines about online qualitative research, see Bloor et al. (2001) and Mann and Stewart (2000).

## USABILITY RESEARCH: A TECHNOLOGICAL APPROACH TO INTERACTIVE AUDIENCES

*IT systems should be easy enough for people to be able to just use them.*

(Nielsen and Coyne 2001)

We stated above that the concrete nature of the more interactive technologies sometimes requires tailor-made research designs, which may put the focus on the interactivity itself, as a navigational process that users engage in. This need has to do with the fact that in order to use some of the new ICTs efficiently, a body–mind coordination and a navigational logic are required that do not always come easy to the non-expert user. As technologies, the first many generations of ICTs have simply been difficult for most people, and even when users have learned to master the technological hardware, each new software product poses a new challenge.

Usability research has established itself through the 1990s as a way to test computer 'user interfaces' (such as a website or a CD-ROM), but in principle, any technological appliance (like a microwave oven or a video recorder) can be subjected to usability testing (Nielsen 1993: 2000). The rationale for the method is summarized by web design guru Jakob Nielsen:

> *Users have infinite potential for making unexpected misunderstandings of interface elements and for performing their job in a different way than you imagine. Your design will be much better if you work on the basis of an*

*understanding of the users and their tasks. Then, by all means design the best interface you can, but make sure to validate it with user tests.*

(Nielsen 1993: 10)

Usability is not a cultural discipline, but basically 'an engineering discipline' (Nielsen 1993: 26), where it is distinguished from social usefulness, or 'utility': 'Utility is the question of whether the functionality of the system in principle can do what is needed, and usability is the question of how well users can use that functionality' (Nielsen 1993: 25). This means that the sociocultural relevance or usefulness of a website or a CD-ROM are absent from the testing process. Instead, usability prophets in the human/computer interface business use, as their unique selling point, the fact that usability testing is a cost-saving device: 'Usability testing costs, but it pays for itself in the long run' (Nielsen and Coyne 2001), including the image-improving effects for the company of offering users easy-to-use software. It is thus oriented towards rational work-based uses, producer- rather than consumer-oriented, as it is promoted as a costly, but necessary evil for the software producer.

## Box 18.1 Five usability attributes

*Learnability*: the system should be easy to learn so that the user can rapidly start getting some work done with the system.

*Efficiency*: the system should be efficient to use so that once the user has learned the system, a high level of productivity is possible.

*Memorability*: the system should be easy to remember, so that the casual user is able to return to the system after some period of not having used it.

*Errors*: the system should have low error rate, and function in such a way that if users make errors they can easily recover from them.

*Satisfaction*: the system should be pleasant to use. Users should like it.

Source: based on Nielsen (1993: 26)

Most relevant for the readers of this book, usability typically has to do with the design-oriented improvement of the functional and aesthetic signs on a user interface, in order to help users find the path leading to the desired goal, such as finding the information sought on the website, or being able to make a contribution to a chat forum.

The goal of increased user-friendliness is achieved by a four-stage research and testing process, beginning with an *observation* visit to the customer location in order to simply observe users, 'keep quiet and let the users work as they normally would without interfer-ence' (Nielsen 1993: 18). Second, when the new type of software is introduced, the producer may benefit from testing a *prototype* that does not challenge users with the full system right away. Third, users are invited to *think aloud* – that is, to verbalize their thoughts about what they are doing and why they are doing it – so that the researcher can pinpoint both the errors made and their likely causes. The think-aloud data can be recorded either by videotaping the users, and/or by having the researcher take notes. Finally, the data are analysed in order to arrive, through *heuristic evaluation*, at the implications for redesigning the user interface. Among the frequent design recommendations arrived at, Nielsen mentions the need to use simpler and more natural language in dialogue boxes, to speak the users' language, to be consistent in the use of key technical terms, and to use clearly marked exits when users have messed up and need to get back to the point of departure.

One of Nielsen's examples reports from a classic study of the usability of icons in a graphical user interface, the objective being to test their intuitive comprehensibility. The test was conducted experimentally with four different prototype sets of icons and four different groups of users. Both quantitative and qualitative methods of analysis were used: Scores were calculated for the proportion of correct icon identifications, for users' reaction times, and for their subjective like or dislike of the set of icons, while the fuzzier data of the think-aloud process were used to understand the practices leading to specific scores. In the evaluation process

> *for the final system, a fifth set of icons was designed, mostly being based on one of the four original sets, but with some variations based on lessons from the tests as well as the aesthetic sensibilities of the graphic designers.*

(Nielsen 1993: 39)

## EMBEDDING USABILITY IN SOCIAL AND CULTURAL CONTEXTS

If usability research is to be of value for the kind of audience and user research dealt with in this book, it must conceptualize the user as a whole human being who is situated in the social and cultural environment in which use of 'the system' acquires its relevance and therefore its potential *usefulness*. There is thus no sense in testing the navigational skills of potential users of, say, an interactive dating site on the web, if one does not take into consideration why users would visit such a site in the first place. This means that before any kind of usability test is carried out, the researcher must study the contemporary phenomenon of 'dating' in its multiple manifestations: for some, as a stage in the serious process of romantic courtship leading to lifelong marriage; for others, as a stage in a process of serial monogamy of shorter or longer duration, or as a pursuit of sexual excitement with no great emotional attachment, or as an exhilarating online computer game with no intention of making the move to a meeting in real life.

The researcher would thus need to familiarize him/herself with social research about the meaning of partnership in our culture, and therefore look at marital practices, divorce rates, 'single culture' and same-sex partnerships. Similarly, the researcher would need to consult cultural research about the personal columns in newspapers, *Blind Date*-type programmes on television, and so on. Only then will the user–researcher be fully prepared to 'test' the usability of the dating web service in question.

As an example of usability research that is connected to wider cultural concerns, we shall conclude by looking at a study that springs from educational concerns about the pedagogical value of multimedia teaching materials. Luckin and her colleagues (1998) wanted to explore and evaluate 'how design features elicit and foster different kinds of learner behaviour and how these cue users into various styles of interaction as they endeavour to make sense of the learning technology' (Luckin et al. 1998; see also Plowman 1996).

Given that 'narrative' was deemed to be important for efficient learning, the study focused on the role of narrative in the creation of meaning for learners using multimedia, looking in a comparative perspective at the narrative qualities of the learning materials and the narratively organized knowledge acquired by the students. They therefore adopted an experimental design to explore the consequences of offering students differently structured narratives about a biology topic (Darwin's discovery of the principle of natural selection in the Galapagos Islands), using three CD-ROM presentations of the topic, constructed to be different with respect to narrative design.

One version adopted a *linear* narrative, close to the format of an educational film, where the user doesn't have to be very active. The second version, called *resource-based*, was organized on encyclopaedic principles, and required students to define their own task sequence. The third version, called *guided discovery*, adopted a narrative format between the first and second versions, so that users were offered guided paths through the learning material. All versions included a notepad facility for composing the student group's written assignment about Darwin's discovery. The purpose of the manipulation was:

> to see to what extent the 'shape' and style of the narrative elements of the interface (a) affect learner behaviour, (b) affect the ease with which they accomplish the task and (c) affect how well they can recall their learning after having completed the task.

(Luckin et al. 1998: 3)

Each version was shown to four groups of students – two from a comprehensive school, two from further education – and the experiment took place in the school environment, contextually anchored in their ordinary biology curriculum. The fieldwork methods comprised double video recording – of the group of students during the learning task and of the image on the computer screen via a scan converter – and mixed these two recordings onto one tape for later analysis. After the biology session, the students were interviewed individually by handing them a sheet of questions and a simple tape recorder for recording their spoken responses to questions such as the following:

- Imagine your friend couldn't get to today's lesson and asked you to fill them in on what they've missed. Try to give them a good idea by describing the lesson in plenty of detail.

- Why were the Galapagos Islands interesting to Darwin?

Their previous experience with computers and the teacher's assessment of their previous learning performance were also taken into consideration. The notepad assignments were assessed by a biology teacher.

The data analysis took many different perspectives into consideration, using both quantitative and qualitative methods: a spreadsheet log was created, registering the amount of time spent by each group on the different theme sections of the CD-ROM; a path chart was constructed tracing the groups' navigation between the different theme sections, including visits to the notepad; notepad content was registered in a transcript; group dialogues were monitored for 'interesting moments' from the perspective of both biological subject matter and CD-ROM navigation – an interface feature that could have been captured through a think-aloud procedure, if the experiment had used individual learners instead of groups; and, finally, transcripts were produced of the individual group member's verbalized subjective experience with the interactive material, looking particularly for the narrative properties. Some of these types of data were cross-analysed – for instance, by combining group negotiation transcripts with screen visual and audio records, and with notepad content in a multi-column table – in order to create a complex picture of the multiple interactivity of the learning process.

Restricting ourselves here to report only a few findings, it was found that both with the encyclopaedic and the guided discovery narratives, learners started their answer construction before they had seen all the theme sections, whereas with the 'film' version they waited until they had viewed all theme sections. On the whole, neither of the narrative extremes functioned very well – for instance, the linear version was found to evoke well-formed user narratives to a greater extent than the less tightly structured versions. However, 'these narratives contain quite major misconceptions, perhaps because learners are not encouraged to reflect on their answer construction' (Luckin et al. 1998: 12) – they simply watch the whole 'programme' and then produce the notepad assignment on the basis of what they can remember.

The study therefore ended up with the following overall conclusion about the pedagogical utility of interactive teaching materials:

> *Productive learning experiences benefit from the interplay between the processes of narrative guidance and narrative construction, and software needs to be designed for both, so learners both find a given narrative coherence and generate it for themselves.*

(Luckin et al. 1998: 13)

In other words, as so often before, the golden mean – the narrative version between the 'film' and the 'encyclopaedia' – was found to be superior.

## AUDIENCE RESEARCH AS REFLEXIVITY LAB

The study by Luckin and her colleagues (1998) shows how the sender- and system-oriented classic usability approach to interactive media can easily be developed into a more user- and context-oriented approach that both involves informants reflecting on their interaction with the user interface, and researchers reflecting on the complex meaning patterns produced by the different qualitative and quantitative methods employed. Research findings thus become the product of a 'reflexivity lab' (a concept borrowed from Gjedde and Ingemann 2002), in which the social and cultural uses and implications of interactive media take precedence over technological ones. This is in accordance with our view that audience research is a multilayered communicative signifying process, as shown in figure 1.1 at the beginning of the book.

So let us end this book by concluding, after the lengthy methodological travels of 18 chapters, that reflexivity remains the most important concern for the committed audience researcher in the age of methodological and media convergence. To be reflexive about our methodological practices will help us both to determine the explanatory potential of our research procedures and remind us of the incompleteness and temporariness of our findings, no matter how multiple the methods we use to understand audience and user practices.

While no amount of triangulation can finally unpack the endless complexities of sociocultural meaning processes, we can nevertheless approximate a relevant and 'truthlike' picture of the audience phenomenon we wish to illuminate. Ultimately, any piece that research can contribute, through methodological rigour and reflexivity, to the vast jigsaw puzzle of the audience map is illuminating and valuable. This means that, if methodologically reflexive, even the small-scale, empirical study undertaken by students as part of their audience coursework, is always worthwhile.

# Bibliography ▢

Adorno, T.W. 1950: *The Authoritarian Personality*. New York: Harper.

Adorno, T.W. 1976: 'Sociology and empirical research'. In P. Connerton (ed.) *Critical Sociology: Selected Readings*. New York: Penguin, 237–76.

Adorno, T.W. and Horkheimer, M. 1947/1972: *The Dialectic of Enlightenment*. New York: Herder and Herder.

Afifi, A.A. and Clark, V. 1996: *Computer-aided Multivariate Analysis*. London: Chapman & Hall.

Alasuutari, P. 1995: *Researching Culture: Qualitative Method and Cultural Studies*. London: Sage Publications.

Alexander, J.C. and Seidman, S. (eds.) 1990: *Culture and Society: Contemporary Debates*. Cambridge: Cambridge University Press.

Anderson, C.A. and Bushman, B.J. 2001: 'Effects of violent video games on aggressive behaviour, aggressive cognition, aggressive affect, physiological arousal, and prosocial behaviour: a meta-analytic review of the scientific literature'. *Psychological Science* 12, 353–9.

Anderson, C.A. and Bushman, B.J. 2002: 'Psychology. The effects of media violence on society'. *Science* 295, 2377–9.

Anderson, D.R. and Collins, P.A. 1988: *The Impact of Children's Education: Television's Influence on Cognitive Development*. Washington, DC: Office of Educational Research and Improvement, US Dept of Education.

Anderson, D.R., Huston, A.C., Schmitt, K.L., Linebarger, D.L. and Wright, J.C. 2001: 'Early childhood television viewing and adolescent behaviour: the recontact study'. *Monographs of the Society for Research in Child Development* 66, I–VIII, 1–147.

Ang, I. 1985: *Watching Dallas*. London: Methuen.

Ang, I. 1990: 'Culture and communication: towards an ethnographic critique of media consumption in the transnational media system'. *European Journal of Communication* 5, 239–60.

Ang, I. 1991: *Desperately Seeking the Audience*. London: Routledge.

Ang, I. 2001: 'On the politics of empirical audience research'. In Durham, M.G. and Kellner, D. (eds.) *Media and Cultural Studies: Keyworks*. Oxford: Blackwell Publishers, 177–97.

Argenta, D.M., Stoneman, Z. and Brody, G.H. 1986: 'The effects of three different television programmes on young children's peer interactions and toy play'. *Journal of Applied Developmental Psychology* 7, 355–71.

Aristotle, Creed, J.L., Wardman, A.E. and Bambrough, R. 1963: *Philosophy of Aristotle. A New Selection*, with Introduction and Commentary by Renford Bambrough. New translations by A.E. Wardman and J.L. Creed. New York: New American Library.

Arlen, M.J. 1982: 'Good morning'. In Gumpert, G. and Cathcart, R. (eds.) *Intermedia: Interpersonal Communication in a Media World*. Oxford: Oxford University Press, 3–8.

Austin, J. 1962: *How to Do Things with Words*. Oxford: Oxford University Press.

Baacke, D. et al. 1990: *Lebenswelten sind Medienwelten: Medienwelten Jugendlicher, Vol. I. Lebensgeschichten sind Mediengeschichten: Medienwelten Jugendlicher, Vol. II* Leverkusen: Leske und Budrich.

Babbie, E. 1990: *Survey Research Methods* (2nd edn). Belmont, CA: Wadsworth.

Babbie, E. 1999: *The Basics of Social Research*. Belmont, CA: Wadsworth.

Baeker, G. 2000: *Cultural Policies and Cultural Diversity in Canada*. Report to the Council of Europe, January, www.pch.gc.ca/.

Bandura, A. 1973: *Aggression: A Social Learning Analysis*. Englewood Cliffs, NJ: Prentice-Hall.

Bandura, A., Ross, D. and Ross, S.A. 1961: 'Transmission of aggression through imitation of aggressive models'. *Journal of Abnormal and Social Psychology* 63, 575–82.

Bandura, A., Ross, D. and Ross, S.A. 1963a: 'Imitation of film-mediated aggressive models'. *Journal of Abnormal and Social Psychology* 66, 3–11.

Bandura, A., Ross, D. and Ross, S.A. 1963b: 'Vicarious reinforcement and imitative learning'. *Journal of Abnormal and Social Psychology* 67, 601–7.

Barker, C. 1999: *TV, Globalization and Cultural Identity*. Buckingham, UK: Open University Press.

Barker, M. and Brooks, K. 1998: 'On looking into Bourdieu's black box'. In Dickinson, R., Harindranath, R. and Linné, O. (eds.) *Approaches to Audiences: A Reader*. London: Arnold, 218–33.

Barker, M. and Petley, J. 1997: 'From bad research to worse'. In Barker, M. and Petley, J. (eds.) *Ill Effects: The Media/Violence Debate*. London: Routledge, 1–26.

Barker, M. and Petley, J. (eds.) 1997: *Ill Effects: The Media/Violence Debate*. London: Routledge.

Batra, R. and Ray, M. 1986: 'Affective responses mediating acceptance of advertising'. *Journal of Consumer Research* 13, 234–49.

Bausinger, H. 1984: 'Media, technology and everyday life'. *Media, Culture & Society* 4, 343–51.

Baym, N.K. 2000: *Tune In, Log On: Soaps, Fandom and Online Community*. London: Sage.

BBC 1995: *People and Programmes: BBC Radio and Television in an Age of Choice*. London: BBC.

Beale, A. 1999: 'Development and destatisation in European cultural policy'. *MIA Culture and Policy* 90, February, 90–105.

Bearden, W.O, Netemeyer, R.G. and Mobley, M.F. 1993: *Handbook of Marketing Scales: Multi Item Measures for Marketing and Consumer Behaviour Research*. Newbury Park, CA: Sage.

Beauchamp, T. et al. 1982: 'Introduction'. In T. Beauchamp et al. (eds.) *Ethical Issues in Social Science Research*. Baltimore, MD: Johns Hopkins University Press, 3–39.

Beck, U., Giddens, A. and Lash, S. 1994: *Reflexive Modernization. Politics, Tradition and Aesthetics in the Modern Social Order*. Cambridge: Polity.

Belch, G. 1982: 'The effects of television commercial repetition on cognitive response and message acceptance'. *Journal of Consumer Research* 9, 56–65.

Bennett, C. 1992: *Regulating Privacy: Data Protection and Public Policy in Europe and the US*. Ithaca: Cornell University Press.

Bennett, T. 1997: 'Towards a pragmatics for cultural studies'. In McGuigan, J. (ed.) *Cultural Methodologies*. Thousand Oaks, CA: Sage, 42–62.

Bennett, T., Emmison, M. and Frow, J. 1999: *Accounting for Tastes: Australian Everyday Cultures*. Cambridge: Cambridge University Press.

Berger, A.A. 2000: *Media and Communication Research Methods*. Thousand Oaks, CA: Sage.

Bergman, S. 1998: 'How a rabbit is pulled out of a hat: repertoire analysis as a tool for reconstructing the meaning of ICTs in daily life'. In Silverstone, R. and Hartmann, M. (eds.) *Methodologies for Media and Information Technology Research in Everyday Life*, research report. The Graduate Research Centre in Culture and Communication, University of Sussex.

Berkaak, O.A. and Ruud, E. 1994: *Sunwheels: Fortellinger om et rockeband [Sunwheels: Narratives of a Rock Band]*. Oslo: University Press.

Berkowitz, L. 1964: 'The effects of observing violence'. *Scientific American* 210, 35–41.

Bernstein, D. 1984: *Company Image and Reality. A Critique of Corporate Communications.* Eastbourne: Holt Rinehart and Winston.

Bertaux, D. (ed.) 1981: *Biography and Society: The Life History Approach in the Social Sciences.* Beverly Hills, CA: Sage.

Bhaskar, R. 1978: *A Realist Theory of Science.* Hassocks: Harvester Press.

Biltereyst, D. 1991: 'Resisting the American hegemony: a comparative analysis of the reception of domestic and US fiction'. *European Journal of Communication* 6, 469–97.

Birdwhistell, R.L. 1970: *Kinesics and Context: Essays on Body Motion Communication.* Philadelphia: University of Philadelphia Press.

Bloor, M., Frankland, J., Thomas, M. and Robson, K. 2001: *Focus Groups in Social Research.* London: Sage.

Blumer, H. 1969: *Symbolic Interactions: Perspectives and Method.* Englewood Cliffs, NJ: Prentice-Hall.

Blumler, J.G. and Katz, E. (eds.) 1974: *The Uses of Mass Communications.* Beverly Hills: Sage.

Blumler, J.C., Gurevitch, M. and Katz, E. 1985: 'Reaching out: a future for gratifications research'. In Rosengren, K.E., Wenner, L.A. and Palmgreen, P. (eds.) *Media Gratifications Research.* Beverly Hills: Sage, 225–74.

Bolin, G. 1998: *Filmbytare: Videovåld, kulturell produktion och unga män* [*Film Swappers: Video Violence, Cultural Production and Young Men*]. Umeaa: Boréa.

Bordewijk, J.L, and van Kaam, B. 1986: 'Towards a new classification of tele-information services'. *InterMedia* 14(1).

Bourdieu, P. 1984: *Distinction.* Cambridge: Polity Press. (Originally published in French 1979).

Bradford-Hill, A. 1965: 'The environment and disease: association or causation?' President's address, *Proceedings of the Royal Society of Medicine* 9, 295–300.

Bradford-Hill, A. 1966: 'The environment and disease: association or causation?', *Proceedings of the Royal Society of Medicine* 58, 295.

Brown, J.D. and Schulze, L. 1990: 'The effects of race, gender, and fandom on audience interpretations of Madonna's music videos'. *Journal of Communication* 40(2), 88–102.

Brown, S.R. 1993: 'A primer on Q methodology'. *Operant Subjectivity* 16, 91–138.

Brunsdon, C. 1981: '*Crossroads*: notes on soap opera'. *Screen* 22, 32–7.

Bryce, J.W. 1980: *Television and the Family: An Ethnographic Approach*. Columbia University: Teachers College, dissertation.

Buckingham, D. 1993: *Reading Audiences: Young People and the Media*. Manchester: Manchester University Press.

Buckingham, D. 1998: *Teaching Popular Culture: Beyond Radical Pedagogy*. London: UCL Press.

Buckingham, D. 2000: 'Studying children's media cultures: a new agenda for cultural studies'. In van den Bergh, B. and van den Bulck, J. (eds.) *Children and Media: Multidisciplinary Approaches*. Leuven: Garant, 49–66.

Budd, M., Craig, S. and Steinman, C.M. 1999: *Consuming Environments: Television and Commercial Culture*. New Brunswick, NJ: Rutgers University Press.

Buonanno, M. 2001: *Eurofiction 2001*. Florence: Council of Europe Audio Visual Observatory.

Burke, M.C. and Edell, J.A. 1989: 'The impact of feelings on ad-based affect and cognition'. *Journal of Marketing Research* 26, 69–83.

Burton, D. (ed.) 2000: *Research Training for Social Scientists*. London: Sage.

Calvert, S.L. 1999: *Children's Journeys Through the Information Age*. Boston: McGraw-Hill.

Campbell, A., Converse, P., Stokes, D. and Miller, W. 1960: *The American Voter*. New York: John Wiley.

Campbell, A., Curin, G. and Miller, W. 1954: 'Television and the election'. In Katz, D., Cartwright, D., Eldersveld, S. and McClung Lee, A. *Public Opinion and Propaganda: A Book of Readings*. New York: Dryden Press, 287–91.

Campbell, D.T. 1963: 'Social attitudes and other acquired behavioural dispositions'. In Koch, S. (eds.) *Psychology: A Study of a Science*. New York: McGraw-Hill, 94–172.

Canclini, N.G. 1988: 'Culture and power: the state of research'. *Media, Culture & Society* 10(4), 467–98.

Carey, J.W. 1985: 'Overcoming resistance to cultural studies'. In Gurevitch, M. and Levy, M.R. (eds.) *Mass Communication Review Yearbook* 5. Beverly Hills, CA: Sage. 27–40.

Carey, J.W. 1989: *Communication as Culture*. Boston: Unwin Hyman.

Carey, J.W. 1992: *Communication as Culture: Essays on Media and Society*. London: Routledge. (First published 1989.)

Carlsson, U. and von Feilitzen, C. 1998: *Children and Media Violence*. Yearbook from the Unesco clearing house on children and violence on the screen'. Gothenburg: Nordicom.

Carlsson, U. and Harrie, E. (eds.) 2001: *Media Trends 2001 in Denmark, Finland, Iceland, Norway and Sweden. Statistics and Analyses*. Gothenburg: Nordicom.

Castells, M. 1998: *The Rise of the Network Society*. Malden, MA: Blackwell. (First published 1996.)

Cawson, A., Haddon, L. and Miles, D. 1995: *The Shape of Things to Consume*. London: Avebury.

Chaffee, S.H. (ed.) 1975: *Political Communication: Issues and Strategies for Research*. Beverly Hills, CA: Sage.

Chahdi, L. and Laurent, R. 1999: 'Calibrating meter and diary data on television viewing'. *Focus on Culture*. Ottawa: Statistics Canada, Vol. 11, 4.

Chaiken, S. and Eagly, A. 1976: 'Communication modality as a determinant of message persuasiveness and message comprehensibility'. *Journal of Personality and Social Psychology* 34, 605–14.

Charmaz, K. 1995: 'Grounded theory'. In Smith, J.A., Harré, R. and Langenhove, L.V. (eds.). *Rethinking Methods in Psychology*. London: Sage.

Clarke, D. 2000: 'The active pursuit of active viewers: directions in audience research'. *Canadian Journal of Communication* 25, 39–59.

Clifford, J. and Marcus, G. (eds.) 1986: *Writing Culture: The Poetics and Politics of Ethnography*. Berkeley, CA: University of California Press.

Cohen, P. 1980: 'Subcultural conflict and working-class community'. In Hall, S., Hobson, D., Lowe, A. and Willis, P. (eds.) 1980: *Culture, Media, Language*. London: Hutchinson, 78–87. (First published 1972.)

Comstock, G.A. and Paik, H.-J. 1991: *Television and the American Child*. Academic Press.

Comstock, G.A., Rubinstein, E.A. and Murray, J.P. (eds.) 1972: *Television and Social Behaviour*. Reports and papers; a technical report to the Surgeon General's Scientific Advisory Committee on Television and Social Behaviour. Rockville, MD: National Institute of Mental Health.

Connell, R.W. et al. 1982: *Making the Difference: Schools, Families, and Social Division*. Sydney: Allen and Unwin.

Connerton, P. (ed.) 1976: *Critical Sociology: Selected Readings*. New York: Penguin.

Cooper, E. and Jahoda, M. 1954: 'The evasion of propaganda: how prejudiced people respond to anti-prejudice propaganda'. In Katz, D., Cartwright, D., Eldersveld, S. and MCclung Lee, A. (eds.) 1954: *Public Opinion and Propaganda: A Book of Readings*. New York: Dryden Press, 313–19.

Corner, J. 1980: 'Codes and cultural analysis'. *Media, Culture & Society* 2, 73–86.

Corradi, C. 1991: 'Text, context and individual meaning: rethinking life stories in a hermeneutic framework'. *Discourse and Society* 1, 105–18.

Correll, S. 1995: 'The ethnography of an electronic bar: the lesbian café. *Journal of Contemporary Ethnography* 24, 270–98.

Corteen, R.S. and Williams, T.M. 1986: 'Television and reading skills'. In Williams, T.M. (ed.) *The Impact of Television: A Natural Experiment in Three Communities*. Orlando: Academic Press, 39–86.

Crawford, P.I. 1993: 'Tekst og kontekst i etnografiske film: eller 'To Whom It May Concern'. *Mediekultur* 21, 34–44.

Crawford, P.I. and Turton, D. (eds.) 1992: *Film as Ethnography*. Manchester: Manchester University Press.

Cresswell, J.W. 1994: *Research Design*. Thousand Oaks, CA: Sage.

Creswell, J. 1998: *Qualitative Inquiry and Research Design: Choosing Among Five Traditions*. Thousand Oaks, CA: Sage.

Cronbach, L.J. and Shapiro, K. 1982: *Designing Evaluations of Educational and Social Programs*. San Francisco: Jossey-Bass.

Cumberbatch, G. 2001: 'Video violence: villain or victim?' At www.videostandards. org.uk/video_violence.htm.

Curran, J. 1990: 'The "New Revisionism" in mass communications research'. *European Journal of Communication* 5, 135–64.

Dahlgren, P. 1981: 'TV news as a social relation'. *Media, Culture & Society* 3(3).

Dahlgren, P. 1998: 'Critique: elusive audiences'. In Dickinson, R., Harindranath, R. and Linné, O. (eds.) *Approaches to Audiences*. London: Arnold.

Danermark, B., Ekström, M., Jakobsen L. and Karlsson, S.C. 2002: *Explaining Society. Critical Realism in the Social Sciences*. London: Routledge.

Davidsen-Nielsen, M. 1996: I folkets tjeneste. Om prætest og TV-seere som målgruppe [In the service of the people: About pre-tests and TV viewers as a target group]. *MedieKultur* 24. Aarhus, Denmark.

Deacon, D. 2003: 'Holism, communion and conversion: integrating media consumption and production research'. *Media, Culture & Society* 25(2).

Deacon, D., Fenton, N. and Bryman, A. 1999: 'From inception to reception: the natural history of a news item'. *Media, Culture & Society* 21, 5–31.

Deacon, D., Pickering, M., Golding, P., Murdock, G. 1999: *Researching Communications. A Practical Guide to Methods in Media and Cultural Analysis*. London: Arnold.

Decima Research and Les Consultants Cultur'Inc. 1992: *Canadian Arts Consumer Profile 1990–1991*. Ottawa: Department of Communications. May.

Defleur, M.L. and Ball-Rokeach, S. 1982: *Theories of Mass Communication* (4th edn). New York: Longman.

Denzin, N. 1970: *The Research Act: A Theoretical Introduction to Sociological Methods*. Englewood Cliffs, NJ: Prentice-Hall.

Denzin, N. 1978: *The Research Act: A Theoretical Introduction to Sociological Methods* (2nd edn). Chicago: Aldine. (First published 1970.)

Dervin, B. 1989: 'Audience as listener and learner, teacher and confidante: the sense-making approach'. In Rice, R.E. and Atkin, C.K. (eds.) *Public Communication Campaigns*. London: Sage, 67–86.

Descartes, R. 1954: *Philosophical Writings*. Edinburgh: Nelson.

Desmond, R.J., Singer, J.L. and Singer, D.G. 1990: 'Family mediation: parental communication patterns and the influences of television on children'. In Bryant, J. (ed.) *Television and the American Family*. Hillsdale, NJ: Lawrence Erlbaum Associated Publishers, 293–309.

De Vaus, D.A. 1995: *Surveys in Social Research* (4th edn). St Leonards, Australia: Allen and Unwin.

Devereux, G. 1967: *From Anxiety to Method in the Behavioural Sciences*. The Hague: Mouton.

Dilthey, W. 1974: 'On the special character of the human sciences'. In M. Truzzi (ed.) *Verstehen: Subjective Understanding in the Social Sciences*. Reading, MA: Addison-Wesley, 8–17. (First published in English 1944.)

Dovey, J. 2000: *Freakshow. First Person Media and Factual Television*. London: Pluto Press.

Drew, P. 1995: 'Conversation analysis'. In Smith, J.A., Harré, R. and Langenhove, L.V. (eds.) 1995: *Rethinking Methods in Psychology*. London: Sage.

Drotner, K. 1989: 'Girl meets boy: aesthetic production, reception, and gender identity'. *Cultural Studies* 2, 208–25.

Drotner, K. 1991: *At skabe sig – selv: ungdom, æstetik, pædagogik*. Copenhagen: Gyldendal.

Drotner, K. 1992: 'Modernity and media panics'. In Skovmand, M. and Schrøder, K.C. (eds.).

Drotner, K. 1993: 'Media ethnography: an other story?' In Ulla Carlsson (ed.) *Nordisk forskning om kvinnor och medier*. Gothenberg: Nordicom, 25–40.

Drotner, K. 1994: 'Ethnographic enigmas: "the everyday" in recent media studies'. *Cultural Studies* 8(2).

Drotner, K. 2001: 'Global media through youthful eyes'. In Livingstone, S. and Bovill, M. (eds.) *Children and their Changing Media Environment*. Mahwah, NJ: Lawrence Erlbaum Associates, 283–306.

Eco, U. 1979: *The Role of the Reader*. Bloomington: Indiana University Press.

Elliott, P. 1974: 'Uses and gratifications research: a critique and a sociological alternative'. In Blumler, J.G. and Katz, E. (eds.) *The Uses of Mass Communications*. Beverly Hills: Sage.

Eron, L.D. 1997: 'The development of antisocial behaviour from a learning perspective'. In Stoff, D.M., Breiling, J. and Maser, J.D. (eds.) *Handbook of Antisocial Behaviour*. New York: Wiley, 140–7.

Evans, W.A. 1990: 'The interpretative turn in media research: innovation, iteration, or illusion?' *Critical Studies in Mass Communication* 7, 147–68.

Ewen, S. 1996: *PR!: A Social History of Spin*. New York: Basic Books.

Fairclough, N. 1992: *Discourse and Social Change*. Cambridge: Polity Press.

Fairclough, N. 1993: 'Critical discourse analysis and the marketization of public discourse: the universities'. *Discourse & Society* 4(2), 133–68.

Fairclough, N. 1995: *Media Discourse*. London: Edward Arnold.

Farquhar, J.W. 1978: 'The community-based model of life style intervention trials'. *American Journal of Epidemiology* 108, 103–11.

Farquhar, J.W., Maccoby, N., Wood, P.D., Alexander, J.K., Breitrose, H., Brown, Jr, B.W., Haskell, W.L., McAlister, A.L., Meyer, A.J., Nash, J.D. and Stern, M.P. 1977: 'Community education for cardiovascular health'. *Lancet* 1, 1192–5.

Ferguson, M. and Golding, P. (eds.) 1997: *Cultural Studies in Question*. London: Sage.

Fernback, J. 1999: 'There is a there there: notes towards a definition of cybercommunity'. In Jones, S. (ed.) *Doing Internet Research*. London: Sage.

Festinger, L. 1957: *A Theory of Cognitive Dissonance*. Evenaston, IL: Row, Peterson.

Festinger, L. and Maccoby, N. 1964: 'On resistance to persuasive communications'. *Journal of Abnormal and Social Psychology* 68, 359–66.

Fidler, R. 1997: *MEDIAMORPHOSIS: Understanding New Media*. Thousand Oaks, CA: Pine Forge Press.

Fielding, N. 1993: 'Qualitative interviewing'. In Gilbert, N. (ed.) *Researching Social Life*. London: Sage.

Findahl, O. and Höijer, B. 1984: *Begriplighetsanalys*. Lund, Sweden: Studentlitteratur.

Finkelstein, M.J., Zanot, E.J. and Newhagen, J. 1994: 'A longitudinal content analysis of environmentally related advertisements in consumer magazines from 1966 through 1991', Research paper, School of Journalism, University of Maryland.

Fish, S. 1979: *Is There a Text in this Class? The Authority of Interpretative Communities.* Cambridge, MA: Harvard University Press.

Fiske, J. 1986: 'Television: polysemy and popularity'. *Critical Studies in Mass Communication* 3(2), 391–408.

Fiske, J. 1987: '*Television Culture.* London: Methuen.

Fiske, J. 1989: 'Moments of television: neither the text nor the audience'. In Seiter, E., Borchers, H., Kreutzner, G. and Warth, E.-M. (eds.) *Remote Control: Television, Audiences and Cultural Power*, London: Routledge

Fiske, J. 1990: *Introduction to Communication Studies.* London: Routledge.

Foddy, W. 1993: *Constructing Questions for Interviews and Questionnaires: Theory and Practice.* Cambridge, UK: Cambridge University Press.

Fornäs, J. et al. 1995: *Garageland: Rock, Youth and Modernity.* London: Routledge. (First published 1988.)

Fornäs, J. et al. 1990: *Speglad ungdom: forskningsreception i tre rockband.* Stockholm, Stehag: Symposion.

Forrester Research, Inc. 1996: *People and Technology: Why Consumers Buy.* Cambridge: www.forrester.com.

Foucault, M. and Gordon, C. 1980: *Power/Knowledge: Selected Interviews and Other Writings, 1972–1977.* New York: Pantheon Books.

Fowler, B. (ed.) 2000: *Reading Bourdieu on Society and Culture.* London: Blackwell Publishing.

Fowler, Jr, F.J. 1993: *Survey Research Methods* (2nd edn). Newbury Park, CA: Sage.

Freedman, J.L. 2002: *Media Violence and its Effect on Aggression: Assessing the Scientific Evidence.* Toronto: University of Toronto Press.

Frey, L.R., Botan, C.H., Friedman, P.G. and Kreps, G.L. 1991: *Investigating Communication. An Introduction to Research Methods.* Englewood Cliffs, NJ: Prentice-Hall.

Friessen, V. and Punie, Y. 1998: 'Never mind the gap – integrating qualitative and quantitative methods in ICT user research: the case of busy households'. In Silverstone, R. and Hartmann, M. (eds.) *Methodologies for Media and Information Technology Research in Everyday Life.* Research Report, The Graduate Research Centre in Culture and Communication, University of Sussex.

Fuglesang, M. 1994: *Veils and Videos: Female Youth Culture on the Kenyan Coast, Stockholm Studies in Social Anthropology* 32 Dept. of Social Anthropology, Stockholm University, dissertation.

Gamson, W. 1992: *Talking Politics.* Cambridge: Cambridge University Press.

Gans, H. 1979: *Deciding What's News*. New York: Pantheon.

Gantz, W. 1996: 'An examination of the range and salience of gratifications research associated with entertainment programming'. *Journal of Behavioural and Social Sciences* 1. Japan: Tokai University.

Garbarino, J. 2001: 'Violent children: where do we point the finger of blame?' *Archives of Pediatrics & Adolescent Medicine* 155, 13–14.

Garfinkel, H. 1967: *Studies in Ethnomethodology*. Englewood Cliffs, NJ: Prentice-Hall.

Garnham, N. 1993: 'Bourdieu, the cultural arbitrary, and television'. In Calhoun, C., LiPuma, E. and Posatone, M. (eds.) *Bourdieu: Critical Perspectives*. Cambridge: Polity Press, 178–92.

Gauntlett, D. 2001: 'The worrying influence of "media effects" studies'. In Barker, M. and Petley, J. (eds.) 1997: *Ill Effects: The Media/Violence Debate*. London: Routledge, 47–62.

Gavin, N.T. (ed.) 1998: *The Economy, Media and Public Knowledge*. London: Leicester University Press.

Geertz, C. 1973: *The Interpretation of Cultures*. New York: Basic Books.

Geertz, C. 1989: *Works and Lives: The Anthropologist as Author*. Cambridge: Polity Press. (First published 1988.)

Gerbner, G., Gross, L., Jackson-Beeck, M., Jeffries-Fox, S. and Signorielli, N. 1978: 'Cultural indicators: violence profile no. 9'. *Journal of Communication* 28, 176–207.

Giddens, A. 1978: 'Positivism and its critics'. In Bottomore, T.B. and Nisbet, R.A. (eds.) *A History of Sociological Analysis*. London: Basic Books, 237–86.

Giddens, A. 1984: *The Constitution of Society*. Cambridge: Polity Press.

Giddens, A. 1987: *Social Theory and Modern Sociology*. Cambridge: Polity Press.

Giddens, A. 1991: *Modernity and Self-Identity: Self and Society in the Late Modern Age*. Cambridge: Polity Press.

Gilham, B. 2000: *Developing A Questionnaire*. London: Continuum.

Gillespie, M. 1995: *Television, Ethnicity, and Cultural Change*. London: Routledge.

Ginsburg, F. 1989: *Contested Lives: The Abortion Debate in an American Community*. Berkeley, CA: University of California Press.

Giorgi, A. 1975: 'An application of phenomenological method in psychology'. In Giorgi, A., Fischer, C. and Murray, E. (eds.) *Duquesne Studies in Phenomenological Psychology II*. Pittsburgh, PA: Duquesne University Press, 82–103.

Gitlin, T. 1978: 'Media sociology: the dominant paradigm'. *Theory and Society* 6.

Gitlin, T. 1979: 'Prime time ideology: the hegemonic process in television entertainment'. *Social Problems* 26, 251–66.

Gjedde, L. and Ingemann, B. 2002: 'WebArt. Methods for investigating design and user experience through a reflexivity lab'. *The Nordicom Review* 23(2).

Glaser, B.G. and Strauss, A.L. 1967: *The Discovery of Grounded Theory: Strategies for Qualitative Research.* Chicago: Aldine.

Goffman, E. 1959: *The Presentation of Self in Everyday Life.* New York: Doubleday.

Goldstein, J.H. (ed.) 1998: *Why We Watch: The Attractions of Violent Entertainment.* New York: Oxford University Press.

Graber, D. 1984: *Processing the News: How People Tame the Information Tide.* New York: Longman.

Gray, A. 1987: 'Behind closed doors: video recorders in the home'. In Baehr, H. and Dyer, G. (eds.) *Boxed In: Women and Television.* London: Pandora.

Gray, A. 1992: *Video Playtime: The Gendering of a Leisure Technology.* London: Routledge.

Gray, G. and Guppy, N. 1999: *Successful Surveys: Research Methods and Practice.* Toronto: Harcourt Brace.

Greenbaum, T. 1998: *The Handbook for Focus Groups.* Thousand Oaks, CA: Sage.

Greenberg, B. 1974: 'Gratifications of television viewing and their correlates for British children'. In Blumler, J.G. and Katz, E. (eds.) *The Uses of Mass Communications.* Beverly Hills: Sage.

Greenberg, B. and Hnilo, L.R. 1996: 'Demographic differences in media gratifications'. *Journal of Behavioural and Social Sciences* 1. Japan: Tokai University.

Greenhouse, C.J. and Kheshti, R. (eds.) 1998: *Democracy and Ethnography.* Albany: State University of New York.

Greenwald, A.G. and Gillmore, G.M. 1997: 'No pain, no gain? The importance of measuring course workload in student ratings of instruction'. *Journal of Educational Psychology* 89, 743–51.

Griffin, C. 1980: 'Feminist ethnography'. CCCS Stencilled Occasional Paper, University of Birmingham.

Groeben, N. 1977: *Rezeptionsforschung als empirische litteraturwissenschaft.* Kronberg/Ts: Athenäum.

Grossberg, L., Nelson, C., Treichler, P.A. (eds.) 1992: *Cultural Studies.* New York: Routledge.

Grunig, J.E. and Hunt, T. 1984: *Managing Public Relations.* New York, NY: Holt, Rinehart and Winston.

Gumperz, J.J. and Hymes, D. (eds.) 1964: *The Ethnography of Communication.* Special issue of the *American Anthropologist* 66, 6 (Part II).

Gunter, B. 2000: *Media Research Methods.* London: Sage.

Gunter, B. and Furnham, A. 1992: *Consumer Profiles: An Introduction to Psychographics.* London: Routledge.

Habermas, J. 1962: *Strukturwandel der Öffentlichkeit.* Hermann Luchterland Verlag. (English translation: The structural transformation of the public sphere.) Cambridge, MA: MIT Press.

Hagen, I. 1994: 'The ambivalences of TV news viewing: between ideals and everyday practices'. *European Journal of Communication* 9.

Hagen, I. 1998a: *Medias publikum.* Oslo: Ad Notam Gyldendal.

Hagen, I. 1998b: 'Creation of socio-cultural meaning: media reception research and cognitive psychology'. In Höijer, B. and Werner, A. (eds.) *Cultural Cognition. New Perspectives in Media Audience Research.* Gothenburg: Nordicom.

Halkier, B. 2001: 'Consuming ambivalences: consumer handling of environmentally related risks in food'. *Journal of Consumer Culture* 1, 205–24.

Halkier, B. 2002: *Fokusgrupper* Copenhagen: Samfundslitteratur.

Hall, E.T. 1959: *The Silent Language.* Garden City, NY: Doubleday.

Hall S. 1973: 'Encoding and decoding in the television discourse'. CCCS Stencilled Occasional Paper, Media Series 7, Centre for Contemporary Cultural Studies, University of Birmingham. Abridged version in Hall, S. et al. 1980.

Hall S. 1980: 'Cultural studies: two paradigms'. In *Media, Culture & Society* 2, 57–72.

Hall S. 1994: 'Reflections upon the encoding/decoding model: an interview with Stuart Hall. In Cruz, J. and Lewis, J. *Viewing, Reading, Listening.* Boulder, CO: Westview Press.

Hall, S. and Jefferson, T. (eds.) 1976: *Resistance Through Rituals.* London: Hutchinson.

Hall, S., Connell, I. and Curti, L. 1976: 'The "unity" of current affairs television'. In *Cultural Studies* 9, Centre for Contemporary Cultural Studies, University of Birmingham.

Hall, S., Clarke, J., Critcher, C., Jefferson, T. and Roberts, B. 1978: *Policing the Crisis.* London: Macmillan.

Hall, S., Hobson, D., Lowe, A. and Willis, P. (eds.) 1980: *Culture, Media, Language.* London: Hutchinson.

Halliday, M.A.K. 1978: *Language as Social Semiotic: The Social Interpretation of Language and Meaning.* London: Arnold.

Halloran, J.D. 1970: *The Effects of Television*. London: Panther Modern Society.

Hammersley, M. 1992: 'Ethnography and realism'. In Hammersley, M., *What's Wrong with Ethnography? Methodological Explorations*. London, New York: Routledge, 43–56.

Hammersley, M. and Atkinson, P. 1989: *Ethnography: Principles in Practice*. London, New York: Routledge. (First published 1983.)

Hansen, A., Cottle, S., Negrine, R. and Newbold, C. 1998: *Mass Communication Research Methods*. London: Macmillan.

Harker, R., Mahar, C. and Wilkes, C. 1990: *An Introduction to the Work of Pierre Bourdieu: The Practice of Theory*. London: Macmillan.

Harris, R.J. 1999: *A Cognitive Psychology of Mass Communication* (3rd edn). Mahwah, NJ: Lawrence Erlbaum Associates.

Have, P. ten 1999: *Doing Conversation Analysis. A Practical Guide*. London: Sage.

Hebdige, D. 1979: *Subculture: The Meaning of Style*. London: Methuen.

Helland, K. 1993: *Public Service and Commercial News*. Bergen: Department of Media Studies.

Hempel, C.G. 1963: 'Typological methods in the social sciences'. In Natanson, M.A. (ed.) *Philosophy of the Social Sciences, a Reader*. New York: Random House, 210–30.

Herman, E. and Chomsky, N. 1988: *Manufacturing Consent: The Political Economy of Mass Media*. New York: Pantheon.

Hermes, J. 1995: *Reading Women's Magazines: An Analysis of Everyday Media Use*. Oxford: Polity Press.

Herzog, H. 1944: 'What do we really know about daytime serial listeners?' In Lazarsfeld, P.F. and Stanton, F. (eds.) *Radio Research 1942–1943*. New York: Duell, Sloan & Pearce.

Himmelweit, H.T. 1958: *Television and the Child: An Empirical Study of the Effect of Television on the Young*. London: Oxford University Press.

Hine, C. 2000: *Virtual Ethnography*. London: Sage.

Hjort, A. 1986: 'When women watch TV: How Danish women perceive the American series *Dallas* and the Danish series *Daughters of the War*'. Research report, Danish Broadcasting Corporation.

Hobson, D. 1982: *'Crossroads': The Drama of Soap Opera*. London: Methuen.

Hodge, R. and Kress, G. 1988: *Social Semiotics*. Cambridge: Polity Press.

Hodge, R. and Tripp, D. 1986: *Children and Television*. Cambridge: Polity Press.

Hoggart, R. 1957: *The Uses of Literacy*. Harmondsworth: Penguin.

Höijer, B. 1990: 'Reliability, validity and generalizability: three questions for qualitative reception research'. *The Nordicom Review* 1, 15–20.

Höijer, B. 1992: 'Socio-cognitive structure and television reception'. *Media, Culture & Society* 14, 583–603.

Höijer, B. 1998: 'Audiences' expectations of and interpretations of different television genres: a socio-cognitive approach'. Hagen, I. and Wasko, J. (eds.) *Consuming Audiences? Production and Reception in Media Research*. Hampton Press.

Holbrook, M.B. 1987: 'The study of signs in consumer esthetics: an egocentric view'. In Umiker-Sebeok, J. (ed.) *Marketing and Semiotics*. Berlin: Mouton de Gruyter, 73–121.

Hollonquist, T. and Suchman, E.A. 1944: 'Listening to the listener'. In Lazarsfeld, P.F. and Stanton, F.N. (eds.) *Radio Research 1942–1943*. New York: Duell, Sloan & Pearce, 265–334.

Holub, R.C. 1984: *Reception Theory. A Critical Introduction*. London: Methuen.

Horkheimer, M. 1976: 'Traditional and critical theory'. In Connerton P. (ed.) *Critical Sociology: Selected Readings*. New York: Penguin, 206–24.

Houtkoop-Steenstra, H. 2000: *Interaction and the Standardized Survey Interview: The Living Questionnaire*. Cambridge: Cambridge University Press.

Hovland, C.I. 1959: 'Reconciling conflicting results derived from experimental and survey studies of attitude change'. *American Psychologist* 14, 8–17.

Hovland, C.I., Lumsdaine, A.A. and Sheffield, F.D. 1949: *Experiments on Mass Communication*. Princeton, NJ: Princeton University Press.

Hovland, C.I. and Weiss, W. 1954: 'The influence of source credibility on communication effectiveness'. In Katz, D., Cartwright, D., Eldersveld, S. and McClung Lee, A. (eds.) 1954: *Public Opinion and Propaganda: A Book of Readings*. New York: Dryden Press, 337–47.

Howard, G.S. 1985: *Basic Research Methods in the Social Sciences*. Glenview, IL: Scott Foresman.

Huesmann, L.R. and Eron, L.D. 1986: *Television and the Aggressive Child: A Cross-National Comparison*. Hillsdale, NJ: Lawrence Erlbaum Associates.

Huesmann, L.R., Moise, J.F. and Podolski, C.-L. 1997: 'The effects of media violence on the development of antisocial behaviour'. In Stoff, D.M., Breiling, J. and Maser, J.D. (eds.) *Handbook of Antisocial Behaviour*. New York: Wiley, 181–93.

Husén, T. 1986: *The Learning Society Revisited*. Oxford: Pergamon Press.

Huston, A.C. and Wright, J.C. 1996: 'Television and socialization of young children'. In MacBeth, T.M. (ed.) *Tuning in to Young Viewers: Social Science Perspectives on Television*. Thousand Oaks, CA: Sage, 37–60.

Hyman, H.H. and Sheatsley, P.B. 1954: 'Some reasons why information campaigns fail'. In Katz, D., Cartwright, D., Eldersveld, S. and McClung Lee, A. (eds.) *Public Opinion and Propaganda: A Book of Readings*. New York: Dryden Press, 522–31.

Hymes, D. 1962: 'The ethnography of speaking'. In Gladwin, T. and Sturtevant, W. (eds.) *Anthopology and Human Behaviour*. Washington: Anthropological Society of Washington, 15–53.

Iser, W. 1974: *The Implied Reader: Patterns of Communication in Prose Fiction from Bunyan to Beckett*. Baltimore: Johns Hopkins University Press.

Iser, W. 1978: *The Act of Reading: A Theory of Aesthetic Response*. Baltimore: Johns Hopkins University Press.

Jackson, S.A. 1992: *Message Effects Research: Principles of Design and Analysis*. New York: Guilford Press.

Jackson, W. 1999: *Methods: Doing Social Research* (2nd edn). Scarborough: Prentice-Hall Canada, Inc.

Janis, I.L. 1951: *Air War and Emotional Stress*. New York: McGraw-Hill.

Janis, I.L. and Feshbach, S. 1954: 'Effects of fear-arousing communications'. In Katz, D., Cartwright, D., Eldersveld, S. and McClung Lee, A. (eds.) *Public Opinion and Propaganda: A Book of Readings*. New York: Dryden Press, 320–36.

Janis, I.L., Lumsdaine, A.A. and Gladstone, A.I. 1954: 'Effects of preparatory communications on reactions to a subsequent news event'. In Katz, D., Cartwright, D., Eldersveld, S. and McClung Lee, A. (eds.) *Public Opinion and Propaganda: A Book of Readings*. New York: Dryden Press, 347–62.

Jankowski, N.W. and Wester, F. 1991: 'The qualitative tradition in social science inquiry: contributions to mass communication research'. In Jensen, K.B. and Jankowski, N.W. (eds.) *A Handbook of Qualitative Methodologies for Mass Communication Research*. London: Routledge, 44–74.

Jauss, H.R. 1975: 'The idealist embarrassment: observations on Marxist aesthetics'. *New Literary History* 7, 191–208.

Jauss, H.R. 1982: *Aesthetic Experience and Literary Hermeneutics*. Minneapolis: University of Minnesota Press. (Published in German 1977.)

Jenkins, H. 1991: *Textual Poachers: Television Fans and Participatory Culture*. London: Routledge.

Jensen, J.F. 2001: '"So, what do you think, Linda?" Media typologies for interactive television'. In Agger, G. and Nielsen, J.F. (eds.) *The Aesthetics of Television*. Aalborg, Denmark: Aalborg University Press.

Jensen, K.B. 1986: *Making Sense of the News*. Aarhus, Denmark: Aarhus University Press.

Jensen, K.B. 1987: *Seernes TV-avis*. Research report 2B/87, Copenhagen: Danish Broadcasting Corporation.

Jensen, K.B. 1988: 'News as a social resource'. *European Journal of Communication* 3, 275–301.

Jensen, K.B. 1989: 'Discourses of interviewing: validating qualitative research findings through textual analysis'. In Kvale, S. (ed.) *Issues of Validity in Qualitative Research*. Lund, Sweden: Studentlitteratur, 93–108.

Jensen, K.B. 1990: 'The politics of polysemy: television news, everyday consciousness and political action'. *Media, Culture & Society* 12, 74–90.

Jensen, K.B. 1991a: 'Reception analysis: mass communication as the social production of meaning'. In Jensen, K.B. and Jankowski, N.W. (eds.) 135–48.

Jensen, K.B. 1991b: 'When is meaning? Communication theory, pragmatism, and mass media reception'. In Anderson, J. (ed.) *Communication Yearbook*, vol. 14. Newbury Park, CA: Sage.

Jensen, K.B. 1995: *The Social Semiotics of Mass Communication*. London: Sage Publications.

Jensen, K.B. (ed.) 1998: *News of the World. World Cultures Look at Television News*. London: Routledge.

Jensen, K.B. (ed.) 2002a: *A Handbook of Media and Communication Research. Qualitative and Quantitative Methodologies*. London: Routledge.

Jensen, K.B. 2002b: 'Media reception: qualitative traditions'. In Jensen, K.B. (ed.)

Jensen, K.B. 2002c: 'The complementarity of qualitative and quantitative methodologies in media and communication research'. In Jensen, K.B. (ed.).

Jensen, K.B. and Jankowski, N.W. (eds.) 1991: *A Handbook of Qualitative Methodologies for Mass Communication Research*. London: Routledge.

Jensen, K.B. and Rosengren, K.E. 1990: 'Five traditions in search of the audience'. *European Journal of Communication* 5, 207–38.

Jensen, K.B., Schrøder, K.C., Stampe, T., Søndergaard, H. and Topsøe-Jensen, J. 1994: 'Super flow, channel flow, and audience flows. A study of viewers' reception of television as flow'. *The Nordicom Review* 2, 1–13.

Jhally, S. and Lewis, J. 1992: *Enlightened Racism: The 'Cosby Show', Audiences and the Myth of the American Dream*. Boulder, CO: Westview Press.

Johnson, J.G., Cohen, P., Smailes, E.M., Kasen, S. and Brook, J.S. 2002: 'Television viewing and aggressive behaviour during adolescence and adulthood'. *Science* 295, 2468–71.

Johnson, M. 1987: *The Body and the Mind: The Bodily Basis of Meaning, Imagination, and Reason*. Chicago, London: University of Chicago Press.

Johnston, R.T. 2001: *Selling Themselves: The Emergence of Canadian Advertising*. Toronto: University of Toronto Press.

Jones, S. 1999a: 'Studying the net. Intricacies and issues'. In Jones, J. (ed.)

Jones, S. (ed.) 1999b: *Doing Internet Research*. London: Sage.

Jørgensen, M.W. and Phillips, L. 2002: *Discourse Analysis as Theory and Method*. London: Sage.

Joy, L.A., Kimball, M.M. and Zabrack, M.L. 1986: 'Television and children's aggressive behaviour'. In Williams, T.M. (ed.) *The Impact of Television: A Natural Experiment in Three Communities*. Orlando: Academic Press, 303–60.

Katz, D., Cartwright, D., Eldersveld, S. and McClung Lee, A. (eds.) 1954: *Public Opinion and Propaganda: A Book of Readings*. New York: Dryden Press.

Katz, E. 1957: 'The two-step flow of communication'. *Public Opinion Quarterly* 21, 61–78.

Katz, E. and Lazarsfeld, P.F. 1955: *Personal Influence: The Part Played by People in the Flow of Mass Communications*. Glencoe, IL: Free Press.

Katz, E., Gurevitch, M. and Haas, H. 1973: 'On the use of mass media for important things'. *American Sociological Review* 38, 164–81.

Katz, E., Blumler, J.G. and Gurevitch, M. 1974: 'Utilization of mass communication by the individual'. In Blumler, J.G. and Katz, E. (eds.) *The Uses of Mass Communications*. Beverly Hills: Sage.

Katz, E. and Liebes, T. 1984: 'Once upon a time in Dallas'. *Intermedia* 12, 3.

Kelman, H.C. 1958: 'Compliance, identification, and internalization: three processes of attitude change'. *The Journal of Conflict Resolution* 2, 51–60.

Kent, R. (ed.) 1994: *Measuring Media*. London: Routledge.

Kiefl, B. 1995: 'In search of a new "black box": the consumer's view of interactive TV, satellites, multi-media and video on demand'. A paper presented to the Canadian Institute. CBC Audience Research, November.

Kimmel, H.D. 1970: *Experimental Principles and Design in Psychology*. New York: Ronald Press Co.

Klapper, J.T. 1960: *The Effects of Mass Communication*. Glencoe, IL: Free Press, 302.

Kline, S. 1997: 'Image politics: negative advertising strategies and the election audience'. In Nava, M. et al. (eds.).

Koosis, D.J. and Coladarci, A.P. 1985: *Statistics*. New York: Wiley.

Korzenny, F. 1977: *Styles of Parent–Child Interaction as a Mediating Factor in Children's Learning from Antisocial Television Portrayals.* East Lansing: Michigan State University, 165.

Korzenny, F., Ting-Toomey, S. and Schiff, E. (eds.) 1992: *Mass Media Effects Across Cultures.* Newbury Park, CA: Sage.

Krosnick, J.A. and Fabrigrar, L.R. 1997: 'Designing rating scales for effective measurement in surveys'. In Lyberg, L. et al. (eds.) *Survey Measurement and Process Quality.* New York: John Wiley & Sons, 141–64.

Krueger, R.A. 1994: *Focus Groups: A Practical Guide for Applied Research.* Thousand Oaks, CA: Sage.

Krugman, H.E. 1965: 'The impact of television advertising: learning without involvement'. *Public Opinion Quarterly* 29, 349–56.

Krugman, H.E. 1972: 'Why three exposures may be enough'. *Journal of Advertising Research* 12, 11–14.

Kubey, R.W. and Csikszentmihalyi, M. 1990a: *Television and the Quality of Life: How Viewing Shapes Everyday Experience.* Hillsdale, NJ: Lawrence Erlbaum Associates.

Kubey, R.W. and Csikszentmihalyi, M. 1990b: 'Television as escape: subjective experience before an evening of heavy viewing'. *Communication Reports* 3, 92–100.

Kuhn, A. 1984: 'Women's genres'. *Screen* 25(1): 18–28.

Kvale, S. 1996: *InterViews: Introduction to Qualitative Research Interviewing.* Thousand Oaks, CA: Sage.

Labov, W. 1972a: *Sociolinguistic Patterns.* Philadelphia: University of Pennsylvania Press.

Labov, W. 1972b: 'The study of language in its social context'. In Labov, W. *Sociolinguistic Patterns.* Philadelphia: University of Pennsylvania Press, 183–259.

Laclau, E. 1990: *New Reflections on the Revolution of Our Time.* London: Verso.

Laclau, E. and Mouffe, C. 1985: *Hegemony and Socialist Strategy. Towards a Radical Democratic Politics.* London: Verso.

Lang, K. and Lang, G.E. 1966: 'The mass media and voting'. In Berelson, B. and Janowitz, M. (eds.) *Reader in Public Opinion and Communication.* New York: Free Press, 455–72.

Larsen, P. 1988: 'Exposure: noter om medier og subjektivitet'. *Samtiden* 3, Oslo 1988.

Larson, E. 1992: 'Watching Americans watch TV'. *Atlantic Monthly*, March, 66–80.

Lasswell, H. 1948: 'The structure and function of communication in society'. In Bryson, L. (ed.) *The Communication of Ideas.* New York: Harper, 32–51.

Lazarsfeld, P.F. 1941: 'Remarks on administrative and critical communications research'. *Zeitschrift für Sozialforschung/Studies in Philosophy and Social Science* 9.

Lazarsfeld, P.F. 1955: 'Why is so little known about the effects of television and what can be done?' *Public Opinion Quarterly* 19, 243–51.

Lazarsfeld, P.F. 1969: *Mathematical Thinking in the Social Sciences.* New York: Russell & Russell.

Lazarsfeld, P.F., Berelson, B. and Gaudet, H. 1948: *The People's Choice: How the Voter Makes up his Mind in a Presidential Campaign.* New York: Columbia University Press.

Lazarsfeld, P.F. and Rosenberg, M. 1955: *The Language of Social Research: A Reader in the Methodology of Social Research.* Glencoe, IL: Free Press.

Leal, O.F. 1986: *A Leitura Social da Novela das Oito.* Petropolis: Vozes.

Leal, O.F. 1990: 'Popular taste and erudite repertoire: the place and space of television in Brazil'. *Cultural Studies* 1, 19–29.

Lee, M. and Cho, Chong H. 1995: 'Women watching together: an ethnographic study of Korean soap opera fans in the United States'. In Dines, G. and Humez, J.M. (eds.) *Gender, Race and Class in Media.* Thousand Oaks, CA: Sage, 355–61.

Lemish, D. 1982: 'The rules of viewing television in public places'. *Journal of Broadcasting* 26: 757–91.

Lesser, G.S. 1974: *Children and Television: Lessons from Sesame Street.* New York: Random House.

Lewis, J. 1983: 'The encoding/decoding model: criticisms and redevelopments for research on decoding'. *Media, Culture & Society* 5, 179–97.

Lewis, J. 1991: *The Ideological Octopus. An Exploration of Television and its Audience.* New York: Routledge.

Lewis, J. 1997: 'What counts in cultural studies'. *Media, Culture & Society* 19(1), 83–97.

Lewis, J. 2001: *Constructing Public Opinion.* New York: Columbia University Press.

Lewis, L.A. (ed.) 1991: *The Adoring Audience: Fan Culture and Popular Media.* London: Routledge.

Liebes, T. 1984: 'Ethnocriticism: Israelis of Moroccan ethnicity negotiate the meaning of *Dallas*'. *Studies in Visual Communication* 10(3).

Liebes, T. and Katz, E. 1990: *The Export of Meaning.* New York: Oxford University Press.

Lindlof, T.R. (ed.) 1987: *Natural Audiences: Qualitative Research of Media Uses and Effects.* Norwood, NJ: Ablex.

Lindlof, T.R. 1995: *Qualitative Communication Research Methods.* London: Sage.

Lindlof, T.R. and Meyer, T.P. 1987: 'Mediated communication as ways of seeing, acting, and constructing culture: the tools and foundations of qualitative research'. In Lindlof (ed.) 1–30. 1987: *Natural Audiences Qualitative Research of Media Users and Effects*. Norwood, NJ: Ablex.

Lindlof, T.R. and Shatzer, M.J. 1989: 'Subjective differences in spousal perceptions of family video'. *Journal of Broadcasting & Electronic Media* 33, 375–95.

Livingstone, S. 1990: *Making Sense of Television. The Psychology of Audience Interpretation.* Oxford: Pergamon Press.

Livingstone, S. 1998: *Making Sense of Television: The Psychology of Audience Interpretation* (2nd edn). London: Routledge.

Livingstone, S. and Lunt, P. 1994: *Talk on Television*. London: Routledge.

Livingstone, S. and Bovill, M. (eds.) 2001: *Children and their Changing Media Environment: A European Comparative Study*. Mahwah, NJ: Lawrence Erlbaum Associates.

Loizos, P. 1993: *Innovation in Ethnographic Film: From Innocence to Self-Consciousness, 1955–1985*. Manchester: Manchester University Press.

Lowery, S.A. and Defleur, M. 1995: *Milestones in Mass Communication*. White Plains, NY: Longmans.

Luckin, R., Plowman, L., Gjedde, L., Laurillard, D., Stratfold, M. and Taylor, J. 1998: 'An evaluator's toolkit for tracking interactivity and learning'. In Oliver, M. (ed.) *Innovation in the Evaluation of Learning Technologies*. London: University of North London Press.

Lull, J. 1978: 'Choosing television programs by family vote'. *Communication Quarterly* 26(1), 53–7.

Lull, J. 1980: 'The social uses of television'. *Human Communication Research* 6, 197–209.

Lull, J. 1985: 'The naturalistic study of media use and youth culture'. In Rosengren, K.E. (ed.) 1994: *Media Effects and Beyond: Culture, Socialization and Lifestyles*. London: Routledge.

Lull, J. 1988: 'Critical response: the audience as nuisance'. *Critical Studies in Mass Communication* 5, 239–43.

Lull, J. 1995: *Media, Communication, Culture*. New York: Columbia University Press.

Luttbeg, N.R. (ed.) 1981: *Public Opinion and Public Policy: Models of Political Linkage*. Itasca, IL: F.E. Peacock Publishers.

Macbeth, T.M. (ed.) 1996: *Tuning in to Young Viewers: Social Science Perspectives on Television*. Thousand Oaks, CA: Sage.

Maccoby, N., Farquhar, J.W., Wood, P.D. and Alexander, J. 1977: 'Reducing the risk of cardiovascular disease: effects of a community-based campaign on knowledge and behaviour'. *Journal of Community Health* 3, 100–14.

Malinowski, B. 1922: *Argonauts of the Western Pacific: An Account of Native Enterprise and Adventure in the Archipelagoes of Melanesian New Guinea.* London, New York: Routledge and Kegan Paul.

McCombs, M.E. and Shaw, D.L. 1972: 'The agenda-setting function of the press'. *Public Opinion Quarterly* 36, 176–87.

McCracken, G. 1988: *The Long Interview.* Thousand Oaks, CA: Sage.

McDaniel, Jr, C. and Gates, R. 1996: *Contemporary Marketing Research* (3rd edn). St Paul, MN: West Publishing.

McGuigan, J. 1992: *Cultural Populism.* New York: Routledge.

McGuire, W.J. 1962: 'Persistence of the resistance to persuasion induced by various types of prior belief defenses'. *Journal of Abnormal and Social Psychology* 64, 241–8.

McLaren, P. 1986: *Schooling as a Ritual Performance: Towards a Political Economy of Educational Symbols.* London: Routledge and Kegan Paul.

McLeod, J.M., Becker, L.B. and Byrnes, J.E. 1974: 'Another look at the agenda-setting function of the press'. *Communication Research* 1, 131–65.

McLuhan, M. 1964: *Understanding Media: The Extensions of Man.* New York: McGraw-Hill.

McQuail, D. 1997: *Audience Analysis.* Thousand Oaks, CA: Sage.

McQuail, D. 1998: 'With the benefit of hindsight: reflections on uses and gratifications research'. In Dickinson, R., Harindranath, R. and Linné, O. (eds.) *Approaches to the Audience: A Reader.* London: Arnold, 151–65.

McQuail, D. 2000: *McQuail's Mass Communication Theory* (4th edn). London: Sage.

McRobbie, A. 1978: 'Working class girls and the culture of femininity'. In *Women Take Issue. Aspects of Women's Subordination.* The Women's Studies Group, Centre for Contemporary Cultural Studies, University of Birmingham. London: Hutchinson, 96–108.

Mann, C. and Stewart, F. 2000: *Internet Communication and Qualitative Research. A Handbook for Researching Online.* London: Sage.

Marcus, G. 1998: *Ethnography Through Thick and Thin.* Princeton, NJ: Princeton University Press.

Marcus, G. and Fischer, M. 1986: *Anthropology as Cultural Critique: An Experimental Moment in the Social Sciences.* Chicago: University of Chicago Press.

Marcuse, H. 1964: *One-Dimensional Man*. London: Routledge and Kegan Paul.

Marsh, C. 1982: *The Survey Method: The Contribution of Surveys to Sociological Explanation*. London: George Allen & Unwin.

Martín-Barbero, J. 1993: *Communication, Culture and Hegemony*. London: Sage. (First published 1987.)

Martín-Barbero, J. 2000: 'The cultural mediations of television consumption'. In Hagen, I. and Wasko, J. (eds.) *Consuming Audiences? Production and Reception in Media Research*. Creskill, NJ: Hampton Press, 145–61.

Masuda, Y. 1980: *The Information Society*. Tokyo: Institute for the Information Society.

Mattelart A. and Mattelart, M. 1998: *Theories of Communication: A Short Introduction*. London: Sage.

Mead, G.H. 1934: *Mind, Self, and Society*. Chicago: Chicago University Press.

Mehrabian, A. 1972: *Nonverbal Communication*. Chicago: Aldine-Atherton.

Menneer, P. 1987: 'Audience appreciation – a different story from audience numbers'. *Journal of the Market Research Society* 29, 241–64.

Merton, R.K. and Kendall, P.L. 1946: 'The focused interview'. *American Journal of Sociology* 51, 541–57.

Merton, R.K. and Lazarsfeld, P.F. (eds.) 1950: *Studies in the Scope and Method of 'The American Soldier'*. Glencoe, IL: Free Press.

Mick, D.G. and Politi, L. 1989: 'Consumers' interpretation of audience imagery: a visit to the hell of connotation'. In Hirschman, E.C. (ed.) *Interpretative Consumer Research*. Provo, UT: Association for Consumer Research.

Mick, D.G. and Buhl, C. 1992: 'A meaning-based model of advertising experiences'. *Journal of Consumer Research* 19, 317–38.

Milcs, M.B. and Huberman, A.M. 1994: *Qualitative Data Analysis: An Expanded Sourcebook*. London: Sage.

Mishler, E. 1986: *Research Interviewing: Context and Narrative*. Cambridge, MA: Harvard University Press.

Mitchell, A. 1983: 'The effects of visual and emotional advertising: an information processing approach'. In Percy, L. and Woodside, A.G. (eds.) *Advertising and Consumer Psychology*. Lexington, MA: Lexington Books, 197–218.

Moore, H. 1994: *A Passion for Difference: Essays in Anthropology and Gender*. Cambridge: Polity Press.

Moores, S. 1993: *Interpreting Audiences: The Ethnography of Media Consumption*. London: Sage.

Morgan, D.L. 1988: *Focus Groups as Qualitative Research*. Beverly Hills, CA: Sage.

Morley, D. 1980: *The 'Nationwide' Audience*. London: British Film Institute.

Morley, D. 1981: 'The *Nationwide* audience: a critical postscript'. *Screen Education* 39, 3–14.

Morley, D. 1986: *Family Television*. London: Comedia

Morley, D. 1989: 'Changing paradigms in audience studies'. In Seiter, B., Borchers, H., Kreutzner, G. and Warth, E.-M. (eds.) *Remote Control: Television, Audiences and Cultural Power*. London: Routledge.

Morley, D. 1992: *Television, Audiences and Cultural Studies*. London: Routledge.

Morley, D. and Silverstone, R. 1990: 'Domestic communication: technologies and meanings'. *Media, Culture and Society* 1, 31–55.

Morley, D. and Silverstone, R. 1991: 'Communication and context: ethnographic perspectives on the media audience'. In Jensen, K.B. and Jankowski, N.W. (eds.). *A Handbook of Qualitative Methodologies for Mass Communication Research*. London: Routledge, 149–62.

Morrison, D. 1986: *Invisible Citizens: British Public Opinions and the Future of Broadcasting*. London: BBC Broadcasting Unit.

Mulvey, L. 1975: 'Visual pleasure and narrative cinema'. *Screen* 16(3), 8–18.

Murdock, G. 1997: 'Thin descriptions: questions of method in cultural analysis'. In McGuigan, J. (ed.) *Cultural Methodologies*. Thousand Oaks. CA: Sage, 178–92.

Murray, C.A. 1994: *The BC Arts Consumer Profile*. Cultural Services Branch: British Columbia Ministry of Tourism and Culture.

Murray, C.A., De La Garde, R. and Martin, C. 2001: 'The Eurofiction 2000 Report'. Florence: Council of Europe, at www.sfu.ca/communication/ecf/.

Myers, G. 1998: 'Displaying opinions: topics and disagreement in focus groups'. *Language in Society* 27, 85–111.

Natanson, M.A. (ed.) 1963: *Philosophy of the Social Sciences, A Reader*. New York: Random House.

Nava, M. and Nava, O. 1990: 'Discriminating or duped? Young people as consumers of advertising/art'. *The Magazine of Cultural Studies*, March, 15–21.

Nava, M., Blake, A., MacRury, I. and Richards, B. (eds.) 1997: *Buy This Book: Studies in Advertising and Consumption*. London: Routledge.

Negrine, R. 1996: *The Communication of Politics*. London: Sage.

Negroponte, N. 1995: *Being Digital*. London: Hodder & Stoughton.

Neuman, L.W. 2000: *Social Research Methods: Qualitative and Quantitative Approaches*. Needham Heights, MA: Allyn & Bacon.

Neuman, R.W. 1991: *The Future of the Mass Audience*. New York: Cambridge University Press.

Neuman, S.B. 1995: *Literacy in the Television Age: The Myth of the TV Effect*. Norwood, New Jersey: Ablex.

Newcomb, H. 1978: 'Assessing the violence profile studies of Gerbner and Gross: a humanistic critique and suggestion'. *Communication Research* 5 (3).

Nightingale, V. 1989: 'What's "Ethnographic" about ethnographic audience research?' *Australian Journal of Communication* 16, 50–63.

Nielsen, J. 1993: *Usability Engineering*. San Francisco: Morgan Kaufmann Publishers, Inc.

Nielsen, J. 2000: *Designing Web Usability*. Indianapolis: New Riders.

Nielsen, J. and Coyne, K.P. 2001: 'A useful investment'. *CIO Magazine*, 15 February, at www.cio.com/archive/021501/et_pundits_content.html.

Nissen, J. 1993: *Pojkarna vid datorn: unga entusiaster i datateknikens värld*. Stockholm: Symposion, dissertation.

Nofsinger, R.E. 1991: *Everyday Conversation*. Newbury Park, CA: Sage.

O'Donohoe, S. 1997: 'Leaky boundaries: intertextuality and young adult experiences of advertising'. In Nava, M. et al. (eds.).

O'Guinn, T.C. and Shrum, L.J. 1997: 'The role of television in the construction of consumer reality'. *Journal of Consumer Research* 23, 278–94.

Olsen, C. 2000: *Tjeck – et gratis magasin for unge i det moderne*. [Tjeck – a free magazine for young people in modernity.] MA dissertation, Department of Communication, Roskilde University, Denmark.

Ortner, S. 1984: 'Theory in anthropology since the sixties'. *Comparative Studies in Society and History* 26(1), 126–66.

Osgood, C.E., Suci, G.J. and Tannenbaum, P.H. 1957: *The Measurement of Meaning*. Urbana: University of Illinois Press.

Packard, V.O. 1959: *The Status Seekers: An Exploration of Class Behaviour in America and the Hidden Barriers That Affect You, Your Community, Your Future*. New York: D. McKay Co.

Palmer, E.L. 1988: *Television & America's Children: A Crisis of Neglect*. New York: Oxford University Press.

Palmgreen, P., Wenner, L.A. and Rosengren, K.E. 1985: 'Uses and gratifications research: the past ten years'. In Rosengren, K.E., Wenner, L.A. and Palmgreen, P. (eds.) 1985: *Media Gratifications Research*. Beverly Hills: Sage, 11–37.

Palter, R. (ed.) 1969: *Toward Modern Science: Studies in Ancient, Medieval, and Renaissance Science*. New York: E.P. Dutton & Co., Inc.

Paredes, A. and Bauman, R. (eds.) 1972: *Toward New Perspectives in Folklore*. Austin, TX: University of Texas Press.

Park, R.E., Burgess, E.W., McKenzie, R.D. and Wirth, L. 1925: *The City*. Chicago, IL: The University of Chicago Press.

Parkin, F. 1971: *Class Inequality and Political Order*. London: Paladin.

Pateman, T. 1983: 'How is understanding an advertisement possible?' In Davis, H. and Walton, P. (eds.) *Language, Image, Media*. Oxford: Basil Blackwell.

Patterson, T.E. and McClure, R.D. 1976: *The Unseeing Eye: The Myth of Television Power in National Politics*. New York: Putnam.

Pavitt, C. 1999: 'The third way: scientific realism and communication theory'. *Communication Theory* 9(2), 162–88.

Pavlik, J.V. 1996: *New Media Technology: Cultural and Commercial Perspectives*. Boston: Allyn & Bacon.

Pearl, D., Bouthilet, L. and Lazar, J.B. (eds.) 1982: *Television and Behaviour: Ten Years of Scientific Progress and Implications for the Eighties*. Rockville, MD: US Dept of Health and Human Services Public Health Service Alcohol Drug Abuse and Mental Health Administration National Institute of Mental Health: Supt. of Docs. US GPO distributor.

Peirce, C.S. 1985: 'Logic as semiotic: the theory of signs'. In Innis, H. (ed.) *Semiotics: An Introductory Anthology*. Bloomington: Indiana University Press.

Petty, R.E. and Cacioppo, J.T. 1985: 'Central and peripheral routes to persuasion'. In Alwitt, L.F. and Mitchell, A.A. (eds.) *Psychological Processes and Advertising Effects: Theory, Research, and Applications*. Hillsdale, NJ: Lawrence Erlbaum Associates.

Pike, K. 1967: *Language in Relation to a Unified Theory of the Structure of Human Behaviour*. The Hague: Mouton. (First published 1954.)

Plowman, L. 1996: 'Narrative, linearity and interactivity: making sense of interactive multimedia'. *British Journal of Educational Technology* 27(2).

Pollock, F. 1976: 'Empirical research into public opinion'. In Connerton, P. (ed.) 1976: *Critical Sociology: Selected Readings*. New York: Penguin, 225–36.

Popovich, M., Gustafson, R.L. and Thomsen, S.R. 2000: 'High school girls' perceptions of female advertising stereotypes and eating-disordered thinking: a Q method analysis'.

Paper for the International Society for the Scientific Study of Subjectivity, Oklahoma State University, October.

Postman, N. 1985: *Amusing Ourselves to Death*. New York: Viking.

Potter, J. 1996: *Representing Reality: Discourse, Rhetoric and Social Construction*. London: Sage.

Potter, J. and Wetherell, M. 1987: *Discourse and Social Psychology*. London: Sage.

Poulsen, I. 1992: *Uge 39. En eksperimentaluge på radioavisen*. Research report 1B/1992, Copenhagen: Danish Broadcasting Corporation.

Price, V. 1992: *Public Opinion*. Newbury Park, CA: Sage.

Professional Marketing Research Society 1997: 'Measuring refusal rates'. *Canadian Journal of Marketing Research* 16: 31–42.

Putnam, R. 1995: 'Tuning in, tuning out: the strange disappearance of social capital in America'. In *PS: Political Science and Politics* 28(4), 17–29.

Radway, J. 1984: *Reading the Romance: Women, Patriarchy and Popular Literature*. Chapel Hill: University of North Carolina Press.

Radway, J. 1988: 'Reception study: ethnography and the problem of dispersed audiences and nomadic subjects'. *Cultural Studies* 2(3), 359–76.

Rasmussen, D. in press: *Det mobile samtalerum [Mobile spaces of communication]*. Department of Language and Communication, University of Southern Denmark, dissertation.

Rasmussen, T.A. 1990: *'Tror du kun det er dig der har øjne': actionfilm og drengekultur*. Aalborg: Department of Communication, Aalborg University, dissertation.

Ray, M. 1973: 'Marketing communication and the hierarchy-of-effects'. In Clarke, P. (ed.) *New Models for Mass Communication Research*. Beverly Hills, CA: Sage, 147–76.

Richards, T.J. and Richards, L. 1994: 'Using computers in qualitative research'. In Denzin, N.K. and Lincoln, Y.S. (eds.) *Handbook of Qualitative Research*. London: Sage.

Richards, Jr, W.D. 1998: *The Zen of Empirical Research*. Cresskill, NJ: Hampton Press.

Roberts, D.F. and Bachen, C.M. 1981: 'Mass communication effects'. *Annual Review of Psychology* 32, 307–56.

Robinson, T.N. 2001: 'Television viewing and childhood obesity'. *Pediatric Clinics of North America* 48, 1017–25.

Robinson, T.N., Saphir, M.N., Kraemer, H.C., Varady, A. and Haydel, K.F. 2001: 'Effects of reducing television viewing on children's requests for toys: a randomized controlled trial'. *Journal of Developmental and Behavioural Pediatrics* 22, 179–84.

Rochberg-Halton, E. 1986: *Meaning and Modernity*. Chicago: Chicago University Press.

Roe, I. 1996: 'Corporate affiliations and advertising: a qualitative study for The United Way of the Lower Mainland'. Research report, School of Communication, Simon Fraser University, Burnaby, Canada.

Roe, K. 1994: 'Media use and social mobility'. In Rosengren, K.E. (ed.) *Media Effects and Beyond: Culture, Socialization and Lifestyle*. London: Routledge, 183–204.

Roe, K. 1996: 'The uses and gratifications approach: a review of some methodological issues'. *Journal of Behavioural and Social Sciences* 1. Japan: Tokai University.

Roe, K. and Muijs, D. 1995: *Literacy in the Media Age: Results from the First Wave of a Longitudinal Study of Children's Media Use and Educational Achievement*. Research report, the Centre for Audience Research, Department of Communication, Katholieke Universiteit Leuven, Belgium.

Rogers, E. 1986: *Communication Technology: The New Media in Society*. New York: Free Press.

Rogers, R.S. 1995: 'Q methodology'. In Smith, J.A., Harré, R. and Langenhove, L.V. (eds.) *Rethinking Methods in Psychology*. London: Sage.

Rogge, J.-U. 1991: 'The media in everyday family life: some biographical and typological aspects'. In Seiter, E., Borchers, H., Kreutzner, G. and Warth, E.-M. (eds.) *Remote Control: Television, Audiences and Cultural Power*. London: Routledge, 168–79.

Rogge, J.-U. and Jensen, K. 1988: 'Everyday life and television in West Germany: an empathic–interpretative perspective on the family as a system'. In Lull, J. (ed.) *World Families Watch Television*. Newbury Park: Sage, 80–115.

Rosaldo, M. 1980: 'The use and abuse of anthropology: reflections on feminism and cross-cultural understanding'. *Signs* 5(3), 389–417.

Rose, G.M., Bush, V.D. and Kahle, L.R. 1998: 'The influence of family communication patterns on parental reactions toward advertising: a cross-national examination'. *Journal of Advertising* 27, 71–86.

Rosengren, K.E. 1993: 'From "field" to "frog ponds"'. *Journal of Communication* 43(3), 6–17.

Rosengren, K.E. (ed.) 1994: *Media Effects and Beyond: Culture, Socialization and Lifestyles*. London: Routledge.

Rosengren, K.E. 1996: 'Review of Klaus Bruhn Jensen, The social semiotics of mass communication'. *European Journal of Communication* 11(1).

Rosengren, K.E., Wenner, L.A. and Palmgreen, P. (eds.) 1985: *Media Gratifications Research*. Beverly Hills, CA: Sage.

Rubin, A. 1979: 'Television use by children and adolescents'. *Human Communication Research* 5(2), 100–20.

Rubin, A. 1981: 'An examination of television viewing motivations'. *Communication Research* 8, 141–65.

Rubin, R.B., Palmgreen, P. and Sypher, H.E. (eds.) 1994: *Communication Research Measures: A Sourcebook.* New York: Guildford Press.

Rubin, R.B., Rubin, A.M. and Piele, L.J. 1999: *Communication Research: Strategies and Sources,* Belmont, CA: Wadsworth.

Ruud, E. 1995: 'Music in the media: the soundtrack behind the construction of identity'. *Young: Nordic Journal of Youth Research* 3(2), 34–45.

Ryan, A. 1970: *The Philosophy of the Social Sciences.* London: Macmillan.

Salomon, G. 1983: *Interaction of Media, Cognition and Learning.* San Francisco: Jossey-Bass.

Sapsford, R. 1999: *Survey Research.* London: Sage.

Savage, P. 1993: 'Why do academics abdicate to advertisers?' Unpublished paper from CBC Audience Research, presented to the Canadian Communication Association, Ottawa, June.

Schiller, H. 1969: *Mass Communication and American Empire.* New York: Augustus M. Kelly.

Schramm, W.L., Lyle, J. and Parker, E.B. 1961: *Television in the Lives of Our Children.* Stanford, CA: Stanford University Press.

Schrøder, K.C. 1987: 'Convergence of antagonistic traditions – the case of audience research'. *European Journal of Communication* 2, 7–31.

Schrøder, K.C. 1988: 'The pleasure of *Dynasty*'. In Drummond, P. and Paterson, R. (eds.) *Television and its Audience.* London: British Film Institute.

Schrøder, K.C. 1989: 'The playful audience: the continuity of the popular cultural tradition in America'. In Skovmand, M. (ed.) *Media Fictions.* Aarhus, Denmark: Aarhus Univeristy Press.

Schrøder, K.C.1992: 'Cultural quality: search for a phantom? A reception perspective on judgements of cultural value'. In Skovmand, M. and Schrøder, K.C. (eds.).

Schrøder, K.C. 1993: 'Corporate advertising from senders to receivers'. *Nordicom Review.* Gothenburg.

Schrøder, K.C. 1994: 'Audience semiotics, interpretative communities and the "ethnographic turn" in media research'. *Media, Culture & Society,* 16, 337–47.

Schrøder, K.C. 1995: *Danskerne og medierne: dagligdag og demokrati* [The Danes and the media: daily life and democracy]. Report for the Commission on the Media, Copenhagen: Prime Minister's Office.

Schrøder, K.C. 1997: 'Cynicism and ambiguity: British corporate responsibility advertisements and their readers in the 1990s'. In Nava, M. et al. (eds.).

Schrøder, K.C. 1999: 'The best of both worlds? Media audience research between rival paradigms'. In P. Alasuutari (ed.) *Rethinking the Media Audience. The New Agenda*. London: Sage, 38–68.

Schrøder, K.C. 2000: 'Making sense of audience discourses: towards a multidimensional model of mass media reception'. *European Journal of Cultural Studies* 3(2), May, 233–258.

Schrøder, K.C. 2002: 'Discourses of fact'. In Jensen, K.B. (ed.) 2002.

Schrøder, K.C. and Hansen, S.E. 2002: 'Beyond duality. Danes' views on Denmark and the European Union 2001'. http://akira.ruc.dk/~kimsc/Beyond_Duality.pdf.

Schudson, M. 1987: 'The new validation of popular culture: sense and sentimentality in academia'. *Critical Studies in Mass Communication* 4(1).

Schuman, H. and Presser, S. 1981: *Questions and Answers in Attitude Surveys*. London: Academic Press.

Schumann, D.W., Hathcote, J.M. and West, S. 1991: 'Corporate advertising in America: a review of published studies on use, measurement, and effectiveness'. *Journal of Advertising* 20(3), 35–56.

Schutz, A. 1964: 'The stranger: an essay in social psychology'. In *Collected Papers. Vol. II*. The Hague: Martinus Nijhoff.

Schwichtenberg, C. (ed.) 1993: *The Madonna Connection: Representational Politics, Subcultural Identities, and Cultural Theory*. Boulder: Westview Press.

Scott, W.D. 1903: *The Theory of Advertising: A Simple Exposition of the Principles of Psychology in Their Relation to Successful Advertising*. Boston, MA: Small Maynard & Company.

Seiter, E. 1999: *Television and New Media Audiences*. Oxford: Clarendon Press.

Seiter, E., Borchers, H., Kreutzner, G. and Warth, E.-M. (eds.) 1989: *Remote Control: Television, Audiences and Cultural Power*. London: Routledge

Serena, W. and Schramm, W. 1969: 'The mass media as sources of public affairs, science and health knowledge'. *Public Opinion Quarterly* 33, 197–209.

Shepard, V. 1993: 'Does it pay to advertise?' *International Magazine of the BP Group*. Spring.

Silverman, D. 1998: 'Qualitative/quantitative'. In Jenkins, C. (ed.) *Core Sociological Dichotomies*. London: Sage, 78–95.

Silverman, D. 2000: *Doing Qualitative Research: A Practical Handbook*. London: Sage.

Silverstone, R. and Hirsch, E. 1992: *Consuming Technologies: Media and Information in Domestic Spaces*. London: Routledge.

Silverstone, R. and Hartmann, M. (eds.) 1998: *Methodologies for Media and Information Technology Research in Everyday Life.* Research report, The Graduate Research Centre in Culture and Communication, University of Sussex.

Singer, J.L., Singer, D.G. and Rapaczynski, W.S. 1984: 'Family patterns and television viewing as predictors of children's beliefs and aggression'. *Journal of Communication* 34, 73–89.

Skeggs, B. 1997: *Formations of Class of Gender: Becoming Respectable.* London: Sage.

Skinner, C.J., Holt, D. and Smith, T.M.F. (eds.) 1989: *Analysis of Complex Surveys.* Chichester: Wiley.

Skovmand, M. and Schrøder, K.C. (eds.) 1992: *Media Cultures. Reappraising Transnational Media.* London: Routledge.

Smith, D. 1987: *The Everyday World as Problematic: A Feminist Sociology.* Boston, MA: New England University Press.

Smith, M.J. 1988: *Contemporary Communication Research Methods.* Belmont, CA: Wadsworth.

Smith, N.C. 1990: *Morality and the Market. Consumer Pressure for Corporate Accountability.* London: Routledge.

Smythe, D. 1977: 'Communications: blindspots of western Marxism'. *Canadian Journal of Political and Social Theory* 1, 120–7.

Spradley, J.P. 1979: *The Ethnographic Interview.* Fort Worth, TX: Harcourt, Brace Jovanovich.

Spradley, J.P. 1980: *Participant Observation.* Fort Worth, TX: Harcourt College Publishers.

Stacey, J. 1988: 'Can there be a feminist ethnography?' *Women's Studies International Forum* 11(1), 21–7.

Stald, G. 1999: 'Living with computers. Young Danes' uses of and thoughts on the uses of computers'. *Sekvens 1998*, Yearbook of the Department of Film and Media Studies, University of Copenhagen.

Stangor, C. 1998: *Research Methods for the Behavioural Sciences.* Boston, MA: Houghton Mifflin.

Starch, D. 1923: *Principles of Advertising.* Chicago, IL: A.W. Shaw.

Starch, D. 1966: *Measuring Advertising Readership and Results.* New York: McGraw-Hill.

Stax, P. 2000: '"And then what was the question again?" – Text and Talk in Standardized Interviews'. *American Statistical Association 2000 Proceedings of the Section on Survey Methods.* Alexandria, 913–17.

Stehr, N. 1994: *Knowledge Societies*. London: Sage.

Stein, A.H., Friedrich, L.K. and Vondracek, F. 1972: 'Television content and young children's behaviour'. In Comstock, G.A. and Paik, H.-J. 1991: *Television and the American Child*. Academic Press, 202–317.

Stempel, G.H. and Westley, B.H. (eds.) 1989: *Research Methods in Mass Communication*. Englewood Cliffs, NJ: Prentice-Hall.

Stokes, D.E. 1968: 'Some dynamic elements of contests for the presidency'. In Luttbeg, N.R. (ed.) *Public Opinion and Public Policy: Models of Political Linkage*. Homewood, IL: Dorsey Press, 33–45.

Strinati, D. 1995: *An Introduction to Theories of Popular Culture*. London: Routledge.

Suchman, L. and Jordan, B. 1990: 'Interactional troubles in face-to-face interviews'. *Journal of the American Statistical Association* 85, 409.

Suleiman, S.R. and Crosman, I. (eds.) 1980: *The Reader in the Text*. Princeton, NJ: Princeton University Press.

Sumser, J. 2001: *A Guide to Empirical Research in Communication: Rules for Looking*. Thousands Oaks, CA: Sage.

Tanur, J.M. (ed.) 1991: *Questions about Questions*. New York: Russell Sage Foundation.

Tomlinson, J. 1991: *Cultural Imperialism: A Critical Introduction*. Baltimore: Johns Hopkins University Press.

Tufte, B. 1998: *TV på tavlen: Om børn, skole og medier?* Copenhagen: Akademisk Forlag.

Tufte, T. 2000: *Living with the Rubbish Queen: Telenovelas, Culture and Modernity in Brazil*. Luton: University of Luton Press.

Tulloch, J. 2000: *Watching Television Audiences*. London: Arnold.

Turkle, S. 1995: *Life on the Screen: Identity in the Age of the Internet*. New York: Simon & Schuster.

Unesco 1997: *Cultural Indicators of Development*. Geneva: UNRISD.

Upton, G.J.G. 1978: *The Analysis of Cross-Tabulated Data*. Chichester: Wiley.

Valkenburg, P.M., Krcmar, M. and De Roos, S. 1998: 'The impact of a cultural children's programme and adult mediation on children's knowledge of and attitudes towards opera'. *Journal of Broadcasting and Electronic Media* 42, 315–26.

van den Bergh, B. and van den Bulck, J. (eds.) 2000: *Children and Media: Multidisciplinary Approaches*. Leuven: Garant.

van der Voort, T. 1997: 'The effects of television on children: parental perceptions and mediation'. *Trends in Communication* 2, 5–29.

Van Dijk, T. (ed.) 1997: *Discourse Studies: A Multidisciplinary Introduction*, Vols 1–2. London: Sage.

Vernoy, M.W. and Vernoy, J. 1997: *Behavioural Statistics in Action*. Pacific Grove: Brooks/Cole.

Wade, S. and Schramm, W. 1969: 'The mass media as sources of public affairs, science, and health knowledge'. *Public Opinion Quarterly* 33, 197–209.

Walkerdine, V. (with the Girls and Mathematics Unit) 1989: *Counting Girls Out: Girls and Mathematics*. London: Virago.

Walsh, D.F. 1998: 'Structure and agency'. In Jenks, C. (ed.) *Core Sociological Dichotomies*. Thousand Oaks, CA: Sage, 8–33.

Warner, W.L. and Henry, W.E. 1948: 'The radio daytime serial: a symbolic analysis'. *Genetic Psychology Monographs* 37, 3–71.

Wasko, J. (ed.) 2001: *Dazzled by Disney*. Leicester: Leicester University Press.

Weaver, D.H.E.A. 1976: 'Influence of the mass media on issues, images and political interest: the agenda-setting function of mass communication during the 1976 campaign'. Paper presented at the Midwest Association for Public Opinion Research, Chicago, IL.

Webster, J.G. and Phalen, P.F. 1997: *The Mass Audience: Rediscovering the Dominant Model*. Mahwah, NJ: Lawrence Erlbaum Associates.

White, J. 1991: *How to Understand and Manage Public Relations*. London: Business Books.

Williams, R. 1974: 'Communications as cultural science'. *Journal of Communication* 24, 17–25.

Williams, T.M. (ed.) 1986: *The Impact of Television: A Natural Experiment in Three Communities* Orlando: Academic Press.

Williams, R. 1990: *Television: Technology and Cultural Form*. London: Fontana. (First published 1974.)

Williamson, J. 1978: *Decoding Advertisements. Ideology and Meaning in Advertising*. London: Marion Boyars.

Willis, P. 1977: *Learning to Labour: How Working Class Kids get Working Class Jobs*. London: Saxon House.

Willis, P. 1980: 'Notes on method'. In Hall, S., Hobson, D., Lowe, A. and Willis, P. (eds.) *Culture, Media, Language*. London: Hutchinson, 89–95.

Wilson, B.J., Kunkel, D., Linz, D., Potter, W.J., Donnerstein, E., Smith, S.L., Blumenthal, E., Berry, M. and Federman, J. 1998: 'The nature and context of violence on American television'. In Carlsson, U. and von Feilitzen, C. (eds.) *Children and Media*

411

*Violence*. Goteborg, Sweden: Unesco International Clearing House on Children and Violence on the Screen, 63–79.

Windahl, S., Signitzer, B. and Olson, J.T. 1992: *Using Communication Theory. An Introduction to Planned Communication*. London: Sage.

Witmer, D.F., Colman, R.W. and Katzmann, S.L. 1999: 'From paper-and-pencil to screen-and-keyboard. Toward a methodology for survey research on the Internet'. In Jones, S. (ed.) 1999b: *Doing Internet Research*. London: Sage.

*Women Take Issue. Aspects of Women's Subordination*. 1978: 'The Women's Studies Group, Centre for Contemporary Cultural Studies, University of Birmingham. London: Hutchinson.

Woodworth, R.S. 1921: *Psychology: A Study of Mental Life*. New York: Holt.

Wulff, H. 1995: 'Inter-racial friendship: consuming youth styles, ethnicity and teenage femininity in South London'. In Amit-Talai, V. and Wulff, H. (eds.) *Youth Cultures: A Cross-Cultural Perspective*. London, New York: Routledge.

Zillman, D. 1978: 'Attribution and misattribution of excitatory reactions'. In Harvey, J.H., Ickes, W. and Kidd, R.F. (eds.) *New Directions in Attribution Research*. Hillsdale, NJ: Lawrence Erlbaum Associates, 335–68.

Zillman, D. 1985: 'The experimental explorations of gratifications from media entertainment'. In Zillman, D, and Bryant, J. (eds.) *Selective Exposure to Communication*. Hillsdale, NJ: Lawrence Erlbaum, 225–39.

Zillman, D. and Bryant, J. (eds.) 1985: *Selective Exposure to Communication*. Hillsdale, NJ: Lawrence Erlbaum Associates.

# Index